The Cultural Revolution and Post-Mao Reforms

A HISTORICAL PERSPECTIVE

The Cultural Revolution and Post-Mao Reforms

A HISTORICAL PERSPECTIVE

TANG TSOU

The University of Chicago Press
Chicago and London

TANG TSOU is the Homer J. Livingston Professor in political
science and Far Eastern languages and civilizations at the
University of Chicago. He is the author of *America's Failure
in China, 1941–1950* and a coeditor of *China in Crisis*, both
published by the University of Chicago Press.

The University of Chicago Press, Chicago 60637
The University of Chicago Press, Ltd., London
© 1986 by The University of Chicago
All rights reserved. Published 1986
Printed in the United States of America

95 94 93 92 91 90 89 88 87 86   5 4 3 2 1

Library of Congress Cataloging in Publication Data

Tsou, Tang, 1918–
    The Cultural Revolution and post-Mao reforms.

    Includes index.
    1. China—History—Cultural Revolution, 1966–1969.
2. China—Politics and government—1976–   .
I. Title.
DS778.7.T76   1986   951.05′6   85-8608
ISBN 0-226-81513-7

This book is dedicated to

Students who took my courses in which the ideas expounded in this book were first developed and tested.

My former and present colleagues in the Department of Political Science from whom I have learned more than they have ever realized.

Professor Clifford Gurney, our family physician, who has sought to promote both the longevity and productivity of his scholarly colleagues as well as to look after their personal welfare and to treat them as whole persons.

We can learn the nature of anything only when it has reached—and passed—its maturation. Events and processes, theories and actions, appear in a new perspective. . . . We see how with a new liberation went a new servitude. . . . We stand at a new vantage point, looking down, after the earthquake, on the ruined temples of our cherished gods. We see the weakness of the exposed foundations—perhaps we can learn how, and where, to rebuild the institutional fabric so that it may better withstand the shocks of change.

Robert MacIver

Contents

Acknowledgments

For a person born in a divided family living near the center of the stormy politics of twentieth-century China, life's journey began like a solitary nighttime voyage in a small boat on a turbulent sea. With no stars to orient him and no knowledge of what his destination was or could be, he drifted with the current, buffeted by high waves and sudden storms, his ultimate destiny a matter of circumstance and accident, beyond his control. An instinct for survival helped him through the squalls, and unexpected good fortune eventually gave him a chance to find a place and a home in a bountiful land.

Having now reached the last stage of my journey, I take the happy opportunity afforded by publication of this book to acknowledge the unexpected bounties conferred upon me by some of those who knowingly or unknowingly, by design or by accident, have directly or indirectly shaped the outcome of that voyage. My wife, who publishes under her own name, Yi-chuang Lu, came early aboard my leaking boat and helped steer me away from the treacherous currents of *realpolitik* and onto a course of lifelong intellectual endeavor. At a time when my academic career was foundering, Hans J. Morgenthau took a great chance in selecting me as one of the research associates in his prestigious Center for the Study of American Foreign Policy. He directed me to write on American policy toward China, giving me a totally free hand in the choice of the period to be covered, the focus of the research, and the political, methodological, and philosophical assumptions underlying my analysis. When the results of my work were submitted to the University of Chicago Press in the form of a book manuscript, Roger Shugg, then director of the Press, showed gratifying audacity in flatly rejecting the hostile appraisal and the suggestions for changes made by one of the readers, leaving the manuscript intact, preserving its integrity, and publishing it under the title *America's Failure in China*. Edward Banfield, who had been my fellow graduate student, took the initiative in suggesting to the Department of Political Science that it offer me a position as assistant professor.

My chance to shift from the study of international relations to the examination of the internal politics of China came when Edward Levi, then provost of the university, established a Center for Policy Study. As its inaugural project, from March 1966 to February 1967, he and Vice-President Charles U. Daly decided to undertake a yearlong examination of China. One of the products was *China in Crisis*, consisting of three books in two volumes, in which the first chapter of the present collection originally appeared. This first scholarly work published in the United States on the Cultural Revolution was carefully and beautifully produced by the same Press. Throughout the "China year" and as I worked to prepare the book for publication, Jonathan Kleinbard, now a vice-president of the university, assumed all administrative responsibilities, thus giving me the time necessary to deal with academic matters. The "China year" gave the university a deserved place in the field of studies on contemporary China. The conference held in early 1967 and *China in Crisis* are still remembered for their timeliness and scholarly contributions. For many reasons, both good and bad, the program of contemporary Chinese studies did not expand as quickly as had been hoped, and, sadly enough, it probably fell short of Mr. Levi's and Mr. Daly's expectations.

Still, many years later, the Center for Far Eastern Studies received a four-year grant from the National Endowment for Humanities for its Modern China Project, of which Philip Kuhn was the moving spirit and I the principal investigator. Chapters 4, 5, and 6 were all written during the period of the grant. Two volumes of *Select Papers from the Far Eastern Center* were published to provide other scholars with the preliminary findings of the project. Other publications that were partly supported by the NEH grant have just begun to come out, the first one being William Rowe's *Hankow* (Stanford University Press, 1984).

A research grant from the Luce Foundation enabled me to write chapters 7 and 8 of this volume. It also gave me an opportunity to inaugurate a research project on Chen Duxiu as a point of entry into my study of Chinese politics in the first half of the twentieth century. The Luce Foundation's innovative and profoundly significant program for Asian scholars has also contributed greatly both to the writing of these two essays and to my new enterprise. I refer specifically to the help of Professor Zhou Shiqiu and Xiang Qing.

In addition to the NEH and the Luce Foundation, my research over the years has been supported by grants from the Joint Committee on Contemporary China of the Social Science Research Council and the American Council of Learned Societies, the Rockefeller Foundation, the Center for Far Eastern Studies, the Center for International Studies under the direction of Chauncy Harris, and the Social Sciences Divisional Research Committee of the University of Chicago. To all these organizations, I want to extend my deep appreciation.

In the course of writing these essays, I benefited from the work and frequent personal comments of many of my colleagues in both political science and Chinese studies. I shall not single out any of them here, except for the two readers of the present work for the University of Chicago Press who must remain anonymous. As some book-review editors have adopted the rule of never sending a book to be reviewed to scholars whose help is acknowledged, my book would have few reviewers if I thanked everyone individually. There are so many to whom I owe so much.

Over the past several years, my research has been greatly facilitated by the extraordinarily successful efforts of James Cheng, now curator of the Far Eastern Library, in building one of the country's most outstanding collections of books and serials on post-Mao China. In this task, Wen-pai Tai, Tai-loi Ma, and Chiung-jen Chien have all made individual contributions in their own areas of specialization.

Throughout the writing of the last four essays, and in preparing the manuscript for publication, I received welcome help from three of my research assistants, help far beyond the call of duty. Edmond Lee turned my virtually unintelligible, cut-and-paste, handwritten manuscripts into neatly typed and vastly improved pieces, correcting many errors in the process. So did Chi-keung Ko, who has also become a skilled user of word processors and computers. Between them, they romanized the Chinese characters I included in my handwritten manuscript according to the pin-yin system and converted the Wade-Giles romanizations used in most of the earlier essays into the pin-yin system for publication in this volume. King K. Tsao rendered many indispensable services in the course of my writing and preparation of this collection. He also took on the tedious tasks of proofreading the galleys and preparing the index.

Finally, I want to note that this book would not have been completed had my wife not urged me to go on in spite of her illness.

Preface

This volume consists of eight essays on the Chinese Communist movement and regime, written over a period of eighteen years. All but one of them were drafted soon after some major development had taken place in China. The essay printed here as chapter 3, which does not deal with specific events, was extracted from a paper presented in 1973 at a conference held at Columbia University and published in 1976 in the *China Quarterly*. It is included in this volume at the suggestion of one of the readers for the University of Chicago Press because it deals with the behavioral pattern of factions within the Chinese Communist party and the broader question of "factionalism."

The time lag between the first drafts of the essays and their publication varied from several months to three years, depending mainly on whether they were printed in journals or in books edited by other scholars or by me. In this collection they are arranged in the order of their writing rather than publication. I have made no substantive changes in the texts of the seven previously published papers except to delete a micropolitical case study in chapter 6 which was too detailed to be included in a volume of essays dealing with broad historical trends on the macropolitical level. The eighth paper was originally written for presentation at the Conference on the Foundations and Limits of State Power in China under the sponsorship of the European Science Foundation. An expanded and revised version is published in this volume. I have added an introduction to the collection to clarify the methodological thinking underlying the essays and to link the substantive themes developed in them. I have also appended a chronology of events pertinent to the subject matter of the essays.

In some cases, when later revelations have contradicted the reports that were available to me at the time of writing or when the historical narrative needs to be supplemented by later information, I have added new footnotes; these are indicated by asterisks to distinguish them from the original footnotes. I have also felt free to correct typographical errors. In the first footnote in each chapter, I have inserted, in brackets, information about the date and the journals, books, or conferences in which the various chapters were first published or presented as well as acknowledgments for permissions to publish them in this volume. In a very few cases, I have inserted, also in brackets, words inadvertently omitted in the process of original publication. Finally, all names originally romanized according to the Wade-Giles or some other system, including names in quoted matter, are here rendered in accordance with the pin-yin system, except for such familiar names as Sun Yat-sen and Chiang Kai-shek. But I have left unchanged the names of the authors of books or articles published in English, the titles of these books and articles, and the place of their publication, so that they can be readily traced.

Introduction

Methodological Notes

Scholars who study macropolitical developments in the People's Republic of China often find themselves in a highly unenviable position: they are expected to analyze major events that have only just occurred. Moreover, scholarship must be sharply distinguished from intelligence research.[1] Social scientists cannot rest content with simply rendering an account of the events on the basis of available published materials or of intelligence reports, even when the former, properly read, are quite informative on some matters and the latter frequently reveal important facts hidden from ordinary observers. Their task is rather to look at these events in a broad historical perspective and to interpret them from theoretical and comparative points of view, after ascertaining on the basis of available information what has actually happened.

This is the kind of task which the essays collected in this volume sought to discharge. In attempting this I have assumed that in so doing, an outside observer must take seriously the ideas, viewpoints, perceptions, and pronouncements of the participants whose actions he is studying. This assumption is particularly significant for studies of China: the cultural gap between China and the West is wide, the two societies are at different periods of economic development, and their political systems stand in sharp contrast to each other.

Particularly important for Western observers is the fact that for millennia the Chinese have given great weight to ideas, and they continue to do so in the twentieth century. Thus, the interplay between ideas and politics, or more precisely the interaction between ideology and political development, lies at the core of each of the essays in this volume. It is around this central phenomenon that the essays address the questions of the changes in the state-society relationship, the process of state rebuilding, the nature of the political system, the role of the Leninist party, the organizations and institutions of the Party and the state, the inner-Party

For general readers or undergraduate students without much knowledge about China or interest in social science methodology and theory, this introduction should be consulted only after the individual essays have been read. Each of the individual essays has a unity of its own and can be read without reference to each other.

1. See Chalmers Johnson's perceptive article, "The Role of Social Science in China Scholarship," *World Politics* 17 (January 1965): 256–71.

struggle for power, the process of decision making, the specific policies adopted, and the impact of policies on society and vice versa.

To make the interplay between ideology and politics the central focus of these essays does not commit us to a single-factor theory or model—one in which ideology is used as the sole independent variable to explain other parts of a sociopolitical system, which are then viewed as dependent variables. Such an approach is just as indefensible as vulgar Marxism, which uses the economic base as the sole independent variable to explain other elements of a system. On the contrary, one begins with the commonplace that the complex process of sociopolitical development in twentieth-century China, together with its outcomes, has been the product of many factors, one of which is an ideology borrowed from abroad. The adaptation of this foreign ideology to Chinese conditions—the sinification of Marxism, or the emergence of Mao Zedong Thought—was the outcome of a political process whose prominent features were the politicomilitary confrontation between the Chinese Communist party (CCP) and the Guomindang, as well as the debates and struggles within the CCP itself. If one uses the terminology of the social sciences, Mao Zedong Thought at its formative stage can be considered a dependent variable, and a function of various independent variables. But once Mao Zedong Thought took shape, and particularly after it was defined as the guide to the CCP's entire work, it acquired a force of its own. To use a contemporary term, it became a "system element," with a degree of independence and functional autonomy. It acted on the political process itself. It became an intervening variable between the socioeconomic conditions in China and the outcomes of Chinese political development. Thus to take the interplay between ideology and politics as central to these studies assumes that more than one factor determines the processes of change and the characteristics of a sociopolitical system at any particular time, while suggesting that ideology gives shape to the process and to the system, even as it is itself shaped by other factors.

This brief, inadequate discussion is undertaken to provide an appropriate context for my more technically inclined readers. In the individual essays, I prefer to place upon my analyses of particular historical situations the burden of characterizing the interrelationships among the many factors at work, the directions of influence, and the relative weight of the various system elements involved.[2]

One's understanding of the interplay between ideology and politics in recent Chinese politics—as well as other related questions—rests on how one interprets the unfolding historical events. Since no one can look at

2. Cf. Alvin W. Gouldner, *The Coming Crisis of Western Sociology* (New York: Basic Books, 1970), 226–31, particularly his "stratified system model."

the history of any particular period, particularly history in the making, with a mind devoid of preconceptions, a writer necessarily brings to the task of writing and interpreting history a set of theoretical ideas, a framework of cross-comparisons among national histories, and knowledge about the past history of the nation concerned. Thus the chief methodological issue in this age of rapid theoretical development in the social sciences is the mutual relationship between history and theory. This issue has two aspects: first, how historical studies contribute to the development of theory, and second, how theory contributes to the study of history. Obviously, this introduction cannot deal on a general level with this twofold issue, which has been a subject of dispute for generations of historians, philosophers, and theorists. Moreover, any distinction between the two aspects of historical study is an artificial one for the purposes of exposition. Basically, historical generalizations and even historical narrative itself are shaped by implicit or explicit theories of human action and historical development, and historical narratives frequently carry within themselves explanations and interpretations of events. Conversely, these theories and generalizations have no validity unless they are grounded in historical and empirical evidence. But here I need to state explicitly under this twofold distinction what I have sought to accomplish in writing the essays included in this volume, as well as what I have *not* attempted to do.

Collectively, the essays attempt to undertake "a theoretically informed and theoretically relevant case study" of the Chinese Communist movement and regime. Individually, each represents a study of a particular period or series of related events, as, for example, the Cultural Revolution, the struggle for succession to Mao Zedong, and post-Mao developments. Over a period of eighteen years, I have gradually developed a changing and more theoretically interesting, but perhaps less explicit, framework of analysis for the overall case. In none of the essays have I tried to arrive at universally valid generalizations or even what many scholars call middle-range theories or generalizations. Obviously, these generalizations can be reached only by comparing a number of cases which are either exhaustive of a particular universe of events or carefully selected according to the canons of comparative method.

Insofar as I have arrived at any generalizations, most of them are valid only within the confines of the single case; and some of them may even be effectively challenged within this stringent limit. Moreover, many of these generalizations have been based on a comparison of specific events during different periods of the Chinese Communist movement and regime under some implicitly assumed or explicitly stated systemic or macrosociopolitical conditions. Some of them are generalizations at a very low level of abstraction, rising only slightly above a historical description of the specific events. When the systemic conditions change, these generalizations may no longer hold and new generalizations need to be sought. The generalizations regarding the behavioral patterns of Party factions developed in the essay "Prolegomenon to the Study of Informal Groups in CCP Politics," written in 1973, fall into this category. This essay takes exception to Andrew Nathan's elegant and theoretically sophisticated "factional model for CCP politics." Nathan's central assumption is that "one faction may for the moment enjoy somewhat greater power than rival factions, but this power will not be so much greater that the victorious faction is capable of expunging its rival and ensuring permanent dominance" and that "a faction engaging in conflict with other factions must therefore operate on the assumption that it will not be able decisively and finally to eliminate its rivals." In contrast, I argue that "the basic assumption of CCP politics has been that a group or a coalition of groups can and does decisively defeat a major rival group or coalition and eliminate it."[3] The generalizations and abstract constructs about CCP politics developed in the essay are linked to this basic point of departure.

This assumption and the related generalizations were proved to be correct in the subsequent conflict between the "gang of four" and the more moderate Party leaders in 1975 and 1976. As we know, this ended with the arrest of the "gang of four" in October 1976, and their trial in late 1980, events which were accompanied and have been followed step by step by the decisive rejection of their theories and the resolute reversal of their

3. Chap. 3. On the level of theory, I argue that an analysis of politics and political systems should be broadened from a preoccupation with "factions" alone to an examination of all types of informal groups and networks. I suggest that informal groups and processes, or at least some types of informal groups and processes, may become formal organizational units and processes, and that informal roles or positions have a tendency to develop into formal roles and positions. In retrospect, this generalization appears to explain at least in part the processes leading to the formation of the CCP in the period 1920–21.

I do agree with Nathan that "the hierarchy and established communications and authority flow of the existing organization provides a trellis upon which the complex faction is able to extend its own informal, personal loyalties and relations." I also take note of the post-Weberian emphasis on informal groups, interpersonal relationship, and the decision-making processes that involve negotiations, bargaining, and compromise. In a later essay, I observe that formal structure and procedures cannot function "effectively and efficiently without informal structures and processes" (chap. 7). Perhaps the study of informal groups in politics will have to start from the assumption that informal groups should be given as much weight as formal structures, if not even greater weight *in certain historical conditions*. In other words, in certain periods of history and under specific circumstances, informal groups may play the primary and decisive role in the political process, generally unaffected and unrestrained by the formal structure, as they did during the Cultural Revolution. John Padgett is exploring this problem in his theoretical, historical, and comparative study of informal groups and networks.

policies and programs, particularly after 1978. But whether the learning process of the Party leaders, the reforms instituted since 1978, the rapidly changing economic parameters, etc., will alter the systemic conditions in such a way as to foster a different and durable pattern of inner-Party struggle and factional behavior remains to be seen.

Some generalizations based on the Chinese case may invalidate generalizations that take no account of the Chinese experience, or they may serve as exceptions to the latter or throw light on entirely different aspects of the subject. For example, Robert C. Tucker in "The Deradicalization of Marxist Movements" concludes with this generalization: "It appears to be the fate of radical movements that *survive and flourish* for long *without* remaking the world that they undergo eventually a process of deradicalization."[4] Yet the Chinese Communist movement in the period from 1927 to 1936 suggests a different generalization, to wit: "It appears to be the fate of radical movements that *cannot survive and flourish* after a period of attempting to remake the world by radical methods that they will undergo a process of deradicalization."[5] In China, it was worldly failure not worldly success that led to deradicalization. The Cultural Revolution of 1966–76, together with Chinese political development after 1978, is simply another case which reaffirms once more the validity of this generalization within the Chinese setting. More important, a process of reradicalization began after 1946 in the form of open civil war and reversion to a program of land reform after the CCP had survived and flourished under its deradicalized program during the period between 1937 and 1945.[6]

But Chinese events may also confirm generalizations derived originally from study of other countries. The contrast between the year of Cultural Revolution and the period since 1978 confirms Richard Lowenthal's generalization on "the existence of a long-term trend toward the victory of modernization over utopianism," as well as Samuel Huntington's observa-

4. Robert C. Tucker, "The Deradicalization of Marxist Movements," *American Political Science Review* 61 (June 1967): 347–48. Emphasis in the original.

5. "Letter to the Editor" by Tang Tsou, ibid. (December 1967): 1101–3. Emphasis added. This letter consists of my comments on Tucker's article in my capacity as a discussant when he read his paper at the annual meeting of the American Political Science Association in 1966.

6. The examination of these periods of the history of the Chinese Communist movement and regime may be labeled a "theory-infirming case study," to use Arend Lijphart's term, or more accurately, a "generalization-infirming case study," to modify his terminology. Arend Lijphart, "Comparative Politics and the Comparative Method," *American Political Science Review* 65 (September 1971): 682–93. One of the specialists on China whose thinking is obviously influenced by Lijphart's article is Elizabeth Perry. See her *Rebels and Revolutionaries in North China, 1845–1945* (Stanford, Calif.: Stanford University Press, 1980): ix.

tion about the development of a "revolutionary one-party system" into an "established one-party system."[7]

Mao's well-known strategy of "surrounding the cities from the countryside" can be considered a deviant case when viewed from the perspective of the French and Russian revolutions.[8] Although this point is generally accepted, its implications for the study of political development after 1949 remains to be systematically explored. This deviant case can also be seen as a case establishing a new pattern of revolutionary actions, which has been repeated with some variation in other cases such as the Vietnamese and Cuban revolutions.

The history of the Chinese Communist movement and regime from 1927 to the present, when juxtaposed to the Western experience of state building since the seventeenth century, suggests, at least tentatively, a new theme. The processes and outcomes of state building or state rebuilding based on the concept of the masses are different from those based on the concept of citizenship. This tentative theme can be further examined in the Chinese setting itself and then tested against other cases of state building or state rebuilding.[9]

These various ways in which study of the Chinese case can contribute to the search for generalization and the building of theories clarify the meaning of the term "a theoretically relevant case study."

But a theoretically relevant case study cannot be undertaken unless the study is from the beginning informed by theory. To be informed by theory means, among other things, to interpret historical events or cases in the light of theories: their concepts and generalizations, or insights derived from them.[10] In this volume, the use of theories is, for the most part, implicit rather than explicit so that the historical narrative and analyses may not be too obtrusively and too frequently interrupted. Moreover, there is no attempt to apply a readily available general model to explain historical instances.[11] Political development in twentieth-century China, particularly the history of the Chinese Communist movement and regime, is so complex and unprecedented that no general model readily fits the Chinese case. Applying a general model, or grand theory, misleads rather

7. See chap. 5. This is what can be called a theory- or generalization-confirming case study.

8. This falls into Lijphart's category of "deviant case studies."

9. This tentative theme is developed in chap. 8. This endeavor is analogous to what Lijphart calls "hypothesis-generating case studies." None of the ideas or themes generated in this volume can be called hypotheses in the strict sense of the term.

10. This intellectual effort corresponds to Lijphart's "interpretative case studies."

11. The difficulties and the shortcomings of this approach have been underscored in Theda Skocpol's conclusion to *Vision and Method in Historical Sociology*, ed. Theda Skocpol (Cambridge: Cambridge University Press, 1984).

than enlightens us. It results either in the distortion of the general model or the forcing of historical facts to fit a Procrustean bed.

Instead, the essays in this volume endeavor to use concepts and theories to develop a meaningful historical interpretation, to use Theda Skocpol's terms.[12] Employing this approach, one is confronted at the outset by the problem of selecting the relevant concepts and theories at various levels of abstraction and with different scopes of coverage from various fields of social studies and their subfields.

Obviously, specialists on China cannot but be influenced by the intellectual currents in the related disciplines. But the difficulty arises from the fact that China in the twentieth century has undergone fundamental changes in a shorter period than most other nations of the past or present. These changes have occurred in the cultural, social, economic, and political spheres or, to use Marxist terminology, in the economic base and the "superstructure," which for some neo-Marxists includes "the civil society" and "the political society," or state. Thus a scholar studying Chinese development on the "macro" level must read widely in various disciplines and pay constant attention to their insights. With luck he may then discover concepts, generalizations, and theories which fit the Chinese case almost perfectly, such as Clifford Geertz's notion of ideology and his generalization on its saliency at a specific historical juncture.

Beyond the use of concepts, generalizations, and theories in the manner just suggested, one may also see Chinese political development as the outcome of the interaction of a series of strategic choices made by the various actors in conflict or in cooperation with each other. The available alternatives are shaped by the perceived and/or actual structures of constraint and opportunity, and the choice of one of these alternatives is an intentional and deliberate act to maximize the chances of a preferred outcome and to achieve self-consciously selected goals. This way of looking at political development and historical change has not been fully exploited in the essays in this volume, although my earlier work, *America's Failure in China,* can be fitted more neatly into such a framework of analysis.

My attempt to use concepts and theories from various disciplines and even those that are anchored in conflicting theoretical systems and philosophical assumptions gives the appearance of theoretical "eclecticism"— a term of opprobrium in both traditional philosophical discourse and the contemporary social sciences. But eclecticism in this sense is a matter of necessity in an endeavor to achieve an informed understanding of Chinese development and perhaps a new systematic interpretation.

12. Theda Skocpol calls this approach "interpretive historical sociology." My aim is more modest. Perhaps the essays in this volume can be labeled "interpretive political history" or "an interpretation of political history."

In many cases even a specifically selected concept or model must be clarified, modified, reinterpreted, given a somewhat different meaning, and further developed in order to throw light on historical events. My adoption of the concept of "totalitarianism" in all the essays, from the first one written in 1966 to the last one written in 1983, has met with criticism rather than approval by many of my colleagues in the field of Chinese studies, particularly during the years of the Vietnam war. It has probably made these essays unacceptable to Chinese scholars and political leaders alike, just as my statement in *America's Failure in China* that "more than any other single person, Generalissmo Chiang Kai-shek was responsible for what happened in China" antagonized many Chinese leaders and scholars on Taiwan.

One of the many reasons for this disapproval is that the first, most systematically developed, and most widely known conceptualization of "totalitarianism" was that of Carl J. Friedrich, with his list of six specific traits. At the outset, I want to emphasize that I reject his concrete characterization of "totalitarianism" in terms of these specific traits. Instead, I have adopted the more general and fundamental meaning of totalitarianism as used by T. S. Timasheff to denote, in his terms, the "unlimited extension of state functions," "a trait isolated by means of abstraction and apt to appear in societies of various types."[13] Thus, the concept of totalitarianism used in this volume is a polar concept at one extreme end of the continuum in the state-society relationship. Within this section of the continuum, one can even speak of "degrees of totalitarianism" or "totalitarian-ness," measured by the penetration of political power into other spheres of social life. At the other pole of the continuum stands "anarchism." Between these two poles can be found societies with varying degrees of "stateness," to use the term popularized by J. P. Nettl. When used as a term referring to state-society relationships, authoritarianism is usually characterized by a high degree of "stateness," whereas nineteenth-century laissez-faire liberalism is marked by a low degree of "stateness" and falls into a position closer to the pole of anarchism than does twentieth-century democratic liberalism, with its orientation toward the socioeconomic rights or welfare of the disadvantaged. Qualitatively, the segment of this continuum from laissez-faire liberalism to totalitarianism parallels the different types of state-society relationship conceptualized by Lloyd and Susanne Rudolph as "reflexive, constrained, autonomous and totalistic."[14]

Authoritarianism in traditional societies, including old China, is funda-

13. See chap. 5 in this volume.
14. Lloyd I. Rudolph and Susanne Hoeber Rudolph, "The Subcontinental Empire and the Regional Kingdom in Indian State Formation," p. 2 in Paul Wallace, ed., *Region and Nation in India* (Forthcoming).

mentally different from modern totalitarianism, inasmuch as the traditional state lacks the capability of penetrating society very deeply. In traditional China, moreover, and perhaps also in other premodern societies, conceptions of man and the state in the cosmological order may have had some influence on the state-society relationship, constraining the penetration of political power into society. In short, then, traditional China is authoritarian but not totalitarian.[15] It is true that civil society in traditional China was weaker than in Europe, where in some countries the church was a powerful force and in others cities with some autonomy existed. But the formal, centralized bureaucracy of the Chinese state extended downward only to the *xian* level. In the countryside, there was what can be called a system of precapitalist "free enterprise" in agricultural production, landownership, and rural trade.[16] Local-level associations were quite strong vis-à-vis the formal bureaucracy, although they were dominated by what I call the "scholar-official-landlord class," which also controlled the latter.

These are all analytic concepts. In real life, fully developed totalitarian societies are difficult to find. Stalin's Soviet Union is the prime example or at least came closest to it. During the Cultural Revolution in China, Lin Biao and the "gang of four," with Mao's sometimes implicit and sometimes explicit support, aspired to establish a fully totalitarian society, under the banner of "continued revolution under the dictatorship of the proletariat" and "all-round dictatorship over the bourgeoisie." But they encountered some active opposition and a good deal of passive resistance from Party leaders and various social groups at a time when the ability of the state, the Party, the "gang of four," and even Mao himself to control society were at a low ebb. Political power as exercised by Mao and the Ultra-leftists with the support of mobilized masses did indeed penetrate Chi-

15. The eminent historian of China, Etienne Balazs, asserts that "Chinese society was to a high degree totalitarian." Etienne Balazs, *Chinese Civilization and Bureaucracy*, ed. Arthur F. Wright (New Haven, Conn.: Yale University Press, 1964): 10.

More plausibly, Barrington Moore, Jr., talks about "totalitarian elements" in the Qin dynasty. But he also notes that "the Qin state was unable to focus these energies [of the Qin society] to the extent possible under a modern dictatorship" and that the economic controls "were mainly attempts to preserve an agrarian ethic against the erosion of commercial life and luxury." Barrington Moore, Jr., *Political Power and Social Theory* (New Haven, Conn.: Yale University Press, 1958): 45.

In other words, the Qin state lacked the capability of penetrating society. According to Moore, it attempted to preserve a subsystem in society rather than to effect a total change in the social structure. In my opinion, making first an analytic distinction between the level of state-society relationship and the level of the structure of political power and then trying to see the empirical relationship between these two levels will lead to clarity in understanding and exposition.

16. See Tang Tsou, Introduction to *Select Papers from the Center for Far Eastern Studies*, no. 4, 1979–80 (Chicago: Center for Far Eastern Studies, 1981): v–xii.

nese society more deeply than before. But what in this volume I call "revolutionary-'feudal' totalitarianism"[17] was in actuality not a fully developed totalitarianism as was that in Stalin's Soviet Union, even though in the realm of theory and the aspirations of the Ultraleftists, totalitarianism reached its highest point in China at that time.

If we limit our use of the term "totalitarianism" to the content of the state-society relationship (or political power-society relationship), we must immediately add another level of analysis. This second level deals with the structure of political power, or types of regime. If we conceive the state-society relationship as a continuum, which in principle can be divided into sections at ascertainable points of demarcation, or thresholds, we analyze the nature of political structure itself in terms of a typology. Underlying the essays of this volume is a typology that is derived and adapted from Juan Linz's widely known works. We are concerned here only with totalitarian and posttotalitarian regimes, traditional and modern authoritarian regimes, and liberal democratic regimes as developed in the West. The dimensions that must be included in any construction of regime types are the centralization or decentralization of power within the political system, the presence or absence of a formal system of checks and balances, the degree of participation and/or mobilization, the modality in the use of coercion and persuasion, and the existence or nonexistence of a sphere of individual immunities protected either by law or by custom or by both.

The inclusion of the last dimension suggests that the two levels of analysis are convenient devices adopted for heuristic purposes in order to achieve clarity of exposition and that they cannot be entirely separated even analytically. Liberal democracy as a regime type rests ultimately on the existence of a sphere of immunities, whereas a totalitarian regime is characterized by the absence of such a sphere. In the latter, there exists at best a "zone of indifference" which political power on its own volition does not try to penetrate or control, for whatever reasons.[18] Hence, the state-society relationships in these two regime types differ basically. On this dimension, authoritarian regimes in traditional societies also differ from modern totalitarian regimes. In the former, there still exist a few individual immunities that are protected by custom, religious beliefs, or moral conventions (though not by formal constitution or law) whereas in the latter none of these provides any effective protection against political power. But even in a modern totalitarian regime, the Party is not a

17. See chap. 5.

18. I use the term "zone of indifference" in an unpublished article, "Political Totalism, Authoritarianism, and Hegemony: A Proposed Framework for the Study of the Transition of a Traditional Sociopolitical System into a Communist Regime in China," written in November 1982.

"monolith" although in principle it is the "monistic" center of power in society, to use Juan Linz's formulation with a slight change.

The distinction between these two levels of analysis allows us to raise some interesting questions. It forces us to relate the other dimensions at the second level to the various sections of the continuum at the first level. For example, what is the relationship of participation and/or mobilization, the modality in the use of coercion and persuasion, and the centralization or decentralization of political power to totalitarianism, authoritarianism, and democratic liberalism? To ask a seemingly absurd question for the purpose of illustrating the extreme form of this complex relationship, is it theoretically possible to have a "democratic totalitarian" society in which the people or the masses participate actively in the selection of their governors and express a preference for the state to penetrate all spheres of society or at least exhibit a spontaneous willingness to allow the state to do so? In this imaginary society, could political power be decentralized and persuasion be substituted for coercion?

Empirically and historically, effective totalitarian penetration of society has almost always been associated with the centralization of political power at the top while coercion overwhelms persuasion as a method of rule. This has been true of the Chinese Communist regime, or at least the top Chinese leaders, particularly Mao and the Ultraleftists, acted along these lines during the Cultural Revolution. Generally, parties are better suited to penetrate society than the state and its bureaucracy. Penetration by a Leninist party must be sharply distinguished from expansion of the functions of the state in liberal democratic regimes—which also involves the penetration of society by the state. But the Cultural Revolution furnishes scholars with a case in which the supreme leader of a Leninist party, working with a small number of his lieutenants and supported by mobilized masses, could partially dismantle the Party and push totalitarianism to a higher level than the Party organization. Still, Mao and the Ultraleftists recognized the utility and effectiveness of the Party in their attempt to bring about yet another social revolution and penetrate society still further. Thus Mao tried to reconstruct the Party and put it under his absolute control after it had been partially destroyed, and the "gang of four" endeavored to capture supreme power over the Party both in anticipation of his death and immediately after it. If the "gang of four" had been successful in this attempt, China would have become very similar to Stalin's Soviet Union in the arbitrary use of political power by the top leader, in the merciless elimination of the defeated leaders, in the ruthless suppression of dissent, and in the stifling of civil society. The major difference would have been that the mobilized masses and their leaders would have occupied those positions of power or influence which in Stalin's time and thereafter have been occupied by the technocrats and the technical intelligentsia. Perhaps a uniquely Chinese type of fully developed totalitarianism, different from both Stalin's totalitarianism and the Chinese polity in the years between 1949 and 1965, would have emerged. As it turned out, the quest for centralized power and absolute control antagonized most of the other leaders, while the deep political penetration of society alienated most social groups and individuals. The "gang of four" was easily removed. After 1978, China seems to have been in a period of transition from a totalitarian regime to an authoritarian regime of some kind. At this moment, the process is continuing. The outcome is by no means certain. A retrogression is not entirely impossible. I shall leave comment on these unresolved problems to others.

As none of the essays in this volume, including this introduction, is an exercise in pure theory, two methodological reasons underlie the foregoing discussion of "totalitarianism." The first is to illustrate how I adapt and modify a concept developed in the social sciences for the purpose of analyzing the Chinese Communist movement and regime. The second is that I owe it to the readers of this volume to clarify my use of the term, however simplified and inadequate the discussion. For these reasons, this excursion into the concept of "totalitarianism" in the introduction or any theoretical remarks in the essays themselves have only heuristic purposes. They are of little value in themselves. Their worth depends on whether they enable us to gain understanding or insight into Chinese development and whether the interpretation based on them makes sense. At the moment, I am still trying to arrive at definitions of "totalitarianism" and "totalitarian regime" at once more systematically formulated and defensible. This task will continue to be one of my preoccupations in the years to come.

None of the essays in this volume is explicitly, systematically comparative for the purpose of arriving at hypotheses on causal regularities. But I hope that my use of concepts and theories from the social sciences in the analysis of Chinese development may facilitate systematic comparison. Indeed, to compare cases one must first examine them in terms of common concepts or generalizations. To undertake theoretically informed and relevant case studies is one way to prepare the ground for comparative studies. In the few places where the essays implicitly or explicitly juxtapose China with other nations, these juxtapositions are intended mainly to highlight differences rather than similarities, and thus to underscore the specific features of Chinese development. As the field of comparative politics, including contemporary Chinese studies, is moving toward systematic comparison and the search for cross-national regularities, these essays may serve as a point of departure for future, more ambitious efforts.

Continuity and Change in the Substantive Themes and the Framework of Analysis
The First Two Attempts to Analyze the Basic Sources of the Cultural Revolution

Seven of the eight essays in this volume were written to analyze specific major events and to develop substantive themes on the Chinese Communist movement and regime.[19] The first essay in the volume, completed during the first week of January 1967, deals with the origins of the Cultural Revolution in the broad perspective of China's tradition and twentieth-century Chinese politics. Most of the themes that in later essays are developed more fully, reformulated, supplemented, or set in a broader and theoretically better-grounded analytical framework are either explicitly stated or are implied in this essay. Insofar as the theory, practice, and institutions of the Chinese Communist movement and regime are concerned, the unprecedented nature of the crisis is conveyed in the following summary statements: "The Great Proletarian Cultural Revolution cannot properly be called a purge, since a purge is an institutionalized practice in the system. It is rather a profound crisis in the institutions of the party themselves. In this sense, the present inner-party struggle is different in nature from all the previous purges since 1935."

As for the future, this essay renders a tentative judgment on the likelihood of one of the three possible outcomes:

> A Maoist victory will establish a precedent under which the Chairman of the party may violate many, if not all, of its most important norms and prescribed procedures and ignore its regular structural arrangements, and under which personal legitimacy may be used to override structural legitimacy. It will restore the position of the charismatic leader and his thought and weaken the party as an institution. It will delay the process of routinization. The important change in the interrelationship of the leader, the ideology, and the organization will make institutionalization in the political sphere more difficult and the political stability achieved at any particular time more precarious than before. This precedent can, however, be nullified if Mao's successors repudiate implicitly or explicitly this particular aspect of the Cultural Revolution. This is a likely development in the long run. A victory by the opposition will make it necessary to reject, revise, or reinterpret the thought of Mao and/or to develop new doctrines to replace or to supplement it. In either case, the effectiveness and legitimacy of the regime will not be easy to re-establish quickly. Even if an

19. As these essays were first published separately or presented at conferences with different participants, they had to offer rounded analyses which could stand on their own and be read without constant reference to earlier essays. Hence, it was necessary to repeat some ideas and facts. But it is hoped that these repetitions in the context of the discussion of a new series of events or in a different framework of analysis may bring out new meaning in what is repeated and may contribute to better understanding of the new developments.

uneasy compromise emerges out of a stalemate, the authority and capacity of the regime to act will be diminished, and public confidence will not be easy to restore soon. China's search for a reintegrated political community has suffered a setback. It will have to begin again with a battered political system.

This statement of the nature of the crisis departs from the most widely accepted interpretation at the time, which saw the Cultural Revolution as nothing but another pure case of struggle for power by factions within the Party or as just another purge. Instead, the essay traces the struggle for power between Mao and his followers and the heir apparent and his to disagreements over policies. In turn, it attributes the disagreements to the growing divergence between Mao Zedong Thought and social reality. Mao Zedong Thought, which had its roots in the backward countryside, was not only transposed to a modernizing China as a whole, it was also radicalized by Mao himself. This widening gap was aggravated by the special position occupied by Mao Zedong Thought in the political system. There it served as the ideological foundation of the regime. Legitimized by its contribution to the success of the revolutionary civil war, it either shaped policies or served to justify them after 1949. More important, Mao at that time was regarded almost instinctively by many other leaders and by the masses as the authoritative interpreter of the system of ideas bearing his name. The essay also analyzes the power struggle in terms of the conflict between a charismatic leader and the routinizing organization. The concepts underlying this analysis are familiar to all social scientists. But this initial attempt led eventually to a conclusion drawn in the last essay: that political development in China since 1978 "must be characterized not as 'routinization of charisma' but as routinization through the repudiation of charisma."

The second essay was written in 1968, as the Cultural Revolution proceeded and as Red Guard materials became available abroad. In addition to describing the events of the first three years of the Cultural Revolution, it attempts to specify and analyze four points of difference in basic outlook between Mao and Liu Shaoqi—again in terms of ideas generally accepted in the social sciences. Their first point of difference was whether a revolutionary regime "should rapidly implement its revolutionary programme or give priority to the consolidation of revolutionary gains and the newly established institutions." The second was "how the Party, in implementing its revolutionary programme and in establishing new institutions, should treat the various social groups and subgroups which were most directly affected" and how it should deal with their "material and personal interests." The third centered on "the issue of the extent to which functional specialization and creativity should be promoted even at the expense of relaxing ideological control and reducing ideological fervor." The final difference lay in the preferred "methods used to control men": indoctrination or organizational measures.

In retrospect, the most theoretically important part of this paper is the sharpening of a thesis already adumbrated in the first essay. This thesis is that ideology and organization may indeed come into conflict and that an ideology that at some earlier time was inseparable from an organization may in new circumstances be used against the organization. In a discussion of how Mao sought to legitimize his attack on the Party organization and how Mao Zedong Thought was elevated to a new peak, I concluded that: "this cult of Mao and his thought served a definite political purpose. It set a new standard of legitimacy and correctness with which the actions and opinions of top leaders were to be judged." "The Maoist vision is both a long-term goal and an immediate available means to destroy the opposition."

In making and documenting this point, both the first and second essays bring out another aspect of the relationship between ideology and organization, neglected in Franz Schurmann's monumental and still useful work. His analysis of Mao Zedong Thought and the Party is based on the commonly accepted generalization in sociology that ideology is the manner of thinking characteristic of an organization. When applied to China, this generalization holds for the period from 1935 to 1958. But Schurmann completed his work just before the Cultural Revolution. He naturally did not see that Mao Zedong Thought could be used as a means of attacking the organization. For intellectual historians, with whom I partially identify myself, ideas have their own force, and the thinking of a man and an organization may change in different directions. The conflict between ideology as developed or reinterpreted by a leader and by the organization that he leads is an always present possibility. As Theda Skocpol suggests in a personal comment, "Mao was a strategically placed man" and "his ideas could count outside of organizational routine."

The second essay reaffirms the characterization of the crisis and the forecast of the outcome in the long run. It gives even greater emphasis to "the demoralization, resentment, and frustrated hopes" as well as "the loss of confidence on the part of the Chinese Communist leaders in their own political institutions and their own wisdom" which could be seen quite readily from outside. But it gives Mao credit for being "motivated by a noble vision." This judgment on that aspect of Mao's mentality still stands. While affirming that "the full realization of this vision is impossible," chapter 2 also states that "it is just possible that somehow the Cultural Revolution will leave as a legacy a higher degree of political participation and economic equality, even if the former means merely a wider sharing of the high political risks and the latter is nothing more than an equality in poverty." This possibility of a higher degree of economic equality is now being called into question every day by the present regime's reversal of socioeconomic policies pursued during the Cultural Revolution. The nature of political participation has also changed dramatically in the last few years. Still, whatever will be the impact of these policies on the structure of income distribution and in turn on the pattern of participation, "a wider sharing of the high political risks" and "an equality in poverty" remain good descriptions of two aspects of the human condition during the Cultural Revolution.

In retrospect, even such a characterization of the crisis confronting the Chinese during the first three years of the Cultural Revolution is inadequate to portray the catastrophe that befell on the Chinese people and the damage inflicted on the political system in the subsequent seven years. For those years witnessed the life-and-death struggle between Mao and Lin Biao and between the "gang of four" and its opponents which made some of the other Chinese leaders, themselves disgraced or clinging precariously to positions of power, aware of fundamental defects in their political theory and practice. As Robert MacIver observes in his foreword to *The Great Transformation* by Karl Polanyi:

> We can learn the nature of anything only when it has reached—and passed—its maturation. Events and processes, theories and actions, appear in a new perspective. . . . We see how with a new liberation went a new servitude. . . . We stand at a new vantage point, looking down, after the earthquake, on the ruined temples of our cherished gods. We see the weakness of the exposed foundations—perhaps we can learn how, and where, to rebuild the institutional fabric so that it may better withstand the shocks of change.[20]

In the light of the continuing and worsening crisis, as well as of the problems revealed during the ensuing years, it became clearer to me that the Cultural Revolution was only the latest in a series of crises that had confronted China since the turn of the twentieth century. This series of crises was the product of both the collapse of the traditional system and the lingering influence of Chinese tradition. The Cultural Revolution occurred because the Chinese Communists had not yet found a satisfactory solution to the persistent problems that had bedeviled China for seven decades. The only difference between the earlier crises and the Cultural Revolution was simply that the latter erupted unexpectedly after the Chinese Communists had for longer than any previous regime established an apparently effective political system, made greater progress in managing

20. Robert M. MacIver, foreword to Karl Polanyi, *The Great Transformation: The Political and Economic Origins of Our Time* (Boston: Beacon Press, 1944): ix, x, xi.

affairs in various social spheres, and carried greater weight in international affairs.

Reflecting on this continuing and worsening crisis from the long perspective of history, I became increasingly dissatisfied with my characterization of the Chinese situation and aware of the limitation of the analytic framework used in the first two essays. In these two essays, the term "disintegration," derived from the then popular concept "integration," is adopted to characterize the situation confronting China in the early twentieth century. The term "reintegration of a political community" is used to describe the process in which the Chinese Communist elite after 1935 developed a unified party, adopted a moderate pattern of conflict resolution within the Party, and built a solid linkage with the various social groups through use of the mass line and the united front, and established an effectively functioning regime and "political community." Finally, the crisis of the Cultural Revolution is conceived in terms of "disintegration" brought about by the conflict between the charismatic leader and the routinizing organization, the incongruence between radicalized Mao Zedong Thought and the emergent reality of a modernizing society, and the alienation of individuals and groups from the faction in ultimate control. This analysis of the development of the Chinese Communist movement and regime does accurately reflect and put in general categories some salient aspects of the events described in the historical narrative and is not without value in our attempt to reveal the underlying processes of change.

But the term "disintegration" is inadequate for the purpose of characterizing the crisis facing China in the first four decades of the twentieth century. It cannot fully reflect the perceptions of the Chinese actors. At the same time the concept of "the reintegration of a political community" does not pinpoint the concrete problems confronting them and fails to focus our attention on many questions of theoretical interest. Thus a better way to characterize the past and the present, to describe the passage from one phase of history to another, and to link abstract ideas to concrete facts had to be found. To put these analyses together has led to a changing framework less explicit and more eclectic than that of "the integration, reintegration, and disintegration of a political community."

Crisis in Twentieth-Century China: External Sources, Internal Manifestations, and the Chinese Communist Attempt to Solve the Two Problems of Rebuilding the State and Redefining the State-Society Relationship

A new characterization of the human condition in the early decades of twentieth-century China is first made in chapter 5 and is discussed more fully in the final essay in the form of some tentative observations. Instead of using the term "disintegration," I now use in these two essays the words "total crisis" and "the sense or the perception of total crisis," while the earlier term is retained to refer to the political disunity of China. As I do not have any social-scientific definition of either the term "total" or the term "crisis,"[21] I owe it to my readers to clarify in this introduction the commonsense meaning of these terms when I apply them to the case of China. "Crisis" denotes dangers so imminent or problems so pressing as to raise the question of survival, and which in the view of a group of people are beyond their ability to avert or resolve by means of their usual ways of thinking and acting. The term "total" suggests that these dangers and problems confront many or even most of the nation's institutions and spheres of activity (or, in neo-Marxist terminology, political society, civil society, and the economic base alike). The Chinese sense or perception of crisis was most vividly revealed in their constant fear of "the extinction of the nation."

The external sources of this "total crisis" are classified under three analytical categories; first, the changes in the international structure of power and China's place in it; second, the challenge of Western examples or models; and, third, the impact of the capitalist world economy. In this introduction, I wish to suggest that, insofar as the external sources of crisis can be separated from each other, the first was instrumental in initiating the crisis, or perception of the crisis; it also decisively affected the fortunes of competing political groups during the crucial period of the Sino-Japanese War of 1937–45 and thus decisively influenced the direction of China's internal development. The impact of the second factor cannot be so easily pinpointed in time, but it provided the Chinese with alternatives in their search for solutions and still does. It has long and pervasively influenced Chinese development. However, its impact will be increasingly less formidable as the Chinese move along their path of searching for "socialism with Chinese characteristics." In contrast, the capitalist world system, whose impact on Chinese political development was in the past relatively slight, has begun to exert a direct, highly visible influence during the past few years and may carry even greater weight in the future.

The impact of the international environment resulted in the abandonment of the examination system in 1905, the collapse of the imperial system in 1911–12, and the attack on Confucianism and other traditional systems of thought and social institutions during the May Fourth period.[22] The May Fourth period and the ensuing six years also witnessed the development of warlordism, marking the highest point of political disin-

21. For an exercise in using the term "crisis" as the organizing concept in a study of sociopolitical development, see Leonard Binder et al., *Crises and Sequences in Political Development* (Princeton, N.J.: Princeton University Press, 1971).

22. The term "May Fourth period" is used in this volume to refer to the years 1915–21.

tegration in twentieth-century China. The collapse of the state institutions, the erosion of the official ideology, and the disintegration of China
into warlord rule brought about a fundamental change of immense consequences. This was the destruction of the unified traditional elite that had
governed the state and society of China for centuries and was responsible
for the continuity and longevity of Chinese civilization. In the first essay,
the term "ruling elite" is used denotatively without any theoretical un-
derpinning. In chapter 8 it is replaced by the controversial label "scholar-
official-landlord class," accompanied by the assertion that each of its three
components was rooted respectively in the hierarchy of status in civil
society, positions of authority in state institutions, and the control of the
principal means of production in the economic base. The mechanisms
that unified these three components into an integrated ruling class were
the examination system, the bureaucracy, and the imperial system. Thus
the destruction of this unified class was the ultimate manifestation of the
crisis at the macrosociopolitical level. At the microeconomic level, the
radical Chinese intellectuals' perception of the countryside in the 1920s
and 1930s was expressed in the widely used phrase, "the bankrupcy of the
villages," although this view has been challenged by recent American
scholarship.

When the crisis at the macrosociopolitical level was total and profound,
the process of rebuilding the state had to begin in civil society, with free-
floating intellectuals playing a role even more crucial in the long run than
that of the militarists. The crisis generated a need for an ideology as "a
map of problematic social reality and matrices for the creation of collective conscience"[23] and an urgent demand for rebuilding a system of political authority, while creating conditions favorable to the emergence of new
types of political elites. Marxism and the Leninist principles of organization were borrowed and developed to meet these needs, and they finally
triumphed over other contending alternatives.

In the final essay, an attempt is made to add to or underscore some of
the generally accepted explanations of this development by adapting
ideas current in the social sciences and applying them to China. As a theory of total crisis and total transformation, Marxism resonated with many
Chinese intellectuals' perceptions of total crisis and their initially vague
and unstructured demands for total transformation. Marxism-Leninism
eventually played an important role in "creating a new history" and in
"collaborating in the formation of a new system of authority."[24] Indeed,
the Chinese Leninist party itself was from the very beginning a system of

23. Clifford Geertz, "Ideology as a Cultural Symbol," in Clifford Geertz, *The Interpretation of Cultures* (New York: Basic Books, 1973) p. 220.
24. Cf. Noberto Bobbio, "Gramsci and the Conception of Civil Society," in Chantel
Mouffe, ed., *Gramsci and Marxist Theory* (London: Routledge and Paul, 1979): 36.

authority in a highly disorganized society, where intellectuals sought to reestablish an effective political system for the nation and where a tightly organized party satisfied their sense of belonging by giving them a well-defined place in that society. It provided information and assurance that change was necessary, possible, and inevitable. It proved to be better suited to China than liberal parties in the Western style, which presuppose the existence of a stable and effective political system and which have as one of their primary functions the imposition of limits on the power of the government and the maintenance of checks and balances within the political system. But the ideology and organizational form borrowed from abroad played their important roles in creating a new history and the formation of a system of political authority under concrete historical situations: the continuing influence of the traditional culture, the constraints imposed by the system of social stratification, the balance of political-military forces within China, and finally the international environment. They were themselves modified by the existential conditions.

These explanations reinforce rather than contradict those offered in the first essay, which can be summarized (and slightly augmented) as follows: The form of the sociopoliticocultural system developed under the Chinese Communist movement and regime paralleled that of traditional China. But there was a change in content. In this process, Confucianism was replaced by Marxism-Leninism, the traditional ruling class was replaced by the new Chinese Communist elite, and the traditional system of imperial power supported by a bureaucracy was replaced by a Party-state.[25] But the substantive content of some Chinese traditions also facilitated the acceptance of Marxism and the Leninist party and affected later developments under the Communist regime. In the specific conditions of China, traditional authoritarianism could easily develop into totalitarianism. The cult of the emperor gave implicit support to the cult of personality. Traditional bureaucracy facilitated the acceptance and development of the hierarchical and concentric-circle structure[26] of the Leninist party. In the final essay I summarize my observations on the historic change and continuity in the following way: "Political life in China is now governed by a new 'paradigm' which is the product of the century-old confrontation between China and the West. In this paradigm, traditional and modern elements, the old and the new, foreign examples and Chinese reality, Western knowledge and Chinese mentality, are sometimes merely juxtaposed, sometimes combined in unstable mixtures, and sometimes fully integrated. But the paradigm is mainly modern in its totality, its explicit

25. This formulation suggests the influence of Franz Schurmann's *Ideology and Organization in Communist China*.

26. For the notion of a "concentric-circle structure" of organization, see chap. 8 of this volume.

orientation, its substantive contents, and its posited goals, even though it is traditional in some of its parts, its implicit supports, its structural forms, and its methods."

During the May Fourth period and thereafter, the CCP's program was one of the totalistic responses to the total crisis. It attempted to make a social revolution through political means and the use of violent methods. It was committed to waging class struggle so as to change the social structure. Such a movement contained within itself totalitarian tendencies that would be actualized in different forms in various sociopolitical spheres under appropriate historical circumstances. It had to penetrate society in one way or another. But its relationship with society varied over time in accordance with changes in the objective situation and its leaders' perception of it.

In trying to capture power and to make a social revolution, the CCP had to establish intimate links with the various social groups and strata. The Marxist concept of class struggle, the Maoist notion of the mass line, and the Chinese use of the united-front policy contributed to the CCP's success in mobilizing and organizing the peasants, who ordinarily were not active participants in the political process and who were dominated and organized by the traditional ruling class. It also established effective alliances with other social classes and groups. Thus it expanded the scope of mobilization and participation in China, organized a large coalition of social forces, changed the social basis of political power, and established new rules for the political game. In other words, it succeeded in developing and mobilizing the energy, capabilities, and creativity of various groups and individuals for the immediate purpose of fighting a battle or waging a political struggle. At a deeper level of analysis one can say that it gradually developed a satisfactory relationship with society by adopting a series of moderate policies which took adequately into account of the perceived interests of the various groups and individuals without sacrificing its fundamental revolutionary goals. Helped by the defeats and degeneration suffered by the Guomindang during the Sino-Japanese War and taking full advantage of new opportunities, the CCP achieved total victory on the Chinese mainland earlier than it had expected. It then built a state in its own image. All these concrete developments correspond to the first of the three phases of Chinese Marxism after 1927 to which we shall now turn.

Three Phases of Chinese Marxism

Under the impact of Chinese reality and in the heat of struggles with opposing political forces and intra-Party conflicts, Marxism underwent three phases of development in China after 1927. In the first period between 1927 and 1955–57, Mao developed a sinified Marxism. It was first given the name of Mao Zedong Thought in official publications in 1943 after the decision had been taken by the Comintern to dissolve itself. In the first essay, there are various references to Mao Zedong Thought as developed in the Yanan period. But these references did not go beyond a restatement of the conventional wisdom.

It is not until chapter 4 that I arrive at a parsimonious characterization of the basic, original features of Mao's synthesis in this period. In that article, I suggest that this synthesis rested ultimately on the integration of a new tenet of historical materialism with Mao's explication of his practice of making policies, solving problems, and developing new ideas. This new tenet was that "in certain conditions such aspects as the relations of production, *theory,* and *superstructure* in turn manifest themselves in the *principal and decisive* role."[27] This proposition involved a subtle but significant modification of Engels's formulation of the basic principle of historical materialism in his letter to Joseph Bloch in 1890. Mao's reformulation of historical materialism was not only a descriptive generalization of the process of ideological, political, social, and economic changes in twentieth-century China, but also a programmatic prescription for revolutionary action. Mao's explication of his practice of making policy, solving problems, and developing new ideas did not stem from or lead to any new proposition in epistemology, but it demonstrated how he used Marx's notion of unity of theory and practice not only to criticize the ideas advanced by the Wang Ming and the "returned-students group" but to serve his cause in the realm of policy decision.[28] The new tenet of historical materialism legitimized revolutionary action in a country where capitalism was underdeveloped, while Mao's explication of his practice of uniting theory and practice was frequently used as a principle of prudence to guide, balance, and control the revolutionary impulse, the formulation of revolutionary programs, and revolutionary action. In that essay, written in early 1977, I suggest that of the two components of Mao's synthesis, the second one is "perhaps [the] more basic and lasting heritage which Mao has left for the Chinese."

During the second period, 1955–57 to 1976, Mao's synthesis was broken down by the Leftward swerve made by Mao himself and his Leftist followers. In the first essay, I characterize Mao Zedong Thought in the years immediately preceding the Cultural Revolution and during its first year in terms of five characteristics: first, the idea of conflict, struggle,

27. Mao Tse-tung, *Selected Works of Mao Tse-tung,* 1:336. Emphasis added. Careful readers will notice that for theoretical reasons the phrase "the relations of production" is not italicized. A personal communication from Jon Elster led to the decision not to underscore that phrase but only the terms "theory" and "superstructure."

28. For some of the ideas in this sentence, see Brantly Womack, "Theory and Practice in the Thought of Mao Tse-tung," in James Hsiung, ed., *The Logic of Maoism* (New York: Praeger, 1974): 15.

and combat; second, the tendency toward polarization; third, the centrality of man; fourth, the politicization of almost all spheres of social life; and, fifth, the emphasis on the importance of ideas over material conditions. With the possible exception of the tendency toward polarization, all these ideas were rooted in Mao's new tenet of historical materialism and formed part of its concrete contents.

The ideological, political, and policy implications of this new tenet of historical materialism were fully developed by Mao and (particularly) by the Ultraleftists in 1975 and the first nine months of 1976, when the thrust toward the Left reached its highest point in theoretical development. On the basis of some remarks by Mao, Zhang Chunqiao, the leading Ultraleftist theoretician, advanced the view that "the correctness of the ideological and political line and the control of leadership in the hands of one class or another decides which class owns a factory in reality."[29] The notion of "the class of bureaucratic officials," used by Mao in 1964 and repeated in some Red Guard publications, was officially published and expanded in a joint editorial of *Renmin ribao*, *Hongqi*, and *Jiefangjun bao* on July 1, 1976. Not only were the bureaucratic officials labeled a "class," but they were also implicitly equated with "those leading cadres who are taking the capitalist road" and identified as "bourgeois elements," They were designated unequivocally as the chief target of the revolution. Thus the political structure was seen as the direct source and foundation of a "class." This is a popular view among liberals and non-Communist leftists in the West, but is difficult to reconcile with traditional Marxism.

The Ultraleftists also developed a theory of "bourgeois right." They alleged that bourgeois right was still prevalent to a serious extent in the relations between men and held a dominant position in distribution.[30] By "bourgeois right" they referred particularly to the eight-grade system of wages and material incentive in the cities as well as to the private plots and the private trading at rural markets in the countryside. Even in a socialist society where the means of production were publicly owned, "bourgeois right" was, according to their theory, the source of new bourgeois elements and a new bourgeois class. The proletariat had to exercise "all-round dictatorship over the bourgeoisie." More ominous was the unqualified assertion that "the bourgeoisie was right [here] within the Party." Thus, they reversed the Marxist theory of the relationship between class and party. This reversal was one of the many absurd ideas and slogans developed during the Cultural Revolution. All these points are discussed and documented in detail in chapter 4 and more systematically

29. Chang Ch'un-ch'iao (Zhang Chunqiao), "On Exercising All-Round Dictatorship over the Bourgeoisie," *Peking Review*, April 4, 1975: 7. For discussion, see chaps. 4 and 8.

30. Chang (Zhang), "All-Round Dictatorship," 8.

and succinctly summarized in chapter 8, though with a slightly different emphasis from that of the discussion here and with the additional thought that by simultaneously attacking both "hierarchies" and "markets"—the only two feasible methods to organize a modern economy—Mao precluded any rational solution to the problems of economic growth.

During this period, the Marxist notion of unity of theory and practice and Mao's own phrase of "seeking truth from facts" became empty slogans, being totally overwhelmed by Mao's new tenet of historical materialism. The incongruence between ideology and reality was more glaring than at any time since the early years of the Jiangxi period.

The third phase of Chinese Marxism began in 1978 and is still going on. The basic characteristic of this period has been the reinterpretation and revision of Mao Zedong Thought to bring it closer to reality—a process which Peter Ludz calls the "refunctionalization of ideology." The most significant change is the elevation to first rank of the epistemological and methodological postulate finalized in the Resolution on Party History (adopted June 1981) in the following terms: "Seeking truth from facts . . . means proceeding from reality, combining theory with practice, that is, integrating the universal principles of Marxism-Leninism with the concrete practice of the Chinese revolution." This epistemological and methodological postulate is characterized as the first of the three basic points of "the living soul of Mao Zedong Thought," which is "the stand, viewpoint, and method embodied in its [Mao Zedong Thought's] component parts."[31]

By emphasizing "facts," "reality," and "practice," the revived epistemological and methodological postulate justifies, as it did in the earlier period, the Party's attention to, and orientation toward, the needs, interests, demands, life situations, and behavioral patterns of social groups and individuals. The obverse side of the reelevation of this postulate is the questioning, or at least qualification, of Mao's new tenet of historical materialism. The latter is not invoked as a justification for the Party's program, even when the Party admittedly alters the relations of production in order to develop the forces of production, as when it rapidly implemented the system of responsibility in agricultural production. At the same time, the Chinese theorists have developed what I call a "sociological postulate" in their reexamination of the notion of "politics in command" and their restatement of the relationship between politics and other spheres of social life. This sociological postulate can be reconstructed as follows. Every sphere of social life has its special characteristics and is governed by special laws of an objective, scientific nature. Political lead-

31. "On Questions of Party History—Resolution on Certain Questions in the History of Our Party since the Founding of the People's Republic of China," *Beijing Review*, July 6, 1981: 33.

ership can and should create general conditions and a framework favorable to the operation of these laws. It can use these laws to promote the desired development. But it cannot violate these laws without suffering serious consequences.[32] The search for general laws of socialist modernization and special laws governing each social sphere is the order of the day. To construct "socialism with Chinese characteristics" is defined as the task of the Party.

The Historic Change in Direction and Continuity with the Past: The Middle Course

The third phase of Chinese Marxism has coincided with a historic change in direction—of which the Third Plenary Session of the Eleventh Central Committee held in December 1978 is the landmark. The third plenum signaled the end of nearly three-quarters of a century of revolutionary ferment and upheaval. It marked the beginning of the reversal of that trend toward increasing penetration of society by the state which had begun after the May Fourth period and which reached its highest point during the Cultural Revolution. But this historic change has been accompanied by an effort to maintain continuity with the past of the Chinese Communist movement and regime. Within three months of the third plenum the Party reaffirmed that Chinese political and social life was to be guided by four fundamental principles: socialism, the dictatorship of the proletariat, the leadership of the Party, and Marxism-Leninism-Mao Zedong Thought. Thus the process of reversal and the new trend toward more autonomy for social groups and individuals have definite limits. These points are made and documented in chapter 5 and chapter 7.

In chapter 7 the metaphor "the middle course" is used to characterize the general direction of change and its limits in all spheres of Chinese life. This middle course is bordered by two "zones of demarcation." The latter term suggests that the middle course lacks precise, well-defined boundaries. Instead, the zone is itself a broad, ambiguous, imprecise area subject to change, as the political tide ebbs and flows. The zone of demarcation on one side is the general orientation adopted by the third plenum, as well as the development in that direction afterwards. The zone of demarcation on the other side is symbolized by the four fundamental principles. The orientations represented by these two zones balance each other, and both form an integral part of the middle course. Moreover, there have been constant conflicts between those leaders who endeavor to push forward even faster and farther the general orientation of the Third Plenum and those who give greater weight to the four fundamental principles. These conflicts will continue. The translations of the complex

32. For a more detailed discussion, see chaps. 5 and 8.

relationship between these two orientations into a general program or a specific policy depends on the changing balance of political and social forces over time in general and in a particular policy area. Thus the middle course is not a straight line but oscillates over time between the two zones of demarcation. To use the more straightforward formulation suggested by one of my readers, the middle course of the present may not be either the middle course of the past or that of the future.

But the "middle course" metaphor does have concrete meanings. On the one hand, it signifies the repudiation of the lingering influence of the Cultural Revolution and the "two-whatever" doctrine of Hua Guofeng. On the other hand, it entails the rejection of "bourgeois liberalization" and of liberal democracy. Positively, it means the granting of a greater degree of autonomy to social groups and individuals, the loosening of the Party's control over all other social and political institutions and organizations, some relaxation of ideological control over academic discussion and literary works, a search for a more subtle way of handling dissent and disagreements, and finally but not least important, use of the market mechanism to supplement central planning. But all this is done within the limit of maintaining the framework of the Party-state and indeed for the purpose of strengthening it. To use Gramscian terminology, the Party has reduced in different degrees its direct domination or command over the various spheres of social life so as to strengthen its hegemony over the civil society as a whole. The "middle course" metaphor also reflects without much distortion the thinking of top Chinese leaders in control, the imprecise Chinese official pronouncements, and the leaders' groping for ways to achieve their goals. It finds support in the Chinese abandonment of the notion of "the struggle *between two lines*" and the simultaneous revival of the idea of "the struggle *on two fronts*" against both Leftist and Rightist errors. It suggests that the moderate reformers in the Party have been trying to occupy the middle position in their relationship to the two other major political tendencies, playing both ends against the middle in order to pursue the program they prefer.

The terms "Left" and "Right" used throughout the essays in this volume are adopted directly from the Chinese usage. I have not been concerned with the meaning of the terms from the social-scientific viewpoint—a problem beyond my present ability to tackle. But looking at the Chinese case as an outside observer, I venture here to suggest that the terms "Left" and "Right" each represent one of the two opposite tendencies in Mao's synthesis during the first period of Chinese Marxism after 1927. The term "Left" denotes the emphasis on Mao's new tenet of historical materialism, revolutionary theory, revolutionary impulse, class struggle, coercive power, mass mobilization, and the political penetration of society. Correspondingly, the term "Right" refers to the emphasis on the notion of unity of theory and practice, the slogan of "seeking truth from facts," prudent respect for reality, the mass line, persuasion, the perceived interests and felt needs of social groups and individuals, and the energies flowing from civil society.

I should also like to suggest here that the move toward the Right since 1978 and the middle course followed at present do not represent a total return to Mao's synthesis of the first period. The revolution is over, the revolutionary impulse has disappeared, "turbulent class struggles on a large scale" no longer exist, limits on the use of coercive power are more clearly recognized than before, mass movements have been abandoned not only as an effective technique but also as something possessing intrinsic value, and finally political power has retreated from its deep penetration of society. If the Yanan synthesis represented a tactical adjustment to reality, the middle course of the present reflects the strategy adopted to achieve nonrevolutionary goals.

Chapter 7 also seeks to clarify what is a paradox to many observers outside China but actually an easily understood phenomenon if we grasp fully both the significance of the change in direction since 1978 and the continuity of the Party-state. This paradox puzzles outside observers, particularly those in Taiwan and Hong Kong, who use the model developed to analyze Maoist China to gauge events in post-Mao China. Their analyses and forecasts have frequently turned out to be wrong. During the Maoist era, when a movement began, it swept through all spheres of society; a movement toward the Left in the sphere of literature was usually a harbinger of things to come in all other areas. But in the post-Mao period, an attack by the Left on the more liberal and less orthodox writers has not been followed by movement toward the Left in other fields. On the contrary, the changes going on in many areas have continued their Rightward movement.

To make the same point at a different level of analysis, one can suggest that the change in the relationship between political power (or more precisely, the Party-state) and society is uneven in different social sectors. The changes in the relationship between political power and the economy have occurred faster and have gone farther than those in the relationship between political power and civil society. Within the economy, changes in the agricultural and rural sector have gone far ahead of changes in other sectors and have followed a steady course. In civil society, the sphere of literature and art has encountered more visible difficulties than most other professions. The developments there exhibit cycles of relaxation and reimposition of stricter control. Chapter 6, which documents the initial establishment of the responsibility system in agriculture, and chapter 7, which gives an account of the reimposition of stricter control over literature symbolized by the criticism of Bai Hua's screenplay *Bitter Love* and updates the rapid development of the responsibility system, can best be read in reverse order to get a full view of the contrast. In the area of abstract questions of ideology which affect the literary writers directly, there have also been cycles of oscillation, with the launching of the campaign against "spiritual pollution" and its quick contraction and termination as the latest episode. This development in late 1983 and early 1984 is not analyzed in this volume. But it is mentioned briefly and indirectly in chapter 8. It is quite possible that these uneven developments in various sectors can be traced to an idea emphasized since 1978, that each sphere of social life has its own special characteristics and is governed by "special laws." It is also possible that political leaders controlling or directing these areas entertain different views and that there exists a limited degree of institutional pluralism. At the moment I am not in a position to make and document either of these arguments. It is also possible that successful reforms in the economic sphere will gradually and eventually bring about changes in the ideological sphere, not through the launching of campaigns but through their long-term cumulative effects. As a result, the developments in various social spheres will be more closely aligned with one another. Even so, this closer alignment will be brought about by processes very different from methods used in the Maoist era.

The Continuing Process of Rebuilding the State and Reforming the Party-State in the Post-Mao Period

The process of state rebuilding did not end in the first few years after 1949 as many people expected. The process of institutionalization and routinization was constantly interrupted, first by the continuing process of revolutionizing the social structure and later by the struggle between the charismatic leader and the routinizing organization which finally produced the unprecedented Cultural Revolution.

The course of recent events, and particularly the discourse among Chinese over their past, present, and future, underscore the importance of reforming and institutionalizing the Party-state. This significant development is elaborated in the final essay in great detail and need not be belabored in this introduction. But the reappraisal by the Chinese of their own past and the reforms adopted or proposed have alerted us to some aspects of the process of state rebuilding in China which I should like to call attention to in this introduction. One superficial aspect is that, in contrast to the Western experience of state building long ago, the central tasks of state rebuilding in China in the twentieth century have not been the building of the army and the establishment of a tax system to extract resources from society. They have been precisely the opposite—establishing a system of civilian authority over the military and downgrading the latter's importance and power. As for taxation and the extraction of resources, the problem has been their excess rather than their insufficiency, as well as the misuse of taxes collected and the misallocation of resources. So far as the common need to build a strong state is concerned, the Chinese problem has always been the overconcentration of power and the arbitrary use of power by one man. This is easy to see.

But pursuing further the comparison with the West and taking advantage of the Chinese reexamination of their past, I try to make two controversial points in chapter 8, which I want to note here. One is that the process of state rebuilding has been based on the concept of "masses" and its two derivatives, the mass line and mass movement or mobilization. This process and its outcomes are fundamentally different from the process of state building based on the Western concept of "citizenship." The Chinese concept of "masses" is not the same as that used by such Western scholars as Kornhauser and Hannah Arendt. It denotes segments of the various social strata or classes with socioeconomic needs and demands. The masses in China during the revolutionary period were not rootless individuals in an anomic society, although some intellectuals and students could be so characterized. The Chinese state that was built on the concepts of masses, the mass line, and mass movement has emphasized the task of satisfying these socioeconomic demands and needs, while civil rights and freedoms have been ignored or even constantly violated in practice, and political rights have been subordinated to the quest for socioeconomic rights and, for other deeper reasons as well, have had little real meaning. In contrast, the concept of citizenship takes the individual to be an isolated entity endowed with a system of formal, legal rights and freedoms, which are protected by the state and society from infringement. The state built on this concept proceeded to secure the protection and development of civil rights in the eighteenth century, of political rights in the nineteenth, and of socioeconomic rights in the twentieth.

The Chinese Party-state has been fairly successful in promoting the socioeconomic rights of the disadvantaged masses, particularly in the city. During the land reform movement that terminated in 1952 it also achieved remarkable success in the countryside. In the past three or four years, it has begun to take the concept of citizenship more seriously than ever before in its attempt to establish a system of "socialist legality," "socialist democracy," and "democracy on a high level." The last is interpreted as a democracy more advanced than Western liberal democracies in that it aims at achieving a full development of civil, political, and socioeconomic rights and combines a high level of "material civilization" with a high level of "spiritual civilization." The theoretical and practical question that confronts outside observers is twofold. Can a state initially built on the concept of masses move from the promotion of socioeconomic rights to the promotion of genuine political and civil rights? More fundamentally, can a

Leninist party-state permit in practice the existence of a meaningful system of political and civil rights?

As regards the two derivatives of the notion of the masses, reflections on the Chinese Communist movement and regime up to the present have deepened our understanding of the mass line and its relationship to mass movement. In the first essay, I merely repeat the conventional wisdom. In chapter 8 I arrive at a better formulation of the nature of the mass line. It is characterized as the method through which "the CCP succeeded during the revolutionary period in finding and maintaining an adequate balance between the Party's fundamental revolutionary interests, which had to prevail, and such immediate, economic interests as were perceived by the peasants and other social groups, which should not (or could not) be sacrificed." I also suggest that the mass line was not a mere method of implementing class struggle and cannot be traced exclusively to this concept. In actuality, it also served as a balance to radical policies derived from the notion of class struggle. "It was an idea which, together with the notion of seeking truth from facts and the impact of the political, economic, and military realities of both the Jiangxi and Yanan periods, led Mao to advocate increasingly moderate policies in many areas." In contrast to the mass line, mass movements and mobilization were merely means of waging class struggle, implementing radical policies, or fighting among Party factions. The recent reemphasis of the mass line on the one hand and abandonment of mass movements on the other enable us to see this distinction clearly.

The Unending Tasks

It is clear from what I have said in this introduction that I have broadened my analytical framework and that some general insights gained from reading works on systems analysis and rational-choice theory have increasingly shaped or served implicitly to undergird that changing framework. This is not the place to discuss how and to what extent ideas derived from these theoretical and methodological viewpoints can be applied to the Chinese case. But I do want to note that when used in the larger context of systems analysis, insights derived from theories of human action and rational choice, including the theory of learning, will enable us to gain new understanding of the strategic and tactical decisions made by the Chinese Communist leaders, particularly during the period after 1927. This task will be greatly facilitated by the publication of selected works of Chinese leaders, their memoirs, diaries, and reminiscences, as well as articles and books based on the ongoing research in China on Party history.

The use of insights from these two bodies of literature would also be helpful in an emerging area of study which holds great promise for the future. This is the study of the interrelationship of the macrosociopolitical and microsociopolitical levels.[33]

As the Chinese are collecting and publishing their economic data more systematically than before and the economists in the field of Chinese studies are pushing their research forward rapidly, it is not only possible but imperative to examine systematically the impact of politics on economics and of economics on politics. This important aspect of Chinese development finds no expression in this volume. To undertake that task, a third level of analysis, dealing with economic development, income distribution, and the nature of the economic system itself, must be detached from the first level of analysis, which deals only in general terms with the state-society relationship. The empirical and historical connection of the Chinese economy with the state-civil society relationship and with the changes in the configuration of political power can then be examined in detail. This task must be left to others.

In the essays collected in this volume, the historical narratives are derived from serious research based mainly on primary Chinese sources. They can stand on their own. But they carry within them explanations and interpretations of events that had occurred shortly before the time of writing. In some cases, explicit generalizations on the Chinese Communist movement and regime are drawn. I hope that these narratives and generalizations can serve as a point of departure for the trend toward systematic comparison with other cases.[34]

In this introduction, I am taking the risk of clarifying my use of terms, concepts, and theories at a time when my thinking on these subjects has not gone very far and is vulnerable to criticism both on purely theoretical grounds and in their application to the Chinese case. I assume this risk willingly in order to give additional impetus to the rapidly developing trend toward an integration of the social sciences with Chinese studies. I also wish to enrich the dialogue between China scholars and the specialists in the disciplines, just as I have constantly tried to do with my former and present colleagues in Chicago. I hope that this volume will be taken seriously by China scholars, specialists in comparative politics, and theorists in the social sciences alike. If so, my intellectual effort over a period of eighteen years will not have been expended in vain.

33. For those who are interested in this endeavor, see Tang Tsou, Marc Blecher, and Mitchell Meisner, "The Responsibility System in Agriculture: Its Implementation in Xiyang and Dazhai," *Modern China* 8 (January 1982): 41–96. Although this paper appears here as chap. 6, the section dealing with the microsociopolitical level has been deleted.

34. Many political scientists in the field of Chinese studies are already doing research in all the areas indicated in this section. It would be impossible in this introduction to name them all.

The Cultural Revolution and Post-Mao Reforms

A HISTORICAL PERSPECTIVE

Revolution, Reintegration, and Crisis in Communist China: A Framework for Analysis

Introductory Remarks

The totalitarian regime in China emerged as a reaction against the country's political disintegration during the early part of the twentieth century.[1] This response followed the failure of the Nationalists to build up a unified party and a reintegrated polity soon enough to withstand the disruptive effects of the Sino-Japanese War. One of the most remarkable achievements of the political leadership of the Chinese Communists up to 1959 was their ability to maintain the unity of their party and an adequate degree of political integration, despite both the unprecedented problems confronting them and the inevitable clashes of views on policy issues. They tried to promote political integration in their own way with policies entailing obvious economic and sometimes even political costs.

Total control and total mobilization, two distinguishing features of a totalitarian polity, were indispensable ingredients of the Beijing regime's stability and success. But the Chinese Communists seemed to have realized that total control without political integration would create tremendous reaction against them which would have to be dealt with by the intensified use of secret police and physical terror. Repression would soon reach a point of diminishing returns and control could break down during a period of prolonged crisis. Success in mobilization probably correlates with the degree of integration achieved within the elite and between the elite and the masses. Upon closer examination, measures undertaken to mobilize the masses are sometimes integrative measures as well. As Karl W. Deutsch defines it, social mobilization is "the process in which major

1. [This essay was first published in Ping-ti Ho and Tang Tsou, ed., *China in Crisis*, vol. 1, bk. 1 (Chicago: University of Chicago Press, 1968): 277–347, © 1968 by The University of Chicago.] This paper was completed in the first week of January, 1967. The written comments on it by Professors Charles P. FitzGerald and Jerome Cohen were completed in March on the basis of their oral remarks made at the conference in the first week of February. [Their comments are not published in this volume.] No extensive revisions have been made in the paper to take account of developments since early January and the voluminous new materials available. Some footnotes have, however, been added to include new materials [available to the author later in that year] which throw light on the Cultural Revolution.

The author wishes to acknowledge the research grant given him by the Rockefeller Foundation during the academic year 1965–66, and the research support given by the Social Science Divisional Research Committee, the Center for International Studies, and the Committee on Far Eastern Studies of the University of Chicago.

clusters of old social, economic and psychological commitments are eroded or broken and people become available for new patterns of socialization and behavior."[2] The erosion of old social, economic, and psychological commitments is one aspect of the process of social disintegration. The development of new patterns of socialization and behavior is one facet of the process of social integration.

While the Chinese Communists succeeded in bringing into existence a polity with a higher degree of integration than the Nationalists, they have encountered mounting difficulties in adjusting their integrative measures to the trends toward functional differentiation, specialization, professionalism, and some amount of routinization which occur in all stable, modern, and industrializing societies. The achievement of a degree of integration enabled the regime to survive and to recover from the extraordinary crisis of three consecutive years of agicultural failure and the ever escalating dispute with the Soviet Union—difficulties which would have brought down most other governments. But the intensified attack on the intellectuals since November, 1965, the Great Proletarian Cultural Revolution, and the current purges make it clear that setbacks in both domestic and foreign policies activated two conflicting opinion groups which the integrative measures of the regime have failed to harmonize and harness. The struggle for power between these two groups has centered precisely around the issue of the extent to which the thought of Mao Zedong should be the integrative myth[3] of the political community and should shape policies and guide activities in various spheres of social life. This conflict raises the very question of how well the ideology and the pattern of integrative measures which had been developed in the revolutionary period in relatively backward base areas fitted the new situation and emerging trends.[4] Since Communist China offers an example of an experiment in one type of political integration, an examination of her past achievements enables us to see the conditions facilitating this type of political integration and to discern the methods employed to promote it. Insofar as this experiment has created its own problems, subjecting it to analysis helps us to discover the limits of its success and the roots of its difficulties.

The Political Community

Analytically speaking, political integration has three different aspects, although emipirically they are linked together: integration among the elite,

2. Karl W. Deutsch, "Social Mobilization and Political Development," *American Political Science Review*, 55 (September, 1961): 494.

3. For the term "integrative myth," see Chalmers Johnson, "The Role of Social Science in China Scholarship," *World Politics*, 17 (January, 1965): 268.

4. John W. Lewis, "The Study of Chinese Political Culture," *World Politics*, 18 (April, 1966): 511.

integration between the elite and the masses, and integration of a political community. Logically and historically, one takes precedence over the other in the order given. Without integration among the elite, integration between the elite and the masses is difficult to achieve; without integration between the elite and the masses, there cannot be an integrated political community. In a disintegrated political community, the process of political integration begins historically with the integration of the elite or a counter-elite and ends with a reintegrated political community through the integration between the elite and the masses. To the degree that integration is achieved, the reintegrated political community furnishes a general framework within which the elite and the masses find their places. Thus, a study of the process of integration must start with the elite, but a study of the system of integrative measures can start with the political community.

As Herbert Spiro suggests, "most communities are political systems."[5] Conversely, a political system is inseparable from a political community. As Talcott Parsons observes, "a relatively established 'politically organized society' is clearly a 'moral community' to some degree, its members sharing common norms, values, and culture."[6] But the choice of the political community rather than the political system per se as our focus of attention is a deliberate one. In a situation where profound changes take place in all spheres of human life (social, economic, political, intellectual, moral, ideological, cultural, religious, artistic, technological), the environment and the political system interact continuously. From the environment, demands arise which lead to the disruption of the traditional political system.[7] Then a new political system emerges which makes the restructuring of the environment its principal preoccupation. To encompass the interactions between the political system and its environment, the term "political community" is used.[8]

A political community presupposes a set of basic principles governing social and political life. In a democratic or a traditional community, there is an agreement on these fundamental principles, and the political system

5. Herbert J. Spiro, "Comparative Politics: A Comprehensive Approach," *American Political Science Review*, 56 (September, 1962): 577.

6. Talcott Parsons, "Some Reflections on the Place of Force in Social Process," in *Internal War*, ed. Harry Eckstein (New York: Free Press of Glencoe, 1964), p. 34.

7. For a discussion of the political system and its environment, see David Easton, *A Framework for Political Analysis* (Englewood Cliffs, N.J.: Prentice-Hall, 1965), chap. 7.

8. Presumably, the term "political system" may be used synonymously with the term "political community." But sometimes the former term is used in a narrower sense. For example, Gabriel Almond observes that every political system is embedded in a particular pattern of orientations to political action, i.e., political culture (Gabriel Almond, "Comparative Political Systems," *Journal of Politics*, 18 [August, 1956]: 396). Statements of this kind suggest that orientation to political action is not part of the political system per se as the

is based on this consensus. This agreement on fundamentals (political consensus) has its origin in the ideologies or schools of thought which once divided the politically active men into various groupings. After a revolution and through a long process of evolution and change, there then emerges an ideological agreement which, generally speaking, draws upon selected ideologies in different proportions to serve as the foundation of an integrated political community.

The collapse of the traditional order in China left in its wake a highly disintegrated political community. It produced a total response in the form of a totalitarian movement and regime with a total ideology which contained an all-inclusive criticism of the existing society and justified total change and reconstruction. In a totalitarian system, the official ideology backed directly by the coercive power of the state serves as a substitute for the agreement on fundamentals characteristic of both democratic and traditional political communities.

Ideology performs several important functions in a political community. It helps to integrate the various functional groups in the society by laying down the basic principles of social life which distinguish between "right" and "wrong." It prescribes the "rules of the game" guiding competition for power and material resources. It sets the general orientation of the political community by defining the common purposes. It provides schematic images of social and political realities which enable the actors to "understand" their environment and to cope with it. It enlists commitments, motivates action, and creates a collective conscience to the extent that it is accepted by the actors and internalized in their personality through a process of socialization. Finally, it legitimizes the political system and transforms power into authority.[9]

These usual functions of ideology are magnified in the case of Communist China for the following reasons. First and most obviously, the possession of an all-embracing official ideology is a basic characteristic of totalitarian regimes. Second, Communist China has a newly established regime in which revolutionary dynamism and momentum have not entirely lost their force. The notion of "the end of ideology" is a view developed by intellectuals in a stable society to characterize a phenomenon which occurs typically in mature regimes. What it actually denotes is the decline of

---

term was used by Almond. The term "political community" has the advantage of encompassing "political culture" as well as other things which interest us.

9. Clifford Geertz, "Ideology as a Cultural System," in *Ideology and Discontent*, ed. David Apter (New York: Free Press of Glencoe, 1964), pp. 47–71. Apter, "Introduction," *ibid.*, pp. 15–46. David Easton, *A Systems Analysis of Political Life* (New York: John Wiley & Sons, 1965), pp. 286–88, 289–90. Johnson, "Social Science in China Scholarship," p. 268. Talcott Parsons, *The Social System* (Glencoe, Ill.: Free Press, 1951), pp. 349–59.

a particular *type* of ideology, that is, such total ideologies as Marxism and Leninism. Far from meaning the end of ideology, it refers to the achievement of an "ideological agreement" which has become "the ideology of the major parties in the developed states of Europe and America."[10] In a sense, the "end of ideology" signifies the triumph of one type of ideology. As applied to a mature totalitarian regime such as the Soviet Union, this notion refers to the process of ideological erosion, a process that in the Soviet Union has gone rather far under the impact of socioeconomic reality and emerging problems for which the ideology has provided no adequate answers. By contrast, Mao Zedong, Lin Biao, and their followers have been making a determined effort to reassert the thought of Mao Zedong in order to preserve the original revolutionary dynamism and momentum.

Third, in contrast to the Bolsheviks, the Chinese Communists came to power after a protracted political-military struggle within China. The thought of Mao Zedong evolved out of practical actions and policy decisions undertaken in the past. It consists essentially of the rationale behind these undertakings and of the justification and rationalization of them. It is the codification of the revolutionary experience of the Chinese Communist Party (CCP). It guided the revolutionary struggle from defeat to victory. It gained its legitimacy and appeal by its proven effectiveness in the past. Furthermore, the CCP from 1927 to 1949 was a Communist party without a proletarian base. Instead of social origin, the Chinese Communists therefore stressed the acceptance of Marxist-Leninist-Maoist ideology as the criterion of a Communist. Ideological indoctrination thus became an absolute necessity and the sole guaranty of the self-identity of the party.

Fourth, in the traditional political system in China an explicit system of official ideology in the form of Confucianism played an important role in legitimizing the regime, in humanizing the autocratic rule, in determining the content of education, and in defining the proper rules governing human relationships. The rejection of the specific content of Confucianism created a moral and intellectual void, while the breakdown of age-old political institutions produced a long period of chaos. The Chinese were confronted with novel social situations which seemed unstructured and incomprehensible to them at a time when institutionalized guides for behavior and thought were weak or absent. It is during times like these that men urgently need what Clifford Geertz calls "maps of problematic social

---

10. Seymour Martin Lipset, "Some Further Comments on 'The End of Ideology,'" *American Political Science Review*, 60 (March, 1966): 17. See also Joseph La Palombara, "Decline of Ideology: A Dissent and an Interpretation," *ibid.*, pp. 1–16.

reality" and "a template or blueprint for the organization of social and psychological processes."[11] Marxism-Leninism and the thought of Mao constituted such a map and blueprint. Even today, the Chinese Communists stress the importance of ideological unity. Lin Biao in his important letter of March 11, 1966, states: "China is a great socialist state of the dictatorship of the proletariat and has a population of 700 million. It needs unified thinking. . . . This is Mao Zedong's thinking."[12] This continued emphasis on ideological unity may very well be a reaction against the moral and intellectual chaos which characterized the period of political disintegration. It may also represent the persistence of a cultural pattern.

Fifth, the Chinese Communists have undertaken to modernize and industrialize their country under more difficult material conditions, but with greater success, than any other underdeveloped nation after World War II.* In overcoming the difficulties and achieving success, they have relied on mobilizing human resources in China, on creating new social, economic, and psychological commitments, and on transforming the attitudes, habits, and customs of the people. In these endeavors, indoctrination has played a principal role. The Chinese Communists' emphasis on the importance of ideological transformation indicates a recognition of a strategic or limiting factor in social change, that is, the moral basis of the society, to use Edward Banfield's term.[13] Without a drastic change in the ethos of the Chinese society, the rapid modernization and industrialization to date would have been impossible.

The political community in China has been held together by the elite through a structure of political institutions and mass organizations and on the foundation of a single faith. In questioning the concept of the elite as developed and applied to the American system by C. Wright Mills and Floyd Hunter, Robert A. Dahl has in effect outlined an operational definition of the concept and challenged us to apply it to any specific political system or community.[14] For the purpose of opening a dialogue between political scientists and specialists on China, one might submit the proposition that the political systems in both traditional and Communist China can pass the three tests proposed by Dahl for the existence of a ruling elite. First, in both systems the ruling elite can be shown to be a fairly well-defined group. In traditional China, the ruling elite—which was also the social elite—was composed of the emperor, the aristocracy, the em-

---

11. Geertz, "Ideology as a Cultural System," pp. 62–64.

12. *Peking Review,* June 24, 1966, p. 6.

* In retrospect, the words "up to 1958" should be added after "World War II."

13. Edward Banfield, *The Moral Basis of a Backward Society* (Glencoe, Ill.: Free Press, 1958), p. 163.

14. Robert A. Dahl, "Critique of the Ruling Elite Model," *American Political Science Review,* 51 (July, 1958): 463–69.

peror's personal retainers, and what Ping-ti Ho calls "the ruling class," consisting of "officials, people holding official ranks and titles, subofficials, and degree-holders above *sheng- yuan* for the Ming period, with the same definition for the Ch'ing period except for the exclusion of *chien-sheng.*"[15] In Communist China there has been a bifurcation between a political and a social elite.[16] But there is still no question that the political elite of party leaders, cadres, and members constitutes the ruling elite or class. Second, there is a fair sample of cases involving key political decisions in which the preferences of the elite ran counter to those of any other likely group that might be suggested. Third, in each case, the preferences of the ruling elite have prevailed.[17]

In a totalitarian society, elite integration is the key to political integration. The governmental institutions and the mass organizations created by the elite are transmission belts which the elite use to mobilize, control, and integrate the people. But to a greater extent than in the Soviet Union, the CCP has created these institutions and organizations in its own image. Their structures and principles of organization parallel closely those of the party, with such modification as fits their specific functions. For example, the structure of the people's congresses of the state parallels the structure of congresses in the party. The Standing Committee of the National People's Congress and the State Council parallel the Central Committee, the Secretariat, and the various departments of the party. On the local levels, the structure of the people's councils parallels the structure of party committees. The principle of "democratic centralism," originally used in the party, is supposed to govern all state organs and mass organizations.[18] The method of "criticism and self-criticism," first developed within the party, is now extended to "all our factories, co-operatives, business establishments, schools, government offices, public bodies, in a word, all the six hundred million of our people. . . ."[19] The "small groups" in which some five to twenty people meet frequently for various purposes follow much the same procedures and have similar power structures as the party small groups. Thus the congruence of the patterns of authority, which is

15. Ping-ti Ho, "Aspects of Social Mobility in China, 1368–1911," *Comparative Studies in Society and History*, 1 (June, 1959): 342. See also Ping-ti Ho, *The Ladder of Success in Imperial China* (New York: Columbia University Press, 1962), p. 40. S.N. Eisenstadt, *The Political Systems of Empires* (London: Macmillan Co., 1963), pp. 116, 157, 160–61.

16. Franz Schurmann, *Ideology and Organization in Communist China* (Berkeley: University of California Press, 1966), pp. 51–53, 171.

17. In the Great Proletarian Cultural Revolution, the ruling elite is split into two major groups. Intra-elite struggle is a different phenomenon from a conflict between the elite and any other group.

18. Mao Zedong, *On the Correct Handling of Contradictions among the People* (Peking: Foreign Languages Press, 1957), p. 13.

19. *Ibid.*, p. 18.

considered by Harry Eckstein as one of the keys to political stability, is fairly close, at least between the party and other secondary groups or organizations. One may lay down as an hypothesis that so long as the party remained united, this parallelism in the structures and organizational and operational principles facilitated the party's control over the government bureaucracy, the army, and all secondary organizations and groups. Party leaders who held leading positions in non-party institutions and organizations could operate with familiar rules. Moreover, since the organizational and operational principles long established in the party served as the norms for other institutions and organizations, the bureaucracies in the latter could not easily obstruct or evade party control by laying down their own complex rules and regulations, or by creating their own traditions which contravened those of the party.

The fact that it was possible for the party to create or reshape the governmental institutions and mass organizations in its own image can ultimately be explained by the weakness and instability of the secondary associations and governmental institutions during the Republican period. The latter were developed in an institutional and organizational vacuum after the collapse of the traditional order. The Chinese Communists' victory in the civil war, together with the lack of strength, tradition, and stability on the part of these non-Communist organizations and institutions, gave the party a carte blanche to remodel them. During the revolutionary period, the party constituted a small political community tied together by ideological, organizational, and personal bonds. This small and tightly knit political community existed in a disorganized society. It attempted to create a reintegrated political community in its own image. Thus, political development in China can be understood as a process in which a small group of men accepted a modern ideology, adapted it to Chinese conditions, perfected a system of organizations, developed a set of practices, and then extended this pattern of ideology, organization, and practices to the whole nation.[20]

Insofar as this attempt achieved some degree of success, it was facilitated by the following factors. First, China is not sharply divided along religious or nationality lines. The Chinese have seldom taken their religion seriously. The problem of national minorities is also not very disrup-

20. Tang Tsou, "Stability and Change in Communist China," in *The United States and Communist China*, ed. William W. Lockwood (Princeton, N.J.: Princeton University Press, 1965), p. 21. For a more extended discussion of this point, particularly the use of mass line as a strategy of economic development, see Chalmers A. Johnson, "Building a Communist Nation in China," in *The Communist Revolution in Asia*, ed. Robert A. Scalapino (Englewood Cliffs, N.J.: Prentice-Hall, 1965), pp. 47–81. For an interpretation of the international behavior of Beijing as a projection of Mao's revolutionary strategy, see Tang Tsou and Morton H. Halperin, "Mao Tse-tung's Revolutionary Strategy and Peking's International Behavior," *American Political Science Review*, 59 (March, 1965): 80–99.

tive. The Manchus absorbed wholeheartedly the Chinese culture during their 267-year rule over China. During the Republican period of thirty-seven years, the barriers between the Manchus and the Hans were completely swept aside. The national minorities account for only 6 per cent of the total population. Second, in the past thousand years or so, regionalism or provincialism constituted a serious problem in traditional China mainly when a ruling dynasty was in decline. When the imperial government was strong, it could generally hold these divisive forces in check by a complex system of political and bureaucratic measures, perfected over several centuries. Third, on the whole it must be said that traditional China was characterized by a high degree of political integration. Although imperial power did not effectively penetrate below the *xian* level, cultural and linguistic (as distinguished from dialectic) homogeneity was a powerful force uniting the Chinese empire. The Confucian tradition permeated to the level of the commoners. Upward social mobility enabled intelligent and hard-working commoners to become members of the ruling class. The gap between the elite and the masses was not wide. Fourth, political disintegration during the Republican period was associated with defeats and humiliations in foreign relations and with civil wars and political chaos in internal affairs. It brought about a deep yearning for a high degree of unity.

Many historical circumstances also helped to establish the legitimacy of the Communist regime. The total bankruptcy of the Nationalist government left the CCP as the only alternative to continued political disintegration and instability which had been the most striking phenomenon on the Chinese political scene after the collapse of the empire. The most salient characteristic of Chinese politics since the period of warlordism between 1916 and 1927 had been a drive toward the reestablishment of a strong central authority. The Nationalist movement and the formation of the Guomindang (GMD) regime in themselves had been steps toward this historic aim. The GMD had succeeded in fashioning the largest coalition of forces in the 1930's under the existing pattern of political participation and rules of the political game. But the Sino-Japanese War intervened before the authority of the Nationalist regime could be fully consolidated. The war also undermined whatever achievements the regime had attained. At the same time, the war produced a chaotic situation in which the CCP could expand its power and influence by appealing both to Chinese nationalism and to a widespread desire for reforms. This contrast suggests the advantage which an ideologically motivated and effectively organized totalitarian movement has over a neo-traditionalist and disunited nationalist movement, even in the very attempt to capture nationalism as a source of power.

Using nationalism as an effective appeal and as one element in its program, the CCP succeeded in winning the cooperation of many groups and in forming a latent united front against the GMD within the broader united front with the Nationalists against the Japanese. In other words, Chinese Communist ideology directed the party's attention to the importance of social groups which had not been active participants in the political process. By changing the pattern of political participation and the rules of the political game, the CCP succeeded in organizing a coalition of social groups much larger and more powerful than that headed by the GMD. During the civil war from 1946 to 1949, this latent united front against the GMD came to the surface. As the military fortunes of the GMD ebbed and the inherent weaknesses of the Nationalist regime were glaringly revealed under the strain of the civil war, the progressive isolation of the GMD was accompanied by the building up of an even broader united front by the Chinese Communists, including, as the Communists put it, "90 per cent" of the Chinese people against a handful of reactionaries. To the lack of any other alternative to political chaos was added a second factor which helped the Chinese Communists to establish the "legitimacy" of their regime. This was the popular support which they gained at the time of the founding of the regime.

The third factor was the effectiveness of their military, political, social, and economic programs during both the Sino-Japanese War and the civil war. Obviously, nothing succeeds like success. But the point is that in a society in which most of the traditional rules of conduct had been called into question and new ones had not been established, success through effectiveness could not be challenged on the ground that this success was obtained by illegitimate means. Furthermore, success and effectiveness could themselves be used to justify new rules of conduct, new institutions, and a new ideology which contributed to this success.

It is generally agreed that the Chinese political system which emerged out of the period of disintegration is basically different from the traditional one. Yet traditions cannot and need not be quickly and completely discarded. Some of them will of necessity persist. Others may turn out, upon close examination, to be parallel to modern patterns and therefore make the latter acceptable. While a large part of the efforts of the modernizers or innovators must be employed to demolish those traditions which cannot be reconciled with modernity, their success in building a stable, modern political community will be fostered by a parallel between modern institutions and the persisting traditional patterns and sometimes even by the conscious use of these traditions to support the modern system. Seen in this light, the contemporary question of tradition versus modernity which preoccupies many social scientists emerges as the perennial question of continuity and change in historical development.

As a preliminary framework for a study of the problem of tradition versus modernity, or continuity and change, in China (or elsewhere), a series of distinctions can be made. First, there is the distinction between *whole* and *part*. No doubt the nature of the political system in China, taken as a whole, has basically changed. The Marxist-Leninist-Maoist totalitarian regime is fundamentally different from the Confucian-authoritarian government of the past. The present system is characterized by total mobilization and active participation of the populace directed toward rapid social change, and by total political control which penetrates to the grass roots. In contrast, the traditional system was characterized by the domination of the elite over a passive population.

But certain parts of the Chinese tradition have persisted. The Chinese Communists distinguish between the "feudal" dregs and the "popular" elements in the cultural heritage of China. The former is considered reactionary and must be eliminated, but the latter is accepted as progressive and must be developed in the new culture. What the Chinese Communists call the "feudal" dregs embraces those components which gave the Chinese culture as a totality its character. What they call the "popular" elements consist of those ingredients which occupied a secondary position in the traditional society. Because the total system has changed, some of the surviving traditional elements occupy different positions, have different meanings, and entail different consequences in the new system. For example, anti-bureaucratism was a persistent strand in the peasant rebellions which flared up time and again in Chinese history. This is an element of the "people's culture" which Mao not only seeks to preserve but also to elevate to a central position in the political system. Anti-bureauctatism is now a constant feature in the theory and practice of the Maoist ruling elite. It is used by the top leaders to bridge the gap between the party and the masses, to bring the party and the people together, and to control the cadres through pressures exerted by the masses. In the present Cultural Revolution, Mao uses the masses to attack and destroy various party organizations. Another instance of the survival of a tradition which, however, belongs to a different category is the self-cultivation of the Confucian gentleman, paralleled by the Chinese Communist practice of self-criticism. But it is obvious that self-cultivation as an individual act and self-criticism in a collective setting are two different things. Of particular interest to students of social change in China is the persistence of parts of the traditional social system at the local level. The survival and resurgence (after the Great Leap Forward) of the natural villages, the traditional kinship ties, and the marketing systems in the rural areas constitute a remarkable phenomenon which raises difficult questions regarding the relationship between structural changes at the macro- and micro-societal levels. Moreover, the modern system and the surviving traditional elements may not always complement each other. Under certain circumstances, the tensions between them may become very sharp and contribute to serious disruptions. Some of these tensions underlie the Cultural Revolution.

Second, the traditional and the Communist political systems, including some of their respective components, are similar to each other in *form*, but basically different from each other in *content*. In both the traditional authoritarian system and the modern totalitarian system, ideology has a pervasive influence. Up to the Cultural Revolution which has disrupted the Communist political system, the ruling class in both the traditional and modern systems was a well-defined group, and a single bureaucratized organization played a dominant role in society.[21] All these structural forms have not changed. But, the traditional ideology—with its concept of harmony, with its notion of reciprocal relationships between those occupying superior and inferior positions, with the postulation of limited action by government as one of its strands—had during various periods the function of civilizing, harmonizing, humanizing, and restraining absolute imperial power, or at least could potentially be used for that purpose. In contrast, the Chinese Communist ideology—with its ethic of conflict, its doctrine of dictatorship of the proletariat, and its call for uninterrupted revolution—has the consequence of maximizing the use of power by the state and of vastly expanding the function of government. The parallelism of structural forms in the political system facilitated the acceptance of the totalitarian system and partly accounted for the Chinese Communists' capacity to make it work, but the environmental changes necessitated the replacement of one content by another.

Sometimes traditional forms are consciously used to support new institutions. In 1963, the Maoists began a major effort to use traditional art forms to propagate Communist ideas. The most conspicuous example is the staging of Beijing operas on contemporary themes. Yet sometimes form is inseparable from content; old forms may have to be modified or discarded and new ones developed. As Jiang Qing asked, "Isn't it necessary to make a revolution and introduce changes if the old literature and art do not correspond to the socialist economic base and the classical artistic forms do not entirely fit the socialist content?"[22] Jiang Qing's concern about the lack of correspondence between traditional form and modern content in the realm of literature and art points to one of the causes of the Cultural Revolution—that is, the tension between some of the surviving traditional elements and the new, Maoist components in the sociopolitical system. The Maoists set out to destroy, among other things, the traditions

---

21. In a remark criticizing the regime, Zhou Yang pointed to one of the parallels but presented it in a different way. He said, "Old ideas sometimes appear in other forms, that is, old content in new form. The old content—feudal-patriarchal rule; the new form—the secretary of the Party committee in command" (*Peking Review*, August 19, 1966, p. 31).

22. *Ibid.*, December 9, 1966, p. 7.

of bureaucratism, regionalism, and localism which had persisted or re-emerged. Undoubtedly some of the long-standing Chinese traditions will survive even the Cultural Revolution. At the moment, however, it is difficult to foresee how and in what proportions the traditional and modern elements will again be integrated in the sociopolitical pattern which will emerge after the present crisis.

But the problem of form and content is much more complicated than the above remarks suggest. In such cases as the kinship system, the disruption of the structure may have gone farther than the erosion of the attitudes cultivated by it. In other words, the form of a social institution may have been disrupted, but the content may persist.

Third, one must make a distinction between *ends* and *means*—that is, between the *goals* of a political community and the *methods* of achieving those goals. Most if not all the goals espoused by the Chinese Communists are modern ones. But the Chinese sociopolitical tradition has conditioned their choice of methods or means. For example, the modern goal of industrialization is to be achieved through governmental effort rather than private enterprise. This choice of means is partly conditioned by the long tradition of the domination of the society by a political elite, and partly by the lack of a tradition of truly free enterprise on any large scale. [*]

Fourth, there is the distinction between *values* and *style*. The major values espoused by the Chinese Communists such as progress, equality between men and women, political activism, are totally modern. But the style of leadership is traditional. For example, the Chinese Communists in exercising leadership among the masses use the traditional style of casual conversation, heart-to-heart talks and intimate person-to-person relationships. When some people characterized Mao as the modern Son of Heaven, they were referring mainly to the continuation of the political style.

Finally, there is the distinction between *explicit orientation* and *implicit support*. The explicit orientation may be totally modern, but the implicit support may be traditional. For example, the explicit principle of foreign relations is "proletarian internationalism" and world revolution. The implicit support for this orientation comes from the tradition of a universal empire. Toward Southeast Asia, the explicit policy is to eliminate American imperialist influence by supporting national liberation movements in some cases and by promoting neutralism in others. The implicit support comes from the traditional, cultural, and political hegemony of China in that area.

* I now believe that in traditional China, there existed a "pre-capitalist system of free enterprise in the countryside." See Tang Tsou, ed., *Select Papers from the Center for Far Eastern Studies*, no. 4 (Chicago: Center for Far Eastern Studies, 1981) v.

The logical relationships among these theoretical distinctions await further examination and elaboration. It may very well be that these five distinctions are merely expressions of different aspects of a single pair of fundamental categories. If so, we would achieve a greater degree of economy and elegance in our solution of the problem of tradition versus modernity and the question of historical continuity and change. The present formulation may be a step forward in this endeavor.

In spite of the fact that the Chinese Communists established in their early years a political community with a higher degree of integration than that achieved by the Nationalist regime in the period between 1927 and 1949, the pattern of political integration contained within itself disintegrative forces with which it could not cope. A tentative and perhaps over-simplified explanation of this paradox can be offered here.

In the Chinese Communist political community, an ideology in the form of the thought of Mao Zedong played an extraordinarily important role in setting the general orientation, in bringing about integration of the various functional groups, in legitimizing the regime, and in enlisting commitment. Because of the operational character of Mao's thought and because of the paramount role played by Mao in making the most important decisions, at least before 1959, there was a particularly close association between ideology and policies.

Policies may be associated with ideology in various ways. At one extreme, a policy may be a direct projection or a derivation of ideology, with perhaps some necessary adjustment to reality. At the other extreme, a policy and an ideology may have no other association except that they are formulated by and identified with one and the same leader. If a policy has led to success, it may establish a precedent and become incorporated into the ideology when it is subsequently rationalized in theoretical terms. The policy of establishing base areas and organizing a guerrilla army and the strategy of surrounding the cities with the countryside were not originally part of Marxism-Leninism. But they have subsequently become a central part of the thought of Mao, which also includes ideas borrowed from Marxism and Leninism. Between these extremes lie several other possible forms of connection between policy and ideology. Policy may flow from a convergence between practical and ideological considerations. Perhaps the commune system falls into this category. Or the policy goal may be a reflection of practical needs but may be pursued through methods which are rooted in ideology. The Great Leap Forward is primarily of this type. Or a policy may be adopted on purely pragmatic grounds but may be justified or rationalized by ideological arguments. Perhaps the policy of self-reliance is of this nature.

Given the close association between policy and ideology, criticisms of the regime's policy may easily become criticisms of the ideology. Differences over policy soon become divergences in ideology, and disagreements over policy cannot be resolved on pragmatic grounds alone. Under these circumstances, the failures of Mao's domestic and foreign policies since 1959 produced not only criticisms of these policies but also a questioning of specific elements of Mao's thought. For example, Lin Mohan, a former Vice-Minister of Culture, is quoted as having said in 1960: "In studying the writing of Chairman Mao, there is no need to study their specific viewpoints because some of them have lost their timeliness."[23] The doubters of Mao's thought also resorted to the method of verbally reaffirming its validity but refusing to be guided by it in practice. Thus, the party charged that after 1963 there was a tendency for many party members to be outwardly "left" but to follow the rightist line in actuality and that they were "waving the red flag to oppose the red flag." The dissidents put forward ideas and values which were basically incompatible with a fundamentalist interpretation of the ideology but refrained from launching an open attack on it. Yang Xianzhen's theory of "two combining into one," and the historian's view that theory or doctrine emerges from historical data are cases in point. Syncretism rather than doctrinal purity may come from this process of development. The dissidents tried either to insulate certain areas of activities from the influence of the ideology or even to establish therein values and norms not in harmony with the Maoist doctrine. One example of such attempted insulation can be found in the notion of "purely academic discussion" to be conducted with standards different from those prevailing in the areas of political debate. Another example is the strict enforcement of academic standards at institutions of higher learning in disregard of a policy of favoring students of worker and peasant origin. These developments at once reflected and might accelerate the emergence of relatively well-defined and differentiated sectors in the society, whose norms and values might or might not be easily integrated with each other. The dissidents affirmed the validity of the ideology at a high level of generality but showed both reluctance to propagate it and doubt as to the advisability of extending its sphere of application. The Mao-Lin group charged that the party officials controlling the propaganda apparatus put countless obstacles in the way of printing and distributing Mao's works on a large scale.[24] All this questioning of Mao's thought seems to have taken place in a climate of opinion which was otherwise characterized by apathy and lethargy toward ideological or even political issues. Hence, Mao, Lin, and their followers have found it necessary to call on the people to be actively concerned with political and ideological questions. This questioning of Mao's thought at once reflected

23. *Renmin ribao* [People's Daily], September 22, 1966, p. 6.
24. *Peking Review*, August 12, 1966, p. 15.

and aggravated the tendencies toward disintegration, disorientation, demoralization, and the erosion of the legitimacy of the regime which had been brought about by policy failure.

The association between Mao's thought and policy failures, together with the doubt about the applicability of Mao's thought to many areas of social life, raises the question of congruence between ideology on the one hand and social reality and emerging trends on the other. To answer this question, one must examine the characteristics of Mao's thought, the circumstances under which it was first evolved, and the changed environment under which it has been applied. We shall consider the following aspects of Mao's thought which have always been present but which he has pushed to the extreme since 1958 and particularly since the Cultural Revolution: first, the idea of conflict; second, the tendency toward polarization in the thought pattern; third, the concept of the centrality of man; fourth, the controlling importance of "politics"; and finally, the importance of ideas over material conditions.

The thought of Mao developed out of the imperatives of fighting a guerrilla war in economically backward parts of China against vastly superior GMD and Japanese forces. It is permeated by the ideas of conflict, struggle, and combat.[25] Since the unfavorable balance of forces could be changed and victory achieved only after a long period of time, the concept of a protracted war emerged. The protracted civil war took the form of a series of GMD campaigns of encirclement and annihilation and Chinese Communist counter-campaigns. Except for the last one, each of the four sets of campaigns and counter-campaigns followed a cyclical pattern. The cycle began with the GMD's offensive and the CCP's retreat toward the center of the base area, reached a critical point in a decisive first offensive battle waged by the Chinese Red Army, moved toward a general offensive by the CCP with the GMD in retreat, and terminated in a voluntary halt by the Chinese Communist forces to prevent an overextension of their

25. It is obvious that the Marxist theory of contradiction was the intellectual source of this idea. The theory of contradiction was more congruent with political reality in the first half of the twentieth century in China than the Confucian theory of harmony. The unity of theory and practice or the CCP stood in sharp contrast to the wide discrepancy between the advocacy of Confucian virtues and the practice of *realpolitik* by Generalissimo Chiang.

To justify the attack on various high party officials and party organizations in the Great Proletarian Cultural Revolution, the Maoists repeatedly used Mao's assertion that "in the last analysis, all the myriad principles of Marxism can be summed up in one sentence: 'To rebel is justified'" (*Renmin ribao* [editorial], August 23, 1966, p. 1). This assertion can be found in Mao's talk on December 21, 1939, celebrating Stalin's sixtieth birthday. This talk was reprinted in *Xinhua yuebao* (New China Monthly), 1 (January, 1950): 581–82. When it is used in the context of the Cultural Revolution, it means that to rebel is justified even in a state ruled by a Communist Party and in a socialist society. A Red Guard poster added to this idea a qualification: "We are permitting only the Left to rebel, not the Right." (I am indebted to Stuart Schram for giving me the exact reference to Mao's speech in 1939.)

inadequate military power. During the stalemate phase in the Sino-Japanese War, the Chinese Communist forces also fought campaigns with similar features against the Japanese.

The ideas of combat and protracted struggle have continued to influence the thinking of the leaders since 1949. There has been a series of domestic campaigns, with the Great Proletarian Cultural Revolution as the latest one. At least four of these campaigns—the agrarian reform movement, the two campaigns to set up agricultural producers' cooperatives of the lower and higher types, and the Great Leap Forward-show a cyclical pattern.[26] The idea of combat, the concept of protracted struggle, and the series of campaigns have given content and substance to the goal of building a socialist society and have led to a revival of the theory of uninterrupted revolution. The continued application of this idea, however, has taken place in an environment in which the popular desire for a measure of stability and routinization has increased with time. This desire is reflected in the writings of the dissidents and the Maoists' analysis of these writings. In a widely read book published in 1956, Feng Ding defined social history as the history of the pursuit of happiness by all men. He wrote:

> Happiness in normal life means peace and no war, good food and fine clothing, a spacious and clean house, love between husband and wife, parents and children. There is no doubt about this, and this is also what we all are seeking.[27]

This view was attacked in 1964 as incompatible with the proletarian notion that the highest purpose in life is to serve the majority of the peoples of China and the world, as well as to struggle for the complete victory of communism in China and in the entire world.[28] Deng Tuo, a former member of the Secretariat of the Beijing Municipal Party of the CCP Committee which was reorganized in June, 1966, wrote: "People's attention should be called to treasure one-third of one's life so that after a day's labor or work, everyone can learn some useful knowledge, both ancient and modern, in a relaxed mood."[29] Commenting on this sentence, Yao Wenyuan, whose attack on Wu Han in November, 1965, signaled the prelude to the Cultural Revolution, wrote:

26. G. William Skinner, "Compliance and Leadership in Rural Communist China—A Cyclical Theory" (a paper delivered at the 1965 Annual Meeting of the American Political Science Association, Washington, D.C., September, 1965).

27. Quoted in D.W. Fokkema, "Chinese Criticism of Humanism: Campaigns against the Intellectuals, 1964–1965," *China Quarterly*, no. 26 (April-June, 1966), pp. 71–72.

28. *Ibid.*, p. 72.

29. Deng Tuo, *Yanshan yehua* [Evening Chats at Yanshan] (Beijing: Beijing chuban she, 1961), p. 3. See also, Yao Wen-yuan, "On 'Three-Family Village,'" *Peking Review*, May 27,

In asking everyone to read *Evening Chats at Yanshan* "in a relaxed mood," they [Deng Tuo and his friends] were trying to dull the people's revolutionary vigilance; beginning by corroding "one-third of the life" of those who were not firm in their revolutionary stand, they aimed at corroding the whole of their lives and making them serve as the organized force and social basis for the Three-Family Village clique in recruiting more and more people and promoting peaceful evolution.[30]

Talks about "relaxation" in their writings were considered to be poisonous weeds.[31] The Maoists also acknowledged that in the literary circles there was "opposition to the 'smell of gun-powder.'"[32]

Second, there is a tendency toward polarization in Mao's thought which accompanies the ideas of conflict, combat, and struggle. Fighting a guerrilla war reinforced the Comintern's theory of "two camps" and sharpened the distinction between the "enemy" and "ourselves." To identify the enemy in changing circumstances became one of the main intellectual tasks of the party. In spite of the shifting alliance with various groups and the policy of the united front, there is in the thought of Mao a tendency to polarize all things into two opposites. The dichotomy set up between the "enemy" and the "people" has become the basis of the political system. Recently an editorial of *Renmin ribao* (People's Daily), official organ of the CCP, declared: "Either you crush me or I crush you. Either the East wind prevails over the West wind, or the West wind prevails over the East wind. There is no middle road."[33] (An interesting question to be further explored is whether or not the tendency toward polarization in political struggle existed in traditional China and, to the extent it existed, whether or not it was related to bureaucratic life.) This thought pattern finds expression in the Maoists' policy toward literature and art which sets the writer's tasks as the portrayal of heroic characters and the exposure of the evil nature of the enemy and which condemns the "writing about middle characters."[34]

This tendency toward polarization in Mao's thought is partly an expres-

---

1966, p. 13. This sentence appeared in the first article in Deng Tuo's column, "Evening Chats at Yanshan."

30. Yao Wen-yuan, "On 'Three-Family Village,'" p. 14.

31. *Ibid.*, p. 13.

32. "Long Live the Great Proletarian Cultural Revolution," *The Great Socialist Cultural Revolution in China*, Vol. 3 (Peking: Foreign Languages Press, 1966), p. 9.

33. "A Great Revolution That Touches People to Their Very Souls," *ibid.*, p. 7. For a discussion of this "either-or" polarity as it affects Chinese philosophical discourse, see Donald J. Munro, "The Yang Hsien-chen [Yang Xianzhen] Affair," *China Quarterly*, no. 22 (April-June, 1965), pp. 75–82.

34. "Hold High the Great Red Banner of Mao Tse-tung's Thought and Actively Participate in the Great Socialist Cultural Revolution" (editorial), *Chieh-fang-chün pao* [Liberation Army Daily], April 18, 1966, in *Great Socialist Cultural Revolution*, vol. 1, pp. 4–5, 18–19.

sion of the necessity of most ideologies, including Maoism, to simplify social reality in order to serve as a guide to action, but it has become an obstacle in coping with reality as the simple life of the base areas has been replaced by an increasingly complex society. Thus, the attempt by semi-educated cadres and illiterate masses to apply the thought of Mao to specialized and technical fields of activity or to solve new problems has impressed Mao's critics as "oversimplification," "philistinism," and "practicalism."

The third aspect of Mao's thought relates to the centrality of man. In guerrilla warfare, popular support is the decisive factor in giving the poorly equipped partisans a chance to survive and to achieve ultimate victory. While the military technology is very simple, the human equation is rather complex. The idea that man is more important than weapons is thus a product of guerrilla war. Likewise, there has been a tendency for the Chinese Communists to overstress the role of sheer human effort in economic reconstruction in which the availability of material resources normally makes a crucial difference. The emphasis on the importance of manpower to compensate for the lack of material resources has necessitated a continued accentuation of the demand for personal sacrifice for the good of the collectivity—a demand which was also an essential ingredient in the success of a protracted guerrilla war. Thus, three articles written by Mao in the Yanan period—"In Memory of Norman Bethune," "Serve the People," and "The Foolish Old Man Who Removed the Mountains"—which stress the importance of personal sacrifice and human effort have been designated the *lao san pian* ("three constantly read essays").

But this demand for greater personal sacrifice and human effort could no longer be made on a populace which had once been readily mobilized by the party's promise to give it land or by the Japanese invasion. Rather, it had to be imposed on a people which primarily desired economic betterment. The dissidents therefore assumed the role of promoters of the interests of the people against the demands of the state and the party. In their historical writings and plays, they constantly praised those officials in the Chinese Empire who "pleaded for the people" *(weimin qingming)* in their memorials to the throne. They commended highly the ancient practice of treasuring the labor power of the people.

Fourth, the thought of Mao calls for the politicization of almost all spheres of social life.[35] In turn, "putting politics first" means putting Mao Zedong's thought first, according to the Maoists in the last few years.[36]

35. Even friendship is being replaced by comradeship. See Ezra F. Vogel, "From Friendship to Comradeship: The Change in Personal Relations in Communist China," *China Quarterly,* no. 21 (January-March, 1965), pp. 46–60.

36. *Peking Review,* January 21, 1966, p. 5.

This process of politicization originated in guerrilla warfare, in which popular support must be won by a political program and the institution of a proper relationship between the army and the population. The underlying principles of the Gutian Resolution, drafted by Mao in December, 1929, were that political considerations must prevail in most policy decisions and actions and that the party must control the army.[37] In the "Talks at the Yanan Forum on Literature and Art," Mao stressed that literature and art must serve politics. During the Great Leap Forward, the slogan "let politics take command" was raised; and in the past few years, Lin Biao has urged that everyone give prominence to "politics" in all fields of activity.

The penetration of politics into almost every sphere of social life may have been a short-term expedient to reconstruct new patterns of social relationships in a disintegrated society. But it is basically incompatible with long-term human needs in a stable, modern community. These needs center around the preservation of an autonomous area of social and private life into which "politics" with its emphasis on conflict, struggle, and combat does not intrude. Hence, the orthodox Maoists have found it necessary to attack frequently the "bourgeois" theory of human nature.

Furthermore, giving prominence to politics in every sphere of activity requires that professional criteria be subordinated to political ones in making decisions and judging work performance. The demand for placing politics above expertise increased after the attack on the intellectuals was intensified in November, 1965. *Jiefangjun bao* (Liberation Army Daily) criticized the view that "politics" is given prominence if "politics" produces concrete results in work *(zhengzhi luoshi dao yewu)*. It advocated the notion that giving prominence to "politics" must produce concrete results in men, that is, it must produce men with correct political viewpoints and behavior *(zhengzhi luoshi dao ren)*. This emphasis on politics in the special sense fails to give technical skill its proper place and runs counter to the demands and needs of the professional groups in a society with increasing social differentiation and specialization.[38]

The fifth aspect of Mao's thought emphasizes the importance of ideas over material conditions. To institute a proper relationship between the party and the army, between officers and soldiers, and between the army and the masses so that the army could fight a guerrilla war successfully

37. *Zhongguo Gongchandang Hongjun Dishijun dijiuci daibiao dahui jueyi an* [Resolution of the Ninth Conference of Delegates from the Fourth army of the Red Army of the Chinese Communist Party] (Hong Kong: Xinminzhu chuban she, 1949). Hereafter cited as *Gutian Resolution*.

38. A. Doak Barnett, "Mechanisms for Party Control in the Government Bureaucracy in China," *Asian Survey*, 6 (December, 1966): 659–74.

and also become an instrument in making a revolution, Mao found it necessary to effect a basic change in the values, attitudes, and political-military viewpoints of party members and military personnel. The Gutian Resolution already contained the rudiments of a program of thought reform which was subsequently systematized in the *Zhengfeng* Movement of 1942–44. The successful application of new ideas by Mao and his followers to overcome objective difficulties and to defeat his opponents during the revolutionary period left a permanent legacy in the mentality of Mao and his loyal followers. This is reflected in Lin Biao's concept of "four first," that is, the concept of giving first place to man as between man and weapons, giving first place to political work as between political work and other work, giving first place to ideological work as between ideological and routine tasks in political work, and giving first place to living ideas as between ideas in books and living ideas.[39]

The Maoists claim that the creative application of Mao's thought will in the long run overcome any objective difficulty. In effect, they are standing Marxist materialism on its head. Ostensibly criticizing the followers of Ernst Mach but actually pointing at Mao, Deng Tuo wrote: "The Machians imagined that through reliance on the role of the psychological factor, they could do whatever they pleased, but the result was that they ran their head against the brick wall of reality and went bankrupt in the end."[40] This charge raises the question of the applicability of the thought of Mao to Chinese society seventeen years after the establishment of the regime, to an international environment in which a certain degree of stability is maintained by two strong and dynamic powers[41] and to a world in which the underdeveloped nations are beginning to tackle the various problems of political development. In this connection, Deng Tuo attacked by insinuation Mao's method of leadership in domestic affairs as "the arrogant, subjectivist, and arbitrary way of thinking and style of work of one bent on acting wilfully." This was, he said, "the tyrant's way."[42] Mao's thesis in international affairs that "the East wind is prevailing over the West wind" was obliquely characterized as "empty talk."[43] By the admission of the Maoists, the dissidents indirectly described Mao's policy as "boasting," "indulging in fantasy," "substituting illusion for reality," and as re-

39. *Peking Review,* January 21, 1966, p. 5, n. 1.

40. "Teng T'o's *Evening Chats at Yenshan* Is Anti-Party and Anti-Socialist Double-Talk," *Great Socialist Cultural Revolution,* vol. 2, p. 21.

41. Tsou and Halperin, "Mao Tse-tung's Revolutionary Strategy," pp. 97–99.

42. *Great Socialist Cultural Revolution,* vol. 2, pp. 13–15. Yao Wen-yuan, "On 'Three-Family Village,'" p. 12.

43. *Great Socialist Cultural Revolution,* vol. 2, pp. 28–29; Yao Wen-yuan, "On 'Three-Family Village,'" p. 11.

sulting in "the total destruction" of "the family wealth consisting of one egg." [44]

It is obvious that failure in policies associated with an ideology and the criticisms of these policies leading to the questioning of the validity of the ideology ushered in a profound crisis in the regime. For the proper functioning of the Chinese political system depends more heavily on the general acceptance of an ideology than does that of other regimes, due to the unusually important role played by ideology in providing the basic principles of the political community, in setting the orientation of the regime, in legitimizing the political system, and in enlisting commitment. Political development up to 1965 does not seem to have reached a point where the legitimacy of the regime as distinguished from the correctness of its policy was seriously challenged. But Mao and his followers feared that developments similar to Khrushchev's denunciation of Stalin and the Hungarian Revolution might take place. Quite possibly, some of the Chinese leaders may have feared that policy setbacks and generational changes might at some future point undermine the political system itself. In his famous interview with Edgar Snow on January 9, 1965, Mao admitted the possibility that "youth could negate the revolution, and give a poor performance; make peace with imperialism, bring the remnants of the Chiang Kai-shek clique back to the mainland, and take a stand beside the small percentage of counter-revolutionaries still in this country." [45]

Seriously concerned with the weakening of the ideological foundation of the regime and its future orientation, Mao, Lin, and their followers see the solution in the reaffirmation of the thought of Mao Zedong which in their opinion ought to be the regime's basic ideology. They have attempted to dissociate failure from the policies adopted and to attribute it to extraneous factors and errors in implementation, thus absolving the thought of Mao from any responsibility for the failure. They have endeavored to attribute all kinds of successes—from the explosion of an atomic device to the accomplishments of the Dazhai Brigade to the ideology itself, whether there was a connection or not. They have advocated the study and application of the ideology by everyone and in every field, thus intensifying their program of indoctrination and seeking to enlist the commitment of everyone to the ideology. They have sought to link up class struggle with the struggle for production and scientific experiment, thus endeavoring to cope with practical problems while being engaged in political combat with the dissidents. At a time when the ideology is being questioned and the party itself is divided, they have tried to emphasize

44. Kao Chu, "Open Fire at the Black Anti-Party and Anti-Socialist Line!" *Great Socialist Cultural Revolution*, vol. 2, pp. 2–4.

45. Edgar Snow, "Interview with Mao," *The New Republic*, February 27, 1965, p. 23.

"personal legitimacy" to compensate for the weakening of "ideological legitimacy" and to overcome the problems created by the split between ideological authority and organizational authority. These attempts have pushed the cult of personality to a new height. As the present crisis is without any precedent in the history of the Chinese Communist movement since Mao's capture of the party center, the Maoists have attempted to use new methods or new applications of familiar methods to deal with it. Hence, the Red Guards and the Great Proletarian Cultural Revolution.

This reassertion of Mao's thought has entailed a measure of radicalization in the ideological sphere which has found expression in the savage attacks on traditional, Western, and "revisionist" ideas. Yet the basic problem of how to strengthen the ideological foundation of the regime and yet at the same time cope effectively with political and economic realities remains. In most areas of social life, the Maoists seem to be at a loss to fashion new, constructive programs which are at once in accord with their interpretation of Mao's thought and which would not disrupt what ever progess has been made in the last seventeen years. Hence, the Cultural Revolution has thus far been justified partly by the slogan that without destruction there cannot be construction and that destruction must come before construction.

The Great Proletarian Cultural Revolution and the Red Guards are therefore the expressions of a profound crisis in integration. The Maoists and the dissidents represent two political forces which the integrative measures of the political system cannot reconcile because the integrative myth itself has become a subject of controversy. This divergence on this most fundamental question confronting the regime may have divided the Chinese people in every sector of social life into two opinion groups. But not every sector has been influenced by this controversy to the same extent, and the relative strengths of the two groups may be different in different sectors. In the struggle for power which has ensued, the thought of Mao has also become a symbol. The vested interests of a group in upholding or questioning Mao's thought link ideological debates with *realpolitik* and have accounted for the extreme claims made for Mao's thought. The policy debates, the political division, and the linkage between ideology and vested elite interests are the problems to be discussed in the next two sections.

The Ruling Elite and the Masses

The dynamics of a political community in which there is a recognizable power elite are provided by the relationship between this elite and the other social groups. When the regime was set up in 1949, the CCP succeeded in unifying all major social formations in China under its leadership and excluded from this coalition only the most uncompromising groups, labeling the latter bureaucratic capitalists, compradores, and reactionary landlords. This achievement in integrating the diverse social groups and the masses entailed the implicit, if not explicit, modification of some of the Marxist-Leninist tenets and departed from Soviet practices toward the bourgeoisie and the rich peasants. It was made possible by social conditions of an underdeveloped country in which the capitalist class was relatively weak and in which there was a tradition of bureaucratic domination of the merchants. It was produced by the circumstances confronting the CCP in its prolonged struggle for power. In this struggle, the CCP was forced by the objective conditions to adopt strategy and tactics that paved the way for the initial form and structure of political integration.

Chinese society was seen by Mao as having "a shape bulging in the middle while tapering off towards the two ends."[46] In more concrete terms, this imagery meant that both the proletariat and the "reactionary big landlord and big bourgeoisie" formed only a small minority of the Chinese population while the other intermediate classes constituted the vast majority.[47] Mao's political strategy in the revolutionary struggle was "to develop the progressive forces, to win over the middle-of-the-road forces, and to isolate the die-hards."[48] It formed the basis of Mao's concept of "new democracy" which was to be based on a "joint dictatorship of all the revolutionary classes."[49] In this new democracy, "the proletariat, the peasantry, the intelligentsia and other sections of the petty bourgeoisie are the basic forces determining her fate."[50] But the proletariat should not overlook the partially revolutionary quality of the "bourgeoisie" and the possibility of establishing with it a united front against imperialism and the government of bureaucrats and warlords.[51]

In 1949, these ideas crystallized into the notion of a united front of four classes: the working class, the peasantry, the urban petty bourgeoisie, and the national bourgeoisie under the leadership of the working class, which would create a people's democratic dictatorship.[52] The status of these four classes within the united front by no means gave equal weight to each. But the significant fact is that the national bourgeoisie was considered a

46. *Selected Works*, vol. 3 (London: Lawrence & Wishart, 1954), p. 239.
47. *Ibid.*, p. 260; vol. 4, pp. 25.
48. *Ibid.*, vol. 3, p. 194.
49. *Xinminzhuzhuyi lun* [On New Democracy] (San Francisco: Cooperative Publishers, 1945), p. 8.
50. *Ibid.*, p. 15.
51. *Ibid.*, p. 14.
52. Mao Tse-tung, *Selected Works*, vol. 4 (Peking: Foreign Languages Press, 1960), p. 415.

component class of the "people" who exercised dictatorial power over the "reactionaries" and that the petty bourgeoisie was designated an ally of the working class. The inclusion of the national bourgeoisie within the ranks of the people paved the way for the peaceful transformation of the capitalists by turning the privately owned industrial and commercial enterprises into joint state-private enterprises and by turning the capitalists into managerial personnel under state control.

The concept of the united front and the strategy of uniting 90 per cent of the people against a small group of reactionaries alerted the CCP to the problem of establishing correct relations with other classes and integrating the various classes into a unified polity. But Mao's vision of a socialist society and the very nature of his totalitarian regime rendered it necessary for him to destroy the political influence of these social groups while integrating their members into the political community. Thus, methods had to be evolved to achieve this. The theory of class struggle and the precedent provided by Stalinist Russia favored the use of repressive methods. In the land reform program, an unknown number of "local tyrants and bad gentry" were liquidated. After Beijing entered the Korean War, it ruthlessly suppressed the so-called reactionaries within the country. Yet in comparison with Stalin, Mao employed violence more openly and selectively. This openness in the use of terror suggested that the regime had succeeded in legitimizing terror by the appeal of its political, economic, and social programs more effectively than had the Soviet government. This success can also be attributed to the strict political control over the use of violence, to the careful selection of the targets to attack, to the policy not to use physical coercion except as a last resort (for example, in dealing with the intellectuals and the national bourgeoisie), and to the development of methods of "thought reform" as a functional substitute for terror and as a supplement to its use. Thus, although Mao's programs aimed at achieving social, cultural, and spiritual changes far more sweeping and radical than anything Stalin ever attempted, his methods of action were, at least until the Cultural Revolution, more moderate than Stalin's. Whether or not the Great Proletarian Cultural Revolution, the Red Guards, and the current purges constitute an exception to this generalization is still difficult to determine at the moment of writing early in January, 1967.

The use of violence, no matter how open, selective, and successfully legitimized, could have had seriously disruptive effects if carried too far. Thus, the Chinese Communists restricted the use of suppression and coercive methods to what were defined as contradictions between the people and the enemy, while proposing the use of "democratic methods, methods of discussion, of criticism, of persuasion and education" to resolve the contradictions among the people. It is, of course, quite true that the boundary between the two kinds of contradictions is not fixed. The line of demarcation between the people and the enemy is actually the political standard of supporting or opposing the regime and its policies. It was drawn by the regime itself according to Mao's six criteria.[53] Recently, an overriding criterion has been added—whether or not one wholeheartedly supports and applies Mao's thought and the Maoist line in everyday work. It must also be stressed that if a contradiction among the people cannot be resolved by the "methods of discussion, criticism, persuasion and education," it can become a contradiction between the people and the enemy and be resolved by suppression and other forceful measures. Mao's method of coercive persuasion is still one form of coercion as we understand it, but it was less brutal and perhaps more effective than overt repressive measures. In short, the violent class struggle became a controlled form of class struggle. The aim was to achieve the desired social change with the least disruptive effects so that a relatively high degree of integration and unity could still be established after the contradictions or conflicts among the "people" had been resolved.

In dealing with the various social groups, the elite follows what is called a *mass line*. The mass line is defined by Mao as the principle of "from the masses, to the masses." In Mao's words, "this means summing up . . . the views of the masses (i.e., views scattered and unsystematic), then taking the resulting ideas back to the masses, explaining and popularizing them until the masses embrace the ideas as their own, stand up for them and translate them into action by way of testing their correctness."[54] The mass line legitimizes the programs and policies of the party because these are supposed to have come from the masses, the creators of history. It directs the cadres' attention to the need for ascertaining, articulating, and aggregating the interests of the masses. It goes without saying that in this process of systematizing and co-ordinating the views of the masses, the elite selects some and rejects others in the light of its own notion of the true interests of the masses. It then superimposes on the correct views of

53. In the published and edited version of the speech, Mao said: "We believe that, broadly speaking, words and actions can be judged right if they:
(1) Help to unite the people of our various nationalities, and do not divide them;
(2) Are beneficial, not harmful, to socialist construction;
(3) Help to consolidate, not undermine or weaken, the people's democratic dictatorship;
(4) Help to consolidate, not undermine or weaken, democratic centralism;
(5) Tend to strengthen, not to cast off or weaken, the leadership of the Communist Party;
(6) Are beneficial, not harmful, to international socialist solidarity and the solidarity of the peace-loving peoples of the world.
Of these six criteria, the most important are the socialist path and the leadership of the Party" (Mao Tse-tung, *On the Correct Handling of Contradictions among the People* [Peking: Foreign Languages Press, 1957], pp. 55–56).
54. *Selected Works*, vol. 4 (London: Lawrence & Wishart, 1956), p. 113.

the masses its overall, long-term program and its ideological conceptions. The product of this process may or may not bear any resemblance to the "scattered and unsystematic" views of the masses. It is, however, presented to the masses as their own ideas. It is said to represent the demand of the masses. The mobilization of mass support and the mass participation in the execution of the program mark the final phase of the mass line. The mass line can be a highly effective method for achieving integration between the elite and the masses if the substantive programs adopted by the party reflect the genuine interests of the masses, as was the case in the Yanan period.[55]

To implement the mass line, the party must be able to penetrate the masses and their formal and informal organizations. It has developed a pattern of methods to facilitate this penetration. The cadres are urged to develop a style of work which will bring the party and the masses together. They are told to live the same kind of life as the masses, to share the same hardships, to develop intimate relationships with the masses, to set a personal example for them to follow, to be considerate of the feelings of the people, and to exhibit a selfless devotion to public duties. Party directives abound with injunctions against "isolationism," "bureaucratism," "warlordism," and "sectarianism," which create a gap between the masses and the power elite. This style of work has been institutionalized in various interesting methods of work which run counter to Western ideas of economic use of skilled manpower. The party experimented with a system under which the cadres must regularly participate in physical labor as ordinary workers on a fixed day or days in a week at a fixed job. Leading cadres were told to spend a period of time at the grass roots—in production brigades or teams of a commune, or in factory workships—so that they could learn intimately the conditions of work and the problems confronting the masses at the lowest level.

The Chinese Communists are highly conscious of the gaps between social groups which have been created by modern conditions. To a much greater extent than their counterparts in the Soviet Union, they have tried various methods to minimize the "three antitheses"* between the working class and the peasantry, between the city and the countryside, and between manual and mental labor. One of the bases on which the regime formulates its wage policy is that the wages and living standards of the workers should not be too high in comparison with the earnings and living standards of the peasants. One of the many methods of reducing the antithesis between the city and the countryside is to mobilize the stu-

---

55. See Chalmers Johnson, "Chinese Communist Leadership and Mass Response: The Yenan [Yanan] Period and Socialist Education Campaign Period," in *China in Crisis*, vol. 1, bk. 1, pp. 397–437.

* "The three great differences" is a better phrase than the "three antitheses."

dents in urban areas to help the peasants during the busy season. The Daqing oil field was characterized as "a village-like city or a city-like village—a new social organization which helps eliminate the differences between industry and agriculture and between town and countryside."[56] The policy of participation of cadres in labor is partly based on the need to minimize the antithesis between mental and manual labor. The "half-work, half-study" schools and the "half-farm, half-study" schools are primarily means to provide an education to children from poor families in spite of a lack of financial resources on the part of the state. But they are also justified as a method to obliterate the differences between mental and manual labor. As Franz Schurmann has pointed out, the type of cohesion which the Chinese Communists seek to bring about is similar to Durkheim's notion of "mechanical" solidarity as distinguished from "organic" solidarity.[57]

Yet despite the initial success of the CCP in organizing a united front embracing all the major social groups in the country, and despite the elaborate system of measures to integrate the elite and the masses, political development in Communist China during the past seventeen years has resulted in the vanishing of the united front, in fact if not in theory. At least during one period of time, it led to the alienation of the peasantry so vividly recorded in the *Gongzuo tongxun* (Bulletin of Activities). It has produced increasing tension between the Maoists and the intellectuals inside and outside the party, leading to the Great Proletarian Cultural Revolution and the current purges. These disruptions stand in contrast to the party's success during the Yanan period in gradually unifying all the major social groups under the party's leadership, and to the widespread popular support enjoyed by the party at the time of the establishment of the regime in 1949.

This political development has been paralleled by a radicalization of the domestic programs of the CCP which actually began in 1946, continued with its ups and downs after 1949, accelerated after 1955–56, and reached a climax in the Great Leap Forward in 1958. This trend toward radicalism superseded the moderation of the CCP in the Yanan period. The degree of radicalism can be measured first by the gap between the goal and reality, second, by the length of time in which a goal is supposed to be achieved, and third, by the scope of the radical program as indicated by the number of people affected and the areas to which it is applied.

There are two broad explanations for this radicalization which changed the party's relationships with the various social groups. First, Mao had

56. *Peking Review*, April 22, 1966, p. 20. See also *ibid.*, p. 17.
57. Schurmann, *Ideology and Organization*, pp. 99–100. See also Lucian W. Pye, *Aspect of Political Development* (Boston: Little, Brown & Co., 1966), p. 60.

always envisaged a sweeping transformation of the Chinese society. The deradicalized program adopted after 1935 was a tactical change and forced adjustment to political reality; the moderation of Mao's theory and practice was a function of the balance of forces within China in which the CCP was a minority party. While the CCP's methods of action persisted to a large extent, the changes in the balance of forces particularly since 1949 made it possible for Mao to adopt radical programs for the transformation of Chinese society. These radical programs entailed either the destruction of some of the social groups or the drastic weakening of their political influence. The landlord class was destroyed in the land-reform movement. The influence of the rich peasants was seriously weakened by the establishment of the system of agricultural producers' co-operatives, although there has been a tendency for new rich peasants to appear.[58] The economic foundation of the political influence of the national bourgeoisie was undermined by the system of joint state-private enterprises, although the social and political status of the individual capitalists was maintained by the continued payment of dividends.

The intellectuals constitute the social group which has caused the regime its greatest difficulties. The political influence of the Democratic League—to which most of the politically active non-Communist intellectuals belonged—largely disappeared in the aftermath of the period of "blooming and contending" and the subsequent anti-rightist campaign. But the influence of the old, individual intellectual in his capacity as a specialist, a writer, and a scientist remained. Furthermore, new intellectuals are found in growing numbers in many sectors of a modernizing and industrializing society.[59] Their general knowledge and special skills, which are needed by the regime, also constitute the sources of many ideas opposed to Mao's thought and policies. The conjunction of the old and newly emergent forces has been considered to be a serious threat by the regime, or at least by one group of its leaders. Zhou Enlai was reported to have declared in December, 1964, in his report on the government:

> . . . for quite a long period the landlord class, the bourgeoisie and other exploiting classes which have been overthrown will remain strong and powerful in our socialist society. . . . At the same time, new bourgeois elements, new bourgeois intellectuals and other exploiters will be ceaselessly generated in society, in Party and government organs, in economic organizations and in cultural and educational departments. These new bourgeois elements and other exploiters will invariably try to find their protectors

58. Schurmann, *Ideology and Organization*, pp. 497–500.

59. John W. Lewis, "Political Aspects of Mobility in China's Urban Development," *American Political Science Review*, 60 (December, 1966): 899–912. The author regrets that he could not take full adventage of this article, since it appeared after the final draft of this paper had been completed.

and agents in the higher leading organizations. These old and new bourgeois elements and other exploiters will invariably join hands in opposing socialism and developing capitalism.[60],*

The difficult problem posed by the intellectuals is even more vividly reflected in Chen Yi's recent interview with an editor of a Uruguay newspaper. In trying to explain the "capitalistic degeneration" in the Soviet Union, Chen Yi was quoted as stating:

> . . . At the Twentieth Party Congress, Khrushchev said that Stalin had killed many people. That's not important. That he had stimulated the cult of personality. That's secondary. Maybe Stalin made these mistakes. But there was a more serious one. By stimulating industry and technology [that is, urban work and the intellectuals] without resolving the agricultural problem, he contributed to the process of degeneration.
> He did not take steps to eliminate the capitalist evils of intellectuality. He was too impatient to declare that there was no longer a class struggle in Russia. Stalin did not foresee the possibility of a turn toward capitalism. Because of this, the Soviet people were not prepared to confront revisionism. Molotov, Malenkov, Kamenev did not know how to fight it, and the revisionists reached the cruel extreme of burning [sic] Stalin's corpse. Afterwards, Khrushchev used the intellectuals to restore capitalism. And imperialism spurred him on. . . . We are attempting to eliminate the intellectual class.[61]

It is apparent that in China non-party intellectuals became a major, though unorganized, social force, that some party intellectuals posed a challenge to party ideologues, and that general knowledge and scientific expertise came to be a source of opposition to the thought of Mao. When the party dissident, Deng Tuo, stressed the importance of the *za jia* ("eclectic scholars") in leadership work and scientific research, he was advocating the assignment of generalists-intellectuals to leadership positions in place of the party ideologues.[62] A series of policies adopted by the regime can be understood as measures to curb the influence of the intellectuals, specialists, and experts. The Cultural Revolution involved "a great debate on the relations between politics and particular profession" in

60. *Peking Review*, January 1, 1965, p. 12.

* This statement by Zhou and the following two by Chen and Nie reflected the Party line at that time. Behind the scene, they actually tried very hard to protect the intellectuals and promote their status.

61. *The National Observer*, November 28, 1966, p. 26.

62. Deng Tuo, *Yanshan yehua*, pp. 7–9. In the same article, Deng also denied that there was any pure school of thought in traditional China. He asserted that on the contrary the well-known scholars in the past were eclectics in various degrees. This view ran counter to the Maoists' insistence on the purity of ideology and preference for ideologues over men with broad knowledge and liberal viewpoints.

every department or unit throughout the country, with the party insisting that "putting politics first is fundamental to all work."[63] Even scientific experiment must, according to Vice-Premier Nie Rongzhen, Chairman of the National Scientific-Technical Commission, be guided by Mao Zedong's thought.[64] One of the two major targets of attack in the Cultural Revolution has been the "bourgeois 'experts,' 'scholars,' 'authorities' and respected masters and their like"[65] and "specialists and professors."[66] The understandable emphasis on the importance of techniques was caricatured as the "purely technical viewpoint" and as the idea that "technique decides everything."[67] The alleged monopoly of "technique" by the experts was denounced. The role of the workers in scientific and technical development and in running the enterprise in the "three-in-one combination" was exalted. The workers were praised for having done things "which bourgeois technical 'specialists' lacked the courage to do" and for having achieved "what bourgeois technical 'authorities' failed to achieve."[68] They were said to "have shattered the arrogance of the bourgeois technical 'specialists' and 'authorities' and deprived them of their power."[69] The policy of raising the level of literature and art by giving high salaries, high royalties, and high awards to creative writers and artists was condemned, as was the policy of relying on famous writers, directors, and actors.[70] The old system of enrolling students in institutes of higher learning through competitive examinations was abolished because "it places school marks in command" and "encourages the students to become bourgeois specialists by the bourgeois method of 'making one's own way' and achieving individual fame, wealth and position."[71] Renmin ribao expressed warm support for the "revolutionary proposal" of several students that the period of schooling in the colleges of arts should be reduced from five to one, two, or three years.[72] The domination of the educational system by bourgeois intellectuals was to be changed.[73] Even a professor's exhortation for the students to read more, take more notes, and write more was condemned. Since the intellectuals, scholars, experts, and specialists are

63. *Peking Review*, April 22, 1966, p. 18.
64. "Speech at the Opening Ceremony of the Peking Physics Colloquium," *Peking Review*, July 29, 1966, p. 34.
65. *Great Socialist Cultural Revolution*, vol. 5, p. 1.
66. *Peking Review*, May 6, 1966, p. 30.
67. *Ibid.*, p. 28.
68. *Ibid.*, July 29, 1966, p. 26.
69. *Ibid.*
70. *Ibid.*, August 12, 1966, pp. 35–36.
71. *Ibid.*, June 24, 1966, p. 16.
72. *Ibid.*, July 22, 1966, pp. 20–22.
73. "Decision of the Central Committee of the Chinese Communist Party Concerning the Great Proletarian Cultural Revolution," August 8, 1966, *ibid.*, August 12, 1966, p. 10.

concentrated in the urban areas, the Maoists' attack on them was also an attack on an urban culture which was considered by them as "bourgeois" and as too heavily influenced by the West. Programs justified by the need to eliminate the three antitheses turned out to be directed against the urban intellectuals.

One group of intellectuals not attacked consists of those "scientists, technicians and ordinary members of working staffs," who are patriotic, work energetically, are not against the party and socialism, and maintain no illicit relations with any foreign country. Those scientists and scientific and technical personnel who have made contributions are to be handled with special care. Toward them the policy is to help them gradually transform their world outlook and style of work.[74]

The second explanation for the radicalization of the movement takes as its point of departure an understanding of the Yanan period. The structure of ideology, institutions, organizations, practice, attitudes, values, and style of work perfected during the Yanan period contained a balanced mixture of moderation and radicalism. In the years since 1949 during which this structure has been extended to the whole society, the relative prominence of its moderate and radical features has fluctuated with the passage of time until radicalism has become dominant in the Cultural Revolution and moderation has been overshadowed. Furthermore, the sociopolitical context in which this structure operates has undergone a basic change. With this change, the theory and practice of the Yanan era have taken on different political meaning. These brief remarks need to be amplified.

During the Yanan period, the CCP's theory and practice were developed and applied in the party, the army, and the front organizations which many people voluntarily joined. Their extension and intensified application in all spheres of sociopolitical life has taken place under the auspices of a party in power. Thus, their acceptance has lost the voluntary character of the revolutionary days and has become compulsory. For example, thought reform through criticism and self-criticism as applied in a party which members joined of their own volition and could freely leave is quite a different thing from thought reform as imposed upon everyone in the country. The method remains the same, but the program amounts to what Benjamin Schwartz calls the transformation of the whole Chinese people into a nation of spiritual proletarians. When the mass line was used during the Sino-Japanese War, the CCP's programs corresponded to the genuine interests of the masses in resisting the Japanese forces and in preserving order and security behind the Japanese lines. When the same method was adopted as a strategy of economic development in the period of the Great Leap Forward and in the establishment of the commune sys-

74. *Ibid.*

tem, it was used to change the age-old work organization and habits of the peasants, to drive them to work harder, and to disrupt, in effect, the traditional system of marketing in the rural areas. Thus, it enlisted popular participation and support in the Sino-Japanese War but provoked hostility and slowdown during the Great Leap which contributed to the three years of agricultural crisis.[75]

Second, the theory and practice of the CCP took a comprehensive, coherent, and partially complete form during its revolutionary days, reflecting the simple, undifferentiated life of the guerrilla bands and party activists in the interior of China where division of labor was simple and a type of mechanical solidarity could be easily established. When they were applied in more highly developed areas of China, they clashed with what remained of the relatively complex socioeconomic institutions. When they are applied in a rapidly developing, industrializing, and modernizing society, there is the problem of how to reconcile their assumptions of mechanical solidarity with the principles of specialization and functional integration on which a modern complex society is based.[76]

For example, Mao's experience in the Yanan period reinforced his Marxist prejudice against sharp differentiation of functions among the various social groups. He was reported to have pointed out recently that each army unit should engage in one or two of the three fields of activity—agriculture, industry, and mass work; that where conditions permit, the workers should engage in agricultural production and side occupations; that the peasants should also collectively run some small factories; that the students should in addition to their studies learn other things, that is, industrial work, farming, and military affairs; and that where conditions permit, those working in commerce, in the service trades, and in party and government organizations should also do the same.[77]

The populist and anti-bureaucratic bias of the "democratic" half of the principle of "democratic centralism" challenges the increasingly large and complex system of bureaucracy and management.[78] The clash between the theory and practice of the Chinese Red Army and the Eighth Route Army on the one hand and the Soviet model of a modern, specialized fighting force on the other led to the gradual abandonment of the Soviet model from 1958 onward. The confrontation between the thought of Mao and

75. Chalmers Johnson, "Building a Communist Nation in China," in *The Communist Revolution in Asia*, pp. 57–58. On the relationship between the commune system and the traditional system of rural markets, see G. William Skinner, "Marketing and Social Structure in Rural China, pt. 3," *Journal of Asian Studies*, 24 (1965): 363–99.

76. Schurmann, *Ideology and Organization*, pp. 97–101, 109, 233–38.

77. *Renmin ribao* editorial in commemoration of the Thirty-ninth Anniversary of the Founding of the Chinese People's Liberation Army, in *Peking Review*, August 5, 1966, p. 7.

78. Schurmann, *Ideology and Organization*, pp. 113, 127, 265.

the demands for specialization has produced "the three-unification move-ment" which aims at uniting cadres, technicians, and workers into a work team and in which each is expected to become the other. These develop-ments are radical in the sense that the gap between Mao's policies and the emergent social reality is widened.

Third, the radicalization of the Chinese Communist movement stems from one particular aspect of the thought of Mao. This is best formulated by Vsevolod Holubnychy:

> Mao believes that practice reveals not only the correct or expected truth but also the wrong or unexpected truth. What his whole epistemology calls for is to push practice and experimenting to the utmost—up to the brink of error and failure . . . the rule of procedure is: In your search for truth, push incessantly forward until you come to the brink of the pit. . . . It is more probable than not that in every particular case, he [Mao] would be inclined to go a step farther than one would ordinarily expect and he would be disposed to explore extreme opportunities, advance radical propositions and push them hard until or unless they become utterly impossible.[79]

It has been in this spirit that Mao has tried to extend the application of his theory and practice in one area of social life after another. He did this in the area of agriculture and economic life with his Great Leap Forward and the system of communes. In the Cultural Revolution, characterized as a great innovation in the international Communist movement, he is at-tempting something analogous to the Great Leap Forward in the fields of education, art, literature, and politics. If fully implemented, the tentative proposals to reform the examination and educational system and the movement to discredit the "academic authorities" and "specialists" in various areas of intellectual life promise to produce results as disastrous to China's cultural life as the Great Leap Forward and the commune system were to China's economy, although the effects will not be as obvious and immediate.

If the radicalization of the Chinese Communist movement has come from the extension and selective and intensified application of the theory and practice as developed by the CCP during the revolutionary period, we must ask ourselves the fundamental question: What social condition has made it both necessary and possible for the CCP to do so?

The social condition in twentieth-century China which has made this extension possible can be described as the high degree of disintegration of the traditional sociopolitical system, coupled with the weakness of the emergent, transitional system. A high degree of disintegration meant not

79. "Mao Tse-tung's Materialistic Dialectics," *China Quarterly*, no. 19 (July-September, 1964), p. 27.

only that the core elements of the overall system had been destroyed but also that some of the substructures of the social system were no longer viable. Thirty years ago, we employed the elegant term "the collapse of a civilization" to describe such a condition. Today some of us prefer such terms as systemic and multiple dysfunction. The warlord period from 1916 to 1927 was the political expression of this disintegration. The new institutions and organizations which emerged in the aftermath did not last long enough to stabilize themselves. Collectively, they did not form a functionally integrated system. In the midst of this disintegrated society, the Chinese Communists built a small political community of their own, one tied together by ideological, organizational, and personal bonds. The dislocation in most sectors of social life and the relative weakness of some of the surviving institutions have made it both possible and necessary for the CCP to rebuild the overall sociopolitical system and many of the sub-systems in its own image.

In this situation there could be no boundary between the state and the society or even the state and the individual. Political power of necessity penetrated to every sphere of social life, including the innermost thought of man. This development inevitably resulted in the radicalization of the Chinese Communist movement. Yet the only ideas, practices, and style of work which many of the Maoists have known and prized are those which they themselves developed in the long years of the revolutionary struggle. In a sense, the Maoists can be considered conservatives because they oppose new emergent things in order to perpetuate their original revolutionary tradition.

In sum, the trend toward increased radicalism which replaced the moderation of the Yanan period has brought about a basic change in the relationship between the party and the various social groups since 1949. The high degree of political unity and popular support enjoyed by the regime at the time of its establishment has been eroded as a result of the successive assaults by the elite upon many of these groups. While the capitalists as a class no longer exist and the non-Communist parties and groups have lost almost all their influence, the old ideas and attitudes of these groups have lingered on. These old ideas and attitudes have been reinforced by the trends toward differentiation, specialization, and professionalism in a developing society. While the peasantry has in the past several years been pacified by the restoration of the private plots, the revival of the rural markets, the reorganization of the commune system, and the allocation of a greater amount of resources to agriculture, the old and new intellectuals in and outside of the party have posed a serious challenge to the policies and ideology of the Maoist group. As the dissent of the intellectuals has been the reflection of unresolved problems in various sectors of the society, the tension between them and the Maoists serves as an indicator of the unsatisfactory relationship between the various social groups and a powerful group in the ruling elite. How the Maoists will handle the intellectuals will determine future political developments in China. In any case, the time when effective political integrations can again be achieved seems at this moment to be quite far away. It will probably come only after a long period of cessation of radical changes, of painful readjustment, and of peaceful economic evolution.

The Elite: The Charismatic Leader and the Routinizing Organization

In a political system in which there is a fairly clearly defined power elite, the unity achieved within this elite is at once a measure of the degree of political integration attained and a decisive factor in bringing it about. Similarly, the division and conflicts within the elite mirror the diverse forces within the political system and the society. For a limited period of time, a united elite can bridge the social gaps and control the centrifugal forces in the society without recourse to violent and repressive methods on a large scale. But the diverse interests of the various social groups inevitably find expression within the ranks of the elite. Unless these interests can at least be partially satisfied by the elite's policies and programs, they will, over a period of time, produce fissions within the elite itself. Furthermore, the members of an elite in power in a modernizing society work in different governing institutions which perform increasingly specialized and differentiated functions and which have diverse clienteles. Different sections of the elite may take on some of the attributes of what Western social scientists call institutional interest groups. The system of party committees and party secretaries at various levels is supposed to integrate the work and functions of the diverse institutions and organizations. Yet it may itself become a strongly entrenched vertical institutional group with its own interests and viewpoints. Even within each of these institutional groups, further functional differentiation takes place.[80] Individuals working within these specialized groups may develop diverse viewpoints because of their different social origin, education, experience, and location in the political and social system. How the conflicts and struggle for power will take shape depends on the effects of the policy pursued by the regime on these groups and individuals and varies with the relationship between the ideology and the functions performed by them.

The Chinese Communists succeeded in building up a highly unified party during the revolutionary period. This impressive solidarity persisted for many years after the establishment of the regime. Then in 1966,

---

80. For a description of the existing functional "systems" in the Chinese Communists' political apparatus, see Barnett, "Mechanisms for Party Control," pp. 671–74.

we learned all of a sudden that the unity of this elite had suffered the most serious breakdown in its whole history or at least since 1935.[81] Furthermore, the "structural legitimacy"[82] of the party was weakened, if not destroyed, when the Red Guards were used to attack the top leaders, the various parts of the party apparatus, and the regional and local committees. While it is impossible at this moment of writing to give an adequate analysis of this development, some preliminary and highly tentative thoughts about the initial unity and its subsequent breakdown will be put forth to elicit discussion.

One of the greatest achievements of the Chinese Communists in the revolutionary period was their success in building up a highly unified party whose deep foundation has been seriously shaken and whose elaborate structure has been strongly buffeted by the Cultural Revolution. This achievement in the past was particularly remarkable in view of both the pattern of factional politics in twentieth-century China and the bloody purges used in overcoming factions in the Bolshevik party of the Soviet Union. Political factions in Republican China frequently stemmed from conflict between strong personalities and were based on the selfish interests of individuals or groups of individuals bound by personal ties of some sort, sometimes rationalized by ideology and program, and sometimes not. Frequently, they reflected regional, provincial, and local loyalties. In their most advanced form under the Nationalist regime, they rested upon functional differentiation among the various groups. For example, the Whampoa Clique had its foundation in the Central Army, the C. C. Clique, in the party bureaucracy; and the "Political Science Group," in some high echelons of the government. But even in its most advanced form, factional politics was still highly colored by issues of personality while the various factions themselves were divided into small cliques bound by particularistic ties. Although the factional struggle for power and preferment was very intense, the issues were seldom resolved on the basis of principles.

The CCP, as a product of Chinese society, was confronted with the same divisive forces that rent the other groups into conflicting factions, cliques, and individuals. In its attempt to build up a highly integrated party, it succeeded in reducing factionalism and personal conflicts to manageable proportions by rigorously implementing the Leninist principles of party organization, by developing a new pattern of inner-party life, by checking the divisive forces at their inception, and by firmly establishing the ideological and organizational authority of Mao Zedong. On the basis

81. The Maoists declared that "the struggle between the two lines within the Party [in 1966] . . . is likewise the most profound struggle in the history of our Party" (*Peking Review*, December 23, 1966, p. 19).

82. For the concept, see Easton, *A Systems Analysis of Political Life*, p. 287.

of the Leninist principles, it has tried to keep to a minimum what are called unprincipled disputes and struggles within the party. These are defined as disputes and struggles which are started not for the sake of serving the interests of the entire party but for the sake of promoting individual and factional interests. Also included in this category are disputes and struggles which do not follow organizational procedures but are characterized by secret scheming against some individual members.

The CCP was constantly on the alert for divisive forces within the party and endeavored to control them by achieving unanimity in thought. For this purpose, it waged frequent struggles against "erroneous" ideological tendencies on the basis of a set of principles, that is, Marxism-Leninism and the thought of Mao Zedong. In the conduct of inner-party struggle as a means of unifying the party and of combating ideological deviations, the CCP departed at an early date from Stalin's practice of bloody purges and developed a new style of inner-party life.

As early as 1941, Liu Shaoqi contrasted the conditions under which the Bolshevik and the Chinese parties were established. When Lenin was building the Bolshevik party, his most important consideration was, according to Liu, "the struggle against right opportunism" as symbolized by the Second International. In contrast, the CCP had from the very beginning been established on the basis of Leninist principles. But it had frequently committed the error of waging violent and excessive inner-party struggle and of moving toward "left deviation."[83] In accordance with this diagnosis, the CCP has established a practice of opposing "mechanical and excessive struggle" within the party. Instead of investigation, arrest, imprisonment, and trial in inner-party struggle, it has placed primary reliance on the method of "criticism and self-criticism" in order to resolve inner-party conflicts on the basis of principles, to achieve unanimity in thought, and to "cure the disease and save the person."

The development of this more moderate form of inner-party struggle took place at a time when the CCP was still a minority party constantly threatened with the outbreak of a new civil war and when the Communists had to achieve unity in order to survive. It departed from the Chinese political practice at that time in the party's insistence that no compromise of principles is permitted, but it conformed to that practice by allowing political opponents a route of retreat and a chance to come back to the fold. This moderate form of inner-party struggle was necessary to preserve party unity in the face of powerful enemies, and became a well-established practice. Although the party could not prevent serious challenges by oppositionist elements within the party, notably the "anti-party

83. Liu Shaoqi, "Lun dangnei douzheng," in *Zhengfeng wenxian* [Documents on the Rectification of the Styles of Work] (Xinhua shudian, 1949), pp. 175–76.

faction" of Gao Gang and Rao Shushi and the "right-wing oppositionists" in the Peng Dehuai affair, there was no bloody purge from 1935 to 1965. What has happened to the individuals purged in the current crisis remains unclear.

It was no accident that this moderate form of inner-party struggle was institutionalized simultaneously with the establishment and consolidation of Mao's ideological and organizational authority. Indeed, the latter was probably the precondition of the former. For inner-party struggle can be controlled within set limits and can assume a moderate form only when there is a recognized ideological authority to distinguish between "correct" and "incorrect" principles and an invulnerable organizational authority to regulate and enforce the limits of the struggle. In a Communist party, the ideological authority and the organizational authority must be identical in order for the authority to be fully effective. This identity was achieved in the period between 1935 and 1945.

The historical circumstances under which Mao established and consolidated his ideological and organizational authority greatly facilitated the development of a moderate form of inner-party struggle and the achievement of a high degree of unity and continuity in the CCP leadership. It was Mao who had first developed the guerrilla bases in the hinterland and formulated a pattern of political-military strategy and tactics to guide the Communist forces in their early successes in expanding their control and in their war against the GMD's campaigns of annihilation and encirclement. The Red Army was defeated in 1934 when the returned student group controlled the party apparatus and directed the war effort. Mao captured control over the party center in 1935 during the Long March* when the fortunes of the CCP were at their lowest ebb since 1927. Under his leadership, the CCP entered a period of rapid expansion. His successes legitimized his ideological and organizational authority while his opponents were discredited by their failures. Thus, the establishment and the consolidation of his authority were not accompanied by bloody purges. Most of the leaders in the period from 1927 to 1935 remained the leaders of the regime up to the autumn of 1965.

The conditions which governed the successful development of guerrilla warfare demanded full integration between the military and civilian officials, between the various functional groups within the party, and between the elite and the masses. Thus, the CCP was intensely conscious of the various gaps within and outside the party and took action to close them. In this integration, civilians were given the top positions. Guerrilla warfare depends for its success on popular support, and this is obtained

---

* For recently available information regarding Mao's official position in the Party during and after the Long March, see chapter 8.

by a political, economic, and social program which only civilian leaders can formulate. The political aspects of fighting a successful guerrilla war are very complex, while the military aspects are fairly simple. Therefore, the party leaders could guide the military officers, but military officers could not guide the movement. At the same time, the army took on many political and economic activities which were inseparable from guerrilla fighting. It was, at the same time, a fighting force, a working force, and a production force. Mao became the military strategist and tactician as well as the ideological authority. He was the prophet armed and triumphant. This tradition of civilian control over the military soon became a very powerful force, sanctioned and strengthened by both the Chinese political tradition and Leninist principles, in spite of the fact that the military took active part in political affairs.

It is generally recognized that common experience and memories of the past contribute to the development of a common outlook on the basis of which the present is understood and a decision is made. Most of the top Chinese Communist leaders share the common experience and memories of fighting a guerrilla war in various base areas, although many, of them, particularly those who worked in the field of literature and art, in united-front work, and in student movements, lived for long periods of time in Nationalist-controlled cities and were exposed to the influence of Western ideas and way of life. To the extent that there is a sharing of common experience and memories, unity in thinking and action can be more easily achieved. The bulk of the writings of Mao is a summation of the political-military experience of waging guerrilla warfare. Its abstract principles generalize the lessons of past defeats and success to guide the party's actions. To the extent to which Mao's thought was not questioned, it enhanced the unifying effects of the common experience and memories by providing a systematic and authoritative interpretation of the past. At the time of the establishment of the regime, the Leninist principles of organization, the development of a new pattern of inner-party life, the firm establishment of the ideological and organizational authority of Mao, the continuity of leadership, and a systematic and authoritative interpretation of common experience provided by the thought of Mao helped to bring about a highly unified elite. Thus, an organic unity of the charismatic leader, the ideology, and the organization was created. The harmony among these three fundamental forces during a period of revolutionary upheaval helps to explain the effectiveness of the CCP then and for some time afterward.

In the first few years of the regime, party unity was one of the main factors contributing to the establishment of effective political control. This effective political control enabled the Chinese Communists to regulate the demands of the various groups in the society. It gave them a relatively free hand to establish a new political system, to formulate their socio-economic programs, and to allocate resources in the light of their ideology, revolutionary experience, and estimate of the situation. It rendered feasible the adoption of unpopular policies such as the entry into the Korean War, the campaign for the suppression of counter-revolutionaries and the Three-anti and Five-anti campaigns. These and other unpopular policies inevitably depleted the capital of popular support available to the regime. Yet circumstances helped the party to balance this loss of popular support by demonstrating the effectiveness of the regime and soundness of its policies. Its success in controlling runaway inflation in the last years of Nationalist rule and in rehabilitating the war-torn economy within three years of assuming power made the people's lives tolerable. The defeat of General MacArthur's drive toward the Yalu stirred the national pride of the Chinese to the highest point since the Opium War. The First Five-Year Plan of 1953–57 was a good beginning for industrialization. The land reform program and the establishment of agricultural producers' cooperatives caused relatively little disruption in the countryside. So long as the policies of the regime met with relative success, the struggle for power within the party could be contained and the crisis of party unity minimized, for the issues around which the struggle took place were relatively specific and narrow, as in the case of the purge of Gao Gang and Rao Shushi in 1954 and debate over the military line in 1958.

But the three years of crisis produced at least partly by the Great Leap Forward and the commune system,[84] together with the drastic deterioration in Sino-Soviet relations since 1959, had quite different consequences for party unity. They raised a whole range of policy issues which called into question the basic orientation of the regime in both domestic and foreign affairs. Zhou Enlai declared in his report in December, 1964, on the work of the government:

> From 1959 to 1962 . . . the class enemies at home launched renewed attacks on socialism, and consequently once again fierce class struggle ensued. In the domestic field, quite a few people actively advocated "*sanzi yibao*" (referring to the extension of plots for private use and of free markets, the increase of free enterprises with sole responsibility for their profits or losses, the fixing of output quota based on households), "*dangan feng*" (referring to the restoration of individual economy), "liberalization," "reversing previous decisions," and capitulationism in united front work; in the international field they advocated "*sanhe yishao*" (referring to reconciliation with imperialism, reactionaries, and modern revisionism, and

84. In an article written jointly by the editorial departments of the *Hongqi* and *Renmin ribao*, Liu Shaoqi is charged with having said that the agricultural crisis was made up of "three parts natural calamities and seven parts man-made disasters" (*Hongqi* [Red Flag], no. 13, 1967, p. 11).

reduction of assistance and support to the revolutionary struggle of other peoples). They used their bourgeois and revisionist viewpoints to oppose our general line of socialist construction and the general line of our foreign policy.[85]

At the moment of writing, it is impossible to identify the dissidents, although we do know that, among others, Wu Han, Deng Tuo, Zhou Yang, and Sun Yefang were accused of having expressed some of these views. Nor is it necessary to do so. All that is needed is for us to indicate that there was an intense debate within the party on all the important issues, that this debate led to the questioning of the extent to which Mao's thought can be vigorously applied in various areas of activities, and that the struggle for power within the party has evolved around this last question.[86] One group of leaders has advocated and undertaken an extensive and vigorous application of Mao's thought, while another group has in practice failed to do so or has tried to restrain the Maoists' attack on the dissidents. It is this contrast in approach that has created for the former a vested interest in upholding Mao's thought and for the latter a vested interest in limiting its application. This contrast has also made it possible for one group to use Mao's thought as a weapon to attack and purge its opponents.

One must probe more deeply, however, into the reason for this division within the party. Our explanation is twofold. The first part relates to what Max Weber calls the routinization of charisma.[87] The CCP has long been led by a charismatic leader and at the same time has developed a large organization with a long tradition going back to the revolutionary period. Certain developments in the party point to a process of routinization which diminishes the influence and the control of the charismatic leader over the organization. At the Eighth Party Congress in September, 1956, the statement that "the Communist Party of China takes Marxism-Leninism as its guide to action" was adopted to replace the statement in

85. *Renmin ribao*, December 31, 1964, p. 2. For an English translation, see *Peking Review*, January 1, 1965, pp. 12–13.

86. In his self-criticism, Liu Shaoqi stated that Deng Zihui, Director of Office of Agriculture and Forestry of the State Council, advocated the fixing of output quota based on households at several meetings and that on another occasion Deng spoke on the merits of the "responsible farm system" and that "we did not oppose this view" (Liu's self-criticism as reproduced in a big character poster posted on December 26, 1966, in Beijing by the Jinggangshan Red Guards of the Qing Hua University.) Liu himself was accused of having advocated the fixing of output quota on the basis of households and of having actively encouraged "going it alone" (*Hongqi*, no. 13, 1967, p. 11).

87. Max Weber, *The Theory of Social and Economic Organization*, trans. A. M. Henderson and Talcott Parsons (Oxford: Oxford University Press, 1947), pp. 363–73. *From Max Weber*, trans. H. H. Gerth and C. Wright Mills (New York: Oxford University Press, 1946), pp. 53, 54, 262, 297.

the Party Constitution of 1945 that "the Communist Party of China guides its entire work by the teachings which unite the theories of Marxism-Leninism with the actual practice of the Chinese Revolution—the thought of Mao Zedong." Not only had the phrase "the thought of Mao Zedong" disappeared in the new Party Constitution but also the statement that "no political party or *person* [italics added] can be free from shortcomings and mistakes in work" had been added.[88] At the same time, a provision was adopted under which the party can have an honorary chairman when necessary. This arrangement was apparently intended to give the charismatic leader an honorific post in the party but to remove him from day-to-day control over party affairs. The forces of routinization were headed by two persons engaged principally in organizational work in the party, Liu Shaoqi and Deng Xiaoping. At the 1956 Congress, they delivered, respectively, the political report of the Central Committee and the report on the revision of the party Constitution and were elected, respectively, the ranking Vice-Chairman of the party and the General-Secretary. It was they who would be the chief beneficiaries of Mao's relinquishment of power. This process of routinization was facilitated by Khrushchev's denunciation of Stalin at the Twentieth Party Congress which was a reflection of the same process in the Soviet Union. In December 1958, the Sixth Plenum adopted a decision approving Mao's proposal that he would not stand as a candidate for the chairman of the People's Republic.[89]

There are reasons to believe that during the period between 1959 and 1962 Mao's control over party affairs was further weakened as the party adopted a series of pragmatic policies to extricate China from the economic crisis. According to one report, Mao complained that during these years the party leaders treated him as they would treat a dead parent at his funeral. The latent tension between the charismatic leader and the routinizing and bureaucratized organization increased after the economic recovery in 1962 when Mao began to raise the question of the ideological purity of some of the members of the organization and started a counter-offensive against his critics and the dissidents. This tension was brought to a head by the foreign policy crisis in 1965 and by the leader's attempt to purge the dissidents below the top echelons of the organization. The organization's effort to protect the dissidents and to restrain Mao's attacks led to a split between the leader and the organization. The basic conditions which had moderated the inner-party struggle since 1942, if not since

88. *Eighth National Congress of the Communist Party of China*, vol. 1: Documents (Peking: Foreign Languages Press, 1956), p. 143.
89. For two different interpretations of this event, see Gene T. Hsiao, "The Background and Development of 'The Proletarian Cultural Revolution,'" *Asian Survey*, 7 (June, 1967): 395; Chün-tu Hsüeh, "The Cultural Revolution and Leadership Crisis in Communist China," *Political Science Quarterly*, 82 (June, 1967): 187.

1935, and which accounted for the early effectiveness of the CCP no longer existed. The tremendous prestige of the leader was now pitted against a strongly entrenched organization. A prolonged and intense struggle ensued. Mao tried to divide the organization by using the leaders of a lower rank against the leaders of a higher rank and by setting one functional group within the party against another. He also promoted the formation of new groups, the Red Guard units, to attack the various party units. In this attempt, he exploited the enthusiasms and grievances of the underprivileged youth against the "establishment" and the more privileged groups of the society. His endeavor was facilitated by the revolutionary ideology and heritage which legitimized the spontaneous activism and revolt of the youth.[90] In these developments, the process of routinization of charisma and the struggle for succession in the political system were linked up with the process of functional differentiation in a modern society. This latter process constitutes a second explanation of the current crisis.

In both Chinese society and the CCP, the process of functional differentiation has gone very far in the past seventeen years. It has been facilitated by a policy, followed since the revolutionary days, of assigning the same individual to the same field of activity over a long period of time. But this process has come into conflict with the demands for doctrinal uniformity. The increasingly differentiated and specialized sectors of the society and the party are supposed to be guided in their work by a single ideology with rather specific operational rules. But the operation of Mao's thought may be functional for work in some spheres of sociopolitical activities, dysfunctional for that in others, and quite irrelevant to that in still others. For many party leaders engaged in activities of the first type, for example military affairs, it is possible to retain faith in the ideology, to carry out policies intimately linked to it, to design programs in conformity with it, and even to devise new methods to apply it extensively and vigorously. For many leaders engaged in the second type of work such as literature, art, and higher education, it is difficult to be fully convinced of the validity of the ideology and to implement programs heavily influenced by it. For them, it is necessary to limit the application of the ideology and the policies associated with it in order that their work may be carried out successfully. For leaders engaged in activities of the third type, especially in science and technology (most notably the making of atomic weapons), it is possible to pay only lip service to ideology and to proceed in their work largely according to professional standards. In addition to such immediate

90. Throughout the Cultural Revolution, the following statement addressed by Mao to the youth has been frequently quoted: "The world is yours as well as ours, but in the last analysis, it is yours. . . . Our hope is placed in you" (*Peking Review*, March 31, 1967, p. 12).

considerations, historical circumstances have sometimes had differential effects on the intellectual outlook of those persons engaged in these three different types of work. Their previous education, training, and experience may be closely related to the thought of Mao as in the case of military leaders, unrelated to it as in the case of scientists, or associated with intellectual currents somewhat incompatible with it as in the case of those persons working in the fields of literature, art, and higher education. Finally, new experiences and new situations may affect still further the person's or the group's attitude toward Mao's thought. All the time, the formulator of the ideology has continued to insist on the universal applicability of his thought.[91]

These general propositions help to explain the different approaches toward the thought of Mao adopted since 1959 by many military-political leaders on the one hand and by most party leaders working in the fields of literature, art, and education on the other. The latter's views are apparently widely shared by leaders working in other areas. It is true, however, that there have been serious struggles even within the People's Liberation Army (PLA) over the issue of whether or not Mao's military line should be modified.[92] The first struggle was precipitated by the new experience gained by some high-ranking officers in the Korean War. Let us recall that Lin Biao was the commander of the first phase of China's operations in the Korean War * and that Peng Dehuai became the commander afterward. With his poorly equipped and inadequately supplied army, Lin Biao scored a smashing victory over General MacArthur by adopting a strategy which closely followed the principles laid down by Mao in his article, "Problems of Strategy in China's Revolutionary War" (1936).[93] In contrast, Peng Dehuai conducted regular, positional warfare during the larger part of the war with new and more modern weapons purchased from the Soviet Union. It is perhaps not accidental that Lin Biao has continued to adhere closely to Mao's military thinking while Peng became an advocate of regularization and modernization of the PLA along the lines

91. The intra-elite dissensus in this period provides many materials to support Edward Shils's generalization that "dissensus is apt to arise from persons whose occupational roles are concered with perceiving and promulgating order and those whose roles are concerned with its conduct and management" and that "the most important [source of dissensus] arises from divergent conceptions of the locus and substance of charisma" ("Charisma, Order, and Status," *American Sociological Review*, 30 [April, 1965]: 209–10).

92. For a thorough treatment of this subject up to 1960, see Alice Hsieh, *Communist China's Strategy in the Nuclear Era* (Englewood Cliffs, N.J.: Prentice-Hall, 1962).

* This version of Lin Biao's role was generally accepted at the time. It later became clear that Peng Dehuai was the commander from the very beginning. It remains probable that Peng's experience in conducting a positional warfare in Korea influenced his military thinking.

93. *Selected Military Writings* (Peking: Foreign Languages Press, 1963), pp. 75–145.

of the Soviet army. A recent editorial in *Jiefangjun bao* confirmed Western analyses of the struggles within the army and their relationship to the experience of the Korean War.

> The first big struggle started after the conclusion of the war to resist U.S. aggression and aid Korea. Under the pretext of "regularization" and "modernization," a handful of representatives of the bourgeois military line, making a complete carbon copy of foreign practice, vainly attempted to negate our army's historical experiences and fine traditions and to lead our army on to the road followed by bourgeois armies. . . . Responding to Chairman Mao's call of "Down with the slave mentality! Bury dogmatism!" the 1958 Enlarged Session of the Military Commission of the Central Committee of the Chinese Communist Party smashed their frantic attack and defended Chairman Mao's thinking and line on army building.[94]

Presumably, it was also some time in 1958 that Beijing rejected Moscow's "unreasonable demands designed to bring China under Soviet military control."[95] But this first inner-party struggle in the military sector did not result in any serious purges.[96]

According to Beijing, the second struggle took place in 1959. At an Enlarged Session of the Military Commission which took place after the Eighth Plenum of the Central Committee held at Lushan in August, Peng Dehuai's "bourgeois, revisionist military line" was repudiated. At the Lushan Plenum, Peng was dismissed from the post of Minister of Defense but was allowed to keep his membership in the Political Bureau. Yet, as John Gittings concludes after an exhaustive study, this major upset "involved only seven other leading officers at the most generous estimate."[97] The third struggle occurred in late 1965 or the first half of 1966. Luo Ruiqing, Chief of Staff, was reported to have been purged. How many other leading officers were involved is still not clear.

What is important to us at the moment is the fact that a group of military leaders found it feasible to apply Mao's thought in the PLA and could claim immense success with at least some credibility. After Lin Biao replaced Peng Dehuai as Minister of Defense and as the actual operating

94. *Peking Review,* August 5, 1966, p. 9.

95. *The Polemic on the General Line of the International Communist Movement* (Peking: Foreign Languages Press, 1965), p. 77.

96. General Su Yu, Chief of Staff, was dismissed during the Quemoy Crisis of 1958. We have no knowledge of the reasons for his dismissal. He was soon rehabilitated and appointed to another, though less important, post. During the Cultural Revolution, he appeared frequently on important public functions and was described by a New China News Agency dispatch as a member of the Standing Committee of the Military Commission of the Central Committee.

97. John Gittings, "Military Control and Leadership, 1954–1964," *China Quarterly,* no. 26 (April–June, 1966), p. 100. Cf. Franz Michael, "The Struggle for Power," *Problems of Communism,* 16 (May–June, 1967): 14.

head of the Military Commission, a most significant development took place in the PLA. At the time of the dismissal of Peng, the morale, discipline, ideological commitment, and political reliability of the army had sunk to a low point, partly due to the neglect of political work under Peng's leadership and partly due to the impact of the Great Leap Forward.[98] Beginning with his famous article of September 29, 1959, and continuing through a series of meetings of the Military Commission and PLA Political Work Conferences, Lin Biao vigorously upheld and applied Mao's thought on army building. He proceeded to devise a series of specific policies and to undertake concrete actions for this purpose. The decline in party membership in the companies was reversed, and party branches were established in the one-third of the companies which still lacked them. It was stipulated that every platoon must have a party small group and every squad have some party members. With this strengthened party apparatus, Lin launched a continuous and comprehensive program of political education for the individual soldier. In turn, the successfully indoctrinated soldiers were asked to undertake political work among the masses.

Lin Biao's endeavors met with great success. As John W. Lewis concludes: ". . . The 'revolutionary' leadership techniques must be credited in large measure for salvaging the crumbling social order in 1961 and then for progressively restoring morale and discipline in the army and in the general populace."[99] The application of Mao's thought produced the desired effects in the army for simple and obvious reasons. Military discipline and total control of personnel were again reinforced by intensified political work. The values of public service and self-sacrifice could be more easily instilled in the armed services than elsewhere. The soldiers were young and relatively uneducated men whose thinking was not too difficult to influence. The skills demanded of them were fairly simple; originality and creativity were not essential in day-to-day work in the army. It can be reasonably argued that the "people's war" is still the best method of defense against an American invasion of the mainland and a promising strategy for revolution in some underdeveloped countries. Whatever their causes, Lin's successes made him the leading advocate of the vigorous application of Mao's thought. To Mao, they must have seemed a vindication of his thought at a time when other policies associated with it had brought economic disaster upon China. In retrospect, it seems that in making himself the leading advocate of Mao's thought, Lin Biao fol-

98. John Gittings, "The 'Learn from the Army' Campaign," *China Quarterly*, no. 18 (April-June, 1965), p. 154. Ralph L. Powell, *Politico-Military Relationships in Communist China* (Washington, D.C.: Department of State, 1963), p. 1. John W. Lewis, "China's Secret Military Papers: 'Continuities' and 'Revelations,'" *China Quarterly*, no. 18 (April-June, 1964), p. 76.

99. *Ibid.*, p. 75.

lowed essentially the same path to power that Liu Shaoqi had pursued in the early forties.

In contrast to the successful reassertion of Mao's thought in the PLA under Lin Biao's leadership, some of the party leaders found it impossible to implement vigorously Mao's thought and still carry out their duties successfully. Others became skeptical of the applicability of Mao's thought in various fields. These tendencies were more visible in the fields of literature, art, education, and academic affairs than in many others.[100] This development, following a direction contrary to the one in the PLA, finally led to the most profound upheaval within the party since 1935, alongside of which the Peng Dehuai affair looks like a preliminary skirmish of minor proportions. These contrasting tendencies also determined the form of the current struggle for power.

It is to be recalled that at the Lushan Plenum in August, 1959, Peng Dehuai criticized the commune system and the Great Leap Forward—with the prior knowledge and apparent support of the Soviet leadership. According to a Western report, Mao declared during a prolonged debate that should the dismissal of Peng lead to a revolt of the army, he would go back to the villages and recruit another army.[101] If this report is correct, it is clear that Mao was willing to go to any lengths, including the risk of destroying the army, in order to preserve the basic orientation of the regime, to maintain his position of leadership, and to crush his opponents. In the event, this proved to be unnecessary. But seven years later in the Great Proletarian Cultural Revolution, Mao was quite willing to disrupt the party for the same purposes.[102]

The fact that Mao found it necessary to disrupt the party in order to make his views prevail suggests the strong resistance within the party.

---

100. This point can be inferred from the long series of exaggerated charges made by the regime against these leaders. See, for example, editorial, *Hongqi* [Red Flag], no. 8, 1966; reprinted in *Peking Review,* June 17, 1966, pp. 7–13.

101. David A. Charles, "The Dismissal of Marshal P'eng Teh-huai [Peng Dehuai]," *China Quarterly,* no. 8 (October-December, 1961), p. 63.

102. New materials available have made it emphatically clear that the Cultural Revolution had its origin in the policy disputes and struggles for power in the Peng Dehuai affair. On December 21, 1965, Mao once again pointed out explicitly that "the crux of *Hai Rui Dismissed from Office* was the question of dismissal from office. The emperor Jia Jing dismissed Hai Rui from office. In 1959 we dismissed Peng Dehuai from office. And Peng Dehuai is 'Hai Rui' too" (*Hongqi,* no. 9, 1967). Qi Benyu, a member of the Cultural Revolution Group under the Central Committee, declared in a speech on May 23, 1967: "Particularly during the period of the country's economic difficulties between 1959 and 1962, the handful of counter-revolutionary revisionists, supported by the handful of top Party persons in authority, put out a large number of poisonous weeds such as *Hai Rui Dismissed from Office, Xie Yaohuan* and *Li Huiniang.* In these they insidiously attacked and insulted our great Party in an attempt to reverse the verdicts on the Right opportunist Peng Dehuai and others dismissed from office at the Lushan meeting and to incite people to join them in activities

This strong resistance in turn indicates that the process of bureaucratization and functional differentiation has gone very far. A review of the events leading up to and during the Great Proletarian Cultural Revolution shows that this is the case. During the period from 1959 to 1962, the economic disaster obliged Mao to acquiesce in a policy of liberalization in many fields and prevented him from acting against the dissidents. As Donald Munro points out, "there occurred in China a faint echo of the Hundred Flowers period of 1957."[103]

As soon as the economic crisis eased, Mao began his counterattack. At the Tenth Plenum in September, 1962, he warned the party: "Never forget the class struggle." Since then he has been reported as having pointed out that "some people were making use of the writing of novels to carry on anti-party activities and were creating a public opinion for the restoration of capitalism."[104] He launched the Socialist Education Movement and the three revolutionary movements of class struggle, of struggle for production, and of struggle for scientific experiment. He called on the Chinese people to learn from the PLA, which had successfully applied his thought.

Mao's endeavors encountered serious resistance in the field of literature and art. For the renewed and intensified application of Mao's doctrine that literature and art must serve politics would have imposed further limitations on the creative talents of writers and artists at a time when the quality of works produced had already been declining over a period of years, ever since Mao delivered his "Talks at the Yanan Forum on Literature and Art."[105] As Zhou Yang was reported to have told a group of young writers and scholars, the intellectuals of his generation were inferior to those of the preceding generation and the intellectuals of their generation were in turn inferior to those of his own. He asked what would happen if this trend continued.

aimed at a counter-revolutionary restoration" (*Peking Review*, May 26, 1967, p. 26). The May 16, 1966, circular of the Central Committee drawn up under the personal guidance of Mao reiterated his view that "the key point in Wu Han's drama *Hai Rui Dismissed from Office* is the question of dismissal from office." It attacked Peng Zhen, then the ninth ranking member of the Politbureau and the First Secretary of the Peking Municipal Party Committee, for covering up the serious political nature of the struggle and the heart of the matter, "namely, the dismissal of the Right opportunists at Lushan in 1959 and the opposition of Wu Han and others to the Party and socialism" (*ibid.*, May 19, 1967, p. 7).

103. Donald J. Munro, "Dissent in Communist China," *Current Scene*, June 1, 1966, p. 3. In retrospect, it seems significant that the slogan, "Let a Hundred Flowers Bloom and a Hundred Schools of Thought Contend" was first proposed, in a speech on May 26, 1956, by Lu Dingyi, Director of the Propaganda Department (who was later dismissed in July, 1966), to a gathering of scientists, social scientists, doctors, writers, and others.

104. *Peking Review*, August 22, 1966, p. 36.

105. T. A. Hsia, "Twenty Years after the Yenan [Yanan] Forum," *China Quarterly*, no. 13 (January–March, 1963), pp. 226–53.

Mao noted the resistance to his demands. He has been reported as having pointed out in 1963:

> In all forms of art . . . problems abounded; the people engaged in them were numerous. . . . Wasn't it absurd that many Communists showed enthusiasm in advancing feudal and capitalist art, but no zeal in promoting socialist art.[106]

While his efforts seem to have made some progess in other fields, for instance in the establishment of "political departments" within economic administration after the example of the PLA, his policies still failed to make much headway in the field of literature and art. Thus, a rectification movement was launched in June, 1964, within the All-China Federation of Literary and Art Circles and its affiliated association. At that time, Mao made his most serious warning to date, declaring:

> In the past fifteen years the literary and art circles for the most part . . . had not carried out policies of the Party and had acted as high and mighty bureaucrats. . . . In recent years they have even slid to the verge of revisionism. If serious steps were not taken to remould them, they were bound at some future date to become groups like the Hungarian Petofi Club.[107]

Yang Xianzhen, Shao Zhuanlin, Feng Ding, and Zhou Gucheng were subject to devastating attacks.[108] Still this persecution of the party and nonparty intellectuals was not extensive and far-reaching enough to satisfy Mao. This dissatisfaction is reflected in the recent charge made by the Maoists:

> In this so-called "rectification movement," Zhou Yang in general forbade open criticism of a sinister gang in literary and art circles which was opposed to the Party, opposed to socialism, and opposed to Mao Zedong's thought. As for those few members of the sinister gang like Tian Han, Xia

106. *Peking Review*, July 8, 1966, p. 18. It has become increasingly clear that Jiang Qing (Mrs. Mao Zedong) has played a vital role in the debate in the field of literature and art and the power struggle which finally led to the attack on Liu Shaoqi. In this debate and power struggle, personal bitterness and jealousy were apparently intertwined with important policy issues. For some of the important articles and speeches revealing the role of Jiang Qing, see "Patriotism or National Betrayal?" *Peking Review*, April 7, 1967, pp. 5–16; "On the Revolution in Peking Opera," *ibid.*, pp. 13–15; "Chairman Mao's Talks at the Yenan [Yanan] Forum on Literature and Art' Is a Programme for Building a Mighty Proletarian Cultural Army," *ibid.*, May 26, 1967; "Summary of the Forum of Literature and Art in the Armed Forces with Which Comrade Lin Piao [Lin Biao] Entrusted Comrade Chiang Ch'ing [Jiang Qing]," New China News Agency dispatch (Beijing), May 28, 1967; Speech by Comrade Chiang Ch'ing, *Peking Review*, December 9, 1966, pp. 6–9.

107. *Peking Review*, August 12, 1966, p. 36.

108. Fokkema, "Chinese Criticism of Humanism," pp. 68–81.

Yan and Shao Zhuanlin for whom open criticism was inevitable, he played a series of tricks of sham criticism but actual defense.[109]

This conscious and unconscious resistance was possible because the process of bureaucratization and routinization had gone a long way in the party apparatus controlling the field of literature and art. Zhou Yang was the Secretary of the League of Left-Wing Writers of China in 1931, and became the deputy director of the Propaganda Department of the Central Committee in 1949. He appointed his fellow writers in the 1930's to leading posts in the party propaganda apparatus.[110] This group of party leaders shared the more liberal and critical traditions of the 1930's in literature and art. They were greatly influenced by Western ideas. For example, Zhou Yang was reported, perhaps not without exaggeration, to have lauded "European bourgeois culture of the eighteenth and nineteenth centuries" as "the summit of human culture in the world" and to have advocated "the continuous introduction into China of the bourgeois literature and art of other countries."[111] They were also bound by intimate personal ties developed over a long period of time. This process of bureaucratization is indicated by the Maoists' accusation that "Zhou Yang tried to recruit deserters and enlist renegades, to form a clique to serve their own selfish interests and to usurp the leadership in literary and art circles."[112] Routinization inevitably accompanies bureaucratization. Mao was reported to have said:

109. *Peking Review*, August 12, 1966, p. 36. On January 14, 1965, a National Work Conference called by the Political Bureau adopted a Summary Minutes of Discussion, entitled "Some Current Problems Raised in the Socialist Education Movement in the Rural Area" (the twenty-three-article document), which was "drawn up under the personal leadership of Comrade Mao Zedong" (*Peking Review*, August 19, 1966, p. 6). This secret document was sent down to the Party committees at the level of the *xian* and regiments. In it, the Party Center defined the problem confronting the movement as "the contradiction between socialism and capitalism." The focal point of the movement was to "rectify those persons in authority in the party who are taking the capitalist road." According to this document, some of these persons acted openly; others operated behind the scenes. Some of their supporters were persons at low levels; others were persons at high levels. See, "Nongcun shehuizhuyi jiaoyu yundong zhong muqian de yixie wenti" ["Some Current Problems Raised in the Socialist Education Movement in the Rural Areas"]. Many of the essential points of this document were later incorporated in the Decision Concerning the Great Proletarian Cultural Revolution adopted on August 8, 1966, at the Eleventh Plenum of the Central Committee. In the twenty-three-article document, it was stated for the first time that "the main target of the present movement is those within the party who are in authority and are taking the capitalist road" (*Hongqi*, no. 9, 1967).

110. *Peking Review*, August 12, 1966, p. 35.

111. *Ibid.*, June 17, 1966, p. 7.

112. *Ibid.*, July 12, 1966, p. 36. There is little doubt that Zhou Yang had reservations about Mao's policies in general and his doctrine of literature and art in particular. According to the Maoists, Zhou Yang said that the correctness of the general line had not yet been proved, that the "all-round leap forward" in 1958 had caused a disproportion in the economy, that production would certainly be raised once the fixing of quota was based on the

In a revolutionary period those who only know how to follow routine paths cannot see this enthusiasm of the masses for socialism at all. . . . They can only travel the well-trodden paths. . . . That sort of person is always passive. . . . Someone always has to give him a poke in the back before he will move forward.[113]

Bureaucratization means command method of leadership. Thus, it was charged that these people "are merely accustomed to monopolizing everything themselves, giving orders and reducing the masses to inactivity."[114]

Bureaucratic organizations have their own method of protecting themselves. They control the communications from the top leaders. Zhou Yang was charged with the error of not transmitting Mao's and the Central Committee's instructions on, and severe criticisms of, literary and art work to people at the lower level. Bureaucratic organizations develop their own informal network of communications. Zhou Yang was charged with having said one thing at the open session of a large meeting but to have expressed the opposite view at smaller meetings and outside the meetings.[115] Bureaucratic organizations can try to sabotage the policies of the top leaders. Zhou Yang and others were said to have put numerous hindrances in the way of the Maoists' policy of staging Beijing operas on contemporary themes and to have laid down numerous rules and regulations to prevent the effective implementation of other policies. Bureaucratic organizations can resist penetration by top leaders. The Beijing Municipal Party Committee was accused of erecting a "tight barricade against the Central Committee" and of maintaining "an independent kingdom, water-tight and impenetrable."[116] An undercurrent of distrust between the party intellectuals and the party military leaders is reflected in Zhou Yang's use of the old saying that "it is impossible for scholars to reason with soldiers."[117]

The materials brought to light by the Cultural Revolution and Mao's decision to stage it show the serious limitations of the much-vaunted

---

household, that if socialism does not lead to democracy it is the tyrant's way, that the dissemination of Mao's thought promoted "the cult of the individual and would strangle the people's initiative." He was said to have opposed Mao's policy that literature and art must serve the workers, peasants, and soldiers, and to have considered this idea outdated (*ibid.*, p. 37; *ibid.*, August 19, 1966, pp. 29–30, 36). Apparently, Zhou Yang looked down upon the dominant form of drama and art during the Yanan period which consisted of using artists to do propaganda work among the soldiers and peasants. This form of art was apparently a main source of Mao's ideas on literature and art which, according to Zhou Yang, were based on "art-troupe experience."

113. *Ibid.*, August 19, 1966, p. 20.
114. *Ibid.*
115. *Ibid.*, August 12, 1966, p. 3.
116. *Ibid.*, July 8, 1966, p. 32.
117. *Ibid.*, August 19, 1966, p. 35.

method of thought reform, even when applied within the party. As the Maoists admitted, there are "a considerable number of muddled-headed people inside the Party whose world outlook has not been effectively remoulded."[118] It has become clearer than before that no matter how effective the technique, thought reform can only be successful when the ideology continues to demonstrate its validity by serving as a basis for successful policies and actions, shows its usefulness as a schematic image of reality, and retains its reliability as a crude map in an uncertain situation. When these conditions are not met, thought reform can even be counterproductive, for attempts at indoctrination merely sharpen the psychological conflicts of the individual without leading to the acceptance of the ideology. Mao's method of controlling the party bureaucracy through indoctrination, which had at an earlier period of time been effective, could no longer produce similar results. The Stalinist method of controlling the party by secret police ran counter to his political style. In any case, many secret police units at various levels were under the control of the party organization rather than Mao himself.

In order to reassert the thought of Mao and to preserve the basic orientation of the regime, Mao was forced by the widespread dissidence and resistance to his policies in various sections of the party to broaden his attack until he had purged some of the highest party leaders. Lin Biao apparently took advantage of the same situation to strike down his competitors and to become the heir apparent to Mao. In the case of some of the leaders such as Liu Shaoqi and Deng Xiaoping, lack of reliable information prevents us from determining whether and to what extent they opposed specific policies of Mao, whether they were implicated primarily by the errors of their trusted subordinates, and whether their mistake lay mainly in trying to limit the extent of the purges and to moderate Mao's handling of the Cultural Revolution.[119]

118. *Ibid.*, November 4, 1966, p. 7. See also *ibid.*, August 19, 1966, p. 20.

119. Materials available since the time of writing indicate that Liu Shaoqi came into serious conflict with Mao over the dispatch in June, 1966, of work teams to conduct the Cultural Revolution in various universities, units, and departments. Liu apparently tried to control the "revolutionary teachers and students" through the work teams, to protect some of the leading party officials under attack, and to preserve the integrity of the party organizations as much as possible. In contrast, Mao wanted to carry out a sweeping change of the leadership of the various party units. See "The Confession of Liu Shao-ch'i," *Atlas*, April, 1967, pp. 12–17, and *Mainichi*, January 28, 1967. It also becomes quite clear that Liu, as the manager of the party apparatus, has generally held less radical views than Mao, the leader of the movement and regime, although prior to the failure of the Great Leap Forward the differences between Liu and Mao had been resolved in one way or another and an effective unity between the leader and the party organization had been preserved. To Liu, the party is supreme; to Mao, the leader, his thought as the embodiment of revolutionary principles, is above the party as the final source of authority and truth.

Space does not enable us to review in any detail the more recent events, but there are several interesting points which deserve mention. First, Mao's policies continued to meet with resistance at every important juncture. In September, 1965, at a Central Committee meeting, Mao pointed to the need to subject the "reactionary bourgeoisie" to criticism.[120] Apparently, opposition within the party prevented him from launching the attack until November.[121] By the Maoists' admission, "even after Comrade Mao Zedong criticized the . . . Beijing Municipal Party Committee, they [the party leaders in Beijing] continued to carry out organized and planned resistance in an attempt to save the queen by sacrificing the knight."[122]

On June 3, 1966, the Central Committee announced the reorganization of the Beijing Municipal Party Committee, appointing Li Xuefeng as its First Secretary to replace Peng Zhen.[123] Then, in spite of Mao's reservations, some party leaders hastily sent out work teams for the avowed purpose of carrying out the Cultural Revolution in various units and places.[124] In fact, the persons in charge of various units or those in charge of the work teams "organized counter-attacks against the masses," "spearheaded

120. It is now known that this "work conference of the Central Committee" was a session of the Standing Committee of the Political Bureau attended also by the leading party officials of all the regional bureaus of the Central Committee. At this meeting in September and October of 1965, Mao gave his instructions regarding criticism of Wu Han ("Circular of the Central Committee of the Chinese Communist Party, May 16, 1966," *Peking Review*, May 19, 1966, p. 6).

121. This attack took the form of an article by Yao Wenyuan on Wu Han's historical play, *Hai Rui Dismissed from Office*, published in the *Wenhui bao* in Shanghai on November 10, 1965, and not reprinted in the *Renmin ribao* (pp. 5–6) until November 30. The Maoists now claim that this "first shot at the Peng Zhen counter-revolutionary revisionist clique" was "led by Comrade Jiang Qing." (*Peking Review*, May 26, 1967, P. 27).

122. *Peking Review*, July 8, 1966, p. 30. On April 16, *Frontline* (of which Deng Tuo was the editor-in-chief) and the *Beijing Daily* (an organ controlled by the Beijing Municipal Party Committee) published a collection of materials with comments entitled "A Criticism of Three-Family Village and Evening Chats at Yanshan." The Maoists charged that this criticism was a sham and that its purpose was "to prevent the struggle from going deeper" by sacrificing Deng Tuo. Yao Wen-yuan, "On 'Three-Family Village,'" pp. 5–8. This article was first published in Shanghai's *Jiefang ribao* and *Wenhui bao* on May 10, 1966.

Prior to mid-May, there existed an organ known as the "Group of Five in Charge of the Cultural Revolution." It was headed by Peng Zhen, of all people. Peng prepared a report which was approved by the Central Committee for distribution on February 12, 1966. It minimized the political aspect of Wu Han's play. On May 16, 1966, the Central Committee issued a circular which sharply attacked Peng's report, dissolved the "Group of Five," and set up a new Cultural Revolution Group directly under the Standing Committee of the Political Bureau (*Peking Review*, May 19, 1966, pp. 6–9). How the reversal of the position of the Central Committee between February 12 and May 16 came about remains obscure.

123. *Renmin ribao*, June 4, 1966, p. 1.

124. *Peking Review*, December 9, 1966, p. 8. The decision to send work teams was made by Liu Shaoqi. *Atlas*, April, 1967, p. 13. See also note 86.

the struggle against the revolutionary activists, encircled and attacked the revolutionary left and suppressed the revolutionary left and suppressed the revolutionary mass movement."[125] Thus, "an error on matters of orientation and an error of line took place during a short period."[126] Mao then convened the Eleventh Plenum which met from August 1 to August 12, 1966, and adopted the Decision Concerning the Great Proletarian Cultural Revolution. But the number of members and alternate members of the Central Committee who attended the meeting was not announced.[127] Instead, the communiqué reported that, among others, "representatives of revolutionary leaders and students from institutions of higher learning in Beijing" were present.[128] A few days after the Red Guards were received by Mao in mid-August, "new problems cropped up."[129] Since then, there have been frequent reports of clashes between the Red Guards and other groups or even between Red Guards under different leadership.

The resistance encountered by Mao suggests that he was not in effective control of the party after 1959, that his orders were no longer followed as a matter of course, that he may not always have had majority support in the Political Bureau before August, 1966, and perhaps not even in the Central Committee, and that a politically unorganized majority of top party leaders had serious reservations about his policies. If these speculations are correct, not only was Mao's ideological authority seriously weakened, but also ideological authority and organizational authority were no longer united in one person or one organ of the party as they had been before 1959. This created a serious dilemma for the party, for Mao still had enormous personal prestige and considerable support within the party. Although the other leaders could attempt to persuade Mao to accept their views, argue with him, and could endeavor to restrain, resist, and even sabotage his moves, they could not take positive actions to oppose or attack him openly without undermining the foundation of the party and the regime. They also could not openly criticize the thought of Mao Zedong and formulate and propagate a counter-ideology. They were thus generally on the defensive. In contrast, Mao took the offensive by using Lin Biao and the Red Guards to intimidate and shake up the party organizations in different units and by reorganizing the Standing Committee of the Political Bureau together with the Political Bureau it-

125. *Peking Review*, August 19, 1966, p. 19. The translation used here is slightly different from the text as it appeared in the *Peking Review*.

126. *Ibid.*, August 26, 1966, p. 7.

127. According to Franz Michael, only 80 of the full Central Committee membership were present (47 regular members and 33 candidate members), with 101 absent (44 regular members and 57 candidate members). "The Struggle for Power," *Problems of Communism*, 16 (May–June, 1967): 19.

128. *Peking Review*, August 19, 1966, p. 4.

129. *Ibid.*, December 9, 1966, p. 8.

self. By doing so, he seriously weakened the structural legitimacy of the party and established a precedent under which the all-sacred party organization can be attacked by other units. This will make governing the nation much more difficult from now on.

Second, Mao's attack was gradually broadened and focused at a fairly early stage on persons within the party itself. As the very perceptive report by the editor of *Current Scene* pointed out, "Opposition created during the previous phase became the principal object of attack during the next stage."[130] The Socialist Education Movement was intensified in November, 1965, with Yao Wenyuan's attack on Wu Han's historical play, *Hai Rui Dismissed from Office*. The attack on Wu Han became the attack on the "bourgeois" intellectuals as a whole. By May, the attack was broadened to include Deng Tuo, an influential member of the Secretariat of the Beijing Municipal Party Committee, and Liao Mosha, the director of its United-Front Department. After the Beijing Municipal Party Committee had been reorganized, the leadership in the Propaganda Department of the Central Committee was changed. Party leaders working in the field of literature, art, education, and propaganda in various localities were dismissed or severely criticized. The two concrete targets became first, "those in authority who have wormed their way into the Party and are taking the capitalist road" and, second, "the reactionary bourgeois academic 'authorities.'"[131] But the Maoists also recognized that their opponents enjoyed widespread popular support. By their own admission, the resistance to the Cultural Revolution also came from "the old force of habit in society,"[132] and "the bourgeois reactionary line has its social base which is mainly in the bourgeoisie."[133] Hence, it was necessary to organize such a large-scale "mass movement" as the Red Guards in order "to destroy the social basis on which the handful of bourgeois Rightists rests and to carry through the Great Proletarian Cultural Revolution thoroughly and in depth."[134] But as the Decision Concerning the Great Proletarian Cultural Revolution adopted by the Eleventh Plenum made clear, "the main target of attack in the present movement is those in the Party who are in authority and are taking the capitalist road."[135]

Third, as has been pointed out by many commentators, it was *Jiefang-*

130. "A Year of Revolution," *Current Scene*, December 10, 1966, p. 9.

131. *Peking Review*, August 26, 1966, p. 17.

132. *Ibid.*, August 12, 1966, pp. 6–7.

133. *Ibid.*, November 4, 1966, p. 7.

134. *Ibid.*, September 23, 1966, p. 15. It is quite probable that the majority of the Red Guards consists of children from the less privileged groups in the society, i.e., workers, peasants, and lower cadres. They are motivated by jealousy of children from privileged goups. *Ibid.*, January 1, 1967, p. 10.

135. *Ibid.*, August 12, 1966, p. 8.

jun bao, the organ of the PLA rather than the party's official organ, *Renmin ribao,* which took the lead in the Cultural Revolution. In one case, the army organ criticized a view expressed in an editorial of the party organ. This is only one of the many indications that the political influence of the army has increased greatly while that of the party itself has declined.

Fourth, at least up to the time of the completion of this paper in early January, 1967, there were efforts to preserve continuities with the past amidst the political upheaval. The PLA still has been kept in the background, and the principle of civilian control over the military, although weakened, has been maintained at least in theory. Despite many incidents involving the Red Guards and other groups, an attempt has been made to preserve the rule that reasoning and not violence should be used. An effort has been made to limit the number of persons against whom drastic action is taken. A way has been left open for the deviant party leaders to repent and to come back to the fold. Whatever the role of the secret police in the Red Guard movement, there has been no secret-police terror. For this, Red Guard terror has acted as a substitute.[136] Whether or not the attempts to preserve these traditions have been and will be successful remains in doubt. These traditions were established and further developed during a period when those opposed to Mao had been discredited by the failure of their policies, when Mao had offered the party a promising alternative program, and when Mao's ideological and organizational authority had been consolidated. They could be maintained only so long as there was a unity of the leader, the ideology, and the organizations. But these conditions no longer exist.[137]

136. Under the slogan of eliminating old ideas, old culture, old customs, and old habits, the Red Guards resorted to violent action against some elements of the population. The Red Guards thus replaced the public security forces as the instrument of violence and coercion. The use of violence by these loosely organized and inadequately supervised Red Guard units was indiscriminate and non-selective. Whether or not this was intended by the Maoists, the effect of this indiscriminate use of violence was the creation of an atmosphere of terror in which the personal and organizational ties among individuals were cut or loosened. The expectations of individuals were destabilized, and the activities of the various established organizations were hampered and disrupted. Furthermore, the Red Guards denounced some of the leading officials in wall posters or struggle meetings and subjected them to public humiliation, using some of the techniques which Mao described with high praise in his report on an investigation of the peasant movement in Hunan in 1927. The rampaging Red Guards intimidated the population and deterred them from rallying to the support of the officials under attack, while they undermined the prestige and authority of the latter. All the time the media of mass communication conducted an intensive propaganda campaign to discredit the oppositionists and their anti-Maoist views.

137. Toward the end of 1966, when the Cultural Revolution was launched in the factories and the rural areas, there were many reports that the workers deserted their posts, demanded and received bonuses and supplementary wages, demanded and got better housing accommodations, and even went on strike in some cases. Other reports stated that the peas-

Fifth, the timing of Mao's move seems to have been related to international events. When Mao called for criticism of the "reactionary bourgeoisie" in September and October of 1965, America's sharp escalation of the war in Vietnam had prevented a defeat of the government forces in South Vietnam. There was increasing fear of war with the United States. The Soviet Union was proposing "united action" to counter the American moves. On September 30, 1965, an army coup which was supported by the Communist Party of Indonesia took place and led within a few days to a counter-coup by the army which ended in the slaughter of hundreds of thousands of Indonesian Communists and their followers. In October, Beijing failed to impose its views on the composition and tasks of the Second Bandung Conference, and the much heralded meeting was postponed. The Pakistani-Indian War ended in a setback for Pakistan and in the Tashkent Conference which greatly enhanced Soviet prestige. This series of setbacks in foreign policy must have heightened Mao's sense of urgency regarding the need to take preventive action against the dissidents. Furthermore, during this period there must have been a great debate over the policy toward the Soviet Union. The issues may have been whether, in the face of an increased danger of war with the United States, Beijing should modify, however slightly, her hostile policy toward the So-

---

ants wanted to divide up all the year-end surplus grain harvested by the production teams or even the grain reserves and to use up the public accumulation funds, and that the students and other urban elements sent to the countryside were returning to the cities. The Maoists charged that the oppositionists were using material benefits to bribe the masses to join them, to discredit the Cultural Revolution, and to disrupt the economy. This charge can only be partly correct. The basic explanation is the fact that the whole Chinese system of economy relies more heavily on political control over demands and performance of the workers and peasants for its effective functioning than do many other systems. This political control was imposed by the party committees at different levels and in different units. With some of the party leaders and party committees under attack by the Red Guards, this whole system of political control was weakened. The masses took advantage of this situation to advance their economic demands or simply to relax their efforts. With their political authority shaken, the party officials may have found it difficult to resist these demands or may have been unable to control the behavior of the masses. Because they themselves were under attack, they feared to take up responsibility and in some cases simply gave up their leadership roles. This must be the basic explanation which the Maoists did not mention.

The situation both as perceived by the Maoists and as it actually developed demanded the reimposition of political control by the Maoists. It brought about a new stage of the Cultural Revolution, the stage of the seizure of power in various localities and units by the Maoists from the established party committees. This stage began with the so-called January Revolution. Shanghai was the first city in which the seizure of power took place. This stage was characterized by several features. Mao called on the army to support the revolutionary rebels in their seizure of power. The army units paraded in the streets to demonstrate their power and, in the case of the city of Harbin, actually surrounded an opposition group and disarmed its members. Revolutionary rebels would first seize the public security bureaus and the mass media of communication, and then would assume the power of the party com-

viet Union and whether the Soviet proposal of "united action" in Vietnam should be accepted. By November, a decision must have been made, with Mao insisting on the rejection of "united action," refusing to undertake largescale intervention in the war but at the same time rejecting negotiation with the United States.[138] Presumably, Mao did not want another "Korean War" during which Beijing ran the serious risk of an American attack and the Chinese army bore the brunt of the fighting. Instead, he preferred that the Vietnamese continue to conduct the "people's war" on a basis of "self-reliance." Probably he also hoped to embroil the Soviet Union and the United States in a confrontation so that the American-Soviet conflict would be more serious than the Sino-American conflict. By June 5, 1966, if not two or three months previously, the fear of war with the United States must have receded, either because the pattern of American escalation in Vietnam had been stabilized and had thus become clear to Beijing, and/or because Beijing, after her rejection of united action with the Soviet Union, had reassessed American intentions. Furthermore, the internal struggle for power had become critical by this time. An important document published by *Jiefangjun bao* on June 6 asserted that "if we think only of dealing with the Chiang Kai-shek gang and United States imperialism but neglect the possibility that the bourgeoisie can still work

---

mittee and the government organ of a particular unit or at a particular level. The provisional organ of power, now known as a revolutionary committee, was based on the principle of the three-in-one combination. In other words, it was to be composed of, first, the leaders of the revolutionary mass organization (that is to say, the revolutionary rebels or the Red Guards), second, the representatives of the army units stationed there, and third, the revolutionary leading cadres (that is, those party officials who originally supported Mao or were persuaded to join the Maoists to seize power from the oppositionists or their fellow colleagues on the party committee).

Since the army was the only organization which remained *relatively* unscathed in the Cultural Revolution, it was the only instrument which could supervise industrial production and farm work. Army units were ordered to support the work of industrial production and to help with routine farm work. The workers and the peasants were told to cooperate with them. In mid-March the seizure of power at the production-team and production-brigade level was suspended for the period of the busy spring farming season. Shortly afterward, the Maoists launched an intensive attack on the top party person in authority who was taking the capitalist road and on his book on self-cultivation, i.e., Liu Shaoqi and his book, *Lun Gongchandangyuan de xiuyang* [On the Self-cultivation of a Member of the Chinese Communist Party] (Zhangjiakou: Xinhua shudian, 1946). A revised edition was published in 1962 by Renmin chuban she. English translations were published by the Foreign Languages Press in 1961 and 1964, under the title of *How To Be a Good Communist*.

Thus the January Revolution, Mao's call for the PLA to give active support to the revolutionary left, and the widespread violence in many localities indicate that the party traditions have become further eroded because the objective conditions necessary to their preservation no longer existed.

138. Editorial departments of *Renmin ribao* and *Hongqi*, "Refutation of the New Leaders of the C.P.S.U. on 'United Action,'" *Peking Review*, November 12, 1965, pp. 10–21.

for a come-back and subvert us from within, . . . then history will judge us a criminal."[139] It was only when the fear of an imminent war had receded that Mao and his followers decided to take such a drastic step as the purging of top party leaders and the launching of the Red Guard movement, thus disrupting openly the unity of the party and the nation which would have been imperative for defense in case of war.

Finally, as everyone realizes, the struggle for power was intimately related to the problem of succession to Mao. Inability to provide for orderly transfer of power is an inherent weakness of all totalitarian regimes. But the crisis in China had certain features which distinguish it from the struggle for succession to Lenin's mantle. In China, the masses were mobilized by both sides. The mass-line method of the CCP had been so rigorously applied in the past that the various social groups had to be drawn into the power struggle in order to obtain even temporary results and to legitimize the outcome. In addition, the major political, social, and economic institutions became more deeply and actively involved in the struggle than in Stalin's fight against his opponents. The army played a central and active role, just as it was once the basis of Mao's power before he had gained control of the party apparatus. The tradition of the PLA as a work force in political affairs as well as a military organization apparently affected the nature of the struggle for succession. The party apparatus was strongly entrenched because of the long-established policies on the assignment and promotion of cadres and the tradition of continuity of leadership. At the same time, the thought of Mao still retained considerable influence. Thus, once there occurred a split between the ideological and organizational authority within the party, its early successes and its long traditions not only failed to prevent a rift in the political system but also magnified the scope and intensity of the crisis.

Summary and Conclusion

From 1935 up to the eve of the Great Leap Forward, the CCP was almost unique among all Communist parties and totalitarian movements in the continuity and solidarity of its leadership, in the flexibility of its political strategy and tactics, in the popular support it enjoyed, in its capacity to effect rapid socioeconomic transformation, and in its ability to bring about at least a minimum of sociopolitical integration of different regions and classes.

Many historical circumstances provided favorable conditions for the victory of the CCP and for the acceptance and consolidation of the political system which the party created in its own image. The Chinese Communist movement was the response of a group of men to the problems of a

139. *Ibid.*, July 15, 1966, p. 20.

highly disintegrated political community which demanded a total solution and revolutionary change. Yet the repudiation of the old order and the rejection of the content of many traditions did not preclude the persistence of certain cultural patterns and traditional forms which made the new political system acceptable to the Chinese. The important role played by an explicit, official ideology in the Chinese Empire, the autocratic nature of the political system, the cult of the emperor, the existence of a well-defined elite, the submersion of the individual in a collectivity, are all cases in point.

During the revolutionary period, Marxism-Leninism was adapted to Chinese conditions in the thought of Mao Zedong. Marxism-Leninism-the thought of Mao became one of the few, if not the only, political doctrines which were Western in origin but took deep root in China. This body of Marxist-Leninist-Maoist ideas was congruent with Chinese reality at the time. Certain parts of Marxism-Leninism suited the conditions of a disintegrated society. The theory of contradiction justified the inevitable, violent conflicts which the absence of a stable and acceptable political order made ubiquitous. The sociological analysis of class and class struggle directed the Chinese Communists to the necessity of making the peasantry and other social groups active participants in the political process, thus enabling them to change the whole pattern of political participation and to defeat the ruling group. The concept of the unity of theory and practice corresponded to the great need for resolute action to achieve carefully defined goals. The principles of party-building fitted an environment in which the rebuilding of a new political community had to begin with a tightly organized group of men. Other parts of Marxism-Leninism, such as the concept of an organic tie between a Communist party and the proletariat, were discarded in practice. The thought of Mao itself evolved out of successful practice in handling political work and military affairs in the course of fighting a guerrilla war. Defeat suffered by the party when rival leaders were in power discredited them, while success achieved by the movement under Mao's guidance confirmed his leadership and legitimized his thought. His rivals' failure and his own success gave Mao control over the party without bloody purges. The unity of ideological and organizational authority in the person of Mao and his followers enabled the party to develop a moderate method of inner-party struggle. This united elite with its international orientation proved to be more capable of exploiting nationalism than the Nationalist party. Employing its united-front tactics, it succeeded in acquiring leadership over all the major social groups toward the end of the civil war. Similarly, circumstances and success in domestic and international affairs helped the party to consolidate its control and to legitimize the political system which it had brought into existence.

The early successes were made possible by a system of ideas and practices which contained within itself the seeds of policy failures occurring between 1958 and 1961 and the profound crisis of 1966. This system had made the thought of Mao the doctrinal basis of the regime, the cognitive framework for understanding reality, and a general guide in formulating policies. The more impressive the early successes and the longer the history of the movement, the more tenaciously one group of leaders, particularly the aging formulator of the ideology himself, held on to the doctrine and the memories of the past. But the ideology was no longer congruent with the social conditions of a developing, industrializing, and modernizing society. It no longer reflected the genuine interests and desires of the population. Policies associated with ideology in various ways produced disastrous results. Among the dissident intellectuals inside and outside the party, criticism of these policies led to doubts about the ideology. The ideological authority of Mao was thus weakened, and effective organizational authority gravitated more than ever to another group of party leaders. A split occurred between ideological and organizational authority. At the same time, however, the first group of leaders continued to find the ideology a useful guide in some sectors of an increasingly differentiated society. They sought to reassert the ideology in order to preserve the general orientation of the regime and to strengthen its foundations.

Thus, two opinion groups emerged in opposition to each other. Their conflicts could not be reconciled, harmonized, or resolved on the basis of the ideology, because the applicability of this ideology was itself the central issue in the dispute. There were no longer any fundamental standards by which to judge right and wrong, for the standards as embodied in the ideology were the subject of the debate.[140] The ideology which had performed an integrative function at an early time became itself a disintegrative force. In the struggle for power, it was used as a weapon by one group to attack the other. *Realpolitik* was joined to a conflict over principles. Party unity disappeared. The persistent force of Mao and his followers was confronted with tenacious resistance or opposition by a politically unorganized majority of the party. This confrontation and the widening split between ideological and organizational authority could not be easily resolved by a political system in which it is almost impossible to remove the top leader and in which the strongly entrenched party organizations at various levels were difficult to purge. At this point, the historical accident of the longevity but uncertain health of Mao may have become a factor. All these circumstances introduced a series of complicating

140. An editorial by the *Renmin ribao* and the *Hongqi* charged that some responsible persons in the party "reversed right and wrong, juggled black and white . . ." (*Peking Review,* January 1, 1967, p. 9).

factors into the process of routinization of charisma and turned that process into an open struggle between a charismatic leader and a routinizing and bureaucratized organization.

The Great Proletarian Cultural Revolution cannot properly be called a purge, since a purge is an institutionalized practice in the system. It is rather a profound crisis in the institutions of the party themselves. In this sense, the present inner-party struggle is different in nature from all the previous purges since 1935. The organizational legitimacy of the party center was weakened when, as the editor of *Current Scene* put it, Mao employed his enormous personal prestige and packed the Eleventh Plenum with outsiders "in order to overcome the resistance of what may have been a majority within Party leadership councils,"[141] and rammed through the revolutionary decisions on the Cultural Revolution. The organizational legitimacy of the party apparatus in various units and at different levels was destroyed when the Red Guards were used to attack them.[142] The long-established traditions and rules governing inner-party struggle were violated. In the process of the Cultural Revolution which has been justified by the thought of Mao and has been said to have been under his personal command, the excesses of the Red Guards, the naïveté of their actions, and the turmoil created by them may have further called into question the validity of Mao's thought and his wisdom. The ideological legitimacy of the regime and the personal legitimacy of the leader may have been further weakened. As the party and the ideology constitute the core of the regime, the political system as a whole has been badly shaken.

A Maoist victory will establish a precedent under which the Chairman of the party may violate many, if not all, of its most important norms and prescribed procedures and ignore its regular structural arrangements, and under which personal legitimacy may be used to override structural legitimacy. It will restore the position of the charismatic leader and his thought and weaken the party as an institution. It will delay the process of routinization. The important change in the interrelationship of the leader, the ideology, and the organization will make institutionalization in the political sphere more difficult and the political stability achieved at

141. "A Year of Revolution," *Current Scene*, December 10, 1966, p. 6. Jiang Qing indirectly admitted that the Maoists did not constitute a majority. An official report of her speech on November 28, 1966, contained this intriguing sentence: "Referring to the question of 'minority' and 'majority' she said one could not talk about a 'minority' or 'majority' independent of class viewpoint" (*Peking Review*, December 9, 1966, p. 9).

142. The Red Guards are probably under the very loose control of the Cultural Revolution groups and committees and the guidance of the PLA. There is also no doubt that the army protected and supported the Red Guards; the *Peking Review* reported that in the last few months of 1966, "the Chinese People's Liberation Army sent more than 100,000 commanders and fighters to take part in the colossal work involved in making the visitors feel at home in the capital" (*Peking Review*, January 1, 1967, p. 4).

any particular time more precarious than before. This precedent can, however, be nullified if Mao's successors repudiate implicitly or explicitly this particular aspect of the Cultural Revolution. This is a likely development in the long run. A victory by the opposition will make it necessary to reject, revise, or reinterpret the thought of Mao and/or to develop new doctrines to replace or to supplement it. In either case, the effectiveness and legitimacy of the regime will not be easy to re-establish quickly. Even if an uneasy compromise emerges out of a stalemate, the authority and capacity of the regime to act will be diminished, and public confidence in it will not be easy to restore soon. China's search for a reintegrated political community has suffered a setback. It will have to begin again with a battered political system.

Thus, just as the thought of Mao and his policies in the Great Leap Forward produced an economic disaster, the thought of Mao and his policies in the Great Proletarian Cultural Revolution seem likely to have serious consequences in the next few years not only for cultural and academic life but also for the political system as a whole. What we have witnessed is the tragedy of a once effective doctrine which has outlived its usefulness and the tragedy of a once impressive political system which has rested on the foundation of a total ideology rather than on a consensus or agreement on fundamentals. Only future events can reveal whether the current political upheaval represents the last gasp of a revolution or whether it represents a new totalitarian "breakthrough" in which a leader gains or regains absolute dictatorial control and, together with his heirs, pushes the revolution to a more radical stage of fairly long duration. What cannot be doubted is that the contrast between the early successes and the present turmoil places in high relief the universal problems and difficulties of transition from revolution to the establishment of a new integrated political community.

2 The Cultural Revolution and the Chinese Political System

One of the most extraordinary and puzzling events of the twentieth century is surely the Great Proletarian Cultural Revolution in China.[1] This most profound crisis in the history of the Beijing regime provides us with the best available opportunity to study the Chinese political system. For it is during a crisis that the nature, the strength, and the vulnerabilities of a political system fully reveal themselves. Furthermore, we can attempt not only to note the unique features of this extraordinary event, and of Chinese politics itself, but also to see whether the seemingly unique Chinese experience does not reveal some universal dilemma of the human condition and fundamental problems of the socio-political order in a magnified and easily recognizable form. It is my belief that the Chinese political system prior to the Cultural Revolution is one of the purest forms found in human experience of a type of association in which there is a clear-cut separation between the elite and the masses. If one follows Ralf Dahrendorf in asserting that in every social organization there is a differential distribution of power and authority, a division involving domination and subjection,[2] the Chinese political system can be taken as one of the polar examples of all social organizations, showing clearly their possibilities and limitations, their problems and dilemmas. From this perspective, the Maoist vision as it has revealed itself in its extreme form during the early phases of the Cultural Revolution can be considered a critique of this type of political organization. It represents an attempt to minimize the consequences arising from the division between domination and subjection by changing the pattern of participation of the dominated in the political process within every single organization, by redefining the role of those in positions of authority, and by changing their attitudes and values so that the line between domination and subjection is blurred and a new type of relationship between the two groups will be obtained.

1. [This article was first published in *The China Quarterly*, no. 38 (April–June, 1969) pp. 63–91. The permission by *The China Quarterly* to reproduce it in this volume is gratefully acknowledged.] The research for this article was undertaken under a grant from the Joint Committee on Contemporary China of the Social Science Research Council. The author also wants to acknowledge the support given to him by the Center for International Studies, the Social Science Divisional Research Committee and the Committee on Far Eastern Studies of the University of Chicago.
2. Ralf Dahrendorf, *Class and Class Conflict in Industrial Society* (Stanford, California: Stanford University Press, 1959), pp. 165, 169.

Beyond this, the ideal society in Mao's vision is one in which the absolute validity of its basic values and norms are beyond question, total commitment to societal goals is demanded from the individual, and all powers are employed in repeated efforts to realize his vision. In this totally mobilized society everyone is deeply concerned with public affairs. Every act must be relevant to politics. Every person must actively participate in the political system and processes. It is commonplace to say that Mao's vision has its roots in his experience in conducting guerrilla warfare which requires total commitment and preoccupation with power to achieve a common objective. But, in Mao's view, this vision also contains the proper corrective for an increasingly bureaucratized, modernizing society in which the gap between values and practices widens, idealistic pronouncements become empty rhetoric, commitments to societal goals are weak, and power is used to pursue narrowly defined interests. In the Cultural Revolution, the elevation of the cult of Mao's thought to a new height is meant to be, among other things, a reaffirmation of the societal values and goals. The repeated emphasis on "the three constantly read articles" is intended to bring about total commitment. Power is to be recaptured and used to implement his vision.

Obviously, the establishment and the successful functioning of the Maoist political system requires a concomitant change in public and private morality and indeed in what we call human nature. Marx has written that "the whole of history is nothing but a continual transformation of human nature."[3] Whereas Marx seems, as Robert Tucker puts it, to "look to the future Communist revolution as the source of a radical transformation of man or 'change of self,'" Mao in effect has attempted to make a series of revolutions and to bring Communist society into existence by a radical transformation of man. From this general perspective, let me now first discuss the pre-Cultural Revolution political system and then the course of the Cultural Revolution so that I can give concrete meaning to these abstract generalizations.

Inner-Party Tensions Prior to the Cultural Revolution

Prior to the Cultural Revolution, Party dominance operated not only in the political system as a whole but also in every organization from the top to the lowest levels.[4] As the Three-anti and Five-anti campaigns, the socialist transformation of industry and commerce, and the collectivization

3. Karl Marx, *The Poverty of Philosophy*, p. 160, quoted in Robert C. Tucker, "The Marxian Revolutionary Idea," in Carl J. Friedrich (ed.), *Revolution* (New York: Atherton Press, 1967), p. 219.

4. A. Doak Barnett, *Cadres, Bureaucracy, and Political Power in Communist China* (N.Y.: Columbia University Press, 1967).

of agriculture show, the ruling class of Party leaders, cadres, and members could effectively control the demands of the masses and impose programmes of sweeping change against the wishes of the non-elite. At the only time during which the Party was openly and directly criticized in the spring of 1957, at its own invitation, it could abruptly terminate the blooming of a Hundred Flowers and launch an anti-rightist campaign to eradicate the "poisonous weeds" and to suppress the "freaks and monsters." As the aftermath of the Great Leap Forward and the establishment of the communes demonstrate, only passive resistance and slowdown on a massive scale could thwart the will of the Party.

When such a high degree of centralization of power in the ruling class was combined with a clear-cut division involving domination and subjection, the substantive policies followed by the elite had enormous and immediate effect on the population; and the way in which the elite dealt with the non-elite was also of crucial importance in determining their relationship. Although Mao cast his analysis of political problems in Marxist terms, his actions constantly reflect, and his pronouncements sometimes explicitly reveal, a firm recognition that conflicts arising from differential distribution of authority in the society represents the most basic fact of social life. In his famous speech, "On the Correct Handling of the Contradictions among the People," he departed from Soviet orthodoxy in his open admission of the possibility of contradictions "between the government and the masses," between "those in positions of leadership and the led."[5] His juxtaposition of non-antagonistic contradictions among the people and antagonistic contradictions between the enemy and ourselves suggests that he is quite aware of both the consensual and coercive bases of a political system. His technique of "thought reform" consists essentially of a method of coercive persuasion which skilfully manipulates man's two fundamental motives for obeying political power.

The materials disclosed during the Cultural Revolution, as well as the very fact that it occurred, have added immensely to, and modified in some fundamental aspects, what little we know about the power relation-

5. Mao Tse-tung, *On the Correct Handling of the Contradictions among the People* (Peking: Foreign Languages Press, 1957). For Mao's departure from Soviet orthodoxy, see G. F. Hudson, "Introduction" in Mao Tse-tung, *Let a Hundred Flowers Bloom* (N.Y.: The New Leader). Mao is apparently not the only one who has made this point. According to the Maoists, Liu wrote in his "On Organizational and Disciplinary Self-Cultivation by Communists" that the Party "is a combination of contradictions. It has leaders and those who are led, Party leaders and Party members, the higher Party organizations and lower Party organizations." *Peking Review*, 15 November 1968, p. 18. This was a report delivered by Liu in the early 1940s at the Central Party School. The quotation can be found on page 3 of a mimeographed version in Chinese, *Zuzhi shang he jilü shang de xiuyang*. See also Franz Schurmann, *Ideology and Organization* (Berkeley: University of California Press, 1966), p. 54.

ship among the top leaders and the process of decision-making. Else-where I have tried to show the incongruity between Mao's thought in its radicalized version and the changing social reality in China.[6] I have also attempted to indicate how this incongruity disrupted the pre-existing unity between the ideology, the leader and the Party organization. What needs to be stressed here is that the Party organization has shown greater willingness and ability to adjust itself to the new, emergent social situation than Mao, who had earlier demonstrated a profound realism in political-military affairs during the Civil War. Over the years, the head or heads of the Party organization have developed a perspective and approach to China's problems quite different from those of the supreme leader. These differences between the supreme leader and the Party organization con-stitute the political reality behind Mao's rhetoric on the struggle between the proletariat and the bourgeoisie and on the struggle between two lines.[7] Hopefully, an examination of these differences and the ability or inability to resolve them will deepen our understanding of the decision-making process and political relationships in China.

The first and basic issue confronting a revolutionary regime is whether it should rapidly implement its revolutionary programme or give priority to the consolidation of revolutionary gains and the newly-established in-stitutions. With the possible exception of the Hundred Flowers episode and the subsequent anti-rightist campaign, in which the roles played by Mao and the Party organization are still a matter of doubt,* Mao has al-ways been the promoter and initiator of new radical policies. With the possible exception of the controversial case of the Socialist Education Movement during 1964, Liu has always tried to consolidate the gains and tended to move more slowly. As the head of the party organization, he was more a co-ordinator of activities than an initiator of new policies. In the process of policy-making as distinct from Party management, he gener-ally played the role of approving, supporting, or rejecting ideas or pro-grammes advanced by his subordinates. The programmes which he sup-ported or approved were generally less radical than those later adopted by Mao. Liu was also the spokesman and executor of the more moderate poli-cies of the regime, which in all probability he wholeheartedly favoured.

6. Tang Tsou,"Revolution, Reintegration, and Crisis in Communist China," in Ping-ti Ho and Tang Tsou (eds.), *China's Heritage and the Communist Political System* (Chicago: University of Chicago Press, 1968), pp. 277–347. Reprinted here as chapter 1.

7. For an earlier discussion of the tensions within the Party in terms of the differences in approaches between the guerilla leader and the political commissar, see John W. Lewis, "Leader, Commissar, and Bureaucrat: The Chinese Political System in the Last Days of the Revolution," *ibid.* pp. 449–481.

* Now it is clear that both Mao and the Party organization were agreed that an anti-right-ist campaign should be launched and that Mao took the lead to do so.

The contrast between Mao's drive for rapid revolutionary changes and Liu's preference for consolidation was most clearly documented by the recent revelations regarding the programme of setting up agricultural co-operatives. In his first self-criticism posted by the Red Guards on 26 December 1966, Liu admitted that in 1951 he incorrectly criticized the Shanxi provincial committee's decision to develop the mutual aid teams in the old liberated areas by forming agricultural production co-operatives.[8] In 1955, Liu also gave at least tacit support to the proposal of Vice-Premier Deng Zihui to dissolve 200,000 agricultural co-operatives.* When Mao declared, on 31 July 1955, that some comrades were tottering along like a woman with bound feet, and proposed a progamme of rapid co-operativization, he was referring directly to Deng Zihui and indirectly criticizing Liu. The caution of Liu and Deng reflected the inherent conservative tendency of a vast organization which had to implement policies and to deal with day-to-day problems of a very practical nature.

Within the Marxist framework, this preference for consolidation and for incremental change was justified by emphasizing the limits imposed on human effort by the objective forces of production and by the need to develop production as a precondition for changes in social and economic institutions. Liu has been charged with having said at different times during the early years of the regime that "the socialist revolution is possible" . . . "only when industry accounts for 40 or 50 per cent of the total production," that "short of industrialization, it is categorically impossible to realize the collectivization of agriculture," and that restriction on rich peasants, nationalization and collectivization "prematurely" would "hamper the growth of the productive forces."[9] In contrast to these views, Mao believes that "in certain conditions, such aspects [of the society] as the relations of production, theory and the superstructure in turn manifest themselves in the principal and decisive role."[10]

The different approaches between the supreme leader and the organization are also reflected in the ideological issues of the status of class struggle in China. After the socialist transformation of industry and commerce and the programme of co-operativization were well under way, Liu

8. One of the three slightly different versions of this self-criticism available to the author indicates that this self-criticism was made on 23 November 1966, at a Central Committee Work Conference. There was a central work conference in October 1966. It is possible that this self-criticism was made during that conference.

* According to recent revelation, the number of agricultural cooperatives actually dissolved was only 20,000 plus, and the widely believed story of the dissolutions of 200,000 cooperatives was a trumped-up charge.

9. Editorial Department of *Capital Red Guard*, "Pichou zhongguo heluxiaofu de fangeming shengchanli lun" ("Criticize China's Khrushchev's Reactionary Theory on Production Forces Until It Smells"), *Renmin ribao (People's Daily)*, 3 September 1967.

10. Quoted in *Peking Review*, 13 October 1967, p. 11.

declared in his political report to the Eighth Party Congress that "the question of who will win in the struggle between socialism and capitalism in our country has now been decided."[11] A resolution of the Eighth Party Congress declared that "the contradiction between the proletariat and the bourgeoisie in our country has been basically resolved" and that "the major contradiction in our country is between the advanced social systems and the backward productive forces of society."[12] The authorship of these two statements has been attributed by the Maoists to Liu. Liu himself admitted in his third self-criticism, released on 2 August 1967, that Mao at the time objected to these two statements and that they had never been officially repudiated or revised up to that time.[13]

This first question, of the priority between rapid revolutionary change and consolidation of revolutionary gain, was intimately related to a second: how the Party, in implementing its revolutionary programme and in establishing new institutions, should treat the various social groups and sub-groups which were most directly affected. These groups and sub-groups in various sectors of the society had different statuses, positions, privileges, powers and influence. To what extent should the interests of these various social groups and sub-groups be taken into account and their participation in the political structure and process be provided for?

By now it comes as no surprise to anyone that the Party organization has shown a greater sensitivity to the material and personal interests of the various selectively privileged social groups than Mao. According to the Maoists, Liu wrote in his "instructions to An Ziwen and others," dated 23 January 1950, that "the type of peasant household which owns three horses, a plough, and a cart should increase to 80 per cent [of the total number of rural households] in the next few years."[14] Liu admitted in his first self-criticism that, soon after the Communists captured the large cities, he made a series of statements "to correct the over impatient sentiments towards capitalist industry and commerce and the over hasty methods used against them."[15] According to the Maoists, he said that "exploitation not only is no crime but is a contribution," and that "if socialist steps

11. *The Eighth National Congress of the Chinese Communist Party*, Vol. I (Peking: Foreign Languages Press, 1956), p. 37.

12. *Ibid.* pp. 115–116.

13. *Mainichi*, 3 August 1967.

14. Editorial Departments of the *Renmin ribao*, *Hongqi*, and *Jiefangjun bao*, "Struggle Between the Two Roads in China's Countryside," translated in *Peking Review*, 1 December 1967, p. 12. As the spokesman of the Party's rich peasant line, Liu declared in a report in 1950 that the policy of preserving the rich peasant economy "is of course not a temporary policy but a long-term policy." Liu Shaoqi, "Report on the Problems of Land Reform," *Xinhua yuebao*, Vol. II, No. 3 (15 July 1950), p. 494.

15. Liu Shaoqi's self-criticism, big character poster posted by Jinggangshan Red Guards on 26 December 1966. From a xeroxed handwritten copy in the author's possession.

were taken right now," they would not be "in the interests of the people" and would "damage the enthusiasm of private industries and individual producers"[16] In his third self-criticism, he denies that he had ever said that "exploitation has some merits." But he did not deny that he ordered the records of these talks to be burned.[17] After the Socialist transformation of industry and commerce, the capitalists were not only given fixed dividends for a number of years but also were retained in various positions in their own companies or assigned to state-owned enterprises. The Maoists charged that at one time in the sphere of commerce in Shanghai more than 170 capitalists were appointed to positions of manager or associate manager in over 100 specialized companies and more than 14,000 capitalists were appointed directors or deputy directors, managers or associate managers of factories and stores which were under the socialist ownership of the whole people.[18] Red Guard reports also indicated that many of the technical and management personnel at middle and lower levels not only retained their posts but were also absorbed into the Party later. These actions were in perfect accord with the Party's policy at the time and were apparently approved by Mao. But they are now considered to be errors and anti-socialist acts after Mao became seriously concerned with their "revisionist" implications and wanted to mobilize the under-privileged groups to attack the Party organizations.

The Party organization's sensitivity to the material interests of the various social groups and its ability to work with the privileged groups might surprise an early twentieth-century Marxist. But from the viewpoint of theory of organization they are perfectly understandable. First of all, the most immediate and most important task of a Party organization is the management of men with different social backgrounds, attitudes, interests, and preferences under rapidly changing circumstances. At a very early date Liu Shaoqi realized that even in a revolutionary organization like the Chinese Communist Party (CCP), which drew into its ranks some of the most idealistic, selfless and rootless individuals, he could gain their loyalty and get the best out of them by taking into account their personal interests. After emphatically underscoring the absolute and unconditional subordination of personal interests to Party interests, he nevertheless pointed out in the first Chinese edition of his *How to be a Good Communist:*

16. Editorial Department of *Capital Red Guard*, "Criticize China's Khrushchev's Reactionary Theory on Productive Forces Until It Smells," *Renmin ribao*, 3 September 1967.

17. *Sankei*, 16 August 1967, in *Daily Summary of Japanese Press*, 16 August 1967, p. 12. Liu declared in his political Report to the Eighth Party Congress that "workers in privately-owned factories were saved from unemployment." *The Eighth National Congress of the Communist Party of China*, Vol. I, p. 31.

18. "Thoroughly Criticize the Reactionary and False theory of the Dying out of Class Struggle," *Renmin ribao*, 24 August 1967.

Although the general interests of the Party include within themselves the personal interests of the Party members, they still cannot include these latter interests completely. The Party cannot and should not wipe out the individuality of the Party members. . . . As far as possible, the Party will attend to and safeguard its members' essential interests. . . .[19]

The Maoists attributed to Liu many remarks in which he tried to foster devotion to the Party's interests by appealing to the individual's self-interests.[20] It would seem that Liu Shaoqi's notion of human nature stemmed from his experience in Party management—in the first instance, management of underground Party organizations in the "White" areas. Confronted frequently with the self-interests of its members and having taken them into account in their decisions, the leaders of the organization would not find it too difficult to give the minimum necessary weight to the interests of other social groups.

In contrast, Mao, as the charismatic leader of a revolutionary movement and later of a nation at war, relied on personal, ideological, and nationalistic appeals to mobilize the masses. In dealing with them, he tried to reduce the distance between the leaders and the led not only by encouraging mass participation, but also by urging the leaders to go among the masses and become one of them. In so doing he could exploit spontaneous mass actions for his own purposes and guide them in the desired direction. Just as making the necessary concessions to the interests of the various social groups is the hallmark of Liu's method of leadership, bridging the visible gaps between the leaders and the led is the characteristic feature of Mao's *modus operandi*. Whereas Liu takes a paternalistic attitude towards the masses, Mao appeals to their sense of their own dignity, power, and importance, and to their love and devotion to an omniscient figure. Both techniques are subsumed under the concept of the mass line. But over the years, Liu and Mao have come to place increasing emphasis on one or the other of these two different aspects of the mass line, until in recent years the distinct emphasis has become very clear.

The second explanation for the ability of the leaders of the Party organization to work with the privileged groups in society is that after coming to power, they became—to use a vague, ill-defined, but for some purposes useful word—the establishment, *par excellence*. As heads of a vast organization, they had a proper appreciation for the ability of the mana-

19. Liu Shaoqi, *Lun gongchandangyuan de xiuyang (On the Self-cultivation of a Member of the Communist Party)* (Xinhua shudian, 1946), p. 40.
20. For example, Liu was reported to have said: "A Party member can only achieve his own success in the success of the Party." "By striving for the development, success, and victory of the Party's cause, it is possible to develop oneself and rise to a higher position." See "We Must Use the World View of the Proletariat to Build up a Proletarian Party," *Renmin ribao*, 14 December 1967.

gers of other organizations and the problems of operating these organizations. As the leaders of the establishment, they found it easy to deal with the leaders of other establishments in subordinate positions. Speaking of the capitalists, Liu was reported to have said in 1957 that their level of education is higher than that of other classes, "that they know techniques," and that "their administrative ability surpasses even that of our Party members."[21] Zhou Yang, the former Vice-Director of the Propaganda Department of the Chinese Communist Party, was charged with having adopted towards the intellectuals the policy of giving them high salaries, high royalties, and high rewards and relying on famous writers, famous directors, and famous actors.[22] Through policies of this type which took account of their minimum interests, an establishment, based on political power and holding all material resources in its hands, absorbed into its orbit of control other establishments based on wealth, knowledge, education and skill. The United Front policy, which Mao had taken the initiative in formulating for strategical and tactical reasons in the 1930s, became the ideological foundation of this absorption or merger. In this absorption or merger, the members of the other establishments were never given real power, but their minimum interests were preserved. The process of absorption took place smoothly, not only because the non-Party groups had no alternative, but also because the Chinese Communist Party had become by 1949 a vast bureaucracy with concomitant built-in conservative tendencies. Although the United Front in the narrow, political sense progressively declined in importance after 1949, the merger of the various establishments under the aegis of the Party organization went on as a socio-political fact. The establishments based on political power, education, knowledge and skill formed a fairly cohesive privileged group in China with many personal and organizational ties among them. Judging from over-all performance, these leaders in various fields were very able and efficient men. The Maoists so far have been unable to uncover outright corruption at the upper levels of these establishments. What the Maoists did prove is that they formed a privileged stratum, keeping various levers of power in their hands and living fairly comfortably amidst the general poverty of China even during the years of agricultural crisis.

The fact that the Party worked with and through the establishments and the more privileged groups and individuals in various sectors implied that the interests of the lowest and most underprivileged groups in the society were not given the highest priority by the Party organization. In contrast, Mao's sympathies seem to have been always with the most de-

21. "Thoroughly Criticize the Reactionary and False Theory of the Dying out of Class Struggle," *Renmin ribao*, 24 August 1967.
22. *Peking Review*, 19 August 1966, p. 37.

prived groups in the society, particularly the poor and middle peasants who furnished the manpower for his guerrilla army. The political importance attributed to the poor and lower-middle peasants, and perhaps even a solicitude for their welfare, underlay Mao's drive towards the establishment of the co-operatives to prevent the further "differentiation of classes in the countryside" and to avoid the danger of the "rupture of the worker-peasant alliance." As the poor and lower-middle peasants and the underprivileged groups constitute the overwhelming majority in Chinese society, it is easier for Mao to justify his programme in terms of "public interests" than for the opposition. The contrasting attitudes between Mao and the Party organization can most clearly be seen in recent disclosures on educational policies since 1958. During the Cultural Revolution, Mao was to turn the grievances of all the underprivileged groups against the establishment of Party committees, educators, high intellectuals, well-known artists, popular writers, capitalists and college-trained engineers. The only exceptions were the army and the scientific and engineering personnel in highly sensitive fields, during the early phases of the Cultural Revolution. In short, the Cultural Revolution is a revolt of those outside the establishment against the establishment, or at least a large sector of it. But it is a revolt inspired, supported and manipulated by the supreme leader to perpetuate his revolution—a leader who had lost effective control over a large sector of the establishment.

The third difference in approach and perspective between the Party organization and the supreme leader need only be briefly discussed. It evolved around the issue of the extent to which functional specialization and creativity should be promoted even at the expense of relaxing ideological control and reducing ideological fervour. The vast Party organization consists of men engaged in numerous types of functional activities. The acceptance and promotion of functional differentiation within the Party made it easy for the heads of the organization to see the value of functional differentiation in the society at large. The specialized functional groups within the organization are constantly subject to the innovative and creative influence of the functional social groups. Current Maoist attacks on Liu Shaoqi's slogan, "red and expert," suggest that the formula was intended by Liu to allow functional specialization as much as it was used to enforce ideological uniformity. Contrary to popular impression at an earlier time, Liu is not a rigid ideologue.

In contrast, Mao tenaciously held the simple life of Yanan as the model of his ideal society and his guide to the solution of the problems of a bureaucratized society. He has an almost mystical faith that interchange of roles, the assumption of multiple roles and mutual penetration can somehow bridge the gaps among men of different occupations and statuses, and help to promote ideological uniformity and political unity. In addition, he demands that ideological and political criteria override professional and technical ones in making decisions and judging work performances.

The fourth difference between the supreme leader and the Party organization lies in the methods used to control men. As the ideological leader, Mao sought consensus on the deepest levels of goals. Indoctrination on basic political and philosophical levels are his principal means of controlling the Party bureaucracy.[23] As the head of the organization, Liu sought in the first instance consensus on the level of organizational principles and exercised his control through rules and regulations. Depending on increasing goal-consensus on the deepest levels, Mao relies less on control and co-ordination through a "tall" hierarchical structure and more on spontaneous and decentralized action. Trying to control the organization through rules and procedures, Liu Shaoqi tended to be a disciplinarian and took drastic action against the cadres when it was necessary to enforce strict discipline. In a vast organization, the leaders at a particular level would have many more informal, personal ties with leaders immediately below them than with cadres at the lower levels, and their general outlooks have more similarity than those between these leaders and the cadres at lower levels. Except in the case of factional struggle among the top leaders, the leaders of the organization tend to take more drastic disciplinary actions against cadres at lower levels than at higher levels. For a supreme leader who regards ideological and political deviations as a source of all errors, the mistakes made by the lower cadres tend to be attributed to faulty ideological and political leadership at the high levels. This difference in perspective and approach obviously underlay the Maoist charge that during the Socialist Education Movement of 1964, Liu followed the policy of attacking a larger group of cadres (at the lower levels) to protect a few cadres (at the upper levels).[24]

After having outlined the differences in approach and perspective between the supreme leader and the Party organization, it is necessary to emphasize immediately that these differences did not lead to any serious conflicts in the years between 1949 and 1958—an indisputable fact which the Maoists attempt to deny in their effort to rewrite history. On the contrary, these differences seem to have made possible a more careful assessment of the objective situation and the adoption of a less radical pro-

23. Chalmers Johnson, "China: The Cultural Revolution in Structural Perspective," *Asian Survey*, Vol. VIII, No. 1 (January 1968), p. 4.

24. For an account of the Socialist Education Movement, see Richard Baum and Frederick C. Teiwes, *Ssu-ch'ing: The Socialist Education Movement of 1962–1966* (Berkeley, Calif.: Center for Chinese Studies, 1968); Richard Baum and Frederick C. Teiwes, "Liu Shao-ch'i and the Cadre Question," *Asian Survey*, Vol. VII, No. 4 (April 1968), pp. 323–345. For an exchange of views between Richard Baum and Charles Neuhauser, see *The China Quarterly*, No. 34 (April-June 1968), pp. 133–144.

gramme than would otherwise have been the case until the Great Leap Forward, which divides the history of the regime prior to the Cultural Revolution into two distinct periods. In sharp contrast to the Maoists' current version of history, the Eighth Party Congress of September 1956 provides the best evidence for the high degree of unity within the Party. According to a talk given by him on 25 October 1966, it was Mao himself who proposed the division of the Standing Committee of the Political Bureau into a first line and a second line. Liu Shaoqi, Deng Xiaoping and others manned the first line, Liu directing some of the major meetings and Deng handling daily works.[25] Mao himself held the second line—which presumably means that he was to concern himself only with the most important decisions and with defining policy goals. His avowed purpose was to foster the prestige of the other leaders so that his death would not cause great turmoil in China. Most likely, this proposal was made and adopted at the Eighth Party Congress which produced a new Party Constitution providing for a Politburo Standing Committee.

In the Party Constitution, the sentence that "the CCP takes Marxism-Leninism as its guide to action" replaced the old formula that the CCP "guides its entire work" by "the thought of Mao Zedong." According to a statement made by Peng Dehuai in late December 1966, or early 1967, it was he who suggested the deletion of the phrase, "the thought of Mao," and Liu Shaoqi immediately agreed to the proposal. But a remark of the outspoken Foreign Minister Chen Yi suggests that the decision not to mention the thought of Mao Zedong was made by "Chairman Mao [and] the Political Bureau."[26] Thus, whoever took the initiative, Mao apparently agreed to the suggestion without much ill feeling at that time.

The accomplishments at the Eighth Party Congress marked an immense step toward routinization and institutionalization in China's political development. A preliminary solution of the most difficult problem of succession was apparently reached. The downgrading of the more explicit, operationally more specific, and thus more restrictive principles of the thought of Mao in favour of the more abstract principles of Marxism and the less directly applicable rules of Leninism could furnish more leeway for policy experimentation and lead to the broadening of the ideological foundation of the political system. Mao permitted and perhaps even encouraged others to take these steps toward routinization within the Party, presumably because his place in history was not in doubt, the

25. "Chairman Mao's Talk at the Central Work Conference," printed by Red Guards on 19 December 1966. From an unpublished version in the author's possession.

26. "P'eng Te-huai's [Peng Dehuai's] Statements—Records made in the interrogation of P'eng Te-huai under detention,"28 December 1966–5 January 1967, *Current Background* (Hong Kong: U.S. Consulate General), No. 851, 26 April 1968, p. 17. Chen Yi's remark is in *Hongwei zhanbao (Red Guard Battle Bulletin)*, 8 April 1964, p. 4.

validity of his thought was not directly challenged, the Party organization had been responsive to his wishes (as the rapid implementation of the programme of co-operativization had just demonstrated) and because the Twentieth Congress of the CPSU had recently denounced the cult of personality.

It was the failure of the Great Leap Forward which transformed the inner-Party differences in approaches and perspectives to increasingly sharp political conflict. In its public pronouncements, the regime attributed the agricultural crisis from 1959 to 1961 primarily to natural disaster and secondarily to some shortcomings in the implementation of policies. But many Party leaders at the top had no doubt that the policies themselves were largely responsible for the disaster.[27]

During the period between 1959 and 1962, Mao's control over Party affairs was weakened as the party adopted a series of pragmatic policies to extricate China from the economic crisis.[28] Mao's loss of effective control over the Party organization reveals a great deal about the power relations and pattern of policy-making within the Party. Over the years, Mao tended more and more to limit himself to setting goals of policy and allowed the Party organization to devise methods of achieving them.[29] The highly bureaucratized and quite cohesive Party organization had developed numerous methods to thwart the wishes of the supreme leader.[30] Mao could not use the secret police to control the Party organization, for this ran counter to his style and to the Party's tradition. Although Mao succeeded in gaining control of the Ministry of Public Security at the Central Government prior to the Cultural Revolution, the loyalty of the security forces was still uncertain. The secret police and public security bureau at the provincial levels and below continued to be under the control of the Party committees and their reliability was doubtful. For example, in November and December 1966, in Beijing itself, the Red Guards opposed to the Cultural

27. See for example, "P'eng Te-huai's [Peng Dehuai's] Letter of Opinion," in *Current Background*, No. 851 (26 April 1967), pp. 21–23; Editorial Departments of the *Hongqi* and *Renmin ribao*, "To Follow the Socialist Road or the Capitalist Road?" in *Hongqi*, No. 13 (1967), p. 11; and *Peking Review*, 25 August 1967, p. 10.

28. There are many well-documented accounts of these developments. Only two articles will be cited here. Harry Gelman, "The New Revolution," *Problems of Communism* (November-December 1966), pp. 2–14. Philip Bridgham,"Mao's Cultural Revolution: Origin and Development," *The China Quarterly*, No. 29 (January-March 1967), pp. 1–35.

29. Liu Shaoqi was reported to have said in the summer of 1961: "Chairman Mao concerns himself only with important state affairs. It is enough for him to propose to turn the whole country into a big garden and forest land. He has no time to solve this problem. . . . Therefore, I have to tackle it." Hong Fen, "Exposing the Crimes Perpetrated in Heilongjiang Province by the Biggest Party Person in Authority Taking the Capitalist Road," *Heilongjiang Daily*, 14 June 1967.

30. Tsou, *loc. cit.* (see note 6).

Revolution Group were engaged in serious violent clashes with the Maoist Red Guards, arresting their opponents, establishing detention centres, and setting up "courts." On 18 November 1966, the CCP Municipal Committee of Beijing issued an order prohibiting these actions.[31] For nearly a month this order was not obeyed. On 16 December, Jiang Qing criticized the "organs of dictatorship" for their timid and "non-interventionist" attitude toward the "pickets" in the West, East and Haidian Districts of Beijing.[32] The next day, it was the public security forces of the Ministry of Public Security, led personally by its Vice-Minister, rather than the municipal police, who arrested the leaders of the anti-Maoist Red Guards.[33] As a consequence of such incidents Mao had to use the army to take over the local police apparatus in many localities.

Mao's principal method of controlling the Party had been indoctrination and the system of criticism and self-criticism. The system of criticism and self-criticism was regarded as a very severe sanction and a most humiliating experience even by top leaders. In 1945, just prior to the meeting of the Seventh Congress (April-June 1945), a North China Conference was held, one of its main purposes being criticism of Peng Dehuai.[34] The conference lasted 40 days and Peng was reported to have made a self-criticism reluctantly. During the Lushan Conference in 1959, Peng used obscene language to characterize this experience; and the same words were [used] in his complaint that the conference, which apparently criticised Mao's policies, did not last long enough.[35] During the Cultural Revolution, Zhu De, the former Marshal, was compelled to make a self-criticism. In disclosing this incident, Vice-Chairman Lin Biao said that "it was the Party Centre which made him take off his pants."[36]

The effectiveness of criticism and self-criticism as a sanction depends ultimately on the validity of the ideological premise on which the criticism or self-criticism is made, and on the correctness of the policy which is juxtaposed to the incorrect policy pursued or proposed by those criticized. But the failure of the Great Leap and the Commune system revealed the errors of Mao's policies and their ideological premises. Criticism and self-criticism could no longer be used effectively by Mao to control his subordinates and to mobilize ideological and political support for his policies. One of the many indications of this fact was the wide-

31. *Hongweibing bao (Red Guards' Newspaper)*, No. 15 (22 December 1967), p. 4.
32. *Ibid.* p. 1.
33. *Jinggangshan*, No. 4 (23 December 1966), p. 4.
34. "The Wicked History of Big Conspirator, Big Ambitionist, Big Warlord P'eng Te-huai [Peng Dehuai]," in *Current Background*, No. 851 (26 April 1968), p. 7.
35. *Ibid.* p. 14.
36. *Geming gongren bao (Revolutionary Workers' Newspaper)*, No. 5 (19 February 1967), p. 4.

spread sympathy for Peng Dehuai's criticism of Mao's policy at the Eighth Plenum of 1959 and for his demand in 1961 for a reversal of the decision against him.[37]

By 1962, the Chinese economy showed signs of recovery. The Party organization seems to have preferred to push forward a policy of further retrenchment and to give even greater recognition to material incentives.[38] To call a halt to the tendency towards individual operation in agriculture and to the policy of encouraging small private enterprises in commerce and industry, Mao began his counter-offensive at the Tenth Plenum in September 1962. To regain effective control over the Party organization, he abolished the distinction between the first and second line. To re-establish the old standards of legitimacy, he intensified a drive to restore the authority of his thought and to elevate it once again to its position in the political system before the Eighth Congress. To set the general orientation and to bolster further the position of the army he asked the whole nation to learn from the PLA. To set up new monitoring agencies to control the government bureaucracy, he established within the branches of economic administration political departments patterned after those in the PLA and manned by former political commissars and military officers. He launched the Socialist Education Movement in 1963 and a purge of literary and art circles in 1964. The failure of these efforts to produce results sweeping enough to satisfy Mao was rooted in the fact that many Party leaders remained sceptical of the applicability of Mao's thoughts and the soundness of his policy views. It convinced him of the powerful resistance of the vast party machine and increased his fear of a further growth of revisionism. Thus, in the six years after the failure of the Great Leap, the previously reconcilable differences in approaches toward both modernization and revolution gradually hardened into irreconcilable conflict between the Party organization's conception of the priority needs of modernization and Mao's uppermost concern about the fate of his revolution. During a period of intensifying conflict and open polemic with the CPSU, the Soviet system provided Mao with a vivid negative example of "revisionism" in operation. At the same time, the processes of forced modernization and industrialization under very difficult objective circumstances

37. One of the most interesting sidelights of the Cultural Revolution is that the reports of the Red Guards have confirmed almost every detail of the account by David A. Charles in "The Dismissal of Marshal P'eng Teh-huai [Peng Dehuai]," *The China Quarterly*, No. 8 (October-December 1961), pp. 63–76. Of the numerous materials on Peng Dehuai, the most interesting one is the compilation issued by the Jinggangshan Corps of the Qinghua University. This compilation is translated in *Current Background*, No. 851 (26 April 1968), pp. 1–31. For excerpts of the Resolution of the Eighth Plenum condemning Peng Dehuai, see *Peking Review*, 18 August 1967, pp. 8–10.

38. Liu Shaoqi's first self-criticism, posted on 26 December 1966.

created tremendous social tension just beneath the surface of political stability maintained by the effective control of the Party organization. From Mao's point of view, these developments made it both imperative and possible to develop new methods and new instruments in order to exploit the social tensions, to attack new targets, and to obtain absolute control.

Hence the Great Proletarian Cultural Revolution.

The Disruption of the Political System during the Cultural Revolution

Zhou Enlai told the revolutionary rebels on 25 January 1967 that the "form of mobilization in the early phase" of the Cultural Revolution was "not entirely the same" as that in all other mass movements in the past in Communist China. He explained that whereas these other mass movements were conducted both "from the top to the bottom" and "from the bottom to the top," the unprecedented Cultural Revolution was "essentially" a movement "from the bottom to the top." He then added immediately that "of course, we cannot detach ourselves from the supreme leadership, the leadership of Chairman Mao and the Party Centre." "These [the principle of 'from the bottom to the top' as the essential form and the supreme leadership of Chairman Mao and the Party Centre] are, in our belief, the two fundamental principles."[39] Viewed in the light of the course of the Cultural Revolution, these statements suggest that the Cultural Revolution is a rebellion of the dominated against the establishment in most spheres of Chinese society—a rebellion inspired and manipulated by the supreme leader. The emphasis on "from the bottom to the top," as the essential form, implies that a measure of spontaneity and autonomy on the part of the masses and their own leaders was permitted and encouraged during the early stages of the Cultural Revolution. It indicates that this was so much greater than that permitted in the mass movements in the past as to make the Cultural Revolution qualitatively different and thus unprecedented. Indeed, the masses, i.e. the Red Guards and the revolutionary rebels, constituted Mao's main instrument of attack in the first 18 months.

Even with the Red Guards and the army as his instruments, Mao was confronted with the very difficult problem of justifying his revolution and legitimizing his attack on the Party organization. For the Party and the Party organizations in various units had become symbols of authority, and the policies pursued by the Party organization were eminently successful when measured in terms of practical results. What Mao did essentially was to use personal, moral, and ideological appeals to override pragmatic

39. Premier Zhou Enlai's important talk on 25 January 1966 to a rally of more than 20,000 revolutionary rebels on "the scientific and technological fronts" as reported in *Keji zhanbao (Science and Technology Battle Bulletin)* (Peking), No. 2 (1 February 1967), p. 3.

standards. Immediately before and during the Cultural Revolution, the Maoists elevated the position of Mao's thought to a new peak. Lin Biao made the following statement in May 1966. "Chairman Mao's experience in passing through many events is more profound than that of Marx, Engels, and Lenin. No one can surpass Chairman Mao in his rich revolutionary experience."[40] He also said on another occasion that Mao stands on a much higher level than Marx, Lenin, and Stalin, and that "99 per cent. of the Marxist-Leninist classics which we study should consist of Mao Zedong's writings."[41] Repugnant as it may be to us, this cult of Mao and his thought served a definite political purpose. It set a new standard of legitimacy and correctness with which the actions and opinions of many top leaders were to be judged.

This apotheosis of Mao was accompanied by a further radicalization of his thought by pushing to their extremes its constituent elements: the idea of conflict, the tendency toward polarization, the concept of centrality of man, the controlling importance of politics, and finally, the importance of ideas and revolutionary morality. To exploit the conflict between those in positions of superordination and those in positions of subordination in order to smash a well-entrenched establishment, the Maoists revived and incessantly used a hitherto neglected assertion made in 1939 by Mao in a speech celebrating Stalin's sixtieth birthday: "In the last analysis, all the myriad principles of Marxism can be summed up in one sentence: 'To rebel is justified.'" The destructive purpose of conflict was blatantly extolled: "Without destruction there cannot be construction and destruction must come before construction."

Mao and the Maoists drew the picture of a Party which was polarized into two groups reaching up to the very top. The class struggle became the struggle between the bourgeois and the proletarian lines within the Party. Mao personally called on his followers to bombard the headquarters, i.e. the headquarters of the bourgeoisie within the Party. The Red Guards shouted time and again: "Protect the Proletarian headquarters." Polarization gives rise to double standards. The Red Guards solemnly announced that "we are permitting only the Left to rebel, not the Right." The Chinese people were urged not to obey the orders of their superiors

40. Lin Biao's talk at an enlarged session of the meeting of the Political Bureau in May 1966, quoted in *Jinggangshan*, Nos. 13–14 (1 February 1967), p. 6. It is clear that the cult of Mao was used to overcome the resistance to Mao's thought and policies. Mao himself said in 1967 that at the time when he presided over the drafting of the 16 May 1966 circular, a large group of persons considered his views outmoded and that, at times, only he himself agreed with his own views. *Wuchanzhe zhi sheng (The Voice of the Proletariat)* (Wuzhou, Guangxi), No. 10 (1 January 1968), p. 1.

41. Lin Biao's remark in September 1966 at a talk to members of military academies and colleges. Quoted in *Jinggangshan*, Nos. 13–14 (1 February 1967), p. 6.

blindly. But at the same time, they were told to carry out Mao's instructions and follow his great strategic plans even if they did not understand these for the time being. The ideological and political criteria used in the first phases of the Cultural Revolution to destroy the authority of the Party committees were completely different from those employed during the final phase to establish the authority of the revolutionary committees.

To mobilize the masses to rebel, the role of man, not man as an individual but man as a member of the masses, was glorified. A *Hongqi (Red Flag)* editorial of January 1967 stated that "the masses are reasonable and they are able to distinguish the people from the enemy." Repeatedly, the Maoists declared, "Let the masses liberate themselves and educate themselves." "Trust the masses, rely on them, and respect their initiative." The practice of the mass line has undergone a perceptible change during the Cultural Revolution.[42] Glorifying the creative role of the masses in history also serves the purpose of downgrading the importance of the experts and of refuting the pragmatists' view that material conditions impose a limit on rapid changes.

Likewise, the controlling importance of politics has been pushed a step further. The Maoists consistently pointed out that so long as the general political orientation of individuals or groups is correct—that is to say, so long as they directed their attack against Liu Shaoqi and his followers— their mistakes should be overlooked. The Maoists explained that in a period of great upheaval, great division, and great realigmnent the only thing that counted was the general political orientation, and that mistakes were inevitable, and disturbances, disruptions, and disorder must not be feared. In effect, this meant that laws and traditions, customary standards and humane considerations could be violated with impunuity.

Finally, correct ideology and revolutionary morality must override everything else including such long-established principles of democratic centralism as the minority obeying the majority. Many Western observers doubt whether Mao had majority support within the Party council. According to a Red Guard newspaper, Mao said in one of his "latest instructions" that he had the support of just a little over the majority at the Eleventh Plenum which gave full Party sanction to the Cultural Revolution.[43] Whatever the case may have been at the Eleventh Plenum, there is no doubt that the Red Guards constituted a minority in the various universities, schools, and units for a long period of time. Thus Jiang Qing, the wife of Mao Zedong, justified the right of the minority to impose its view

42. Zhou Enlai's remark cited above, p. 82, is one of the best evidences of the change in the mass line.

43. "A great strategic disposition—Chairman Mao's Latest Instruction," reproduced in *Wuchanzhe zhi sheng (The Voice of the Proletariat)* (Wuzhou, Guangxi), No. 10 (1 January 1968), p. 1.

on the majority on the ground that "one could not talk about a 'minority' or 'majority' independent of class viewpoint."[44] In effect, this meant that the thoughts of Mao and Mao himself were placed above the Party as the ultimate source of authority and standard of right and wrong.[45] Practical results achieved by the Party and government bureaucrats were considered to be contaminated by their appeal to the self-interests of the individuals. Complete devotion to public interests and standards of revolutionary virtues as defined by Mao have been used to judge the actual performance and the motives of the Party leaders and cadres. The Red Guards attempted to set up puritanical rules of behaviour and enforce them on everyone. The new revolutionary committees set up to replace the government administration and Party committees on the provincial level and below adopted stringent regulations on improving their style of work. These regulations were aimed at maintaining collective leadership, preserving the anonymity of the individual members, ensuring constant contact between the officials and the masses, and eliminating the outward differences between the leaders and the led. In turn, these proclaimed virtues were used to justify the revolution and the new revolutionary order. Thus, the Maoist vision is both a long-term goal and an immediately available means to destroy the opposition.

The strategy adopted by Mao in launching and making the revolution bears on the problem of legitimizing his actions. The Maoists have made it clear that the criticism of the "academic authorities" and the intellectuals had the purpose of preparing public opinion for the so-called seizure of power which took place after January 1967 in many units below the top level. The Maoists captured the control of the propaganda agencies and mass media of communication before they attempted to seize power from the Party committees.

At first, Peng Zhen and later Liu Shaoqi were left in charge of the Cultural Revolution. Harry Gelman and Philip Bridgham,[46] two leading U.S. Government analysts in the field of Chinese Communist internal affairs, have developed the theory that Mao put his erstwhile lieutenants through tests to determine their loyalty and purged them when they failed. This interpretation is correct as far as it goes. But Mao's strategy also served the purpose of legitimizing his removal of the top party leaders and mobi-

44. *Peking Review*, 9 December 1968, p. 1.

45. For example, Chen Boda told students at Beijing University, on 26 July 1966, that "this leadership of the Party is the leadership of Mao Zedong's thought and the leadership of the Party Central Committee." On 21 August 1966, Tao Zhu said that "now the only correct leadership is that of Chairman Mao and the Central Committee under his leadership." *Hongse zaofan bao*, 26 December 1966, p. 4, translated in *Joint Research Publication Service (JPRS)*, No. 40, 349 (March 1967), pp. 76–77.

46. See above, p. 75, n. 28.

lizing the masses to attack them. The intellectuals in a totalitarian society, because of their role as the seekers of truth and critics of society, are the most vulnerable targets of attack by the ideologues. Their published writings are indestructible proof of guilt, once a policy of liberalization is replaced by a drive to re-impose strict ideological control. Wu Han and other intellectuals fell victim to this process. There is no question that they also criticized Mao by historical analogy or in Aesopian language. After the cult of Mao and his thought had been pushed to a new peak, their veiled criticism could be made into the most serious political offence. When Peng Zhen tried to protect them, he could be charged with protecting the "freaks and monsters." Similarly, when the work teams endeavoured to restore control over the revolutionary students, a sharp conflict occurred between the establishment and those outside it. The resentment of the revolutionary students against the work teams was transferred to Liu Shaoqi and the other Party leaders responsible for sending them. By adopting the principle of letting the masses liberate themselves, trusting the masses, and relying on them, the time-honoured method of using the work teams became an error in orientation and an error of line. After Mao had criticized the dispatch of the work teams, the top leaders like Liu Shaoqi and Deng Xiaoping could only defend their decision by saying that they were old revolutionaries who encountered new problems, that they had no understanding of new things, and that their failure of understanding stemmed from their lack of a firm grasp of Mao's thought. Once Mao had succeeded in making a case out of a specific mistake, he then generalized his criticism by linking this error with the past and present policies, proposals, and actions of the other leaders and traced them to basic ideological sources. In this process, Mao and the Maoists perverted history and departed from the standards of fair play, which notion they specifically repudiated. But in this way they attempted to present a plausible case for their sweeping purge. There is still another aspect of Mao's strategy which should be noted. Mao is a revolutionary romantic with a radical vision, but he is also a cautious man in his strategy and tactics. Generally speaking, he tends to try out less radical measures first before he resorts to more radical ones. The events from September 1962 to March 1967 suggest that he followed the same rule. The resistance of the Party organization made it necessary for him to escalate his conflict with the party organization until he purged its top leaders.

During the Cultural Revolution, the resistance put up by the Party organization was a matter of self-protection and survival. It has brought out several interesting points about the Chinese political system. In the first period of 50 days, most of the work teams were able to gain ready acceptance of their authority and received adequate support from the students, even though they took fairly stern disciplinary actions against some of the cadres on the one hand and repressive measures against the Red Guards on the other. They succeeded in keeping the Maoist students under control until Mao returned to Beijing, criticized the work teams, and ordered their withdrawal. Although both persuasion and coercion were extensively used by the work teams, it is also true that they enjoyed genuine authority and obtained obedience to their orders without too much difficulty, so long as they were considered the embodiment of the Party. "To oppose the work team is to oppose the Party" was one of the most effective slogans at this time.[47] During the early autumn of 1966, most of the workers and peasants also obeyed the orders of the Party committees in various units when some of them were instigated here and there by the Party committees to attack the Red Guards. This shows that the rule of the Party was accepted as legitimate and that a true relationship of authority existed between those in command and those in subordination. It is precisely because obedience to the orders of the Party organizations had become quite habitual, and because this obedience was based at least partly on the internalization of those values and norms justified in and propagated by Liu Shaoqi's many writings, that the Maoists had to launch an attack on "the slave mentality advocated by China's Khrushchev."

Another significant but not surprising point about the Party committees was their amazing tactical skill and their cohesiveness. In the first seven months, revolutionary committees were established in only six out of 29 units at the provincial level. Leaving aside Shanghai and Beijing as special cases, all the four provinces in which revolutionary committees were successfully set up were those in which one or several Party leaders of fairly high rank came out at a fairly early stage to support Mao. In the rest, the Party committees maintained their solidarity. In some places, they staged what was called sham seizure of power by handing over the office building and the official seals to Red Guard units organized by them or at least sympathetic to them. One of the reasons why revolutionary committees could not be as rapidly set up as Beijing wanted was that most of the top Party and government leaders refused to break with their colleagues and join the Maoists.[48] Hence Beijing's repeated call for the cadres to "stand out," and its constant emphasis that correct treatment of the cadres, by

47. The Maoists had to counteract the tendency to obey the Party committees in various units by constantly reiterating the point that not every Party organization or individual Party member represents leadership by the Party. Qi Benyu told the Red Guards on 12 November 1966: "Leadership by the Party is mainly political and ideological leadership and leadership by Mao Zedong's thought. It is not specifically the leadership of a certain person or a certain organization."

48. As we shall note later, another reason was that Mao made the establishment of a "great alliance" among the revolutionary rebel groups a condition for the establishment of revolutionary committees and their recognition by Beijing.

forgiving their former mistakes and supporting them in their work, was an indispensible condition for successfully establishing the revolutionary committees.

But the tactical skills and the cohesiveness of the local Party committees stand in contrast to another phenomenon. I have uncovered no evidence that Liu Shaoqi, other non-Maoist Party leaders, and the various Party committees, ever had a nationwide, strategic plan to oppose Mao publicly and to take offensive action against him. The opposition to Mao was essentially a case of the Party organization trying to defend itself under the major premises and the rules of the game as laid down by Mao. All the organizations pledged allegiance to Mao and his thought. All of them said that they supported the Cultural Revolution. Mao's prestige, Lin Biao's control over the army, the narrow majority obtained by Mao at the Eleventh Plenum by rather irregular means, are three obvious explanations. But still another explanation is, I suspect, Mao's success in making his thought the sole legitimate criterion of right and wrong, whether one actually agrees with it or not. The disability of the Party organization shows the significance of political ideology and the difficulty of challenging an established doctrine and evolving a new one in a totalitarian system. [49]

Another major target of the attack launched by Red Guards and revolutionary rebels was the government bureaucracy. The disruption of the government bureaucracy has received less publicity in the American press than the fighting and conflicts in the provinces. But a perusal of Red Guard publications shows its seriousness. Still, the government bureaucracy survived the Cultural Revolution in much better shape than the Party. With notable exceptions, like Jiang Nanxiang, the Minister of Higher Education, and Bo Yibo, the Chairman of the State Economic Commission, many of the top government leaders are still at their posts. In contrast to Liu Shaoqi, Premier Zhou Enlai's influence and power increased during the Cultural Revolution. No doubt, Zhou's personality and skills in political manoeuvre and his ability to protect his subordinates constitutes one explanation. Another, and perhaps more basic, reason is that although the government administration, like the Party organization, is also a huge bureaucracy with its tendency towards conservatism and routinization, the Party bureaucracy and the government bureaucracy in the Chinese political system differ from each other in their respective relationship with the supreme leader. First, the Party is the locus of power, whereas the government bureaucracy is one step removed from

49. Tang Tsou, "Cultural Revolution: Causes and Effects," *Proceedings of the Symposium on China*, 13 January 1968 (Berkeley, California: Chinese Students Association and the Center for Chinese Studies, 1968), pp. 34–41.

the centre of authority. When actual conflicts occur over policies, they are inevitably linked up with issues of power, and the Party organization becomes the focus of conflict with the leader. Secondly, ideological matters are one of the main concerns of the Party organization. The innate tendencies of the organization and the attitudes and views of its members would sooner or later find expression in ideological writings or statements. These incipient ideological intrusions into the eminent domain of the supreme leader, and these doctrinal deviations, however slight, can easily be viewed as a challenge to the authority of the leader. Thirdly, in the government bureaucracy each of the various vertical systems has some specialized function. They are usually not the immediate source of generalized political power. In contrast, the core of the Party organization is its system of Party committees and secretaries at the regional, provincial, and local levels, having generalized political authority over most activities. These can more easily become "independent kingdoms." Finally, the tasks performed by the government bureaux are of greater practical use to the supreme leader than the control functions performed by the Party organization.[50]

The army has also behaved in an interesting manner during the Cultural Revolution. Its behaviour stems from its dual, ambiguous role in its relation to Mao and within the Chinese political system. Under Lin Biao, it has been Mao's main basis of power. It has been highly indoctrinated with the thought of Mao Zedong. But it is an organization which has its own professional standards and expertise. It was also a part of the establishment. The ties between the military leaders in various military regions and districts and the Party leaders on the regional and provincial levels were particularly close. Thus, while the army has been one of Mao's two chief instruments during the Cultural Revolution, it has also become a conservative force in the Maoist coalition, frequently resisting the more extreme measures advocated or undertaken by the Cultural Revolution Group and the Red Guards, particularly after Liu Shaoqi had been effectively pushed aside. While it has dutifully carried out what it believes to be Mao's instructions, it has also tended to interpret these orders with a bias toward preserving law and order and limiting the extent of the political purge.[51] This role offers an explanation for the relative compliance of

50. In outlining the steps to be taken in the seizure of power, Zhou Enlai told the Red Guards on 23 January 1967 that as a first step they should merely supervise the business operations of the various agencies. But if the agencies concerned "do not have business operations as in the case of the departments and units within the Party, a thorough-going revolution can be made by the Red Guards." *Youdian fenglei (Thunderstorm in the Postal and Telecommunications Services)*, No. 5 (10 February 1967), p. 3.

51. The worst offender against the Maoist line of supporting the Left was Zhao Yungfu the Deputy Commander of the military district of Qinghai province. See "Order of the Military

the army until its integrity as a whole was threatened in August 1967, when Wang Li and other radicals in the Cultural Revolution Group raised the slogans of "dragging out a small handful in the army." The dismissal of the Acting Chief of Staff Yang Chengwu, in March 1968, suggests that despite the growing power of the People's Liberation Army, China is still not under army dictatorship. Mao remains the pivotal figure who welds together a coalition of forces and maintains a balance among them by throwing his influence on the one side or the other. His purpose has been to keep the Cultural Revolution going without plunging China into intolerable political chaos or a civil war.

While Mao's ultimate source of power was the army, the spearhead of Mao's Cultural Revolution was the Red Guards and the revolutionary rebels. The reasons why Mao had to use them as his offensive forces are obvious. Such a momentous undertaking as the Cultural Revolution must be justified on the ground that it is demanded and supported by the masses. Mao and his followers had no direct control over the mass organizations and thus could not use them as their instruments. Strictly speaking, the Maoists cannot be said to have been an organized faction prior to the Cultural Revolution. They had no organization of any kind under their direct control, with the exception of the army. If the difficulty confronting Liu Shaoqi was Mao's success in making his ideology the only source of legitimacy, the problem confronting Mao was Liu Shaoqi's control over all the organizations with the exception just mentioned. Yet Liu Shaoqi and the numerous persons purged by Mao cannot be called a faction in the strict sense of the term. If there had been a Liu-Deng faction, this must have had almost complete direct control over the Party apparatus. This is shown by the fact that 90 per cent of the work teams were accused of having committed errors in the 50 days in June and July of 1966. Almost all the Regional Bureaux and Party committees at the provincial and municipal levels resisted the Cultural Revolution. Operationally speaking, such a faction would be almost identical with the whole Party organization.[52]

Mao's shrewd sense of politics led him to see the potential conflict between the establishment and those outside the establishment, and he set out to exploit the repressed resentment against the establishment to attack the leaders of the Party organization. Furthermore, the students, unlike the Party leaders engaged in practical work, had no real knowledge

---

Committee of the Central Committee," 6 April 1966, *Zhonggong zhongyang wenjian huiji (Collection of Documents Issued by the Party Centre of the CCP)*, reprinted by the Liaison Station of the Red Guards of the Mentougou district of the city of Beijing (April 1967), pp. 170–173.

52. Tsou, "Cultural Revolution: Causes and Effects," *Proceedings of the Symposium of China*, pp. 34–41.

of the actual consequences of the thought of Mao and his disastrous policies. Instead, they had been exposed in the communication media to nothing but the praise of Mao, his thought, and his achievements. The Party organization's practice of "waving the red flag to oppose the red flag" may have been a necessary expedient, but it also played a part in promoting the cult of Mao among the masses. Brought up under a relatively stable regime and without any personal experience of the social dislocation and ideological confusion of pre-1949 China, the students knew only one set of legitimate values and had a remarkable sense of moral certitude. Thus Mao permitted and indeed encouraged, during the early stages, the Red Guards to take spontaneous action, and granted them a large measure of autonomy. Not only were their mistakes overlooked, but the blame for any conflict between them and those in authority was placed on the latter. Vice-Premier Xie Fuzhi told the students that Chairman Mao had said:

> Where outside cadres assume leadership responsibility, if their relation ship with local cadres is bad, then the outside cadres should bear the main responsibility for it. . . . Where army cadres are actually in leadership positions, under normal circumstances, if their relationship with local cadres is unsatisfactory, the main responsibility should be placed on the army cadres. . . . Where veteran cadres assume the main responsibility of leadership, if the relationship between the old and new cadres is poor, then the former should bear the responsibility.[53]

Then the Vice-Premier added as his own opinion that in regard to the contradictions between the majority and minority factions, the former must bear geater responsibility. After the work teams were withdrawn, every political leader including Chen Boda and Jiang Qing assumed, at least for a brief period, the posture of learning from the students in talk ing to them.[54]

The students and rebels organized themselves into numerous small units with all sorts of strange names. To form or join a Red Guard unit became an absolutely essential means of self-protection and of obtaining power and prestige. Power soon drifted into the hands of Red Guard units sponsored by Maoists like Nie Yuanzi of Beijing University and Kuai Dafu of Qinghua University, and these units maintained close contact with the Cultural Revolution Group. Probably, most of the members of these units

53. "Vice-Premier Xie Fuzhi's Seven Viewpoints," *Wuchanjieji wenhua dageming youguan cailiao bianhui [sic] (Collection of Materials Pertaining to the Great Proletarian Cultural Revolution)* (Canton, 28 October 1966), Vol. II, pp. 25–27, in *JPRS*, No. 40,391 (24 March 1967), p. 7.

54. From the minutes of a forum held by the revolutionary teachers and students of the College of International Relations under the auspices of Deng Xiaoping and Li Fuchun. See also *Current Background*, No. 819 (10 March 1967), p. 72.

were not members of the Party or the League and the majority of them were children of workers, peasants and soldiers.

The exploits of the Red Guards have been reported extensively in the press. But there are several interesting points which ought to be made. Not all the students took an active part in the Revolution. In a remark reminiscent of Karl Marx's description of the Communist utopia, a Red Guard newspaper reported that "in the high schools the students read Mao's *Selected Works* in the morning, took a rest in the afternoon, and learned to swim after four o'clock."[55] The active Red Guards, however, waged their struggle on many fronts. They carried their quarrels and their factionalism everywhere they went. Not long after the Red Guards were sent to the factories to promote the Cultural Revolution, Chen Boda found it necessary to scold them for bringing to the workers the bourgeois and petty bourgeois ideas of small-group mentality and factionalism instead of proletarian influences.[56] Several months later, he bluntly told a group of workers not to be misled by the factionalism of the students into adopting a wrong orientation. The fragmentation of the Red Guard movement reveals one of the general consequences of the breakdown of political authority. It also forcefully demonstrates the impotence of ideology which is not supported by an organization. For ideology and general directives cannot create unity and produce united action unless there is a hierarchy of organizations to give them authoritative interpretation, to translate them into specific decisions, and to enforce them in various units.

The movement to seize power did nothing to improve matters. In a speech in January 1967, Chen Boda said:

> In some units the seizure of power is like this: you want to seize power and I also want to seize power; instead of seizing power from power holders taking the capitalist road, some small groups struggle with one another for power to see who can seize power first. Those groups which did not seize power before now also want to seize power. Thus, internal struggles are created.

He asked: "If, for instance, a small group of yours cannot represent the great majority of a school but still want to take over a nationwide unit, whom can you ask to recognize your seizure of power?" He concluded: "Now, the 'small-group mentality' has become a national problem."[57]

---

55. *Wuchan jieji wenhua dageming dashi ji.* 1965.9 1966.12 (*The Great Proletarian Cultural Revolution—a Record of Major Events. September 1965-December 1966*), in *JPRS*, No. 42,349 (25 August 1967), p. 26.

56. *Youdian fenglei*, No. 5, 10 February 1967.

57. *Ibid.; Huochetou (Locomotive)*, No. 7, 2 February 1967, in *Survey of the China Mainland Press*, No. 3898 (14 March 1967), p. 4.

To counter this development, Mao adopted the policy of making the formation of a great alliance among the various small units a condition for recognizing their seizure of power in various schools, universities, departments, units and localities. But new problems immediately emerged. The Red Guards and revolutionary rebels in power were more concerned with personal prestige and position than with the interests of the whole. What the Maoists call "bourgeois and petty bourgeois ideas" turn out to be simply human tendencies of those in positions of power.

In waging their struggle against the Party leaders, the Red Guards resorted to methods not approved by the Maoist leaders. In a speech to the Red Guards in February 1967, Chen Boda pointed out that such slogans as "Smashing So and So's Dog Head" and such actions as putting a dunce cap on a person and forcing him to kneel down were not advocated by the Cultural Revolution Group. Some of the difficulties confronting the Maoist leaders arose from the amazing organizational and tactical skill of the Red Guard units. In December 1966, Zhou Enlai noted that the Red Guards arrested Peng Zhen, the former mayor of Beijing, in an action lasting only seven minutes, keeping even the Beijing Garrison Command in the dark.[58] Even more serious was the Red Guards' attack on the army and the revolutionary committees and their refusal to obey orders. On 17 September, 1967 Zhou pointed out to the Red Guards that when students went to other localities, they always supported those opposing the established leadership. But he told them that times had changed and they should not act in the same way as they acted in 1966.

Chen Boda is partly correct when he characterized some of the excesses committed by the Red Guards as "the shortcomings of the methods of struggle spontaneously created by the masses." It was also probable that many of the extreme actions taken by the Red Guards were encouraged or backed by a radical faction within the Cultural Revolution Group. But Mao must ultimately bear the responsibility because he explicitly permitted the masses to commit "minor" mistakes so long as their general orientation was correct; and because he praised similar methods of struggle in the famous report on the Hunan Peasant Movement. Furthermore, the Maoists' ideological pronouncements, used at the beginning of the Cultural Revolution to mobilize the students to attack the Party leaders, also served as justification for their excessive acts. It is also apparent that the Red Guards had absorbed the strategic thinking of Mao without accepting his idealistic values. For example, Mao has written that political power grows out of [the barrel of] a gun. The Red Guards have raised the slogan that "political power grows out of strength" and used it to justify their self-serving actions. Repeatedly, the Maoist leaders told them to smash

58. *Douzheng bao (The Struggle Newspaper)*, early January 1967, p. 7.

self-interest and establish public interest, but to no avail. Thus, the Red Guards had ultimately to be brought under control by the workers' teams in mid-1968.

Conclusion

The foregoing analysis of the Cultural Revolution shows that it has not only destroyed the Party organization and badly disrupted the government bureaucracy, but has also inflicted serious damage on the relationship of authority which had been established in Communist China. This damage will be vastly more difficult to repair than the economic disaster produced by the Great Leap. For the rebuilding of a new set of stable political relationships in the aftermath of the demoralization, resentment, cynicism, and frustrated hopes stirred up by the upheaval is a much more complex and intricate task than economic recovery and adjustment of institutions in the economic sphere. The loss of confidence on the part of the Chinese Communist leaders in their own political institutions and their own political wisdom must have been profound. For some time to come, they will be preoccupied with the problems of rebuilding the political system.

The Cultural Revolution had its roots in the increasing divergence between Mao's ideology and the changing social reality. Yet the Cultural Revolution has destroyed the very institution in China which was more able than Mao to accommodate the material interests of the various social groups and the needs for differentiation and specialization in a rapidly developing nation. In the classical revolutions, the alienated intellectuals together with the rising expectations of the people played crucial roles in bringing about the upheaval. In the Cultural Revolution, the intellectuals who were alienated by Mao but supported by the Party organization became its first victims, and the rising expectations of most social groups were denounced as morally wrong. In the long run, many aspects of the Cultural Revolution and many elements in Mao's thought will probably be implicitly or explicitly repudiated.

But one must also not forget that in making the Cultural Revolution Mao has also been motivated by a noble vision. It is a vision of a society in which the division involving domination and subjection will be blurred, the leaders will be less distinguishable from the led in status and privileges, and the led will take part more directly in the policy-making process. The full realization of this vision is an impossibility. But it is just possible that somehow the Cultural Revolution will leave as a legacy a higher degree of political participation and economic equality, even if the former means merely a wider sharing of the high political risks and the latter is nothing more than an equality in poverty.

3 Prolegomenon to the Study of Informal Groups in CCP Politics

Prior to the Cultural Revolution, scholars studying and analysing Chinese Communist politics had long been influenced consciously and unconsciously by the Weberian model of bureaucracy. This model directed our attention to the formal traits of bureaucracy: largeness, the use of achievement as a criterion of recruitment and promotion, "hierarchical organization, impersonality of operations, intensive use of rules, complexity of administrative tasks, secrecy, and employment of specially trained personnel on a career basis."[1] The dynamics of bureaucracy were found essentially in the elaboration of these formal traits. Informal groups, interpersonal ties and informal rules were considered departures from the bureaucratic norms and hindrances to the effective functioning of the bureaucracy which were to be eliminated or at least to be contained. In so far as a more inclusive model was needed to analyse Chinese Communist politics, we relied on elite theories and many of us were unduly swayed by the notion which had been made popular by the theory of totalitarianism of a monolithic elite headed by a supreme leader. The dynamics of elite politics were found mainly in the routinization of charisma. Thus, we fused Weber's two notions of legal-rational order and charisma and attempted to integrate the theories of bureaucracy and elite.

Even as we were formulating these interpretations, several developments had already called these views into question. The post-Weberian theories of bureaucracy and organization had for two decades stressed informal groups, interpersonal relationships and the decision-making processes which involve negotiations, bargaining and compromise—features not sufficiently taken into account before. The theory of totalitarianism had been increasingly challenged for its oversimplified characterization of

[This article was first published in *The China Quarterly*, January, 1976, pp. 98–114.] It was extracted from a paper prepared for the Seminar on the Pursuit of Political Interests in the People's Republic of China under the sponsorship of the Joint Committee on Contemporary China of the American Council of Learned Societies and the Social Science Research Council at Greystone House, N.Y. City, 27–29 December 1973. The revision of this article for publication was made possible by a grant from the Joint Committee on Contemporary China. The author also wishes to acknowledge the research support given by the Social Science Divisional Research Committee and the Center for Far Eastern Studies at the University of Chicago. [The permission of *The China Quarterly* to reproduce the article in this volume is deeply appreciated.]

1. Anthony Downs, *Inside Bureaucracy* (Boston: Little, Brown, 1967), pp. 24–25.

both the political structure and processes in the societies concerned. This intellectual gap between the social sciences and Chinese studies is forever a warning to us. Today, we are rapidly closing the gap but we have not done enough to draw on moral and political philosophy in our attempt to understand the human purpose and the moral foundation of a society which itself stresses man and his moral and political values. Thus, we boldly discuss equality or the lack of it in China without a real understanding of the philosophical principles of equality and the limits placed on any attempt to achieve equality by the imperatives of political order and economic development. We have not given sufficient attention to the extent to which moral and political values influence the definition of individual and political interests and affect their articulation, aggregation and pursuit. Our evaluation of Chinese society and politics relies too much on our inarticulate value premises and not much on an explicit and systematic moral and political philosophy.

But the two most serious blows to pre-Cultural Revolution interpretations have come from the development of Chinese Communist studies themselves. As we looked at Chinese politics and society more closely, we found that our empirical findings could not be encompassed neatly by the Weberian and monolithic models. We began to be impressed by the complexity of Chinese politics, the wide variations in socio-political life in different localities, levels and periods, and the prevalence of bargaining, conflicts, compromises and stalemates. The decisive shift came with the Cultural Revolution and the source materials which it made available to us. In one way or another, all of us have engaged in criticism and self-criticism of our intellectual work and presuppositions. Whereas we formerly used our mental construct of the Yanan period as both our base line and model for the study of Chinese politics, many scholars have now begun to employ their understanding of the Cultural Revolution to re-interpret the whole Chinese Communist movement. This reassessment has taken place in the wider context of the ascendancy of the conflict model over the consensus model in political analysis and the triumph of the bureaucratic politics model over the "rational" model in decision-making theory.

Of the post-Cultural Revolution re-interpretations of Chinese Communist politics, Andrew Nathan's "A factionalism model for CCP politics" is one of the most solidly grounded in social science theory, the most elegantly formulated, and the most sweeping and challenging in its implications. It performs for the profession the service of re-opening the question of the role and behaviour of informal groups in CCP (Chinese Communist Party) politics on a new level of theoretical sophistication. Nathan's model is based on two propositions, one qualification and one basic assumption.

The first proposition is explicitly stated in the following terms: "The hierarchy and established communications and authority flow of the existing organization provides a kind of trellis upon which the complex faction is able to extend its own informal, personal loyalties and relations."[2] This proposition represents a significant step forward in the study of "factions" in CCP politics, but I would substitute the term "informal group" for Nathan's concept of "faction." From my point of view, the significance of this proposition for understanding and research is as follows: by beginning one's analysis with the existing organization or bureaucracy and, in effect, by making the existing organization the pre-condition rather than the product of the development of informal groups, one already makes certain important assumptions about the nature of these groups. Although "informal ties" and "transactional relationships" are by definition essential constitutive elements of informal groups, the dependence of these groups, or at least of one important type among these groups, on the existing organization increases the probability of the following: that in fact these informal groups also share at least some elements of the specialized ideology of that organization, as well as some components of the general ideology of the system of which the organization is a part, that their operational goals do not consist exclusively of the aggrandizement of the power and material interests of the informal groups but are also shaped by the formal goals of the organization, and that their behaviour and actions cannot totally escape the influence of the formal and normative rules of the organization and the encapsulating system. In other words, Nathan's proposition has the merit of immediately raising the problem of the relationship between formal structure and informal groups and makes this problem the focus of our inquiry. This approach is in accord with the thrust of the voluminous literature in the field of sociology.

The change in terminology from "complex faction" to "informal groups" carries with it the following implications: "complex faction" as defined by Nathan is only one possible type of informal group formed around bureaucratic organization. Horizontal and "quasi-horizontal"[3] ties linking colleagues at the same level of a bureaucratic organization are, in some situations, just as important as ties linking leaders at different levels. The

2. Andrew Nathan, "A factionalism model for CCP politics," *The China Quarterly*, No. 53 (1973), p. 44. The results of Nathan's intellectual effort cannot be called a model in the strict sense of the term, but I shall follow his usage for reasons of style.

3. The term "quasi-horizontal ties" includes those linking the formal head of a bureaucratic unit (e.g. the first secretary of a Party Committee) with his lieutenants (e.g. the other secretaries and members of that Party Committee). The ties between Peng Zhen and his lieutenants were hierarchical in terms of his position as a member of the Politburo and a ranking member of the Secretariat. In his capacity as the first secretary of the Beijing Party Committee, his ties with his lieutenants were quasi-horizontal.

"informal groups," including his "complex faction," may or may not function politically in the way Nathan suggests. But the most important point which I want to underscore at the outset is that informal groups and processes, or at least some types of informal group and process, may become formal organizational units and processes, and that informal roles or positions have a tendency to develop into formal roles and positions.[4] The transformation of the informal group consisting of Jiang Qing, Chen Boda and their close followers prior to the Cultural Revolution into the core of the Cultural Revolution Small Group illustrates the transformation of an informal group into a formal unit. The development of the informal secret memorial system during Kang Xi's reign into an elaborate, formal system under Yong Zheng exemplifies the transformation of an informal process into a formal process.[5] The transformation of informal rules, groups and processes into formal ones is one of the most interesting phenomena in the dynamics of bureaucracy and the political system.

Nathan's other proposition is only implicit in scattered statements in his article. At the risk of misinterpreting him for the purposes of clarity, this proposition might nonetheless be stated as follows: once factions are formed, they enter the political arena as distinct actors and largely operate independently of the constraints imposed by the bureaucratic structure or the larger structure of the political system, except those constraints which determine their size and capability. In Nathan's model, the major complex factions have equal and independent status in the political system. They are headed by leaders who occupy positions on the same level of the political system. No organizational or systemic constraints affect the actions of the factions except those which originally enable them to be formed. Although Nathan recognizes that power and policy are inseparably linked, policy considerations do not occupy a central place in his description of the characteristics of factional politics except in a very general and indirect way, which contrasts sharply with his discussion of power interests. He gives an impression that complex factions merely pursue their narrowly defined power interests and that the goals of the organization are irrelevant. In contrast to Nathan, I shall argue here that the con-

4. F. G. Bailey defined "faction" as a group of persons without a common ideology as a basis for co-operation and recruited by a leader with whom they have a transactional relationship. This definition is not adopted in this paper and what is called "informal group" is different from Bailey's "faction" in the sense that it can also derive its strength and solidarity from shared ideology, common goals and agreement on policy. But Bailey's analysis of the processes of the evolution of a "faction" into a formal structure is applicable to our "informal group." F. G. Bailey, *Stratagems and Spoils* (Oxford: Basil Blackwell, 1969), pp. 51–57.

5. Silus Wu, *Communication and Imperial Control in China* (Cambridge, Mass.: Harvard University Press, 1970).

straints imposed by formal bureaucratic organizations and formal political institutions on informal groups fluctuate over time, and that the constraints increase in direct proportion to the vigour and legitimacy of these structures and institutions, and in inverse proportion to the size and capability of the informal groups. In addition to the formal constraints, "constitutional" conventions, unwritten rules of the game and informal understandings also put constraints on the actions and operations of informal groups even at the very top level of the power structure where Nathan finds rampant factionalism of the type he outlines. Most of my qualifications of his second proposition fall into Nathan's category of "organizational-structure" constraints on the behaviour of complex factions or, in my terminology, "informal groups."

Thirdly, Nathan makes an explicit qualification of the usefulness of his model when he writes that "systems are usually mixed, but models are pure" and that "a more complete explanation of behaviour in any political system would have to take into account not only what might be called the 'organizational-structure' constraints . . . , but also cultural constraints, institutional constraints, and ideological constraints."[6]

Finally, Nathan's two propositions and his exclusion from his model of cultural, institutional and ideological constraints have led him to one central assumption on which he has built an elegant model. This fundamental assumption is that "no faction will be able to achieve and maintain overwhelmingly superior power," that "one faction may for the moment enjoy somewhat greater power than rival factions, but this power will not be so much greater that the victorious faction is capable of expunging its rival and assuring permanent dominance."[7] Nathan further argues that the participants themselves act on the basis of this assumption. He writes: "A faction engaging in conflict with other factions must therefore operate on the assumption that it will not be able decisively and finally to eliminate its rivals."[8] His model is based largely on the experience of the Third and Fourth French Republics and on his study of factions in the Chinese parliament in the early years of the Republic. It also reminds his readers of the system of multiple balance of power in international politics theory. But it does not fit CCP politics. For the basic assumption of CCP politics has been that a group or a coalition of groups can and does decisively defeat a major rival group or coalition, and eliminate it. Thus, any model of CCP politics must be built on an assumption diametrically opposite to Nathan's. Such a postulate of CCP politics is rooted in "organizational-

6. Nathan, " A factionalism model," p. 66.
7. *Ibid.* p. 46.
8. *Ibid.*

structure," ideological, environmental and cultural factors and cannot be understood without them. This is one of the major themes of this paper.

I shall introduce the theme in a roundabout way by first confronting CCP political events with the 15 characteristics of factional politics formulated by Nathan, in order to see whether or not they fit each other. Nathan finds that 10 out of the 15 are visible in, or consistent with, the events of the Cultural Revolution. With regard to the existence of the other five characteristics, he does not render a definitive judgment but seems to believe that a *prima facie* case can be made. From this, he proceeds to extend his model backwards and makes the assumption: "factionalism [in his sense of the term] since the earliest days of the party."[9]

My contention is that if we look at the whole history of CCP politics, we shall see, first, that Nathan's model fits certain periods of CCP politics (e.g. the Cultural Revolution) better than other periods (e.g. 1945–56). But even during the Cultural Revolution, CCP politics was based on the assumption that the major rival opponents and groups could defeat and eliminate one another. Secondly, a central tendency in the history of the CCP has been an attempt to break away from the politics of factionalism as described in Nathan's model. Chinese Communist leaders have always assumed, explicitly in certain periods and implicitly in other periods, that "anti-Party factions" will arise and must be defeated and eliminated.

For the purposes of discussion, I shall give the designation "informal groups" to what both outside observers and the Chinese themselves call "factions" and "cliques." Let us also assume that all the major leaders from Chen Duxiu and Li Dazhao to Mao Zedong and Zhou Enlai were leaders of an informal group or a coalition of informal groups. By looking at CCP history closely, we shall find that these leaders and their informal groups behaved very differently from Nathan's "factions" and operated under a very different set of rules. The fundamental fact is that throughout the history of the CCP one informal group or an alliance or coalition of informal groups has always aimed at achieving and keeping overwhelmingly superior power by controlling or capturing the formal institutions of authority within the Party. Some groups have succeeded in this at least to the extent of acquiring sufficient power to defeat and eliminate the major rival group as a political force. That is to say, throughout CCP history, one or more of these groups has entertained hegemonic ambitions. More importantly, there have always been "organizational-structure," ideological, institutional and environmental factors in CCP politics which produce this type of group and which enable it to achieve sufficient power to defeat and eliminate its major rivals.

Subject to further research, one can assert that Chen Duxiu and the

---

9. *Ibid.* p. 58.

group around him achieved overwhelmingly superior power with the support of the Comintern. Li Lisan endeavoured with some success to build his own political machine from 1928 to 1930, gradually removing some of his opponents from positions of power (Xiang Ying, He Mengxiong, Luo Zhanglong and Yun Daiying) and purging others from the Party (Chen Duxiu and his followers). The surprising thing about the Li Lisan line is not Mao's refusal to attend the meeting in Shanghai, his failure to attack Wuhan, his half-hearted 24-hour attack on Nanchang, nor his order to cut short the second attack on Changsha. It is rather the fact that "until September he generally followed the 'Li Lisan line.'"[10]

After June 1931, the core of the returned-students group gradually expanded its power and influence. According to Ilpyong J. Kim, it co-operated with some veteran leaders, made necessary compromises with others and, for a year from early 1933 to February 1934, set up a "collective leadership" with other groups.[11] But there were also signs that the returned students endeavoured to destroy the influence of the other groups and to dominate the Party. This endeavour was considered by Mao and his followers as the main tendency in CCP politics in that period.[12] On his road to supremacy after the Zunyi conference, Mao decisively defeated Zhang Guotao and Wang Ming and absorbed their followers into his apparatus. The Mao-Liu alliance was an alliance of a senior and junior partner. By 1945, this informal alliance or coalition was transformed into a cohesive informal group and a structure of institutionalized authority with Mao as the supreme leader. Up to 1956, this formal structure paralleled closely the informal distribution of power and influence.

From 1959 to the demise of Lin Biao, CCP politics fits Nathan's model more closely. The informal groups formed around Liu became so powerful that they could successfully resist the wishes of Mao and his informal groups. But the stalemate which developed was a strange one: the "supremacy" of Mao and his groups in form, in ideology and in policy orientation but the "supremacy" of Liu and his group in practice and in policy implementation. The Cultural Revolution was undertaken to reclaim the supremacy of Mao in all spheres. In the process, he broke many of the pre-existing rules of the political game, sometimes deliberately and sometimes as a result of the force of circumstance. As Nathan himself writes, Mao's goal "was no longer purely an improved position for his faction in the elite, but an end to factionalism and its associated policy oscillations

10. James P. Harrison, *The Long March to Power: A History of the Chinese Communist Party, 1921–72* (New York: Praeger, 1972), p. 173.

11. Ilpyong J. Kim, *The Politics of Chinese Communism* (Berkeley: University of California Press, 1973), Chaps. III and IV.

12. "Resolution on questions in Party history," *Selected Works of Mao Tse-tung,* Vol. III (Peking: Foreign Languages Press, 1965), pp. 185–93 and 208–10.

and an institutionalization of the Party as an instrument of Maoist will, capable of outliving Mao himself." [13] This statement is important because it describes the dynamic process of CCP politics from 1935 to the purge of Lin Biao. Indeed, if one eliminates the reference to Mao and to the Cultural Revolution, it describes a powerful motivational force in CCP politics from the very beginning.

The obverse side of this drive for supremacy by a leader, an informal group or a coalition of informal groups is the defeat and elimination of the major group or groups once in power or in opposition if the process is allowed to run its course, although the individuals or even the leaders who once belonged to these groups may be absorbed into the winning group or coalition. The groups eliminated once and for all include those led by Chen Duxiu, Li Lisan, the returned students, Zhang Guotao, Wang Ming, Gao Gang and Rao Shushi, Peng Dehuai, Liu Shaoqi and Lin Biao.*

The rules of the game and the mode of conflict in which the ultimate triumph of one group or a coalition of groups is accompanied by the permanent elimination of a defeated group are very different from those laid down by Nathan. In CCP politics, a group engaging in conflict with other groups does not operate on the assumption that "it will not be able decisively and finally to eliminate its rivals." If a coalition of groups is engaged in conflict with other coalitions, the internal politics of these coalitions (i.e. the relations among the various groups forming each coalition) may more closely approach Nathan's model than the relations between the coalitions. But even the groups within a coalition envisage the possibility that one of them and one leader will achieve hegemony or supremacy, that collective leadership will yield to leadership of a single leader who is more than the first among equals, and that the coalition may develop into a group with that leader as its head. The group and the leader endeavour not only to protect their power base but also constantly to increase their own power, and they do so not alone by secret preparation and surprise offensive. CCP politics has not prevented the emergence of strong leaders. On the contrary, only strong leaders can emerge triumphant. In serious power struggles, the principle of legitimacy has always been raised. When Chen Duxiu and his followers were finally expelled from the Party, they were labelled "Trotskyites." The Cultural Revolution involved a sweeping examination of the principle of legitimacy. The notion of the struggle between the two lines is based on a definite conception of legitimacy.

13. Nathan, "A factionalism model," p. 62.

* To be more precise, these groups were eliminated as effective political forces. None of the leaders were executed, although four of them died in the aftermath of the struggle in one way or another.

For whatever reasons, the CCP has made decisions as frequently by the victory of one view over another as by consensus among groups. The opposition to or reservation about the policy of "the bloc within" in 1923 and the doubts about continuing the alliance with the Guomindang (GMD) in early 1927 were suppressed by the order and influence of the Comintern. The Guangzhou Commune was staged in spite of the misgivings of leaders on the scene. The Li Lisan line did not enjoy widespread, wholehearted support. Mao's tactics of the United Front were adopted in 1937 and 1939 against the opposition of Zhang Guotao and Wang Ming. Mao's intervention in 1955 to overrule the Party apparatus and to speed up the process of co-operativization is well known. His policy of "blooming and contending" must have been greeted with doubts by the Party apparatus.[14] The 10th Plenum's decision on the question of class struggle reversed Liu's position stated at the Eighth Party Congress. I doubt if there was any consensus behind the dismissal of Peng Zhen and the launching of the Cultural Revolution. The formula of triple combination was adopted after the Shanghai Commune had been established. Mao and Zhou must have personally made the decision to respond to American overtures and to seek a dialogue with the United States against the resistance of some Party leaders. Mao's decision not to have a chairman of the Republic was made in the face of the strong overt and covert opposition of Lin Biao and Chen Boda.

The whole history of the Chinese Communist movement and regime contradicts the characteristics of *immobilisme* or the inability to carry out an innovative programme as specified in Nathan's model.[15] The CCP may have made many errors but it has not frequently failed to take decisive actions one way or the other. Many of its policies can only be characterized as innovative given the historical and political context. The land reform programme, the peaceful transformation of private industries and commercial firms into joint state-private enterprises, the commune system, mass mobilization as a method of building up the agricultural sector, the system of co-operative health care and barefoot doctors in the countryside, the sending of students and youths to the rural areas, the new education system, etc.—all fall into the category of innovative programmes although one may question the wisdom of many of these policies. A footnote by Nathan extending the meaning of *immobilisme* makes a more plausible case. He writes: "Of course, at any given moment there seemed to be a definite policy line, but the question is whether the line was consistently sustained or whether it gave way to a contradictory line."[16] The implication is that the inconsistency was rooted in the fac-

14. See Roderick MacFarquhar, *The Origins of the Cultural Revolution* (N.Y.: Columbia University Press, 1974), Vol. I.
15. Nathan, "A factionalism model," pp. 49 and 51.
16. *Ibid.* pp. 55 note and 65.

tional system and arose as the influence of one faction or another ebbed or flowed. But many of the inconsistencies and reversals of policies were not necessarily the product of factional struggle but adjustments to changes in circumstance or the results of the perceived failure of a policy.

Our present knowledge of the policy-making process in China does not enable us to separate clearly these three categories of inconsistence and reversals of policy. In many cases, we do not know who reversed the policies and why he did so. But we do know that many of the reversals and changes in policies were initiated by Mao. For example, in early 1946, in anticipation of the outbreak of full-scale civil war, Mao adopted a radical land-reform programme. In late 1947 and in 1948, Mao himself criticized the ultra-Left tendencies of Liu in implementing the programme. In 1957, Mao raised the slogan of "the East wind prevails over the West wind." But in 1970 and 1971, he personally approved the dramatic reversal of policies towards the United States. In other cases, a policy was based at first on a consensus but was changed as Mao shifted his position. The policy of promoting a rich peasant economy is a case in point. The cessation of payment of 5 per cent interest to the national capitalists during the Cultural Revolution is another. One can readily concede that the inconsistencies and reversals of policies during the Cultural Revolution approximate more closely to Nathan's model than in any other period of Mao's ascendency. But CCP politics even during the Cultural Revolution depart from Nathan's model at several fundamental points. First, one "faction" or an alliance of "factions" was out to destroy another and succeeded in amassing sufficient power to do so ("overwhelmingly superior power" would be an overstatement). Secondly, its aim was, as Nathan admits, to destroy the "factional system." Thirdly, the principle of legitimacy was not only discussed but underscored. Fourthly, major new policies and institutions were adopted and implemented. Examples are the three-in-one combination, the new educational policy, the sending of all middle-school graduates to the factories or the countryside, the new system of public health care, the May Seventh cadre schools, etc.

Nathan's article represents the result of an ambitious undertaking in which he proposes to construct a model deductively from certain premises and then to verify it by confronting it with the experience of the CCP. A different approach is to adhere more closely to the history of the CCP to 1971 and to abstract the structural element and behavioural characteristics from different periods of history. In arriving at these constructs, one is guided by one's sense of logical possibilities. Such abstract constructs are only one step removed from reality and should not be called a model. This method leads us to three abstract constructs. All of them are based on a dual premise. On the one hand, one or more of the informal groups and leaders aim at achieving supremacy or hegemony in the Party, destroying some of the other informal groups as significant political forces or subordinating them to their control. On the other hand, there are objective conditions, organizational-structure factors, ideological compulsions, institutional elements and cultural conditions which make it possible for one group or one leader to achieve supremacy or hegemony. It is this dual premise which makes CCP politics entirely different from the type of factionalism described in Nathan's model.

In the first abstract construct, one of the leaders or groups has achieved supremacy or hegemony. I shall return to this construct in a moment. In the second construct, an informal alliance or coalition of two or more of these groups has achieved domination. This second construct may evolve out of a "collective leadership" in which diverse groups with conflicting policy views take part. For this "collective leadership" cannot be stable given the basic premise underlying this abstract construct. Soon an alliance or a coalition of two or more groups within the "collective leadership" achieves a dominant position and defeats the other groups or drastically reduces their power. After the Zunyi conference, a collective leadership emerged with Mao as the director of the Military Affairs Committee,* Zhang Wentian one of the "28½ Bolsheviks," as general secretary, and with Zhang Guotao wielding enormous influence. Mao was the first among equals in this "collective leadership." But with the defection of Zhang Guotao and the defeat of Wang Ming's policy, the "collective leadership" was replaced by a dominant alliance or coalition of groups and leaders centred around Mao Zedong and Liu Shaoqi. The difference between an alliance and a coalition is a matter of degree. An alliance is less cohesive. Within an alliance there are more divergent interests and policy views which are handled through negotiations and bargaining. The elimination of Xiang Ying in the New Fourth Army incident and the failure of the 100-Regiment battle further strengthened Mao's position. At some time after the launching of the *zhengfeng* movement, the alliance became a coalition. An informal coalition of leaders and groups becomes an informal group when the supreme position of one leader is acknowledged by the other leaders and groups and a superordinate subordinate relationship replaces that between equals. The power relations within this informal group and between this dominant group and other groups tend to be institutionalized into a structure of authority. This transformation was formalized in the Seventh Congress of April-June 1945 and the First Plenum of the Seventh Central Committee in June 1945, when Liu Shaoqi led the

---

* Recently published materials show that two months after the Zunyi Conference, Mao became the leading member of a "three-man military command small group." See chapter 8. According to the current official version of Party history, Zhang Wentian did not hold the formal title of "general secretary."

others in promoting the cult of Mao, when Mao's authority was confirmed by his election to the newly created position of chairman of the Central Committee, and when the Party Constitution designated the Thought of Mao Zedong together with the theories of Marxism-Leninism as "the guiding principles" of all work in the party. The dominant informal group can at this point use the hierarchical structure of authority and the formal channels of communication to enhance further its power. An informal structure becomes a part of the formal structure. Real power and formal position are now closely aligned. At this point, the second abstract construct is superseded by the first.

Under the first construct, however, not all the informal groups disappear. Some of them simply become the component parts of the dominant informal group and formal structure. Other new informal groups may emerge in the course of time. But in human affairs, in contrast to theory, authority is seldom absolute and power is seldom undivided. To preserve his authority and his power, a supreme leader of a dominant group must undertake all sorts of manoeuvres to retain the loyalties of his chief lieutenants and followers, to consolidate the support of other groups, to prevent the formation of opposition groups, and to defeat them once they emerge and challenge his authority. He must still resort to the methods of persuasion, negotiation, compromise, bargaining and co-operation. But the achievement of a supreme formal position by a leader of a dominant group does make important differences in his ability to rule. Towards the other groups, he need not resort to these non-authoritative methods as frequently as he previously had to. For now he can also use authoritative commands as an alternative method. With the ultimate sanction in his hand, his non-authoritative methods can yield better results more quickly. Towards the top leaders in his own group, he still uses non-authoritative methods. But his command over resources and his repertoire of measures has greatly increased.

The style of political leadership may vary within the first model from Stalin's use of the secret police to control the Party,[17] through Chiang Kai-shek's method of divide and rule, to Mao's rather unique way of leadership. But whatever the style, a supreme leader is confronted with a real dilemma. If he wishes to enhance the capability of the political system as a whole, he must promote the unity of the various bureaucracies which manage the affairs of the state. This unity can be achieved by placing one of the bureaucracies above the others; in Mao's case, the Party between 1945 and 1959.[18] To run this premier bureaucracy effectively, he must del-

17. Stalin's use of the secret police to control the Party is a prime example of the use of a separate monitoring agency as a device to control a large bureaucracy. For a discussion of monitoring organizations, see Downs, *Inside Bureaucracy*, pp. 144–53.

18. The primacy of one bureaucracy over other bureaucracies can be analytically distin-

egate authority to one man; in Mao's case, Liu Shaoqi. To strengthen the chief bureaucracy and its operational head necessarily entails an increase of the latter's authority and power at the expense of the supreme leader. But to use the method of divide and rule would mean a decline in the political capability of the system as a whole. Generally speaking, Mao opted for the first horn of the dilemma in the period between 1945 and 1959. His style was to intervene at crucial moments when basic issues were at stake. In so doing, he may have been supporting one group or one leader over one issue but another group or leader over another issue at another time; he may have arbitrated and settled the differences among the various conflicting views; or he may have developed his own view and have obtained the support of one group or another. But he did not deliberately play the game of divide and rule; or if he did, then he failed miserably, for events after 1959 show that Liu Shaoqi had accumulated so much power and authority that Mao had to resort to the method of divide and rule by promoting Lin Biao and the People's Liberation Army (PLA) to weaken Liu's control, and then to launch the Cultural Revolution to regain supreme and unchallenged power.

This leads us to the third abstract construct, in which two or more informal groups or coalitions of groups reach a stalemate. Under this construct, at least one of these groups or coalitions of groups will attempt to break the stalemate by building up its coalition or by drawing other groups into the intra-elite struggle, thus enlarging the scope of political participation. This third construct is based on CCP politics between 1959 and 1966. Mao built up the power and prestige of Lin Biao and the PLA to counter Liu's coalition, thus resorting to the policy of divide and rule. He then mobilized the students and workers in a struggle to purge the Party apparatus. Although this third abstract construct is more like Nathan's model than the two others, it is still fundamentally different from his model in that one or more of these groups or coalitions of groups aims at achieving supremacy and the destruction of the opposing group or groups as a political force.

If my analysis is correct, it is incumbent upon me to suggest, however tentatively, some of the conditions or factors which are conducive to the emergence of groups and leaders with ambitions to achieve supremacy in the CCP and which facilitate the achievement of their ambitions. Here,

---

guished from a pattern of control in which one bureaucracy is used merely as an agency to monitor other bureaucracies. In the former pattern, the functions of the premier bureaucracy are comprehensive and diffuse while in the latter pattern the function of the monitoring agencies is narrow and specific. The differences between the two patterns can also be examined in terms of the relationships of the recruitment and promotion systems in the different bureaucracies as well as the frequency and ease of the assumption by a single individual of multiple roles in different bureaucracies and of the exchange of roles from one bureaucracy to another.

one must underscore some organizational-structure factors which Nathan neglects, and bring into the picture ideological, institutional, cultural and historical factors which he deliberately excludes. The ideology and goal structure of the CCP envisage sweeping and profound revolutionary changes in all aspects of society and culture. To achieve these tasks, strong and centralized leadership is required. The quest for strong and centralized leadership has been a prime motif of political history since the 1911 revolution and echoes the traditional concept of political authority. The hierarchical structure and the Leninist principles of organization of the CCP are inseparable from its ideology and goal structure. They vest supreme authority in the Party Centre (the whole Party obeys the Centre) and give important powers to a single person or organ (in different periods to the general secretary, the standing committee of the Political Bureau, and the chairman of the Central Committee and its Political Bureau). Under this organizational structure, the leader of a group or a coalition of groups which captures the formal apparatus of the Party would enjoy legitimate authority over the Party and would necessarily accumulate a tremendous amount of power and influence.[19] The capture of the formal Party apparatus does not mean that the dominant group and its leader can dispense with the normal political methods of political manoeuvres such as negotiation, bargaining, co-optation and compromise in order to keep itself in power, to consolidate and extend its control, and to achieve its objectives. But it does mean that the dominant group and its leader have many more resources and a larger repertoire of instruments of power than any other group. Hence the struggle for power in the CCP has, during most of its history, resulted in the ascendancy of one group or a coalition of groups.

In the early years, the CCP was a branch of the Comintern and was under its strict discipline and close guidance. The successive representatives of the Comintern supported or elevated one group over other groups or one leader over other leaders to a dominant position within the Party so as to facilitate their control and to use the CCP as their instrument. The most blatant case was the ascendancy in 1931 of the "28½ Bolsheviks" under the sponsorship of Pavel Mif.

Its revolutionary ideology and goals in combination with Leninist organizational principles make the CCP a structure of groups which are engaged in conflict with other groups in Chinese society. In these groups there exist a high frequency of interaction and deep personal involvement

19. A vivid description of the use of some of these formal powers can be found in "Summary of Chairman Mao's conversations with responsible comrades in various localities during the period of the inspection tour of the provinces (from Mid-August to September 12, 1971)," *Zhonggong yanjiu (Studies on Chinese Communism)*, September 1972, pp. 81–96.

of members which intensify both sentiments of love and hatred. When conflict breaks out, it is likely to lead to a total disruption of the pre-existing relationship and to the purge of the dissident and defeated members so that new tightly knit groups can again be formed.

Moreover, the CCP in its rise to power was confronted with a series of crises. While a crisis situation tended to create splits within the Party and intensified the struggle for power, it also facilitated the emergence of strong and centralized leadership which held out the promise of extricating the Party from the crisis and leading the movement to victory. In the Chinese cultural setting, this frequently meant the supremacy of a strong leader. The Chinese Communist Party was a product of the reaction against warlord and GMD politics. Its search for a strong and centralized leadership represented an attempt to end the type of factional politics prevalent under those regimes.

In a crisis situation, success and failure of the policies adopted or advocated by a leader or a dominant group constitute an objective test of the quality of leadership. The defeat suffered by the CCP in the Fifth Campaign discredited the returned students. The subsequent successes of Mao legitimized this leadership. The availability of such an objective test at crucial moments alleviated some of the bitterness of intra-Party struggle. Moreover, throughout much of the civil war, the wide disparity of military strength between the GMD and the CCP made it imperative for the CCP to achieve the greatest possible degree of unity. Defection to the GMD by leaders defeated in intra-Party struggle or disillusioned by Party politics was always a possibility and would inflict serious damage on the movement. These three conditions together with the establishment of the ideological and organizational authority of Mao facilitated the development of a moderate pattern of intra-Party struggle which Nathan characterizes as a "code of civility." Far from being the product of the inability of one faction to eliminate the other, this "code of civility" emerged in China side by side with the establishment and consolidation of the ideological and organizational authority of Mao and was facilitated by the conditions arising out of confrontation with a strong enemy outside the Party. This "code of civility" lost much of its lustre during the Cultural Revolution which occurred after Mao had lost some of his ideological authority, and actual organizational control had drifted into the hands of Liu.

But whether the methods of intra-Party struggle are moderate or immoderate, the outstanding fact is that from the viewpoint of the participants, all the contests have resulted in the victory of one group and the defeat of another. The inner-Party directives and the published speeches at the 10th Congress repeatedly stressed the 10 major struggles in the Party's history in which one line was defeated and another emerged triumphant. This tradition of Party history and the perception of both the victors and the vanquished have established a basic rule which we must take into account as the fundamental premise in formulating our abstract constructs.

The above thoughts on the characteristics of political conflict and conflict resolution at the highest reaches of CCP politics are invoked by Nathan's seminal article on "factionalism." They are influenced by the systems approach, particularly the systems approach as applied in international politics. They have an affinity with structural-functionalism. But ultimately, they rest on the assumption that structures and institutions reflect human purposes and, increasingly in modern times, have come to be consciously designed to perform definite functions or preserved and developed to fulfil once latent functions.[20] The present analyses cover some but not all of the rules governing political conflicts among leaders and group-actors in China to 1971. They do not deal with the question of the possible change of the present system into another in which collective leadership is the rule rather than the exception. Above all, they do not attempt to answer the far more difficult questions to some of which Nathan also addresses himself: e.g. the nature of "faction," the internal structure of "faction," the formation and development of "factions" and the coalition of "factions." They merely try to show that the characteristics of political conflict in the CCP are very different from those postulated in Nathan's model, whether these political actors are individuals or groups, whether they are formally designated an "anti-Party faction," an "anti-Party alliance," representatives or leaders of a certain political "line," "military club," "power holders taking the capitalist road," or "bourgeois headquarters," and whether they are characterized by outside observers as "factions," "opinion groups," or "informal groups."

But the major purpose of this methodological commentary is to call for a systematic study of the informal group structure of the CCP, the characteristics of political conflict at the highest reaches of CCP politics, and the rules governing conflict and conflict resolution. The times have long since passed when China scholars could assert with utmost confidence that there was no faction in the CCP. Nor can we be satisfied with concepts such as the monolithic Party or the totalitarian leader. The value and limitations of Nathan's article suggest that a systematic study of the question of "factionalism" must be approached simultaneously from both ends of the abstractness-concreteness continuum. On the one hand, we must try to utilize western social science theories and concepts to help us formulate theoretical "paradigms" or "models," fully bearing in mind that generally speaking they are culture-bound and rooted in western political val-

20. Donald Philip Dore, "Function and cause" in N. J. Demerath III and Richard A. Peterson (eds.), *System, Change, and Conflict* (N.Y.: Free Press, 1967), pp. 403–19.

ues. On the other hand, we must re-examine with utmost detachment the history of political conflicts in the CCP, beginning with a careful analysis of the political actors' perceptions of the nature of their opponents and their own groups, and of the processes, rules and expected outcome of political struggle, both as these perceptions are reflected in public statements and private analyses at the time as well as in the recollections, accounts and collective memory after the event. The "theoretical paradigm" or "model" may help us to detect the significance of the historical data and alert us to the meaning of facts and events. My comments on Nathan's article illustrate how a "paradigm" or "model" can force us to rethink many basic problems. At the same time, the historical data will almost certainly force us to revise our preconceived "paradigms" or "models" and suggest to us necessary modifications or even something totally different. My three abstract constructs are outlined to illustrate how one can move from concrete historical events in all their details and uniqueness to a slightly higher level of abstraction. With intensive effort and working from both directions, we may then be able to discover the nature of the units of political action at the highest reaches in changing historical contexts and over different issues and to specify comprehensively and systematically the set of rules, some permanent and others variable, which govern political conflicts. If we can achieve this, we shall have real knowledge rather than facile speculations about CCP politics.*

* Cf. Albert O. Hirschman, "The Search for Paradigm as a Hindrance to Understanding," *World Politics* (April 1970), pp. 329–43.

4

Mao Zedong Thought, the Last Struggle for Succession, and the Post-Mao Era

I

In a letter to Joseph Bloch, dated 21–22 September 1890, Friedrich Engels wrote: "[W]e make our history ourselves, but in the first place, under very definite assumptions and conditions. Among these the economic ones are *ultimately decisive*. But the political ones, etc., and indeed, even the traditions which haunt human minds also play a part, although not the decisive one."[1] The phrase, "the political ones, etc.," refers to the superstructure and the forms of social consciousness of a society as distinguished from its economic base or the mode of production.

In his article, "On contradiction,"[2] Mao Zedong deals with the same problem of the role of the economic factor in history but goes much further than Engels in recognizing the importance of the superstructure. Mao writes:

> True, the productive forces, practice, and economic base *generally play* the principal and decisive role; whoever denies this is not a materialist. But it must also be admitted that in certain conditions, such aspects as the relations of production, theory, and the superstructure in turn manifest themselves in the *principal and decisive* role. . . . When the superstructure (politics, culture, etc.) obstructs the development of the economic base, political and cultural changes become principal and decisive.[3]

In acknowledging the principal and decisive role of the economic base, Mao uses the term "generally" *(yi ban de)*, which carries, at least in its

This article [first published in *The China Quarterly*, no. 71 (September, 1977) pp. 498–527 and printed by permission of *The China Quarterly*] is an abbreviated version of a paper originally presented at a conference on "What is communism?" held at the University of Chicago in April 1977. The writer benefited from discussions with Professors Adam Przeworski, Ira Katznelson, Philippe Schmitter, Joseph Cropsey, and Bernard Silberman, and comments by Professors John K. Fairbank, Chalmers Johnson, Brantly Womack, and particularly Edward Friedman. He also wants to acknowledge the support of the Social Science Research Committee and the Center for Far Eastern Studies of the University of Chicago and the National Endowment for the Humanities.

1. Lewis S. Feuer, *Marx and Engels: Basic Writings on Politics and Philosophy* (Garden City, New York: Anchor Books, 1959), p. 398. Emphasis added.

2. For the controversy over the precise time of its composition and the extent of its revision, see Arthur A. Cohen, *The Communism of Mao Tse-tung* (Chicago: University of Chicago Press, 1964), pp. 22–28.

Chinese phrase, the notion of frequency rather than the idea of causal flow and finality implied by Engels' term "ultimately." Going beyond Engels, Mao affirms that in certain conditions, political and cultural changes become *principal and decisive,* not merely "playing a part" in the course of human history. Moreover, in the quoted passage as well as in the preceding sentences in which he uses the notion of principal and secondary aspects of a contradiction,[4] Mao puts "productive forces," and "the economic base" together on one side of the contradiction and "relations of production" and "the superstructure" together on the other side.

Mao's reformulation of historical materialism represents not only a descriptive generalization of the process of ideological, political, social, and economic changes in 20th-century China, but also a programmatic prescription for revolutionary action. As such, it comprehends, encompasses, shapes or legitimizes a number of developments in China before 1949 which cannot be understood in terms of the conventional wisdom of Marxism up to that time, but which are familiar to all China scholars. Changes in the sphere of ideology and the political superstructure under the impact of the West far outpaced the development of the "forces of production" or the "economic base." A Communist Party, supposedly the vanguard of the proletariat, led the revolution to victory while its organic ties with the proletariat were severed and few of its leaders were of proletarian origin. It was the ideological form and the political superstructure established in guerrilla bases in the rural areas which gave the Party its character and the movement its direction, while the economic base (in the form of a system of land tenure with an oppressed peasantry) furnished it with the opportunity to gain political support and manpower through a programme of land reform which changed quickly and sharply over a period of 22 years. Correct, flexible political-military strategy and tactics executed by effective, disciplined organizations overwhelmed the vast superiority in economic resources commanded by the other side. Po-

3. *Selected Works,* Vol. I, p. 336. Emphasis added. Many years later, Mao wrote a series of 33 comments on Stalin's *Economic Problems of Socialism* (1952). He began with the following highly critical remarks. "From the beginning to end, this book of Stalin's has not touched upon superstructure. It has not considered man. It saw things but not man. . . . The standpoint of Stalin's last letter ['Reply to Comrades A. V. Sanina and V. G. Venzher,' dated 28 September 1952] is almost totally wrong. The basic error is his distrust of the peasantry." *Mao Zedong sixiang wansui* (no place of pub.; 1967), p. 156. Some of the ideas of Nicos Poulantzas and Antonio Gramsci parallel Mao's emphasis on the superstructure and political and ideological line over economic base. This will be developed in another paper.

4. For a Marxist view of the importance of Mao's distinction between the principal contradiction and secondary contradiction, and the distinction between principal aspect and secondary aspect within a contradiction, see Louis Althusser, *For Marx* (New York: Vintage Books, 1970), pp. 193–96.

litical power grew out of the barrel of a gun in a "peasant war under proletarian leadership" rather than economic power in the most advanced part of the country. The descriptive generalization *cum* programmatic prescription was then raised to the level of a new tenet of historical materialism. This fusion of descriptive generalization, programmatic prescription and general principle is resonant with the traditional principle of Chinese thought.

Mao's qualification of Engels' formulation of historical materialism suggests that an ideology which has its roots in social, economic, and political circumstances vastly different from those existing in China must be modified if it is to serve as useful "maps of problematic social reality," as "templates for the organization of social and psychological processes,"[5] and as guides to actions. In China as well as many other late comers to modernization, this process of adapting a transferred ideology to local conditions was protracted and tortuous. Mao's success in this task produced what he called "sinification of Marxism"[6] or, to use the later official formulation, "the integration of the universal truth of Marxism-Leninism with the concrete practices of the Chinese Revolution." Mao's modification of Engels' formulation of historical materialism is one of the two most significant theoretical developments in this process of sinification.

The sinification of Marxism in turn led Mao to a related significant insight. Mao declared that:

> There is no such thing as abstract Marxism, but only concrete Marxism. What we call concrete Marxism is Marxism that has taken on a national form, that is, Marxism applied to the concrete struggle in the concrete conditions prevailing in China, and not Marxism abstractly used.[7]

This remark reflects a complex of experiences which easily led Mao to the abstract statement that "it is precisely in the particularity of contradiction that the universality of contradiction resides."[8] This seemingly commonsensical statement has nevertheless a significant place in the development of Marxism. Althusser notes: "Mao Zedong begins with contradiction in its 'universality,' but his only serious discussion centers around the con-

5. These phrases are borrowed from Clifford Geertz, *The Interpretation of Culture* (New York: Basic Books, 1973), pp. 216–20.

6. Stuart Schram and Benjamin Schwartz did more than any other China scholars to document and popularize this development of Marxism in China. Stuart Schram, *The Political Thought of Mao Tse-tung* (New York: Praeger, 1969). Revised edit., pp. 171–74. The Chinese text can be conveniently found in *Mao Zedong ji*, Vol. VI, pp. 259–62.

7. Schram, *Political Thought*, p. 172.

8. *Selected Works*, Vol. I, p. 316.

tradiction in the practice of class struggle, by virtue of another 'universal' principle, the principle which Mao reflects, vis à vis contradiction, in the following form: contradiction is always specific and specificity universally appertains to its essence."[9] Althusser makes clear that Mao's formulation is "essential to dialectical materialism, and Marx discusses an illustration of it in the *Introduction* . . . "[10] The point is that whereas Marx used this idea mainly in intellectual, scientific pursuit and academic discourse, Mao brought it to the realm of the practice of revolution and employed it to study the revolutionary situation, to formulate programmes, or at least to rationalize policies and legitimize his struggle with his opponents inside and outside the Party.

The sinification of Marxism is inseparable from the second and perhaps more basic and lasting heritage which Mao has left for the Chinese. This is his development of the notion of the unity of theory and practice and the concrete examples which he provided in this development. Guided in the Jiangxi period only by some vague and imprecise notions of Marxist theories, goals, and values, he took vigorous actions, formulated general programmes, adopted specific policies on the basis of concrete analyses of concrete situations. These programmes and policies underwent frequent changes and modifications in the light of their success or failure and the rapidly changing circumstances. For the purpose of arriving at a correct analysis of the changing situation and for the purpose of policy experimentations, the method of "study and investigation" was developed and employed. The guidelines to action, policies, and programmes, as well as the analyses of concrete situations, were then raised to a higher level of generalization. This process of decision-making and theoretical generalization was justified in terms of the notion of unity of theory and practice which was then self-conciously employed as an epistemological principle, a prudential guide to action, and a criterion of valid theory. As Brantly Womack observes, "there is little propositional novelty in the principles of Mao's theory-practice relations," but "the difference is that what Marx states as a premise for theoretical criticism, Mao takes as a fundamental problem area for action."[11] In so doing, Mao introduced and, through his personal example and his writings, explicated for the Chinese a modern principle which, for the first time since the end of the 19th century, holds out the promise of restoring the Chinese tradition of unity of knowledge and action.

9. Louis Althusser, *For Marx* (New York: Vintage Books, 1970), p. 183.
10. *Ibid.*
11. Brantly Womack, "Theory and practice in the thought of Mao Tse-tung," in James Hsiung [ed.], *The Logic of Maoism* (New York: Praeger, 1974), p. 15.

But one should not overlook a basic difficulty in Mao Zedong Thought which he did not resolve and which has furnished the ideological background for serious political struggles. In his reformulation of historical materialism, he has never explicitly and systematically explained what constitute the *generally* obtained conditions in human history under which productive forces and economic base play the principal and decisive role or, in contrast, what are those "certain conditions" under which the relations of production and the superstructure in turn manifest themselves in the principal and decisive role. The vague phrases, "when it is impossible for the productive forces to develop without a change in the relations of production" and "when the superstructure obstructs the development of the economic base" are poor guides and raise more questions than answers. The reformulated thesis that in certain conditions the superstructure, [theory,] and the relations of production play the principal and decisive role served him well during the period of revolutionary civil and foreign wars. But after 1949 the Party is in power; can it not be said that the productive forces and the economic base now play the principal and decisive role? If it is the case that both theses are still applicable after 1949 in different areas of human activities, under different conditions, and in different periods of time, can one or other thesis be applied? How can the two theses be reconciled at any one period of time? In what way are specific policies and institutional arrangements to be judged or rationalized in terms of these two theses? How to answer these questions is a matter of judgment over which loyal Chinese Communists can and do differ, when they are taking decisions or rationalizing specific policies.

In principle, these questions can be answered through recourse to a vigorous application of the notion of unity of theory and practice as developed in his article "On practice" which gives primacy to practice.[12] The primacy of practice also reflects a common-sense truth that in daily affairs, *a fortiori* in a revolutionary situation, one frequently must act before one has finished theorizing or even thinking, and that the generality of theory and the infinite horizon of thinking cannot supply the basis for any concrete decision with certainty.[13] But there is a basic antinomy in Mao's very notion of theory and practice if one takes his writings and actions as a whole. While the primacy of practice in Mao's epistemology is clear, the relationship between theory and practice in Mao's dialectical materialism and historical materialism and in the sphere of political actions is ambivalent. His writings and actions point to two very different ways of resolving the tension between theory and practice, and of turning

12. In this article, Mao emphasizes the dependence of theory on practice and emphasizes that theory is based on practice and in turn serves practice. *Selected Works*, Vol. I, p. 297.

13. I am indebted to Dr. Theresa Chu for this formulation.

it into unity. In his "On contradiction," on the one hand he writes that in the contradiction between theory and practice, practice *generally* plays the principal and decisive role, and on the other hand underscores the thesis that in certain conditions, theory in turn manifests itself in the principal and decisive role. Mao has not given his followers any criterion to differentiate the two sets of conditions other than the phrase "in those times of which Lenin said, 'without revolutionary theory, there can be no revolution.'"[14] Whether there should be another revolution or a drastic change in the prevailing practice when the Party is in power is a matter of judgment. Indeed, what constitutes a revolution when the Party is in power is a very difficult question to answer. In practice, such a question involves the issue of political survival and self-preservation for a large number of leaders. Of course one can assign the epistemological principle a higher theoretical status than the reformulated thesis in "On contradiction." But the operational test of the validity of theory or policy provided by practice is the test of success or failure which in human affairs involves a prolonged process, a balance between subjective efforts and objective results, and a calculation of costs and benefits. Then the unanswered question, perhaps a question unanswerable in abstract terms, is at what point in the process and the balance one should decide that practice has proved or disproved the validity of a theory or a policy.

Our research does not allow us to ascertain to what extent these abstract ideas shape the perceptions, attitudes, and preferences of the political leaders which in turn influence their policy choices since 1949. We also do not know for certain whether or not policy choices are made "pragmatically" and exclusively in light of the objective demands of the situation and then rationalized by ideology. Nor can we be sure that policies are the product of rational choice according to some objective and subjective criteria or are merely the products of political bargaining constructed out of the personal and special interests of the actors. If policies represent a mixture of rational choice and political bargaining, we cannot easily separate one from the other. Sometimes, leaders espousing different ideological principles share a common view on concrete policies. At other times those who share common ideological principles may differ violently over specific decisions. Political leaders do not usually align themselves neatly into two camps over a period of time or even at any one time. The policy process produces consensus, compromise, domination and submission, violent disagreements, and purges.

But at a minimum we can assert that policy debates, particularly on the more fundamental and persistent issues, are couched or justified in terms of ultimate ideological principles. Ideological debate is an integral part of

14. *Selected Works*, Vol. I, p. 336.

the policy-making process. The rise to ideological eminence of the "gang of four" in 1975 and 1976, the programmes formulated by the veteran political leaders to contain their influence, and the counter-attack against them after their arrest have produced ideological statements and writing richer in quantity and quality and have raised the ideological debate to a higher level than all other intra-Party struggles since 1935, with the possible exception of the *Zhengfeng* movement. Though couched in Marxist and Maoist terminology and principles, the ideological debates evolve around serious concrete policy issues. Some of these issues are common to all developing countries such as the question whether to accord priority to economic growth over equality and participation or vice versa, and what is the proper mix of these desiderata. Policies in education and basic scientific research fall partly into this area. Other issues are pertinent to revolutionary regimes such as the question of whether to consolidate the revolutionary gains already achieved or to push the revolution further into various spheres of social, economic, and political life, or how a society can combine revolutionary change with stability and economic growth. Still other issues are relevant to Marxist regimes, such as whether a new class can emerge after the means of ownership have been socialized, what the basis of this new class is, and how to deal with it. There are issues which are specific to China's response to the West but are also of general relevance to Third World countries—such as the issue of self-reliance and the question of importation of technology and industrial plants. The revival of the terms "foreign affairs faction" and the problem of "substance and function" indicates that the issues confronting the Chinese since the late 19th century have not been completely solved.

But the most significant feature of this ideological debate is that both sides rely ultimately on Mao's reformulated thesis on historical materialism and[/or] his use of the notion of unity of theory and practice to justify their positions on concrete issues. This characteristic points at once to the vitality of these two ideas and to the unresolved problems and antinomy in them.

II

In the last three months of 1974,[15] final preparations were made for the convocation of the Second Plenum of the 10th Central Committee and the Fourth National People's Congress for the purpose of adopting a new constitution of the People's Republic of China, of reorganizing the State Council, and of electing a new Standing Committee of the National People's

---

15. In this paper, we shall not discuss the campaign to "criticize Lin Biao and Confucius" and the movement to "study the historical experience of the struggle between the Confucian and Legalist schools."

Congress. There is little doubt that the struggle between the two groups and the manoeuvring for position were intensified by this process. It is now charged that, in November and December, the "gang of four attempted to exclude Premier Zhou from the preparatory work and to organize their own 'cabinet.'"[16] It is also charged that in October, Wang Hongwen, a vice-chairman of the Party and number three man in the Party hierarchy, went to see Mao and made "false accusations against Zhou."[17] It is said that Mao "severely scolded him." Mao is alleged to have pointed out: "Jiang Qing has ambition. She wants Wang Hongwen to serve as the chairman [of the Standing Committee of the National People's Congress]. She herself wants to be chairman of the Party."[18] Apparently managed by Premier Zhou, the Second Plenum and the first session of the Fourth NPC produced a series of compromises in the choice of personnel and in official documents adopted. But it is clear that the election of Deng Xiaoping at the Plenum to be a vice-chairman of the Party and a member of the Standing Committee of the Politburo, and his confirmation by the Congress as the ranking vice-premier, as well as other appointments, gave the balance of power to the veteran political leaders at least in government administration. Similarly, the operational significance of Zhou's report on the work of the government lies in its emphasis on building a firm foundation for "an independent and relative comprehensive industrial and economic system" by 1980 and "accomplishment of comprehensive modernization of agriculture, industry, national defence, and science and technology before the end of the century." In political terms, Zhou may have endeavoured to build up a collective leadership under Mao and a package of compromises in policies which would, he hoped, prevent the developing inner-Party struggle from erupting into an open break after the death of Mao and himself. Although Mao did not attend either of the two meetings, many of the results must have had his general endorsement, or were not strongly opposed by him.

But Mao probably wanted to balance the emphasis on rapid economic growth with all its social and political consequences by underscoring the need to avoid "revisionism," and to prevent the restoration of the "capitalist system" by further eliminating the existing socio-economic inequalities. Thus, on 26 December 1974, the same date on which he approved Zhou's plan for a new Party constitution and the list of major appointments, he issued a series of "important instructions on the question of theory," which were then made public, beginning with the February 9th issue of the *People's Daily*, just three weeks after the conclusion of

16. Article by Gao Ning, in *Guangming ribao*, 14 November 1976, p. 1.
17. *Guangming ribao*, 2 December 1976, p.3.
18. Gao Ning in *Guangming ribao*, 14 November 1976.

the first session of the Fourth National People's Congress. In these instructions, Mao stressed the importance of "exercising dictatorship over the bourgeoisie." He noted that:

> Our country at present practices a commodity system; the wage system is unequal too, as in the eight-grade wage scale, and so forth. Under the dictatorship of the proletariat such things can only be restricted.[19]

He also pointed out: "Lenin said, '[S]mall production engenders capitalism and the bourgeoisie continuously, daily, hourly, spontaneously and on a mass scale.' This also occurs among a section of the workers and a section of the Party members. Both within the ranks of the proletariat and among the personnel of state organs, there are people who follow the bourgeois style of life."[20]

While the veteran Party leaders were pre-occupied with the formulation and implementation of concrete policies in a variety of fields, particularly scientific research and factory management, the "gang of four" and their followers made a systematic effort to give radical interpretations to Mao's instructions and to draw out the operational significance of these radicalized interpretations. The ideas expressed in the published articles formed the basis of a series of unpublicized attacks on the veteran Party leaders. The limitation of space does not allow me to describe the political struggle in any detail, but these writings do contain some interesting ideas. The published counterattacks launched by the Party veterans after the purge of the "gang of four" show how the latter attempted to rely on the writings of Mao Zedong to legitimize their concrete actions. It is to these theoretical formulations and general policy orientations that we shall turn our attention.

The central theoretical problem which the "gang of four" and their followers tried to solve is to explain in Marxist terms how classes and class struggle can exist after the means of production have been socialized and owned by the state or the collective units, i.e. after the economic base of classes—the private ownership of the means of production—has been destroyed. Up to this time, the existence of classes and class struggle had been explained: first by the remnants of the "feudal" and bourgeois classes and their ideological influence, and secondly by those in power in

19. The English translation can be found in *Peking Review*, 28 February 1975, p. 5. The term "only" as well as the original Chinese phrase is ambiguous. It can be interpreted as "must be" or as "merely" restricted, but not eliminated. It is perhaps highly significant that Mao issued his instructions on the study of theory on the same day after he had listened to Zhou's report on the preparatory work on convening the Fourth National People's Congress. On 23 and 24 December he warned Jiang Qing, "Don't form a faction. Those who formed factions will fall down." *Hongqi*, No. 2 (1977), pp. 13–14.

20. *Peking Review*, 28 February 1975, p. 5.

the Party taking the capitalist road, who were designated as "representatives" or "agents" of the bourgeoisie. In a comment dated 29 January 1965,* on a report concerning the Socialist Education Movement, Mao applied the term "class" to the category of "bureaucratic officials" and declared that "the class of bureaucratic officials [on the one hand] and the working class and poor and lower middle peasants [on the other hand] are two classes in sharp opposition."[21] But this statement by Mao had not been officially published or quoted in major editorials or documents. Standing alone, moreover, it suggests that instead of the economic base, political power and the relationship between superiors and their subordinates, which constitute, in Marxist terms, a part of the superstructure, are the only basis of classes and class struggle. Without abandoning these old explanations, the ultra-leftists endeavoured to find the basis for "newly engendered bourgeois elements" or the "new bourgeoisie" in the socialist system, and more specifically, in the continued existence of "bourgeois right" in a socialist society. They found a convenient point of departure in the three aspects in the relations of production, as generally defined by Marxists: first, ownership of the means of production; secondly, the form of distribution; and thirdly, relations between men. But they gave these familiar notions and the interconnection between their empirical referents a new twist. According to Zhang Chunqiao, public ownership of the means of production took two forms in industry, agriculture and commerce in China: ownership by the whole people (i.e. the state) and collective ownership. While state ownership predominates in industry and commerce, collective ownership held sway in agriculture. He asserts: "the non-existence of bourgeois right in the realm of the system of ownership in a socialist system, as conceived by Marx and Lenin, implies the conversion of all the means of production into common property of the whole society."[22] Moreover, private plots and private trade at rural fairs still exist in China.

Most significantly Zhang followed Mao's modification of Engels' formulation of historical materialism and adopted the same pattern of rea-

* Mao may have made this comment in late 1964. See *infra* pp. 134–35.

21. "Mao Zedong sixiang wansui" (April 1967). This compilation is different from the now generally available Chinese version with the same title. (*Current Background*, 891 p. 49.)

22. Chang Ch'un-ch'iao, "On Exercising All-round Dictatorship over the Bourgeoisie," *Peking Review*, 4 April 1975, p. 7. Zhang did not tell us how Marx and Lenin conceived of a socialist society and how this conception is related to his own conclusion. Zhang is later accused of claiming that the "thought of Zhang Chunqiao "represents the fourth milestone in the development of Marxist thought, following Marx and Engels, Lenin and Stalin, and Mao Zedong. Zhang's concern with equality and "bourgeois right" went back at least as far as 1958. An article of his on the subject was published on 13 October 1958 in the *Renmin ribao*. The editor noted that "Zhang's article is basically correct but somewhat one-sided." This article with the editor's note is reproduced in *Pangu* (Hong Kong), April 1975, pp. 68.

soning to analyse the interconnection between the system of ownership and the remaining two aspects of relations of production. Zhang wrote:

> It is perfectly correct for people to attach importance to the decisive role of the system of ownership in the relations of production. But it is incorrect to attach no importance to whether the issue of the system of ownership has been resolved *in form or in reality*, to the reaction exerted on the system of ownership by the two other aspects of the relations of production—the relations between men and the form of distribution—and to the reaction exerted on the economic base by the superstructure; *these two aspects and the superstructure may play a decisive role under given conditions.* [23]

This assertion that the relations between men and the form of distribution can play a decisive role after the system of ownership has been nationalized or collectivized is absolutely essential for Zhang's purpose. For this formula enabled him to underscore the decisive importance of the fact that in China, "bourgeois right . . . is still prevalent to a serious extent in the relations between men and holds a dominant position in distribution." In so far as the system of distribution and exchange of commodities were concerned, the ultra-leftists referred specifically to the eight-grade system of wages and more generally to "material incentives."

Theoretically, this assertion about the existence of "bourgeois right" was buttressed by quotations from Marx and Lenin which were widely publicized in the official media. [24] Whereas Marx considered the existence of bourgeois right in the socialist society as inevitable birthmarks of the old society and envisaged its gradual disappearance, and whereas Lenin thought that bourgeois right can exist without the bourgeoisie, [25] the ultra-leftists in China pointed to bourgeois right and the socialist economic sys-

---

23. [Chang Ch'un-ch'iao, "On Exercising All-round Dictatorship over the Bourgeoisie," p.7] Emphasis added. Politically speaking, this is very skilful writing which links his new formulation with Mao's familiar formula. But, in terms of Marxist theory, it raises more questions than it answers. Zhang's opponents later pointed out that Zhang's article did not once mention the development of socialist production. *Guangming ribao*, 30 November 1976, p. 4. Another and simpler statement is the following one: "[I]n the process of production, the relations between people and the form of distribution are determined by and react upon the system of ownership, and they played a decisive role under given conditions." "Dictatorship of the proletariat and the renegade Lin Piao," *Peking Review*, 27 June 1975, p. 8.

24. The most relevant quotations are drawn from Karl Marx, *Critique of the Gotha Programme*. Actually, Marx in precisely this work criticized "vulgar socialism" for considering and treating distribution as independent of the means of production and "hence the presentation of socialism as turning principally on distribution." See David Resnick, "Crude communisin and revolution," in *American Political Science Review*, December 1977, p. 1137.

25. Lenin observes: "It follows that under Communism, there remains for a time not only bourgeois right but even the bourgeois state—*without the bourgeoisie!*" Quoted in *Peking Review*, 28 February 1975, p. 9. Emphasis added.

tem which retains it as the source of a new bourgeoisie. Since this state of affairs cannot be changed in a short period, class struggle between the bourgeoisie and the proletariat is inevitable and the proletariat must exercise "all-round dictatorship over the bourgeoisie" to prevent them from seizing power and from restoring capitalism.

As for the "relations between people," the ultra-leftists charged that under Lin Biao and, by implication, under the veteran Party leaders, these had become "relations of buying and selling of commodities." " . . . [P]olitics has become something like a big business transaction. . . . If you pledge loyalty to me, I will offer you higher official posts."[26] Thus, in the writings of the ultra-leftists in China, "the relations between people" become more than the relations between economic classes as these are defined by other Marxists.

Equally important is the Chinese ultra-leftists' distinction between the form and actual content of the system of ownership. Chi Heng wrote: ". . . if the revisionist line should become predominant in a unit, this unit would change its nature, in which case, the ownership would be socialist only in form but capitalist in reality."[27] Referring to the "Lin Biao anti-Party clique," Yao Wenyuan wrote: "in units and departments under their domination and control they turned socialist public ownership into Lin Diao anti-Party clique private property."[*] Whereas Chi Heng was referring to factories and enterprises, Yao's terms "units" and "departments" were applicable to the government, the army, and the Party as well.

As the leading theoretician, Zhang Chunqiao offered an explanation of this distinction between the form and actual content of the system of ownership and the paradox that a unit may be publicly owned in form but capitalist in reality. After having referred to Mao's dictum that the superstructure may play a decisive role under given circumstances, Zhang immediately observed that "the correctness or incorrectness of the ideological and political line, and the control of leadership in the hands of one class or another, decide which class owns a factory in reality."[28] These basic ideas were then linked with other revised concepts. Together these revisions formed the basis of a programme to encourage the workers at the lowest levels to rebel against veteran and middle aged Party cadres

26. "Dictatorship of the proletariat," p. 8. According to the ultra-leftists, the relations between the people should be governed exclusively by the lofty spirit of "utter devotion to others without thought of self."

27. Chih Heng [Chi Heng], "Conscientiously study the theory of the dictatorship of the proletariat," *Peking Review*, 14 February 1975, p. 8.

* Yao Wen-yuan, "On the Social Basis of Lin Piao Anti-Party Clique," *Peking Review*, 7 March 1975, p. 9.

28. Chang [Zhang], "On exercising all-round dictatorship," p. 7. To the extent that "control" and "own" are indistinguishable, that part of Zhang's statement referring to "the control of leadership" is tautological.

who controlled the various units and departments. A number of methods, including slowdowns and strikes, were used in many factories, railroads and enterprises.

Another theoretical weapon of the "gang of four" was the slogan raised by Mao in attacking Peng Dehuai and his followers in 1959 and cited by Yao Wenyuan in his signed article published on 1 March 1975. Mao said: "at present, the main danger lies in empiricism."[29] According to a later account, Zhang Chunqiao, in his capacity as the director of the Political Department of the PLA, praised on the same day Yao's article at a conference held by the PLA. He observed that opposition to empiricism "has realistic meaning."[30] He suggested that opposition to empiricism be considered the "key link" or "the main theme."[31] The operational meaning of this definition of the situation can be found in the ultra-leftists' remark that not only old cadres but also new cadres are influenced by "empiricism." It is made even clearer by the subsequent charge that the ultra-leftists "wanted to put the label of 'empiricism' on a large group of old and new cadres as well as cadres of peasant and worker origins who had been nurtured and trained by our Party in the protracted revolutionary struggle, who firmly upheld Chairman Mao's revolutionary line, and who had had rich *practical experience*."[32] Their intention was to "criticize and overthrow" them all. They were accused of conspiring "to overthrow a large group of responsible comrades in the Party, the government and the army at the Centre and localities." They were said to have criticized many cadres for "following the established ways and adhering to the old," for "resting on the laurels of their seniority." They called the latter "bourgeois democrats who relied only on their own experience to manage affairs," and who were not willing to push forward the socialist revolution.[33] They noted that the army was run by "old fellows."[34]

Unfortunately for the ultra-leftists, their definition of the current situa-

29. Yao Wen-yuan, "On the social basis of the Lin Piao anti-Party clique," *Peking Review*, 7 March 1975, p. 9.

30. *Guangming ribao*, 19 November 1976, p. 1. This is an awkward and literal translation of the Chinese phrase, "*you xianshi yiyi.*" It can perhaps be loosely rendered as "has operational meaning."

31. The term "key link" is used in the official English publication to translate the Chinese character, "*gang.*" The term "*gang*" can also be translated as "the main theme." Mao himself explained that "*gang*" is the "main theme." *Renmin ribao*, 7 February 1977, p. 1.

32. *Guangming ribao*, 14 November 1976, p. 1. Emphasis added.

33. Jiang Qing is reported to have said that "[M]ore than 75 per cent of the old cadres inevitably turn from members of the democratic faction into members of the faction of the capitalist roaders." *Guangming ribao*, 14 December 1976, p. 4. (Article by Zhang Junbo.)

34. *Ibid.* 19 November 1976, p. 1. See also the revealing article under the by-line of the Theoretical Group of the Military Training Department of the General Staff in the *Renmin ribao*, 4 December 1976, p. 2.

tion did not receive the wholehearted support of Mao. Mao's own ambivalence towards the ultra-leftists, his endeavour to strike a balance between them and the veteran leaders, and his attempt to prevent an open break were revealed in a comment written by Mao on 23 April 1975. He declared: "The correct way to raise the problem is opposition to revisionism, including opposition to both empiricism and dogmatism. Both [empiricism and dogmatism] represent a revision of Marxism-Leninism. Do not raise only one item and allow the other item to get away."[35] In his long career, Mao had opposed both "empiricism" and "dogmatism" and at one time or another he considered one or the other as the "main danger." His refusal to endorse the radicals' definition suggests that he had not made up his mind.

Another theoretical concept which the ultra-leftists had stressed as the basis for their attack on the veteran leaders was opposition to the "theory of productive forces." This was the theory which was used by the Cultural Revolutionary Group to deal a devastating blow against Liu Shaoqi. It was, according to the ultra-leftists, embodied in the following remarks made by Liu in the mid-1950s: "[I]n our country, the question of which will win out, socialism or capitalism, has now been settled," "class struggle is over," and "now, the main task of the Chinese people is to develop the productive forces as rapidly as possible."[36] This theory was restated by the ultra-leftists as follows:

> . . . the relations of production were no longer in contradiction with the productive forces, and the socialist revolution on the economic front had ended; the superstructure was no longer in contradiction with the economic base, and the socialist revolution on the political and ideological fronts was entirely unnecessary; classes were eliminated, the bourgeois no longer existed, class struggle was over, and it was quite enough for the working class and other labouring people simply to immerse themselves in production and professional work.[37]

To oppose this theory, the ultra-leftists again borrowed a leaf from Mao: "[T]he productive forces generally play the principal and decisive

35. *Ibid.* 19 November 1976, p. 1. In another statement, Mao said: "As I see it, those who criticize empiricism are themselves empiricists." This statement is more critical of the ultra-leftists; but no data is given for this statement. It is not known whether it was really directed at the ultra-leftists. *Renmin ribao*, 28 November 1976, p. 1. Mao's criticism of the ultra-leftists found expression in an article under the by-line of Li Jun in *Hongqi*, No. 6 (1975), p. 9. This article criticized both "empiricism" and "dogmatism." Mao's support of the veteran Party leaders was also reflected in the article in the same issue which stressed stability and unity and the unified leadership of Party committees and governmental organs at all levels.

36. Hung Hsueh-ping, "The essence of 'theory of productive forces' is to oppose proletarian revolution," *Peking Review*, 19 September 1969, p. 7.

37. *Ibid.*

role. . . . [But the relations of production] react upon the productive forces, promote or hinder their development, and play the decisive role under certain conditions." In this manner, changes in relations of production were given priority by the ultra-leftists over the development of productive forces. Moreover, the ultra-leftists downgraded the existential and theoretical importance of "forces of production" by advancing a peculiar definition of the economic base: "[T]he economic base refers to the economic system at a certain stage of social development, that is, the *sum total of the relations of production.*"[38] This revision of Marxism by the device of a simple definition excludes "forces of production" as a part of the economic base.

These rather abstract ideas formed the justification of slogans and actions with serious consequences not only for economic growth but also for political stability, particularly after February 1976. According to their opponents, the ultra-leftists said that "when the revolution is handled well, production will naturally go up."[39] To achieve the goals of their revolution, they wanted to destroy the rules and regulations adopted to manage the various enterprises. They also wanted to dispense with normal procedures in production. They urged the workers "not to produce for the wrong [ideological and political] line," "not to produce for the faction of those taking the capitalist road."[40] They raised the slogans: "[D]o not fear strikes, do not fear stoppages of production, and do not fear social disorders," "[I]n such a country as China, a little disorder will bring about a lively atmosphere,"[41] "[W]e would rather have socialist low rate of growth than capitalist high rate of growth,"[42] and "we would rather stop production for two years than stop class struggle for one moment." They are also accused of saying that "to disrupt the production of one factory is to put a knot around the neck of the faction in authority," and that "the loss belongs to the state, the responsibility belongs to the faction in authority, and the power belongs to us."[43] With regard to the leadership group of cadres, managers, experts, and knowledgeable persons, they issued the call: "[O]verthrow those who can be overthrown; chase away those who

38. Hung Ou, "Economic base and superstructure," *Peking Review*, 15 August 1975, p. 7. Contrast this definition with the following sentence of Etienne Balibar: ". . . it, the second form of antagonism is *inside the economic base,* typical of a determinate mode of production, and its terms are called, 'the level of the productive forces,' and 'the relations of production'." Louis Althusser and Etienne Balibar, *Reading Capital* (London: 1975), p. 203.

39. *Guangming ribao*, 30 November 1976, p. 6.

40. Article under the by-line of the Great Criticism Group of the State Planning Commission, *Hongqi*, No. 12 (1976), p. 47.

41. *Dagong bao* (Hong Kong), 27 January 1977, p. 1.

42. *Ibid.* 3 December 1976, p. 2. Zhang Chunqiao is charged with having said: "[D]o not fear a decrease in growth rate. It is all right to have a lower rate of growth." *Huaqiao ribao* (New York), 18 February 1977, p. 1.

43. *Hongqi*, No. 12 (1976), p. 48.

cannot be overthrown; as for those who cannot be chased away, attack them until they get sick; attack those who do not get sick until they fear us."[44]

More specifically, the ultra-leftists attacked the management system of the Daqing oilfield as one that "controls, curbs, and oppresses" the workers. They characterized it as merely a model of production, implying that it was not a model of revolution. They attacked the cadres running the railroads for "lowering their head to pull the cart rather than raising their head to look at the road," for allowing "running the trains on time to take command" of all other work, and "for taking the road of the white experts."[45] These charges find support in the strikes, work stoppages, drop in production, and local disorders which were reported in newspapers outside China in 1975 and 1976.

In the field of agriculture, Zhang Chunqiao was, to say the least, sceptical about the movement to learn from Dazhai. He is now accused of advocating the development of the rural areas around Shanghai as a model, and of criticizing certain slogans raised by Dazhai as "reactionary," and as "typical theory of forces of production." He called for an item by item criticism of Hua Guofeng's report on increasing the number of Dazhai-type counties, delivered in mid-October 1975. Jiang Qing is reported to have said that, "Dazhai has been influenced by revisionism."[46]

Mao's attitude towards the ultra-leftists' attempt to push revolutionary changes in the management of the enterprises at the expense of economic growth is even now not entirely clear. But we do know that Mao personally issued a document on China's steel and iron industry on 4 June 1975. This statement placed its emphasis on the political and ideological aspects of managing the enterprise. It called for the examination of seven aspects of work:

> Whether or not the ideological and political line is correct; whether or not the movement to study the theory of the dictatorship of the proletariat has really been developed; whether or not the masses are fully mobilized; whether or not a strong leadership core has been established; whether or not the bourgeois characteristics in the management of the enterprise had been overcome; whether or not the Party's policies have been implemented; and whether or not an effective blow has been struck against the disruptive activities of the class enemy. In sum, whether or not the task of consolidating the dictatorship of the proletariat has been implemented at the basic level.[47]

---

44. *Huaqiao ribao* (New York), 18 February 1977, p. 1. For a different translation, see *Peking Review*, 11 February 1977, p. 13.

45. *Guangming ribao*, 22 November 1976, p. 2. See also *ibid.* 6 December 1976, p. 3.

46. Article under the by-line of the Big Criticism Group of the Ministry of Agriculture and Forestry, *Guangming ribao*, 20 January 1977, p. 1.

47. *Huaqiao ribao* (New York), 28 February 1977, p. 1.

The opponents of the ultra-leftists now claim that Mao's document dealt a serious blow to the "gang of four." But it is also likely that the ultra-leftists derived strong support from this document. What is certain is that both sides claimed the support of the chairman but gave his statements diametrically opposed interpretations. Each side apparently defined the "task of consolidating the dictatorship of the proletariat" in very different terms. For the ultra-leftists, it meant radical changes in the management system and the removal of the experienced leadership groups regardless of the consequences for economic production and political stability and oblivious to the real needs of the people. For the veteran political leaders it meant the consolidation and gradual development of the present political and economic system as a whole.

In the name of giving equal opportunity to the workers and peasants for education and opposing the creation of an "intellectual aristocracy," the ultra-leftists succeeded in blocking the endeavours of the educators to maintain a minimum standard for admission to institutions of higher learning by reintroducing and perfecting a new system of examinations. Zhang Chunqiao argued, in November 1975, that "I would rather have a labourer without culture than to have an exploiter, an 'intellectual aristocrat,' with culture."[48] He is now accused of advocating the elimination of education for the sake of transmission of knowledge and propagating the idea that "it is useless to study." The ultra-leftists also opposed efforts on the part of scientists to put more stress on basic research in order to correct the overemphasis on the practical application of science.[49]

Since the ultra-leftists apparently believed that the introduction of foreign technology would strengthen directly the authority of scientists, engineers and managers and indirectly the political position of the veteran Party leaders who supported the latter, they opposed this policy in the name of the principle of self-reliance. They opposed the export of crude oil in order to obtain foreign exchange to finance the import of technology. The export of oil depended on the rapid expansion of oil production, which would strengthen the hands of the experts and the veteran Party leaders. The ultra-leftists charged that the export of oil and other raw materials represented nothing less than selling out "national sovereignty" and giving away precious resources to please foreign nations at the expense of domestic consumption.[50] They further condemned the export of

48. *Guangming ribao*, 23 November 1976, p. 1. Article by the Great Criticism Group of the Ministry of Education.

49. *Dagong bao*, 16 January 1977, p. 2. Article by the eminent physicist Dr. Zhou Peiyuan. Science and higher education by their very nature contain an element of elitism. In the name of checking and destroying elitism, the ultra-leftists were also destroying science and higher education.

50. One of the most revealing articles giving a retrospective account of the attacks by the

oil as a measure which would help the developed world and hurt the Third World. When the export of oil and raw materials were combined with the importation of advanced technology and plants China would return to the status of a semi-colonial country. They put the 19th-century label "foreign affairs faction" on the veteran political leaders in an attempt to discredit them.

III

While the ultra-leftists were formulating the theory of "bourgeois right" and "all-round dictatorship over the bourgeoisie," the veteran Party leaders pre-occupied themselves with the solution of the concrete problems of industrial management and production, science and technology, education, and foreign policy and trade. While they did not oppose the restriction of "bourgeois right," they tended to adopt a gradual approach. In this respect, Deng Xiaoping, the newly appointed vice-premier and vice-chairman of the Party, probably went further than most other leaders. In his usual forceful and outspoken way, Deng was reported to have said on 5 March 1975: "[I]n order to limit bourgeois right, there must be a material foundation. Without it, how can we limit bourgeois right?"[51] Deng said in June: "[N]ow, everything is called bourgeois right. A greater amount of reward for a greater amount of labour is a correct principle. How can we call it bourgeois right?"[52] At one time or another, he also said that to use revolutionary measures to limit bourgeois right was a policy "fundamentally divorced from reality" and tantamount to an attempt "to establish Communism now."[53]

Apparently taking advantage of Mao's refusal to back the ultra-leftists' designation of empiricism as the principal danger and of Mao's reiteration at a Politburo meeting on 3 May 1975 of the need for unity,[54] Deng di-

---

ultra-leftists is Kuo Chi, "Foreign trade: why the 'gang of four' created confusion," *Peking Review*, 25 February 1977, pp. 16–18.

51. Gong Xiaowen, "Deng Xiaoping and the twenty articles," *Xuexi yu pipan*, No. 6 (1975), p. 15.

52. *Ibid.* p. 16.

53. Article under the by-line of Zhuang Nan, *ibid.* No. 3 (1976), p. 6.

54. According to the retrospective account after the purge of the "gang of four," Mao reiterated the basic principle of "three do's and three don'ts," i.e. "[P]ractice Marxism-Leninism and not revisionism; unite and don't split; be open and above board and don't intrigue and conspire." He added a warning to Jiang Qing and her followers: "[D]on't function as a gang of four, don't do it any more, why do you keep doing it?" This account also quotes Mao's instruction that "if this problem of functioning as a gang of four is not settled in the first half of this year, it should be settled in the second half; if not this year, then next year; if not next year, then the year after." Joint editorial, 25 October 1976, trans. in *Peking Review*, 29 October 1976, p. 15. See also *Qishi niandai* (Hong Kong), February 1977, p. 10.

The Chinese sentence can be rendered as either "should be settled" or "can be settled." If the latter translation is used, it suggests that Mao was trying to counsel restraint on the

rected his subordinates to push forward the drafting of a document entitled, "Certain problems in accelerating industrial development."[55] On 18 July Deng appointed Hu Yaobang, the former general secretary of the Communist Youth League who fell from power during the Cultural Revolution, to be vice-president of the Academy of Sciences. Hu, with the support of Deng, completed on 11 August, a first draft of another important document, entitled, "Outline report on the work of the Academy of Sciences." At the "report meeting," Deng implied that this document was applicable to the scientific and technological personnel of the whole country.[56] An un-named top official in the Ministry of Education began preparation in early October to draft an outline report in the field of education along the same line as that for the Academy of Sciences.[57] Most importantly, Deng's subordinates followed his suggestions and basically completed a draft of a document entitled, "On the general programme for all works of the whole Party and the whole nation."

On the basis of the ultra-leftists' attacks on these three documents,[58] the following points should be noted. First, Deng and his subordinates indirectly criticized their opponents' programme as a case of "Leftist opportunism," like that advocated by Wang Ming, and as "ultra-Leftism" like that of Lin Biao.[59] This designation stands in sharp contrast to the line adopted after the purge of the "gang of four" according to which they are "ultra-rightists." The political meaning of this contrast is explained later.

Secondly, Deng raised Mao's directives on unity and stability and on the development of the national economy to the same level as his directive on the study of the theory of the dictatorship of the proletariat. He desig-

veteran Party leaders while issuing a warning against the "gang of four." At that time, Mao's view on unity is expressed in *Hongqi*, No. 6 (1976), pp. 1–9. Apparently, Deng was also taking advantage of the severe criticism of Jiang Qing at the Politburo meetings during July-September of 1975 for her interview with Roxane Witke in 1972 to push forward his programme. *Qishi niandai*, March 1977, p. 7.

55. The process of drafting this document lasted six months with the final draft completed 25 October. It was intended to be discussed at a national conference at the end of October. But the conference was never held and the draft was stillborn. See Gong, "Deng Xiaoping and the twenty articles," p. 19.

56. Article under the by-line of Kang Li and Yan Feng, *Xuexi yu pipan*, No. 4 (1976), p. 24. See also *Qishi niandai*, March 1976, p. 12.

57. *Xuexi yu pipan*, No. 4 (1976), p. 25.

58. For a detailed report of the contents of these three documents, see the article by Qi Xin, in *Qishi niandai*, March 1977, pp. 9–12. This article was written on the basis of the documents circulated in China after the fall of the "gang of four." The full texts of the "General programme," and "Certain problems in accelerating industrial development" are reproduced in the appendix of Qi Xin, *Sirenbang shijian tansuo* (Hong Kong: The Seventies Publishing Company, 1977), as are excerpts from the "Outline report." *Ming bao* published a text of the twenty articles, by instalments, on 21–29 May 1977.

59. Qi Xin, *Sirenbang shijian tansuo*, pp. 147–48.

nated them together as forming the general programme for all works in the Party, army, and nation not only at the present time but also in the next 25 years. This definition of the general programme downgraded the importance of the "study of the theory" which had contributed to the increased influence of the ultra-leftists. He also tried to limit the applicability of the theory of class struggle by an interpretation of Mao's 1962 slogan regarding the three great movements of class struggle, struggle for production, and struggle for scientific experiment. One passage of "On the general programme . . ." reads:

> Even if we have truly grasped the characteristics and laws of class struggle and solved the specific contradictions in class struggle, this is not tantamount to having grasped the characteristics and laws of the struggle for production and the struggle for scientific experiment, nor to having solved the specific contradictions.[60]

Thirdly, Deng and his subordinates attacked the ultra-leftists for separating politics and economics, revolution and production from each other, talking only about politics and not about economics, only about revolution but not production. Finally, Deng and his followers confronted realistically the "crisis" in the sphere of science and technology, education, and industrial management.[61] "They" were reported to have said that if their proposed programmes were not adopted, "all of us would one day be all finished."[62] Thus, they expressed a willingness to "risk their old age" in order to work out and implement their programme. They boasted that they had put aside all worldly considerations, that they did not fear being labelled "[landlords'] contingents returning to their own villages,"[63] or "royalists attempting a restoration," and that they were not afraid of being overthrown.

Deng's and his followers' concrete programmes were relatively straightforward. In the sphere of economic development they advocated the introduction of advanced technology, machinery, and equipment from foreign countries. To accelerate the development of coal and oil they would use deferred or instalment payment and sign long-term contracts with foreign countries under which the latter would supply a fixed number of coal and oil fields in China with complete sets of modern equipment suitable to China's needs and China would repay them with coal and oil. In industrial management, they advocated the re-establishment of the "responsi-

60. *Xuexi yu pipan*, No. 4 (1976), pp. 16–17; see also Qi Xin, *Sirenbang shijian tansuo*, p. 151.

61. For a vivid description, see *ibid. passim*, particularly pp. 194–200.

62. *Xuexi yu pipan*, No. 4 (1976), p. 21.

63. According to Qi Xin, what Deng actually said was "the proletariat's contingent returning to their own villages." *Qishi niandai*, March 1977.

bility system" under which every kind of work and every post, as well as every cadre, every worker, and every one of the technical personnel, would have clearly defined responsibility and this would find expression in the system of rules and regulations. They sought to establish a strong and independent management and command system to run production with the Party committee exercising only general unified leadership over important policies and refraining from the direct handling of matters large and small. They opposed "absolute egalitarianism" and underscored distribution according to labour. They proposed the implementation of "a system of regular promotions and increase in wages."

This clear emphasis on rapid sustained economic growth is supplemented by an equally strong stress on the rapid development of science and technology. To justify this policy, they quoted or misquoted Marx to the effect that the "productive forces consist, in the first instance, of science and technology."[64] They also cited the view that "philosophy cannot replace natural science."[65] They suggested that in the field of science and technology, the dictatorship of the proletariat should not be mentioned.[66] If non-scientists were put into positions of leadership in research institutions, they ought to be those who were enthusiastic about scientific research. The Party secretaries in research institutes who did not understand the professional work involved were encouraged to follow the advice of the directors of the institutes. Deng was reported to have said that, "[W]hy should we fear the presence of a few white experts? They should be protected and praised."[67] The intellectuals "are also labourers." "In a state, science and technology should take the lead." All these slogans, policies and remarks were directed at a "crisis" situation in which "the role of the specialists is underestimated," people "do not dare" to study technology, to read works in foreign languages, and to read professional literature. In some institutes in the Academy of Sciences, scientists could do research work "only four half-days out of a six-day work week."[68] In addition to the implementation of the reforms to overcome the crisis in science and technology, Deng and his subordinates also proposed rectification in the fields of industry, agriculture, communication, and transportation, finance and trade, culture, education, health, literature and arts, army and the Party.

It is clear that by mid-October 1975, the reform programmes of Deng and his subordinates were running into trouble. The December issue of *Hongqi* published a lead article entitled, "The direction of the revolution in education must not be tampered with." It criticized the idea that in the

64. Article under the by-line of Yan Feng, in *Xuexi yu pipan*, No. 2 (1976), p. 3.
65. *Xuexi yu pipan*, No. 4 (1976), p. 23.
66. *Ibid.* p. 24.
67. *Ibid.*
68. Qi Xin, *Sirenbang shijian tansuo*, p.195.

field of natural sciences, the best students should be selected to go to college directly without first working two years as workers and peasants. It attacked the view that transmission and development of knowledge should have the highest priority in education. It repudiated the charge that the revolution in education had been carried to excess and that the quality of university education was not as good as that of the technical middle schools in the past.

The nearly fatal blow against Deng was dealt by Mao himself in a statement cited in the 1976 New Year's Day editorial by the *Renmin ribao*, *Hongqi*, and *Jiefangjun bao*. Mao said: "Unity and stability do not mean writing off class struggle; class struggle is the key link and everything else hinges on it."[69] After the death of Premier Zhou Enlai on 8 January Hua Guofeng was nominated personally by Mao as the acting premier and was also put in charge of the works of the Politburo.[70] Apparently, Deng no longer functioned as vice-premier, but Zhang Chunqiao was also passed over in favour of Hua, who maintained a close relationship with the veteran Party leaders and had serious conflicts with the "gang of four"[71] In the next two months, Deng's programme in education, science and technology, industrial development and foreign trade, etc., were roundly criticized without naming him. The widely publicized and unprecedented demonstration in the memory of Zhou Enlai on 5 April led to the dismissal of Deng from all posts both inside and outside the Party, and the appointment of Hua as first vice-chairman of the Central Committee and premier of the State Council. The anomaly of allowing Deng to keep his Party membership while defining his problem as one of antagonistic contradiction did not escape the notice of outside observers.

Two points of theoretical interest emerged during this period of criticism of Deng. First, Mao himself used the term "bourgeois right," which had been popularized by the ultra-leftists in their interpretation of these directives. Instead of saying that there were representatives of the bourgeoisie in the Party, he now asserted that "The bourgeoisie are right in the Party." This statement reads in full:

> With the socialist revolution, they themselves [Deng and people like him] come under fire. At the time of the co-operative transformation of agriculture, there were people in the Party [who] opposed it, and when it comes

69. *Hongqi* No. 1 (1976), p. 6; *Peking Review*, 2 January 1976, p. 9. The limitation of space does not allow me to mention other statements.

70. *Renmin ribao* editorial, reprinted in *Guangming ribao*, 22 December 1976, p. 1.

71. Hua Guofeng's important speech at the Conference to develop Dazhai-type counties held from mid-September to mid-October 1975, was not printed in *Hongqi*. It is now charged that Yao Wenyuan was responsible for this decision and that the ultra-leftists criticized Hua's speech as placing too much emphasis on production and as having a touch of revisionism. Zhang's disappointment and resentment were expressed in a poem widely publicized now.

to criticizing the bourgeois right, they resent it. You [referring to Party members] are making the socialist revolution and yet do not know where the bourgeoisie is. It is right in the Communist Party—those in power taking the capitalist road. The capitalist roaders are still on the capitalist road.[72]

The key sentence, "[I]t [the bourgeoisie] is right in the Communist Party—those in power taking the capitalist road," can be interpreted in two different ways with very different political implications. As the veteran political leaders were to insist, the sentence should be read as a whole. The term "bourgeoisie" merely refers to "those in power taking the capitalist road" and its meaning is specified by the latter phrase. Thus interpreted, it is not different in meaning from the frequently used phrase "the representatives of the bourgeoisie." In contrast, the ultra-leftists often use the first half of the sentence ("The bourgeoisie is right in the Communist Party") alone without the specifying phrase.[73] It is now alleged that in a publication controlled by the ultra-leftists there is the following statement: "Chairman Mao says that the bourgeoisie is right in the Communist Party; we believe that the term refers to class as an entity."[74] This concept of a bourgeois class existing within a Party as an entity is an anomaly, as it is now pointed out. But it does not necessarily conflict with the prevailing and accepted point of view that in certain conditions the superstructure can play the principal and decisive role and that the ideological and political line decides everything. It thus became an additional block in the theoretical edifice of the ultra-leftists. It was used as the term of ultimate opprobrium applied to the veteran political leaders. To outside observers, it is clear that in the interpretation given by the ultra-leftists, the word "bourgeoisie" was transformed from a term with fairly clear empirical referents within a given theoretical tradition into a condensation symbol with intended political impact on the mass mind.

Secondly, Mao's statement using the phrase "the class of bureaucratic officials" was published officially in its entirety for the first time and with an important twist in the joint editorial on 1 July 1976, commemorating the 55th anniversary of the founding of the Party.

The order of the three paragraphs of Mao's comment made in 1964 on a report was changed so that the second paragraph of one sentence became the first paragraph. This twist highlighted the sharp opposition between

72. *Hongqi*, No. 4 (1976), pp. 1, 15. The dash in the English version is a comma in the Chinese.

73. For example, in the important joint editorial by the *Renmin ribao*, *Hongqi*, and *Jie-fangjun bao*, *Hongqi*, No. 7 (1976), p. 3.

74. Xiang Qun, "The complete reversal of the relations between the enemy and ourselves," *Renmin ribao*, 4 March 1977, p. 1. The theoretically interesting article by Zhi Feng, *Guangming ribao*, 9 May 1977, p. 2 arrived too late to be included in this article.

the bureaucratic officials on the one hand and the working class together with the poor and lower-middle peasants on the other rather than the questions of management and socialist education. Then, in explaining Mao's statement that the bourgeoisie exists "right in the Communist Party," the joint editorial reads:

> In 1964, Chairman Mao pointed out in a directive concerning the socialist educational movement: "The class of bureaucratic officials on the one hand and the working class together with the poor and lower middle peasants on the other are two classes sharply opposed to each other." Chairman Mao further pointed out, "Management itself is a matter of socialist education. If the managerial staff do not join the workers on the shop floor, work, study, and live with them and modestly learn one or more skills from them, then they will find themselves locked in acute class struggle with the working class all their lives and in the end are bound to be regarded as the bourgeoisie and overthrown by them. If they do not learn any technical skills and remain outsiders for a long time, they would not be able to do management well either. Those in the dark are in no way to light the way for others." Chairman Mao also stated: "Those leading cadres who are taking the capitalist road have turned or are turning into bourgeois elements sucking the blood of the workers; how can they possibly realize fully the imperative need for socialist reform? These people are the target of the struggle, the target of the revolution, and we must never rely on them in any socialist educational movement. We can rely only on those cadres who are not hostile to the workers and are imbued with revolutionary spirit.[75]

Just a month before, another three statements by Mao were cited in *Hongqi*. More than any other statements by Mao, they clarified Mao's common-sense view that political power itself is a source of conflict and a cause of revolution in socialist China, not only at the present time, but also in the remote future. They explain why Mao rejected Marx's utopia. Mao said:

> After the democratic revolution, the workers and the lower middle peasants do not stand still; they want revolution. On the other hand, a number of Party members do not want to go forward; some have moved backward

75. *Hongqi*, No. 7 (1976), p. 6. In the official translation, the phrase, "the bureaucrat class," is used rather than the words, "the class of bureaucratic officials," which has narrower empirical referents than the former. The official translation uses the phrase "sharply antagonistic" rather than the words "sharply opposed," which is the more literal translation of the original Chinese phrase, and which connotes a more moderate tone. The officially published Chinese version includes two changes from the unofficial version distributed by the Red Guards. "Those persons" is changed to "[T]hose leading cadres who are taking the capitalist road." And, the phrase "the imperative need for socialist revolution," is added. These two changes add to the radicalism of Mao's statement.

and opposed the revolution. Why? because they have *become high officials and want to protect the interests of high officials.* [76]

Mao also said:

> Will there be a need for revolution a hundred years from now? There will always be need for revolution. There are always sections of the people who feel themselves oppressed; junior officials, students, workers, peasants, and soldiers do not like bigshots oppressing them. That is why they want revolution. Will contradictions no longer be seen ten thousand years from now? Why not? They will still be seen.

Earlier, Mao had said: "[W]ithout struggle, there is no progress"; asking, "[C]an 800 million people manage without struggle?"

Mao's comments on the "class of bureaucratic officials" were published and used in the joint editorial on 1 July, at a time when Mao's health was deteriorating rapidly [77] and when Yao Wenyuan controlled, or at least dominated, two of the three editorial departments. This altered quotation from Mao served the ideological polemics of the ultra-leftists well. Not only were the bureaucratic officials labelled a "class," but they were also implicitly equated with "those leading cadres who are taking the capitalist road" and then identified as "bourgeois elements." They were designated unequivocally the target of the revolution and "in the end were bound to be overthrown. . . ."

From a theoretical perspective, the publication of Mao's comments enabled the ultra-leftists to round out their theory of the existence of the bourgeoisie in a socialist society and the theory of the struggle between two antagonistic classes which calls for the "all-round dictatorship" of the proletariat over the bourgeoisie in the continuing revolution. The theory developed by the ultra-leftists can be systematized as follows: the bourgeoisie has its source in both the economic base and the superstructure of the socialist society in China. Defined solely in terms of the relations of production (thus excluding forces of production), the economic base has three components: the ownership of the means of production, the form of distribution, and the relations between men. In certain conditions, the form of distribution and the relations between men rather than the ownership of production play a principal and decisive role in determining the nature of the society and its further development into a higher form or its retrogression back to an earlier form.

In the system of distribution in China, particularly commodity ex-

76. Editorial Departments of the *Renmin ribao, Hongqi,* and *Jiefangjun bao,* "The Great Cultural Revolution will shine forever," *Peking Review,* 21 May 1976, p. 7. Emphasis added.

77. See the picture of Mao in his meeting with Prime Minister Lee Kuan-yew of Singapore in *Peking Review,* 14 May 1976, p. 3. This picture caused a great deal of speculation abroad. Mao died less than four months after the appearance of this picture.

change, money economy and the eight-grade wage system, "bourgeois right" continues to be the predominant feature, in spite of the change of the system of ownership of the means of production. As defined by the ultra-leftists on the basis of selected passages from Marx and Lenin, "bourgeois right" is fertile ground for the emergence of "new bourgeois elements" or simply "the bourgeoisie." Here, the ultra-leftists went further than Lenin; for Lenin believed that in a socialist society, bourgeois right exists but not the bourgeoisie.

The relations between men also constitute a fertile ground for the emergence of "new bourgeois elements" or "the bourgeoisie." The relations between men are defined not exclusively as relations between economic classes. They include the relations of exchange of "commodities" broadly defined to include political and social favours granted and received. They also encompass power and personal relations between the superiors and subordinates. In other words, they are analogous to what we call patron-client relations from which a power structure both inside and outside the formal organizations and institutions can be built. To make the picture more complete, the ultra-leftists did not ignore the remaining though, minor, forms of private ownership of means of production, particularly the private plots. Nor did they fail to observe that collective ownership in the vast agricultural sector is still not ownership by the whole people (i.e., the state).

The extensive presence of "bourgeois right" in China's society leads to the emergence of "new bourgeois elements" among Party members, government officials and even workers and peasants. Thus an explanation in terms of "the economic base" is found for the emergence of "the class of bureaucratic officials," "the bourgeoisie." Instead of envisaging the gradual disappearance of "bourgeois right" after the nationalization of the means of production, the ultra-leftists insisted that they must be rigorously restricted by political action. Ominously, the ultra-leftists likened "bourgeois right" to the "fortified villages" during the civil war period, implying that it can only be eliminated by physical violence.[78]

The economic base is only one source of "new bourgeois elements" or "the bourgeoisie." More important and perhaps decisive is the superstructure. The political structure is the direct source and foundation of the class of bureaucratic officials and the "leading cadres who are taking the capitalist road." Moreover, the power of leadership and the ideological and political line followed by the leaders can have a decisive effect on the content of the system of ownership of the means of production as dis-

---

78. Mao said that "bourgeois right can only be restricted." This is a clear difference in emphasis from the position of the ultra-leftists. All the recent articles published in China confirm this interpretation of the meaning of the term "fortified villages."

tinguished from its form. This conclusion is a startling revision of Marxism and goes much further than anything said by Mao. At this point, we quote once more Zhang Chunqiao's extraordinary statement:

> The correctness or the incorrectness of the ideological and political line and the control of leadership in the hands of one class or another decide which class owns a factory in reality.

When this sentence is read in the light of Mao's 1964 remarks now officially published and widely publicized, the "class" in Zhang's sentence can easily be interpreted as the "class of bureaucratic officials," "the bourgeois elements" who would be overthrown by the working class. Thus, a fairly complete and sophisticated theory, by the standards of Chinese polemics, is rounded out. This theory was used to arouse public support for the ultra-leftists, and to legitimize actions to attack the leading cadres at all levels, including the top level veteran Party leaders. This theory was further supported by the old notion that the influence of the ideas of the overthrown landlord and bourgeoisie remains strong and that it penetrates the Party and turns even top level leaders into the spokesmen and representatives of these old classes. The abstract ideas organized by this theory contributed to the views that the reactionary forces are everywhere and that ruthless dictatorial actions must be taken to suppress them, whatever the cost to economic progress and political stability. They also contributed to the sense of righteousness, invincibility, and approaching triumph on the part of the ultra-leftists which made them arrogant and blind to political and economic realities. Hence, their rigorous actions in pushing their programme, in gaining power, and in fomenting disorder to overthrow the veteran Party leaders led only to a sudden and complete disaster for themselves.

IV

As the history of the Chinese Communist movement and regime shows, Mao's reformulated thesis of historical materialism, that in certain conditions, the superstructure, theory, and relations of production rather than the economic base, practice, and forces of production play the principal and decisive role in social change, resonates almost invariably with the revolutionary impulse and frequently with the revolutionary situation in 20th-century China. This thesis is usually thrust into prominence by those, including Mao himself, who are pushing for rapid change and revolutionary policies. The relationship of this thesis to the notion of unity of theory and practice is on one level complementary and on another level antithetical. The notion of unity of theory and practice can be viewed as the epistemological principle with which Mao's reformulated thesis of historical materialism is arrived at or justified. It frequently acts as a principle of prudence to guide and control the revolutionary impulse, the formulation of revolutionary programmes, and revolutionary actions themselves which stem from the revolutionary situation but are structured or rationalized by the reformulated thesis of historical materialism. But the notion of unity of theory and practice is also antithetical to Mao's reformulated thesis of historical materialism because the former gives the primary place to practice whereas the latter assigns the principal and decisive role to theory. Both as a principle of prudence and as an antithesis of the latter, it is given saliency when realistic political and military strategy and tactics, carefully regulated social change, well thought out reforms, and planned economic growth are desired. This relationship between policy-choices and theoretical tenets, or, if you will, the political use of ideological symbols, is brought out more clearly in the struggle between the "gang of four" and the veteran leaders than in most other intra-Party struggles.

The rapid destruction of the "gang of four" as a political force following the death of Mao confronts the veteran leaders with both a challenge and an opportunity to work out a mix between revolutionary change and modernization and to adapt Mao Zedong Thought to such a programme or (allow me the luxury of anticipating a possible formulation some years hence) "to combine Mao Zedong Thought with the concrete practices of revolutionary modernization in China" in the last quarter of the 20th century.*

Naturally, the first and most fundamental step is to elevate once again to its rightful place Mao's notion of unity of theory and practice and his personal example in applying it.[79] Thus, Mao's departure from the Bolsheviks' path to power and Lenin's departure from the theory of Marx and Engels have been underscored. The "gang of four" have been attacked for using such words as "forever" and "everlasting" to describe Mao's ideas as guides to action. In Hua Guofeng's speech to the second conference on learning from Dazhai in December 1976, "integrating theory with practice" was listed ahead of "forging close links with the masses" and practising "criticism and self criticism" as the three major features of the Party's

* The Communique of the Third Plenary Session of the Eleventh Central Committee of the CCP adopted on December 22, 1978 declared that "the lofty task of the Party Central Committee on the theoretical front is to . . . integrate Marxism-Leninism-Mao Zedong Thought with the concrete practice of socialist modernization and develop it under the new historical conditions," *Peking Review*, December 29, 1978, p. 15. The use of the term "socialist modernization" rather than "revolutionary modernization" has turned out to be significant.

79. For a more detailed discussion of the various points in this section, see the up-dated version of the Conference paper, dated 19 May 1977, which will appear in Japanese in *Ajia Kuotari*.

"fine style of work." The ultra-leftists' "so-called opposition to empiricism" is attacked as being in reality "opposition to giving first place to practice," and "opposition to integrating Marxism-Leninism with the concrete practice of the Chinese Revolution."[80]

The next step is to refute the exclusive emphasis made by the ultra-leftists on Mao's reformulated thesis of historical materialism in the making and appraisal of policies, programmes, and institutions. This theoretical task is done much less satisfactorily and elegantly. The Chinese theoreticians now argue that even when superstructure, theory and relations of production play the principal and decisive role, these principal aspects of the contradictions cannot exist without the opposite, though admittedly secondary, aspects of the contradictions—i.e. the economic base, practice, and the forces of production. The principal aspects should receive emphasis but the secondary aspects should not be neglected. To emphasize only one aspect is an expression of "metaphysical" thinking and does not conform to reality. These ideological arguments enable the Chinese to agree with Mao's reformulated thesis and still to push forward vigorously a programme of developing the forces of production and strengthening the economic base by practical actions.

Not unexpectedly, the current leaders launched a strong attack on the ultra-leftists' interpretation of Mao's statement that the bourgeoisie "is right in the Communist Party—those in power taking the capitalist road." Using the interpretation mentioned above, Xiang Qun accuses the "gang of four" of "completely ignoring the minimum common sense of Marxism."[81] Similarly, Jiang Qing's thesis that 75 per cent of the "democratic faction" will turn into the faction of capitalist roaders was refuted by noting the leadership role of the Communist Party in the New Democratic stage of the revolution. The re-emphasis on the notion of unity of theory and practice and the refutation of the charges of "empiricism" have served to underscore the value of the "experience" of the veteran leaders and the validity of their ideas and policies which grew out of revolutionary practice. As to the question of bourgeois right, it is now argued that it can only be limited and cannot be eliminated in one morning and that "as to how and to what extent it is to be restricted, this depends on the material and spiritual conditions at the time."[82]

The characterization of the "gang of four" as ultra-rightists rather than ultra-leftists has puzzled many outside observers and has been criticized

80. *Renmin ribao*, 14 November 1976, p. 2, article by Tian Qing; *Guangming ribao*, 15 November 1976, p. 3, article by Jun Ping; *Renmin ribao*, 17 November 1976, p. 1; Hua Guofeng's speech to the Second Conference on Learning from Dazhai, *Peking Review*, 1 January 1977, p. 40; *Hongqi*, No. 2 (1977), p. 15; and *Guangming ribao*, 14 November 1976, p. 1, article by Gao Ning.

81. *Renmin ribao*, 14 March 1977, p. 1.

82. *Hongqi*, No. 2 (1977), p. 16.

by foreign radicals. From the viewpoint of the new leadership, this characterization can be explained and justified in the following two ways. First, the ultra-leftists advocated a programme so completely divorced from reality and from the demands and sentiments of the masses that its implementation would cause a total and rapid collapse of the regime, or at least political chaos and economic set back. As Edward Friedman observes "the programme of the Left does not summarize or synthesize or reflect the real needs of the citizenry. It is idealism."[83] This could soon lead to an ultra-rightist reaction. In this way, the ultra-leftists are "objectively" ultra-rightists. Furthermore, the ultra-leftists and ultra-rightists have one thing in common. Both are divorced from reality and the masses. Both approaches are therefore "metaphysical."

The second explanation is more pregnant with political significance. Although the ultra-leftists adopted revolutionary phrases and advocated revolutionary programmes in the field of economics and social arrangement, they were using ultra-rightist political methods, adopting an ultra-rightist style of life, and invoking "feudal" ideology to legitimize their attempt to gain power. All the detailed exposures of the political actions, designs, and private life of the "gang of four" are aimed at driving this point home to the masses.

Space does not allow us to document this explanation. But it is important to analyse the political meaning of this characterization. First, it is possible that by characterizing the "gang of four" as ultra-rightists rather than ultra-leftists, the new leaders would find it easier than otherwise to retain specific parts of their ideas which are also Mao's, and which the new leaders consider correct and useful in the new situation. The publication in April 1977 of the fifth volume of Mao's *Selected Works* furnished the occasion for emphasizing the "great theory of continuing the revolution under the dictatorship of the proletariat" which Mao "founded by systematically summing up" historical experience at home and abroad. The prominence given to this theory stands in contrast to its omission in the available version of "On the general programme for work of the whole Party and the whole nation." This contrast may or may not reflect a basic difference between the current leadership and Deng. But it suggests that Hua Guofeng is very careful in preserving the revolutionary tradition while he is vigorously pushing ahead with economic reconstruction.*

In his extremely important report on 4 May 1977 at the National Conference to Learn from Daqing, Vice-premier Yu Qiuli went out of his way to reaffirm the following points:

83. Communication from Edward Friedman.
* In retrospect, it is clear that in the last seven or eight paragraphs written in early 1977, I did not detect the serious conflict between Hua and Deng. Subsequent developments have shown that Hua's specific programs at once to be the rightful heir and sole authoritative in-

It is not enough to have only a revolution in the system of ownership of means of production. The socialist revolution on the political and ideological fronts must continue to be carried out thoroughly. Those parts of the relations of production which do not fit the forces of production and those parts of the superstructure which do not fit the economic base must also be reformed without interruption. If revolution in these spheres is not carried out, socialist institutions cannot be consolidated and publicly owned enterprises would degenerate, change their character, and become capitalist enterprises under the signboard of socialism.[84]

In returning to these ideas of Mao while rigorously pushing forward a programme of rapid industrialization, Hua, Yu and other leaders are re-establishing the vital linkage between politics and economics which was partially severed in the concrete programmes pushed by the ultra-leftists through their cavalier dismissal of the importance of economic growth. The reaffirmation of these Maoist ideas also suggests that the new leadership is trying to find a proper mix between rapid economic growth and continued revolutionary change, so as to maintain and further develop the patterns of Chinese development in which the achievement of a greater degree of economic quality and the expansion of participation have gone hand in hand with a respectable rate of economic growth. It also reflects a determination that China should not and would not become another Soviet Union.

The second and equally important point is the following. By characterizing the "gang of four" as ultra-rightists in their political method and

---

terpreter of Mao's revolutionary tradition and to push rigorously ahead with economic reconstruction were soon challenged by other leaders. In trying to assume the mantle of Mao, he adopted the "two-whatever" slogan, i.e. "we will resolutely uphold whatever policy decisions Chairman Mao made, and unswervingly follow whatever instruction Mao gave." This policy was challenged by Deng. Hua's overambitious and totally unrealistic program of rapid introduction was criticized by Chen Yun and other economists. Hua's power and prestige declined rapidly after Third Plenum held in December, 1978. In 1980, he resigned under pressure from the premiership of the State Council and the chairmanship of both the Party and the Party's Military Commission. The theory of "continued revolution under the dictatorship of the proletariat" was officially repudiated in the "Resolution on Certain Questions in the History of Our Party since the Founding of the People's Republic of China," adopted by the Sixth Plenum in June, 1981. All this was undertaken under Deng's leadership. The differences between Hua and Deng over policies and ideology were wide indeed. But Deng himself has also tried at once to preserve the "scientific principles of Mao Zedong Thought" and to push ahead rapid economic growth. A reinterpretation of Mao Zedong Thought has enabled him to legitimize many innovative policies which are anti-Maoist or non-Maoist. His much more sophisticated methods, realistic programs, and popular policies have so far been quite successful. See the following chapters and the chronology as well as Tang Tsou, "The Historic Change in Direction and Continuity with the Past," *China Quarterly*, 1 June 1984, pp. 320–47.

84. *Dagong bao*, 9 May 1977, p. 4.

programme, the new leaders can find an explanation for the disruption of China's political system since the Cultural Revolution. They can also justify a programme of rebuilding the battered political system. The new leaders admit that the system of democratic centralism, as well as many other rules, regulations and traditions has been disrupted by the methods and conspiratorial activities of the "gang of four." They stress that these must be rebuilt. In the next few years, one would expect to see the revival of many of the Party traditions which were destroyed at the beginning of the Cultural Revolution. In this way, the new Chinese leadership attempts to fulfil Mao's wish and to speed up a recurrent pattern in Chinese history that "great disorder across the land leads to great order."

5 Back from the Brink of Revolutionary-"Feudal" Totalitarianism

An Historic Turning Point

The Third Plenary Session of the Eleventh Central Committee of the Communist Party of China held in December 1978 may turn out to be the landmark of the beginning of a new historic era in China. For the Chinese Communist movement, it may prove to be as important as the Zunyi Conference of January 1935, which made Mao Zedong the head of a three-man group to handle military affairs * and paved the way to Mao's leadership of the party. For the political development of China, it may signal the end of nearly three-quarters of a century of revolutionary ferment and upheaval. In a low-key manner, the communique called on the party to "shift the emphasis of its work to socialist modernization" and to "integrate the universal principles of Marxism-Leninism-Mao Zedong Thought with the concrete practice of socialist modernization and develop it under the new historical conditions."[1]

But what was the earlier emphasis from which the call for socialist modernization represents a shift? The communiqué did not address itself to this question in a forthright manner. But it did state that "as Comrade Mao Zedong pointed out, the large-scale turbulent class struggles of a

This essay was prepared as a framework for analysing politics and social change in twentieth-century China. The support of the Endowment for the Humanities is appreciatively acknowledged. The first draft was completed in early January 1980. It was presented on May 30, 1980, at the Luce Seminar, University of Chicago. The essay was updated in the summer of 1982. In the process of revision, I was greatly benefited by the comments of Professors Ira Katznelson, Adam Przeworski, Philippe Schmitter, Michel Oksenberg, Mark Selden, Edward Friedman, Ross Terrill, Lowell Dittmer, Hong Yung Lee, Marc Blecher, and Brantly Womack. [This chapter is reproduced from *State and Society in Contemporary China*, edited by Victor Nee and David Mozingo (Ithaca, N.Y.: Cornell University Press, 1983). The permission by the Cornell University Press to reprint it here is gratefully acknowledged.]

* The latest sources suggest that the three-man group was established two months after the Zunyi Conference. See chapter 8.

1. "Communiqué of the Third Plenary Session of the Eleventh Central Committee of the Communist Party of China" (adopted on December 22, 1978), *Peking Review*, December 29, 1978, pp. 8, 15.

Later, the phrase to shift the "focus of work" was used in the English translation in place of to shift the "emphasis." For example, see *Beijing Review*, Janury 7, 1980, p. 14.

For an analysis of the events and ideological debates surrounding the struggle for succession to Mao in the years just before and after his death, as well as a forecast on the likelihood

mass character have in the main come to an end."[2] More important, other official statements and numerous articles, as well as the programs and policies adopted and implemented afterward, have made it clear that this "shift of emphasis" may mark the end of a prolonged period of revolutionary transformation of the Chinese Society and the beginning a new era of consolidation, adaptation, and modernization. Thus Richard Lowenthal's insight on "the existence of a long-term trend toward the victory of modernization over utopianism"[3] in Communist regimes may be proved correct by events unfolding in China. Or in Samuel Huntington's terminology, the "revolutionary one-party system" in China has now been developing into an "established one-party system."[4]

Lowenthal makes clear that his analysis is based on a "version of the much criticized totalitarian model of Communist Party dictatorship."[5] He concludes that a postrevolutionary Communist party regime "is neither totalitarian nor democratic, but *authoritarian*."[6] The thrust of his argument agrees generally with Juan Linz's conclusion, which is based on an examination of both Communist and non-Communist regimes whether they are totalitarian or authoritarian.[7] In contrast to the "much criticized totalitarian model," however, "totalitarianism" is defined in this essay not in terms of those fixed institutional traits enumerated by Carl J. Friedrich or reconceptualized by other theorists with great sophistication in the

---

of a revival of the call for integration of universal principles with concrete practice, see Tang Tsou, "Mao Tse-tung Thought, the Last Struggle for Succession, and the Post-Mao Era," *China Quarterly*, no. 71 (September 1977), pp. 498–529, reprinted as chapter 4 in this volume.

2. *Peking Review*, December 29, 1978, p. 11. As published in the revised version of his famous speech, "On the Correct Handling of the Contradictions among the People," Mao's statement reads, "The large scale, turbulent class struggles of the masses characteristic of the times of revolution have in the main come to an end, but the class struggle is by no means entirely over." *Selected Works of Mao Tse-tung*, 5 vols. (Peking: Foreign Languages Press, 1977), vol. 5, p. 395. It has a different emphasis from the way in which it is used in the Communiqué.

3. Richard Lowenthal, "Development vs. Utopia in Communist Policy," in *Change in Communist Systems*, ed. Chalmers Johnson (Stanford: Stanford University Press, 1970), p. 54.

4. Samuel Huntington, "Social and Institutional Dynamics of One-Party System," in Samuel Huntington and Clement H. Moore, eds., *Authoritarian Politics in Modern Society* (New York: Basic Books, 1970), pp. 3–47.

5. Lowenthal, "Development vs. Utopia," p. 108.

6. Ibid., p. 115; italics in the original.

7. Juan Linz, "Totalitarianism and Authoritarianism," in Fred Greenstein and Nelson Polsby, eds., *Handbook of Political Science* (Reading, Mass.: Addison-Wesley, 1975), Vol. 3, pp. 175–411.

light of their improved understanding of developments in totalitarian regimes. Rather, it is simply defined as a central dynamics in the relationship between political power on the one hand and civil society and the economy on the other. As such, "totalitarianism" connotes, to use the words of N. S. Timasheff, "unlimited extension of state functions"; it designates "a trait isolated by means of abstraction and apt to appear in society of various types."[8] But it is a particularly salient feature in a society undergoing a social revolution. One can even suggest that all social revolutions contain within themselves totalitarian tendencies in different degrees. A total social revolution is by definition totalitarian in the full sense of the word. Therefore, we can speak of "the degree of totalitarianism" or "totalitarian-ness" in a continuum, measured by the penetration of political power into other spheres of social life. In a totalitarian society, political power may find concrete embodiment in the state, the party, or a charismatic leader supported by mobilized masses or a combination of all three forms of political power in various proportions.[9]

The Rise and Fall of Revolutionary-"Feudal" Totalitarianism, 1966—1976

Informed by the specific concept of totalitarianism just noted, this essay puts forward the following simple but probably controversial argument. Political developments in the three years from 1978 to 1980 marked an exceedingly rapid retreat from the brink of what I call "revolutionary-'feudal' totalitarianism," which the ultraleftists and Lin Biao with powerful but qualified support from Mao advocated and endeavored to put into action during the Cultural Revolution of 1966–1976. At the same time there was an attempt to find a proper and flexible limit to this retreat. By 1981, the tempo of retreat had slowed down. In such areas of civil society as literature and art and the expression of dissent, there has been some

8. N. S. Timasheff, "Totalitarianism, Despotism, and Dictatorship," in Carl J. Friedrich, ed., *Totalitarianism* (Cambridge, Mass.: Harvard University Press, 1954), p. 39.

9. For a more extended theoretical discussion of the concept of totalitarianism and the definition of politics, see my paper (pp. 3–12) with the same title as this chapter, which was presented on May 30, 1980, at the Luce Seminar, University of Chicago.

For a suggestion to use a new phrase "political totalism" in the place of "totalitarianism," see my paper "Political Totalism, Authoritarianism, and Hegemony: A Proposed Theoretical Scheme for the Study of the Transformation of the Traditional Sociopolitical Order into a Communist System in China," presented at the Northern Illinois University, October 27, 1982.

For a sequel to the present essay, and a more detailed and concrete discussion of events since 1980, see "The Middle Course in Changing the State-Society Relations and in Reforming the Political Structure," a revised and updated version of a paper presented at a conference on China held at the University of Chicago in November 1981. This paper, revised with a new title, was subsequently published and is reproduced here as chapter 7.

retrogression from the high-water mark of 1980, although in other areas such as the relations between the peasants and the state, the trend has continued to move forward. Taken as a whole, the ongoing course of development has been stabilized. Specific reforms and incremental changes reflecting a retreat from the brink have continued to occur.

From a larger historical perspective, the great leap backward in the first three years and the continuing program of reforms mark the reversal of a fundamental trend in China in the twentieth century toward increased penetration of politics into other spheres of society, culminating in the revolutionary-"feudal" totalitarianism of the ultraleftists. Their ideas and programs were "revolutionary," first, because they called for the overthrow of the "new bourgeois class" that had allegedly emerged within the Chinese Communist party; second, because they endeavored to effect fundamental change in the relations of production; and third, because they envisaged the use of both violent and nonviolent methods, bypassing the hitherto officially sanctioned channels and organizations. These ideas and programs were totalitarian because they pushed to the extreme the long-existing tendency of extending political control over every sphere of social life. The concept of "all-round dictatorship over the bourgeoisie" meant, among other things, complete, dictatorial control over all professions because the professionals and the intellectuals were considered by the ultraleftists to be members of either old or new bourgeois class. In the ultraleftists' program, political control over thought, expression of ideas, family life, and individual behavior became even more extensive, penetrating, and repressive, even though this program was not effectively and fully implemented during the chaos of the Cultural Revolution.

In contrast to their revolutionary program and rhetoric, their political actions paralleled the "feudalistic" pattern in the sense that the Chinese Communists use the term, because they derived implicit and in some cases explicit support from the cognitive, evaluative, and emotive orientations of the "feudal" political culture. The notions that "politics can decide everything" and that "with power in one's hand, one has everything" were suggestive. The cult of personality, which the ultraleftists pushed to the extreme, derived implicit support from the previous long history of worship of emperor. Loyalty toward the leader rested on the traditional concept of loyalty toward one's superiors in all political and social ranks. The injunction, "every directive issued by Chairman Mao must be obeyed whether you understand it or not, agree with it or not," drew on the traditional virtue of obedience. The ideas of the Legalist school were revived by the leftists who used historical analogy and allusion as a basis for attacking the veteran leaders and their moderate program.

Thus the revolutionary-"feudal" totalitarianism of the ultraleftists represented a more extreme form of the totalitarian tendency than that which had occurred under the auspices of the organized party. It was first developed in the early phases of the Cultural Revolution when the overwhelming majority of the party organizations were destroyed or paralyzed by the combined action of the leader and the masses. Its fluctuating fortune thereafter varied inversely with the degree to which the party was rebuilt. This totalitarianism of personal leadership plus mass action—an organizational form that existed not exclusively at the highest level but at all levels—is different in principle from the totalitarian tendency of the party. It was much less restrained by any formal rules or norms, and it paid little heed to party traditions. To fill these normative and organizational vacuums, the ultraleftists and their allies fell back on "feudal" values, norms, ideas, and attitudes. To the extent that a party organized along Leninist principles is a modern phenomenon, the totalitarianism organized around Mao's arbitrary personal leadership represented a regression into China's distant past.

But the ultraleftists never achieved total domination. Their increasing influence was opposed by an overwhelming majority of other leaders in the party, army, and government, who received encouragement and support from various social groups and from the unorganized masses in many subtle and unobserved ways. They succeeded only in establishing small enclaves of power. Toward the end of the Cultural Revolution they had little influence over the military, and their effort to build up an urban militia as a second armed force further antagonized the army without achieving any real countervailing power.

Paradoxically, the program of the ultraleftists, which marked the culmination of the totalitarian tendency in the Chinese Communist movement, soon led not only to its total repudiation but, more significantly, also to sweeping historical reexamination by the current leaders. Mao's successors were forced to ask the fundamental question why a movement for class and human liberation had developed into one of the most oppressive systems in Chinese history—what the Chinese Communists call "feudal fascism." This self-examination was undertaken by those who in their youthful and idealistic days joined the revolution to fight against political oppression; who in their middle age became themselves the oppressors, the inquisitors, and the denunciators in an attempt to achieve a revolutionary transformation of the society; who in their late middle or old age were oppressed, condemned, and denounced by others in the name of still another revolution; and who in the remaining few years of their lives regained power and authority. They have indeed been reeducated by the Cultural Revolution but not in the way intended by its originator. The diametrically opposite positions they occupied before and during the Cultural Revolution forced them to view the political system from the bottom as well as from the top, from the outside as well as from the inside, and in their capacity as its victims in contrast to their earlier role as its beneficiaries. Indeed, the pre-1966 oppressors suffered during the Cultural Revolution more grievous harm than those whom they had oppressed. Now they are seriously concerned with their own place in China's history. It is this "second liberation" and the personal experience of the "reborn revolutionary" which gives extraordinary poignancy to their reexamination and soul-searching.

Not long after those who before 1976 had been both the oppressors and the oppressed had been rehabilitated by the post-Mao leadership, one witnessed the deeply moving scene of the erstwhile oppressors recently restored to leading positions of power and influence apologizing publicly to their victims and permitting them to publicize views for which they had been punished before 1976. In October-November 1979, at the Fourth Congress of Writers and Artists, which met for the first time in nineteen years, Zhou Yang publicly apologized to those whom he had unjustly persecuted. By this act of self-criticism, he mollified his critics and was even elected chairman of the All-China Association of Writers and Artists.[10] He and other party leaders have been forgiven by at least some of their victims, in the charitable spirit that, as individuals, "they know not what they do." As Ding Ling observed, what happened in the past was not a question of receiving favors or suffering from personal enmity; what she went through involved the entire society; there was no single person who struck her down.[11] These leaders had not known the harmful effects of the more radical principles and policies they had initiated or implemented for the purpose of strengthening revolutionary power and transforming man and society. The full implications of these ideas and practices were realized only when, pushed to their logical conclusion by the ultraleftists, they were used to persecute many of their originators, champions, and advocates.[12] As Ding Ling saw it, the basic source of these errors was a combination of political power and small group mentality, that is, "sectarianism," which was a concrete expression of "feudalism."[13] At that juncture of history, many though by no means all of those who had been disgraced before 1976 found some common ground in raising fundamental questions about some of these erroneous principles and practices or at least in searching for ways to modify them.

Many of the influential figures probably shared Ba Jin's feeling of deep

10. *Dagong Bao* (Impartial Daily), November 28, 1979, p. 8.

11. Ding Ling, "Some Remarks from the Heart," *Hongqi* (Red Flag), 1980, no. 12, p.51.

12. It is now widely recognized that there were "leftist" errors in the policies toward literature and the arts before the Cultural Revolution. These "leftist" policies helped the ultraleftists to seize control after 1966. See the article by Zheng Wen in *Renmin ribao* (People's Daily), August 10, 1979, p. 4; editorial, November 17, 1979, p. 1.

13. Ding Ling, "Some Remarks from the Heart," p. 52.

regret that he did not perceive the disastrous consequences of the regime's policies toward literature and the arts in time, that he agreed with or at least acquiesced in their implementation, and indeed sometimes even voluntarily helped further them. In the initial period when he himself was victimized, he truly believed in his persecutors' argument. Only later, he discovered that he was being deceived. This discovery led to a feeling of emptiness and total disillusion.[14] For a brief period, the thought of suicide crossed his mind. Finally, he began to analyze both himself and his persecutors objectively. In his account of his own thoughts, past and present, he tells himself with a profound sense of remorse and guilt that the days of political persecution must not be allowed to return.

Self-doubt and the gnawing feeling that the regime's overall policies might be correct were a major subjective factor in the failure of other writers such as Liu Binyan, to resist. After being labeled a rightist in 1957, Liu spent the next three years trying piously to reform himself, to criticize his own class and rightist viewpoint, and to place his trust in the party's words. Only the stark realities of life in the countryside gradually convinced him of the falsity of official propaganda and the errors of the policies of the superior authorities. Still, Liu confided his doubts only to himself and his diary. He continued to perform his assigned tasks obediently. His rightist label was removed in March 1966. Less than three months later, the Cultural Revolution began, and he was again attacked when his diary, which had been copied stealthily by one of his colleagues, was used against him. In 1979, he declared that he would continue to write and speak his mind, come what might, because for him and people like him there was no route of retreat.[15]

The amazing fact that a large number of purged leaders not only survived the Cultural Revolution but have been restored to positions of authority must be attributed to the principle gradually developed during the period of civil and foreign wars that top party leaders who lost out in inner party struggles should not be executed.[16] The practice of sparing these leaders reflected the only norm governing inner party struggle and rectification campaigns which was not openly violated during the Cultural

14. See Ba Jin, "Random Thoughts," a series of short essays and reminiscences published since December 17, 1978, in *Dagong Bao* and *Huaqiao ribao* (China Daily News). See particularly numbers 7, 11, 14, 15, 27, 29, 34, and 36. One of the most moving pieces is number 36, in which he describes the fate of two dogs and his feelings toward his own dog. The force of these short pieces derives from Ba Jin's honesty and frankness in analyzing his thoughts, feelings, and role in these traumatic years as well as from his ability to express an understanding of the reality of that period.

15. Liu Binyan, "The Call of the Times," *Wenyi bao* (Literary Gazette), 1979, nos. 11–12, pp. 36–46. The article consists of his remarks made at the Fourth Congress of Writers and Artists.

16. Some of the lower-level cadres were executed for "counterrevolutionary crimes."

Revolution, although not a few prominent leaders are known to have been hounded to their deaths or driven to commit suicide. This longstanding norm turned out to be the saving grace of the system and has given it a second chance to reform itself at a crucial time in the nation's history.

Because the self-examination was undertaken by veteran political leaders who had deep personal experience of the hopes and promises of the revolutionary movement in its early years and their utter betrayal in the recent past, it seems likely to have lasting significance. For the rehabilitated leaders have seen that the system they built could lead to a disastrous outcome and that certain underlying principles and actual practices, which they had strongly advocated or supported at various times, could have devastating consequences for Chinese society as a whole.[17]

The self-examination and soul-searching by many survivors of the Cultural Revolution has also led to a reconstruction of institutions and to a restatement of basic ideological and sociopolitical principles. These changes mark China's transformation from utopianism to development, as Lowenthal foresaw, and from a revolutionary one-party system to an established one-party system, as Huntington suggests. But the true, historic significance of the reevaluation and resulting changes lies in the reversal of the profound trend that began after the May fourth period and was characterized by increasing penetration of politics into all spheres of social life. This reversal signifies the retreat of politics from the control of society. In other words, the relationship between political power and society in China is beginning to undergo a change in direction. In attempting to sketch an overall view of the post-Mao era as a step toward a larger interpretation of twentieth-century Chinese politics, I can only describe these changes in broad outline. I have not been able to give even preliminary answers to the basic question: What are the larger factors in the Chinese economy, social stratification, relative power among the various social groups, and the international environment which can be induced to account for the rapid collapse of the totalitarianism of the ultraleftists and hence for the current retreat? Description is the first step toward explanation, which will involve difficult theoretical questions and a diligent search for adequate historical data.

The Retreat of Politics as Reflected in Ideological Discourse
The changing relationship between political power and society can be most easily detected in the sphere of ideology, more specifically in a reinterpretation of Mao Zedong Thought. Ideological discussions still fill

17. According to the editor-in-chief of the *Renmin ribao*, Hu Zhiwei, the tragic and painful lessons of the ten years during the Cultural Revolution enabled "us" to realize profoundly and personally that unless "democracy" inside and outside the party was fully devel-

many pages in the official newspapers and various journals, although the proportion of articles on practical problems, factual reports, and empirical studies has sharply increased. Given the salience of ideology and its function as a template for political action in twentieth-century China, the downgrading of ideology must be, as Brantly Womack perceptively noted,[18] the task of ideology. The reversal of many concrete programs, strongly or partially justified by Mao's ideas, as well as the abandonment of many of his explicit directives or policies, is rationalized on the basis of a reinterpretation of Mao Zedong Thought by giving primacy to his theory of knowledge. This rationale basically implies a shift from the emphasis on the substantive conclusions of Marxism-Leninism and Mao Zedong Thought to a stress on their use as a method of analysis; it also implies a transition from the stress on utopian goals to an emphasis on the concrete conditions confronting China. Specifically, the epistemological postulate that "practice is the criterion for testing truth" has been elevated to the status of the most fundamental postulate of Marxism-Leninism and Mao Zedong Thought, thus reversing the emphasis given by Mao in his later years to the decisive role of theory. These ideological shifts explain the formulation adopted by the Third Plenum on the need to "integrate the universal principles of Marxism-Leninism-Mao Zedong Thought with the concrete practice of socialist modernization and develop it under the new historical conditions."

In an article published in September 1977, I pointed out that the emphasis on practice can be understood as a principle of prudence in decision making, a criterion to judge the correctness of policies, a basic justification for the Sinification of Marxism and the development of a revolutionary program suitable to Chinese conditions. From the perspective of the present analysis we can now see that this slightly reformulated epistemological postulate on "practice" obliges the party, the state, and leaders at all levels and in all spheres to take heed of the social practices of the masses, that is, the needs, the interests, the demands, the life situations, and the behavioral patterns of various social groups and individuals. It gives greater weight to the perceived interests and demands of the various social groups and individuals as they impinge on the party and the state, especially the party's ideas about these interests and demands. To be sure, China still has a system in which the party and its leaders guide the national development, coordinate its interdependent parts, and ulti-

---

oped the party's system of centralism could become "feudal autocracy" and a "feudal, fascist, dictatorial system" (Hu, "How to Develop Criticism and Self-Criticism in Newspapers," *Xinwen zhanxian* (The News Battlefront), 1979, no. 6, p. 5).

18. Brantly Womack, "Politics and Epistemology," *China Quarterly*, no. 81 (December 1979), pp. 768–792.

mately control its multifarious groups and individuals. But the inputs and feedback from the society to the party and the state are more direct and have more discernible effects than before.

The process through which the elevation of "practice" to the status of a basic principle was accomplished also suggests that in post-Mao China, the source of new ideological formulations has become more pluralistic and can be found at a much lower level of the party hierarchy. The article, "Practice Is the Sole Criterion for Testing Truth," published on May 11, 1978, in *Guangming ribao*, was given credit for starting the nationwide public discussion on the theory of knowledge. It was written by Hu Fuming, the vice-chairman of the Department of Philosophy at the University of Nanjing and concurrently the deputy secretary of the party branch of that department. It came about as the author's response to the charge that he was defending "revisionist viewpoints" when he noted the disastrous consequences of the educational program of the ultraleftists and when he reaffirmed the "theory of forces of production," which had been declared to be a proper subject of criticism in a document previously adopted by a general meeting of the party. He came to the conclusion that the criterion for judging any idea, theory, law, or decree can only be "practice"—the basic point of departure of the Marxist theory of knowledge.[19] Publication of the article met with widespread positive response from the leaders. On June 2, Vice-Premier Deng Xiaoping used the important occasion of a conference on political work of the People's Liberation Army (PLA) to drive home its major theme in a speech that called on everyone "to use the method of seeking truth from facts, proceeding from reality and integrating theory with practice."[20]

The nationwide discussions that followed were undoubtedly organized and promoted by the moderate veteran leaders at the top, particularly Deng and Hu Yaobang. They provided strong ideological support for the innovative policies of the pragmatic leaders and showed up the theoretical hollowness and practical absurdity of the position of standpatters. From then on, the latter's argument advanced as late as March 1977 in the party's theoretical journal, *Hongqi,* that "whatever the decision made by Chairman Mao was, we will resolutely support; whatever Chairman Mao's directive was, we will unswervingly obey,"[21] became a subject of ridicule and contempt. The endorsement of the national discussions on criterion

19. "The Tree of Practice Is Forever Green," *Renmin ribao*, March 21, 1979, p. 3. This report gives an account of the genesis of Hu's article "Practice Is the Sole Criterion for Testing Truth." The possibility or even likelihood that Hu's article was the product of prompting by leaders at a higher level or of an unannounced meeting of a group of like-minded party leaders and cadres at different levels cannot be excluded.

20. *Peking Review*, June 23, 1978, pp. 14–21, 29.

21. *Hongqi*, 1977, no. 3, p. 18.

of truth by the Third Plenum in December 1978 paved the way for a series of articles demystifying and demythologizing Mao. After intensive soul-searching and internal debate, this process of de-deification of Mao culminated in the "Resolution on Certain Questions in History of Our Party since the Founding of the People's Republic of China" adopted by the Sixth Plenum on June 27, 1981. This historic document reaffirmed Mao's theoretical and practical contributions to the Chinese revolution, particularly his role in leading the CCP from defeat to victory. But it also noted that "chief responsibility for the grave 'left' error of the 'Cultural Revolution' . . . does indeed lie with Comrade Mao Zedong." [22] The "theory of continued revolution under the dictatorship of the proletariat" which incorporated Mao's principal theses justifying the Cultural Revolution was specifically repudiated.

The central ideal of this first systematic and most widely known article on the criterion of truth in the post-Mao era is simply Marxist common sense, as its author emphasized. From the perspective of the philosophy of science, it raises more questions than it answers. More specifically, the criterion of truth for formal logic, mathematics, and all analytic propositions is not "practice." Partly for this reason, the term "sole" has frequently been dropped since 1981 and Mao's phrase "seeking truth from facts" has once again become the standard formulation.

This new epistemological postulate on practice as the criterion of truth which is supposed to inform all decisions and actions is reinforced by a sociological postulate that can be reconstructed as follows. Every sphere of social life has its special characteristics (te dian) and is governed by objective laws. Political leadership can and should create the general conditions and framework that are favorable to the operation of these laws and that promote desired development. But it cannot violate these laws without suffering serious consequences.

This restatement of the relationship between politics and other spheres of social life and the reinterpretation of the principle of "politics in command" can be found in the authoritative article by Hu Qiaomu, then the president of the newly created Academy of the Social Science. Hu re-emerged as one of the regime's leading theoreticians and powerful figures after a long period of obscurity during the Cultural Revolution. [23] In February 1980, he became a member of the reestablished Secretariat, and since September 1982, he has been a member of the Political Bureau.

On the basis of a selective quoting or paraphrasing of Marx, Engels,

22. *Beijing Review*, July 6, 1981, p. 23.

23. For the theoretical problems raised in this article, see "China: New Theories for Old" by the editors, *Monthly Review*, May 1979, pp. 1–19. For a debate over the post-Mao developments, see Charles Bettelheim, "The Great Leap Backward," ibid., July-August 1978, pp. 37–130, and Reader's Comment on *China since Mao*, ibid., May 1979, pp. 21–55.

Lenin, and Mao, Hu made the following points: Economic laws are like "natural laws," and "natural laws" cannot be dispensed with; they cannot be altered at the will of the society, the government, and the authorities. "Over and above the economic laws in objective existence, politics itself cannot create other laws and impose them on the economy. In fact, insofar as the laws of economic developments are concerned, the mission of correct political leadership lies precisely in making the maximum effort to see to it that our socialist economic work operates within the scope of these objective laws." In a socialist society, political power can bring "enormous damage to economic development" if it is misused.[24] Similar views have been expressed by the current leaders in all spheres of social life, particularly those in the areas of science, education, and literature and the arts who had suffered from various forms of persecution and attack dating back to the beginning of the Cultural Revolution in most cases but to the Yanan period in some cases.[25]

The significance of this postulate lies not alone in the impetus it has given to the restoration of a measure of rationality in economic and other policies. Its fundamental meaning is that there exist certain areas of autonomy in economic and social life into which political power cannot and should not intrude. It thus symbolizes and legitimizes the reversal of the historic trend toward the increasing penetration of politics into all social spheres. It may also mark a new beginning in the relationship between political power and society. For it opens up the possibility for the professionals and specialists in various spheres to show what these objective laws are. Hence, the official acceptance of this postulate has coincided with the reemergence of the economists, educators, natural and social scientists, writers, and artists in positions of authority and influence in the political system. "Listen to the views of the specialists" is now a constant refrain. An article in *Hongqi* declares that the term "authority" has two meanings:

> What we commonly call theoretical authority, academic authority, technical authority, . . . etc., is in essence a synonym for truth. The reason

24. Hu Qiaomu, "Observe Economic Laws, Speed up the Four Modernizations," *Peking Review*, November 10, 1978, pp. 8, 9. For more details, see the new or republished works of Xue Muqiao, Sun Yefang, Yu Guangyuan, and Xu Dixin.

25. As a Marxist, Mao recognized that there are laws governing all things. In particular, he urged his comrades to study the "laws of war" and to plan their actions "in accordance with these laws in order to overcome the enemy facing us" (*Selected Readings from the Works of Mao Tse-tung* [Peking: Foreign Languages Press, 1967], pp. 51–52). But Mao also emphasized that war is a continuation of politics and that military strategy must be subordinated to political objectives. This is as it should be. How much Mao's thinking on political-military relations influenced his ideas on the relationship between politics and other spheres is an interesting but unresolved problem.

why authority is called authority is that it represents truth, represents the objective laws of natural and social development, represents correct opinions, and thus also represents the interests of the majority. . . . The other meaning of authority refers to the laws, discipline, rules and regulations, order, directives, etc., which are indispensable in class struggle, struggle for production and scientific experiment.[26]

This postulate also changes the terms of the debate on the question of the relationship between the party and the specialists and between politics and other vocations. To be sure, that relationship was and still is defined primarily as involving "redness" and "expertise." Although it was and still is frequently affirmed that officials and cadres in professional work should be both "red and expert," the debate almost always gave redness an easy victory whenever redness came into conflict with expertness. The salience of ideology in modern China, and the highest priority given to moral values in the Chinese cultural tradition,[27] made the outcome nearly inevitable—quite aside from the question of who had actual political power in the society.

Now the sociological postulate marks out spheres of social activities, supposedly governed by special laws that can be discovered by the experts and cannot be ignored by the politicians without doing damage to the entire society. Thus it bolsters the experts' claims of authority even when the traditional formula is used. In other words, the traditional formula has taken on a new meaning within the changed context of discourse.

The social standing of all specialists in China in all fields is now higher than at any time since 1949, and their impact on policies is also much greater. Western social scientists can legitimately ask what the objective laws governing each sphere of social life are and whether such objective laws can be discovered. From their own experience with "the best and the brightest" in government, they rightly question whether the Chinese are entertaining an illusion. But for the moment, we can leave these questions aside and merely note the significance of this sociological postulate as a signpost of the change of direction in China's political development.

The affirmation of these existential objective laws and the implicit grant of a certain degree of autonomy to various social groups also imply a recognition of the positive functions performed by the various professions and occupations. It represents a reversal of the analysis made by the ultraleftists on the basis of many remarks by Mao on the functions of the various groups in the society. In Maoist analysis, the emphasis was placed on

26. Hua Song, "Repel the Interference of Anarchism" *Hongqi* 1980, no. 2, p. 23; italics added.

27. For example, to establish virtue was considered to be the highest personal achievement, to be followed by the performance of meritorious deeds and formulation of ideas and views, in that order.

what social scientists in the West would call the latent dysfunctions[28] of the various professional and occupational activities, particularly as they affect social stratification and political conflict. For example, the latent dysfunction of education, development of science and technology, and economic management in creating a new bourgeois class and a new intellectual aristocracy was stressed by the ultraleftists, whereas the manifest functions of these professions in the transmission of culture, in economic and technical development, and in the achievement of other aspects of modernization were ignored or given a subordinate place. The ultraleftists were accused of propagating the view that it is better to have workers without culture than a bourgeoisie with culture. The stress on the latent dysfunction of education, science, knowledge, and culture in creating a new class legitimized the intrusion of politics on these spheres as a necessary form of class struggle. Thus the Chinese case provides one more example that functional analysis can be placed in the service of radicalism as well as conservatism. In some cases, the latent dysfunction as seen from the viewpoint of the ultraleftists was interpreted by them as a conscious purpose of those engaged in these activities. Their theory of conspiracy had one of its sources in their functional analysis.

This misuse of functional analysis as a political weapon contributed to the loss of a generation of educated youth, scientists, engineers, physicians, humanists, social scientists, writers, artists, and other specialists. Now the tables are turned, manifest functions are stressed, and latent functions or dysfunctions are deemphasized. Will the Chinese hang themselves on the other horn of the dilemma by creating a new meritocracy? They may do so eventually. But at the moment, the intellectuals and specialists in other fields are only beginning to be liberated from the overcentralized control of the party and government bureaucracies, which generally lack staff sufficiently informed in fields of science, technology, education, and culture. The urgent task is to tame bureaucratism (which is also a legacy of what the Chinese call feudalism) rather than to counterbalance the influence of the intellectuals.

There has also been a deemphasis, reinterpretation, and even repudiation of Mao's reformulation of historical materialism to the effect that in certain conditions theory and the superstructure rather than productive forces, practice, and economic base can and do play the principal and decisive role in social change.[29] Some Chinese theorists assert that Mao's formulation is still correct, but they immediately add that the conditions

---

28. The term "latent dysfunction" is derived from Anthony Giddens, "Functionalism après la lutte," *Social Research*, Summer 1976, pp. 325–366.

29. For a more detailed discussion of this idea of Mao, see Tang Tsou, "Mao Tse-tung Thought." [Reproduced here as chapter 4 in this volume.]

which make it possible for theory and superstructure to play the principal and decisive role are themselves created by the development of productive forces and the economic base. In the writings of other theorists, Mao's formulation was implicitly but directly challenged and the ultraleftists' interpretation of Mao repudiated, usually without naming Mao.

The following passage from an authoritative article from *Hongqi* reveals the degree of change in official Chinese thinking within the party.

> In studying the forms of economy and the laws of economics, many comrades often try to recruit the help of such non-economic factors as ideas, politics, violence, instead of beginning their study with the mode of production. They have been accustomed to use the expressed wishes of certain persons, the [ideological and political] line of a certain period, and certain guiding principles and policies in their efforts to explain the formation, development, and transformation of economic relations and to elucidate the movement and functioning of economic laws. Take a few examples. To explain the coming into being of the socialist relations of ownership, they do not attribute it to the objective needs of the developing productive forces, but instead name the role of the proletarian organ of power as the most fundamental and decisive factor. [For them] whether the nature of ownership is socialist or capitalist depends entirely on what leadership it has and is not to be judged by an actual analysis of the form of ownership; the transition of a form of ownership from its lower level to its higher level is to be decided by the ideological and political levels of the masses and cadres, and not to be decided by whether the level of economic development is favorable to the transition; the law of economics has become something people can dispose of at will and can be utilized and restricted in accordance with all sorts of needs, including political needs. Furthermore, it can be put under the "rule of man."[30]

In short, the economists have replaced the revolutionaries as authoritative interpreters of social change. The central message is that economic considerations cannot and should not always be overridden by the political line and the government's action.

But the return to the classical Marxist formulation of historical materialism must be understood in the broader context of the political-economic development in twentieth-century China. The original Marxist thesis reflected the situation in early capitalist society in which the free market and economic forces played the primary role in the transformation of other aspects of social life. In contrast, Mao's formulation asserted that in the revolution and social changes of twentieth-century China, politics (in-

---

30. Article by Lin Zili, in *Hongqi*, December 1979, p. 2. For a reaffirmation of Mao's formulation coupled with a repudiation of its interpretation and used by the ultraleftists, see Jin Shougeng's article in *Zhexue Yanjiu* (Philosophical Research), 1980, no. 1, pp. 16–23. ["Rule by men" is a better translation.]

cluding ideology, state, party, personalized leadership, and the masses) played the primary role in transforming society. But as capitalism developed, especially in mature capitalist society in the West, politics intervened to ameliorate many undesirable consequences of the free market. Political participation of the lower classes and the labor union movement constituted one of the factors in disproving Marx's prophecy of increasing misery of the proletariat under capitalism. The gap between the classes at the top and the bottom narrowed rather than widened.

In China, the reinterpretation or abandonment of Mao's formulation took place after the attempt to push the transformative role of politics to the extreme had created many serious problems in the economy and other areas of society. The practical and operational consequences of the current ideological discourse are to allow economic forces and other social groups a degree of autonomy in order to ameliorate many of these adverse effects of politics. Politics is still given a primary role to play in economic development, but the market and other social forces will also be allowed to play their own roles in the economy and the society. In other words, the real significance of ideological theses in China can be detected only when they are understood both in their theoretical context and in the light of the real situation confronting the political actors and the society. Thus the restructuring, reformulation, and reinterpretation of the ideological theses frequently signify a change in the rules of the game at the most abstract level and provide the broad framework for decision making. The current theoretical discourse in the various journals and newspapers on matters of ideology can best be understood within this context.

The Reversal of the Position of the Intellectuals and the New Perception of the Class Structure

Of the various groups in the society, the broad class of Chinese intellectuals undoubtedly have gained most in the reversal of the trend in the state-society relationship.[31] During 1968, the term "stinking number nine"[32] emerged as a characterization of the intellectuals as a social group,

31. The New Year's editorial of the *Guangming ribao* (The Light Daily), a newspaper specializing in education, culture, and science, hailed this reversal as "a change of historic significance" (January 1, 1980, p. 1).

The term "intellectual" embraces "professors, scientists, senior engineers and writers who are commonly known as highly qualified intellectuals as well as ordinary technicians in factories, primary school teachers and other mental workers with professional knowledge." In 1949, there were about three million intellectuals. Now, there are twenty-five million intellectuals, including six million scientific and technical workers. Ninety percent of the total trained after 1949 came from "working people's families" (*Beijing Review*, June 23, 1979, p. 14).

32. This term came into vogue after the publication of Yao Wenyuan's article, "The Working Class Must Take Over the Leadership in Everything," *Hongqi*, 1968, no. 2, pp. 3–7.

placing them last on the list of disreputable social groups, the others being landlords, rich peasants, counterrevolutionaries, bad elements, rightists, renegades, special agents (of the enemy), and capitalist-roaders. All were subjected to attacks and discrimination. Now they are classified as "a sector of the working class"[33] engaging in "mental labor." Peng Chong, the former first secretary of Shanghai municipality, stated the matter even more strongly: "The intellectuals in our country are that section of the working class which grasps advanced scientific and cultural knowledge earlier than any other sections. They are the treasure of our nation and our state."[34] The policy of remolding the intellectuals adopted shortly after 1949 is considered to be "no longer applicable in regard to the overwhelming majority of the intellectuals."[35]

The state, the party, or any political leader, however eminent he is, no longer has any automatic and special claims to truth. Formerly, the idea that the natural sciences have no class character had been only intermittently heard. Now it is part of the accepted orthodoxy. The view that the social sciences have class character, however, is still prevalent. But many influential writers assert that truth in social sciences has no class character—undoubtedly a tautology but a tautology with important political implications. The role of the intellectuals as social critics is being recognized. The symbol of this recognition is Ma Yinchu, whose advocacy of population control in the years of 1955–1957 had been vehemently attacked in 1958 and had cost him his job as the president of Beijing University. In his late nineties, Ma was appointed as the honorary president of that university, an accolade given nationwide publicity. Virtually all the disgraced scholars and writers in the original Department of Philosophy and Social Sciences in the Academy of Sciences ranging from those condemned as "counterrevolutionary revisionists" to those labeled as "intellectuals with unreconstructed bourgeois world views" have been rehabilitated and given high positions in the academic world.[36]

The once condemned view that literature must "intervene in life," that is, must be "concerned with and involved in the lives of individuals and

33. Deng's speech at the All-Army Political Work Conference, June 2, 1978, *Peking Review*, June 23, 1978, pp. 14–21, 29.

34. Quoted in *Dagong bao*, December 29, 1979. Peng Chong was elevated to be a member of the Secretariat in February 1980.

35. *Beijing Review*, February 2, 1979, pp. 10–15.

36. *Renmin ribao*, July 14, 1979, p. 1. Before the Cultural Revolution, this department had slightly more than 2,000 researchers and cadres. Before 1976, 1,042 persons were investigated at one time or another. It is not known how many of these persons were disgraced. In July 1979, it was announced that more than 800 of those disgraced had been rehabilitated after 1977, that is, the adverse decisions against them were reversed, the labels removed, and their reputations reaffirmed. (The eminent economist Sun Yefang was denounced as a "counterrevolutionary revisionist.")

groups" and must reflect the dark side of the society as well as its bright spots, has been heard once again. It has been reflected in many loudly acclaimed short stories, poems, journalistic reports, and essays including "Between a Human Being and a Monster," [37] "The Wounds," "The Son of the Commander of the Artillery Forces," and "From Where Silence Reigns." Its once youthful protagonists such as Liu Binyan are now conspicuous figures in the literary world after many years of obscurity. [38] Although there is still a strong undercurrent of opposition to these ideas, and in many places opinion swung away from them in the early months of 1980, the debate has been conducted in the open. [39] The party is apparently attempting to balance those writing which explore the darker side of the society by an advocacy of writings which reflect the endeavors to correct the past mistakes and to build a modernized society. In spite of the criticisms launched against Bai Hua's *Bitter Love* and Ye Wenfu's poems in 1981 and 1982, the slogan "literature and art serve politics" has officially been replaced by "literature and art serve the people and serve socialism." This change was accompanied by the official abandonment of Mao's famous axiom laid down at the Yanan Forum that "literature and art are subordinate to politics" from which the former slogan was derived. [40]

Research institutes and universities have been strengthened and given greater financial support. The expansion of the Academy of Sciences and the transformation of the Department of Philosophy and the Social Sciences into the new Academy of the Social Sciences are merely the most prominent examples. Economists have been playing a very visible role in formulating economic policies. Scientists, engineers, and other technical experts have been given a greater voice in pursuing their own research and in charting the development of their respective fields. Vice-Premier Deng Xiaoping told a group of scientists that he was willing to serve as the head of the department of logistics for their scientific research. [41] Party

37. For the public response to this exposure of a case of corruption, see Liu Binyan, "The Call of the Times."

38. *Dagong bao,* December 14, 1979, p. 1.

39. From January 23 to February 23, 1980, the Chinese Associations of Playwrights, Writers, and Movie Makers held several joint discussions on the new situation and new problems that had emerged during the past two years. The discussion was focused on three plays (*The Impostor, The Female Thief,* and *In the Dossier of the Society*). Although the majority of the participants pointed out the "serious defects" of these plays and scripts, the view of the other side was also put on record. More important, no label was put on the writers.

40. Article by Wang Roxui, *Renmin ribao,* April 28, 1982, p. 5. For a brief report on Hu Qiaomu's talk, see *Dagong bao,* June 28, 1982, p. 1. For the criticism of Bai Hua's *Bitter Love,* see my paper "Paradoxes in Political Reform in China," presented at a conference in November 1981 held at the University of Chicago. [A revised version of this paper is published as chapter 7 in this volume.]

41. Deng's speech at the National Conference on Science, March 18, 1978, *Hongqi,* 1978, no. 4, p. 17.

and government officials were told that although party leadership in the overall programs throughout the nation and in various units must be maintained, outsiders should not interfere with the work of insiders and in technical matters outsiders cannot lead insiders. Indeed, persons with specialized knowledge should shoulder the burden of leadership in party committees and in professional organizations at all levels.[42] One should not be afraid of the charge that one adopts "the line of experts" and allows "the experts to run the factory and the university."

The elevation of the role to be played by scientists and specialists reached a high point in the speech before the National Congress of the All-China Association for Science and Technology made by Party General Secretary Hu Yaobang. He called on the party and the government to place able research workers in positions where they can freely and boldly use their special talents and to promote those specialists with administrative and organizational ability to positions of leadership in the party, government, economic, scientific, and educational works. As a symbolic gesture, he told the assembled scientists that he and his colleagues in the Secretariat were prepared to invite some of the scientists to hold symposiums and seminars on special subjects for their benefit and to invite the scientists to be their "teachers" (laoshi). [43]

Almost all the professional and academic associations that existed before the Cultural Revolution have been reestablished. The first meetings of these associations furnished the occasion for the tearful reunion of old friends and colleagues for the first time in more than ten years and, in some cases, more than twenty years. A participant in the Fourth Congress of Chinese Writers and Artists used the metaphor of "hospital for wounded soldiers" to describe the assemblage of writers and artists.[44] Not only were the participants old and sick, or had suffered physical injuries at the hands of the Red Guards during the Cultural Revolution, they were also spiritually "wounded." The meeting was an occasion for treating these wounds. Xiao Jun, the Manchurian writer who had lived in obscurity after his attack on the behavior of the Soviet Union and the Red Army in his native region, called himself "a cultural relic" recently unearthed. Liu Shaotang, who at the age of twenty-one had been labeled a big rightist in 1957, declared that he would begin his life and writing career again as if he were twenty-one.[45]

In addition, new professional and academic associations have been established as a result of the tendency toward increasing specialization. Lo-

---

42. Article by Zheng Yan, *Hongqi*, 1980, no. 3, p. 35.
43. *Renmin ribao*, March 25, 1980, p. 2.
44. This remark was made by the poet Ke Yan (*Dagong bao*, December 28, 1979, p. 7).
45. *Dagong bao*, December 14, 1979, p. 7; December 28, 1979, p. 7; *Ming bao* (The Bright Daily), November 23, 1979, p. 3.

cal associations have been set up in various provinces and cities to mobilize all human resources to achieve a more decentralized pattern of organization and to take advantage of special talents and conditions in these localities. for example, Nanjing is the center for the study of the Taiping Rebellion, Wuhan for the study of the 1911 Revolution, and Guangzhou for the study of the life of Sun Yat-sen. Most significantly, academics and professionals have been encouraged to take the initiative in organizing specialized associations.[46] These associations are not merely transmission belts. They are beginning actively to promote the interests of their members. The Association of Chinese Writers recently adopted a decision to organize a committee to protect the rights and interests of the writers under the chairmanship of the highly respected veteran writer, Xia Yan.[47] At the National Congress of Associations of Scientific Workers held in March 1980, the veteran scientist Zhou Peiyuan declared that the association must resolutely struggle against any attempt to attack and oppress scientific workers or any action that violates their rights and interests.[48]

The *fanshen* or the reversal of the position of the intellectuals and the reverse flow of their influence to the state and the party on basic policy decisions and institutional reconstruction constitute only one of the many manifestations of the changing relationships between political power and society. Former capitalists, landlords, and rich peasants are also being given a different position in the political system. The then premier and party chairman, Hua Guofeng, solemnly declared at the second session of the Fifth National People's Congress in June 1979 that, as classes, the landlords and rich peasants had ceased to exist. As for the capitalists, Hua said that "the great majority of these people have been transformed into laborers earning their own living in our socialist society" and that "the capitalists no longer exist as a class."[49] An effort has been made to return or replace personal and real properties confiscated or requisitioned during the Cultural Revolution. Former capitalists are again placed in enterprises in accordance with their technical and managerial ability. They are being given a major role in programs to attract foreign and overseas Chinese investments in joint enterprises.

Of great importance for our purpose is the new status conferred on for-

---

46. For a discussion of the functions of these mass organizations in the scientific and technological fields by a leading theoretician in China, Yu Guangyuan, see *Renmin ribao*, March 14, 1980, p. 5. Under the All-China Association for Science and Technology there are more than one hundred societies on special subjects.

47. *Huaqiao ribao*, January 12, 1980. Xia's leg was broken by the mob during the Cultural Revolution and he was permanently crippled. He was also imprisoned for a period of time. Only in 1978 did he become active again (*Dagong bao*, December 28, 1979, p.7).

48. *Dagong bao*, March 24, 1980, p. 1.

49. *Beijing Review*, June 16, 1979, p. 9.

mer landlords and rich peasants in the countryside. In early 1979, the Central Committee adopted a decision to remove the designations of those landlords, rich peasants, counterrevolutionaries, and bad elements who had, over the years, abided by state laws and decrees, worked honestly, and done no evil and to grant them the same rights as enjoyed by rural commune members.[50] They have been reclassified as commune members.[51] It was also decreed that there should be no discrimination against the descendants of the landlords, rich peasants, and members of the national bourgeoisie in the future regarding education, work, and admissions to the Youth League or the party.

The significance of this change is apparent when viewed against the earlier policy. Up to that time, the alleged existence and continuing influence of these two rural classes were used to justify the increasing penetration of state power into the rural society to bring about the dominance of the poor and middle peasant class in the countryside. The repressive measures against the landlords and rich peasants and the discriminatory treatment of their descendants had the latent function of demonstrating the absolute authority and unchallengeable power of the local cadres, which cowed all social groups and individuals, including the poor and lower-middle peasants, into submission to the state's demands for further social change and economic reconstruction. These practices helped stifle the peasants' expression of demands based on felt needs and perceived interests and give the cadres scapegoats for their own errors and shortcomings. Overall they raised tensions in the countryside which prevented the development of a regularized and predictable relationship between the state and society.[52]

The redefinition of the class situation in society was accompanied by a reassessment of the seriousness of class struggle. It is said that although

50. *Beijing Review*, February 16, 1979, p. 8. In 1978, there had been more than five million landlords and rich peasants. By 1979, only fifty thousand retained these labels (*Beijing Review*, January 21, 1980, p. 14). To what extent this change actually occurred in the countryside cannot be ascertained.

In 1950, the State Council adopted a regulation under which the labels of landlord and rich peasant could be removed if the landlord had worked in the field for five years and the rich peasant had worked three years without violating laws and regulations and without doing evil things ("On Certain Problems concerning Classes and Class Struggle," *Xinhua yuebao [Wenzhai ban]* [New China Monthly (Selected Articles)], 1980, no. 10, p. 1). But this regulation was never enforced.

51. *Beijing Review*, June 21, 1980, p. 10.

52. The discriminatory treatment of the descendants of landlords and rich peasants has contributed to the magnification of class struggle in the countryside simply as a result of population growth. For example, there remained in one province about 50,000 persons who had originally been classified as landlords or rich peasants. But their second generation numbered more than 250,000 persons and the third generation, 500,000 (*Hongqi*, 1980, no. 2, p. 29).

class struggle has not died out, the period of large-scale and turbulent class struggle is over. "Class struggle in the days to come will no longer be a struggle between *classes as a whole.*"[53] It is no longer the "principal contradiction" that needs to be resolved at the present time. Vice-Chairman Ye Jianying declared in his historic speech on September 29, 1979, that "we must oppose the view that magnifies it [class struggle], to say nothing of creating so-called class struggles out of the void."[54] Even more significantly, it is asserted that "at all times class struggle is a means; the basic goal of revolution is to liberate and develop the social productive forces."[55] These statements represent a reaffirmation and an extension of the conclusions adopted by the Eighth Party Congress in September 1956, which of course were repudiated during the decade of the Cultural Revolution. Just as the ultraleftists' totalitarian program rested on a special definition of class struggle, the new definition points to a decision not to change the existing social stratification by direct political action. Inputs and feedback from the society to the party and the state will be allowed to have greater impact than before.

Restructuring the Economy and Rediscovering the Importance of the Immediate Material Interests of the Individual

The retreat of politics finds no more concrete expression than in the field of economics. The former trend toward increasing the scope of planning, restricting the use of the market, limiting the function of price, attacking the use of profits, and disparaging material incentives has been reversed. Now, the limitations of planning are underscored. Xue Muqiao, the noted economist who serves as an adviser to the State Planning Commission and the director of the Economic Research Institute attached to it, has observed that the state economic plan should not be all-inclusive and impose many precise targets on grass-roots units because the more specific the terms laid down by the state organs at the top become, the more difficult it is to strike a balance between the supply and demands for products.[56] Xue suggests that on the contrary, most of the final plans of the

53. *Beijing Review,* November 16, 1979, p. 16; italics added. The implications of this view are far-reaching. Would struggle between classes as a whole be replaced by conflicts among institutional interest groups and corporate professional and occupational groups? What role would the party play in the resolution of these conflicts?

54. *Beijing Review,* October 5, 1979, p. 21.

55. *Beijing Review,* November 23, 1979, p. 16. The Chinese now admit their error in their criticism of Stalin's view expressed in 1936 that exploitative classes had disappeared in the Soviet Union. At the same time, they reaffirmed their criticism of Stalin's judgment expressed in 1937 that class struggle had sharpened. See "On Certain Problems Concerning Classes and Class Stuggle," pp. 4–5.

56. "A Study in the Planned Management of the Socialist Economy," *Beijing Review,* October 26, 1979, pp. 14–21.

state-owned enterprises in production and marketing should be decided on by the enterprises themselves after consultation with the upper-level units. Enterprises should be given certain rights over their own incomes and expenditures. Xue also proposes the abandonment of the present procedure of making state plans under which purchasing plans are worked out according to production plans and marketing plans are in turn worked out according to the purchasing plans. Instead, he urges that purchasing plans should be drawn up on the basis of market needs and production plans drawn up on the basis of purchasing plans. In other words, sales in the market should determine production plans. Concrete measures to implement these suggestions are being discussed. Experiments giving the enterprises a large degree of autonomy have been undertaken.[57]

In agriculture, rural free markets have been reopened and expanded.[58] Private plots and sideline production by peasant households have been given added protection. The use of price policy in the promotion of economic growth is nowhere more obvious than in agriculture. In 1979, the state purchase price of grain was increased 20 percent with an added 50 percent for above quota purchases. The prices paid by the state for edible oil, pigs, and eggs were also raised. According to the government's calculations, these changes in prices would increase the peasants' per capita income from the collective unit by 8 *yuan* a year—an increase of more than 10 percent from their average per capita income of 73.90 *yuan* in 1978.[59]

The autonomy of the basic grass-roots units in the countryside—the production teams—has been given greater protection by the regime. In

57. By 1980, these experiments were being undertaken in more than three thousand factories, or 7 percent of the industrial enterprises owned by the state. This 7 percent produced more than 30 percent of the total industrial output or around 40 percent of the total profits derived from industry (speech by Liu Guoguang, *Wenhui bao* [Literary Catchment Daily] [Hong Kong], March 8, 1980, p. 7). On a report on the experiment in one hundred factories in Sichuan in the first half of 1979, see the article by Ren Tao of the Institute of Planned Economy of the State Planning Commission in *Jingji yanjiu* (Economic Research), December 1979, pp. 6–9, 33. Six of these factories were studied more intensively than others. Many of the one hundred factories formerly held the title of "enterprises of the Daqing type." For a report of a survey of these experiments in Sichuan, Anhui, and Zhejiang, see the article by Lin Zili, *Renmin ribao*, April 4, 1980, p. 5. See also ibid., April 4, 1980, p. 1.

58. By early 1980, there were thirty-six thousand rural markets, close to the total number existing in 1965. The monetary transactions at these markets in 1979 increased by 36 percent over 1978 (*Renmin ribao*, March 10, 1980, p. 2). According to G. William Skinner there were forty-five thousand market towns in China in the mid-nineteenth century. There are now approximately fifty thousand communes. The number of rural markets given refers most likely to the large local market and does not include many small ones.

59. According to a later report, the preliminary calculation shows that the peasants' average per capita income from the collective units in 1979 was 84 *yuan*, an average increase of 10 *yuan*, 2 *yuan* more than the projected figure (Report of the Vice-Chairman of the Planning Commission, Li Renjun, by the New China Agency, *Dagong bao*, April 11, 1980, p. 1).

1978, it publicized criticism of the cadres in Xiang Xiang County in Hunan Province for their indiscriminate attempts to use, without compensation, the labor power and material resources of the production teams for projects undertaken at the higher levels and for their misappropriation of state funds intended for the benefits of the teams.[60] Soon thereafter another campaign publicized the arbitrary use of power by the cadres in Xunyi County in Shaanxi Province.[61] Many of the specific examples of abuses reported in the press were related to the attempts of brigade, commune, and county level cadres to use their political authority and influence to restrict the permissible private economic activities of the peasants.

More significantly, since 1979 the regime has promoted the adoption of the responsibility system in agriculture production, under which the contract relation has been given a progressively larger role while authority over work assignment and distribution of rewards has been transferred downward.[62] A primary feature of this system is the linkage between yield and reward received by the peasants. In December 1981, it was reported that more than 90 percent of the 5,870,000 production teams had adopted one or another of the many forms of the responsibility system, 16.9 percent of them were using the household responsibility system (baochan daohu), and 11.3 percent had adopted the household total responsibility system (baogan daohu).[63] By April 1982, it was reported that about half of the teams had adopted either the household responsibility system or the household total responsibility system; that is roughly 21.8 percent more than the figure given in December 1981.[64] The draft constitution published on April 28, 1982, provides for the reestablishment of the xiang-level government,[65] which was eliminated when the commune system was established as both an economic and a government unit. The communes would presumably be retained as a collective economic unit to manage small industrial and other enterprises. In the three xian in which experiments with the reform of the commune system had been undertaken, the production brigade as a level of economic organization was abolished and replaced by a unit with the traditional name of cun for the purpose of administration.[66] Thus the plan to divide political and economic functions and assign them to separate organs has been tried out at the lowest level

60. *Renmin ribao*, July 5, 1978, p. 1.

61. Ibid., August 3, 1978, p. 1.

62. For a detailed discussion, see Tang Tsou, Marc Blecher, and Mitchell Meisner, "The Responsibility System in Agriculture," *Modern China* 8 (January 1982): 41–103.

63. *Wenzhai bao* (Journal of Selected Reports), December 15, 1981, p. 1.

64. *Liaowang* (Outlook), 1982, no. 4, p. 8.

65. *Renmin ribao*, April 28, 1982, p. 4.

66. *Dagong bao*, June 17, 1982, p. 1.

in the countryside. The purpose is to minimize direct political interference in the management of agricultural and other economic activities at the grass roots. The state is to retreat a step further in its control over society.

Urban residents, particularly urban youth seeking employment, are being encouraged to organize themselves into small cooperatives to engage in small industrial and handicraft undertakings and service trades. Licenses for individual traders and handicraftsmen in some activities are again being issued. This decision reverses the political trends since the mid-1950s toward absorbing all family- and individual-owned stores and trades into ever larger state-owned and operated enterprises and cooperatives.

In other words, the state is increasingly relying on indirect methods to control China's economy. This new system is helping to replace, to some extent, centralized bureaucratic measures by the use of market forces and price mechanisms to create a structure in which basic-level units and individuals are given a much larger measure of autonomy than before to respond to economic incentives.[67] Individuals, collective units in both urban and rural areas, and state-owned enterprises are encouraged to play a more active role and to take greater initiative in increasing their own earnings and thus in promoting economic development of the society. At the height of the trend toward economic liberalization, the slogan that China's economy was based on an integration of planned and market economies was frequently heard. Since then, it has been replaced by the formula that China's economy is primarily planned and market economy is to be used as a supplement.

Such changes in economic thinking and practice took place in the larger context of renewed attention to the immediate material interests and pressing needs of the masses, as distinguished from supposedly objective, long-term interests and needs as defined by the party and the state. The party repeatedly noted in its analyses that during the periods of the revolutionary wars, the relationship between the party and the masses was analogous to that between fishes and water.[68] The party survived because it received wholehearted support from the masses. According to the party's own estimates, this support was given because the party attended

67. Xu Dixin, Dong Fureng, and Liu Guoguang, in their capacities then as respectively the director and vice-directors of the Institute of Economic Research of the Chinese Academy of the Social Sciences, made three informative speeches in Hong Kong on the new policies. The full texts are printed in *Wenhui bao* (Hong Kong), March 8, 1980, pp. 6–7. These speeches are among the best summaries of the policies at that time. See also Xue Muqiao's three-part article in *Beijing Review*, February 4, 1980, pp. 16–21; March 24, 1980, pp. 21–25; and April 7, 1980, pp. 20–25.

68. For example, "Never Forget the Relationship between Fishes and Water," by "our special commentator," *Renmin ribao*, August 19, 1978, p. 2.

to the masses' material interests and felt needs and advocated programs designed to link its historic mission to everyday questions of people's livelihood and to their hopes and demands. This relationship gradually eroded after the party came to power. Now wide gaps existed between the party and the masses. The masses kept the party at a distance and did not express their real views and true feelings in the presence of party and government cadres, for they no longer trusted the cadres and they had no confidence in the party. Moreover, they were in constant fear that no matter what policies the party should adopt today, they will be changed after a little while. The party's statements no longer had any credibility; its promises no longer inspired confidence. In other words, the party recognized realistically the existence of a profound crisis of confidence and authority. It was taking steps to overcome this crisis.

To this end, the material interests of individuals are being given a prominent place in ideology and policy decisions. A *Renmin ribao* special commentator asserts: "Personal interests are the base on which class interests are concentrated; without this base there are no such things as common class interests. Moreover, the common interests of a class will eventually find expression in terms of its members' personal interests. . . . To deny personal interests means also to deny common class interests; the so-called 'common interests' divorced from the laborers' personal interests, in fact, can only mean the interests of a few. . . . In building socialism, we must not ignore the laborers' personal interests; on the contrary, we must pay close attention to their material interests; otherwise it will be impossible to bring about socialism."[69] In effect, the material interests of individuals are being given a larger place in the traditional formula that the socialist economy should integrate the material interests of the state, the collective units, and the individuals in various fields.

"Socialist Legality" and "Socialist Democracy"

The relationship between the individual and the state is also changing. The direction is toward granting the individual a limited sphere of immunity in which he can be assured of some degree of regularity and predictability in his daily life. The full significance of this new direction cannot be found by an examination of the slight changes in the provisions in the draft constitution for individual rights, or in the reaffirmation of such principles as "all citizens of the People's Republic of China are equal before the law," and the independence of the judiciary. It can be understood only as a profound reaction against the arbitrary use by a minority group of political leaders of the authority of the state and the power of the mob to harass, attack, detain, arrest, and incarcerate a large number of other

69. The translation used is taken from *Peking Review*, October 13, 1978, p. 7.

leaders and to oppress most social strata.[70] The ability of the ultraleftists and the Lin Biao group to grasp a share of power with the support of the mob is attributed, among other things, to the nonexistence of a legal framework that limits the authority of the state and protects individuals from mob actions. The current emphasis on "socialist legality" is intended to prevent the recurrence of the terror unleashed by the Cultural Revolution, which is now regarded as a "catastrophe."[71]

China's basic criminal code, which had gone through more than thirty drafts before the Cultural Revolution, was finally adopted, together with a law on criminal procedures. However imperfect these laws are, they give the Chinese a structure of expectations in their daily life, or at least a set of standards to measure the actions of government organs and officials when these impinge on their personal freedom and physical security. In the legal provisions on the relationships among the police, the procuracy, and the courts, the Chinese now underscore more strongly than before the principle of checks and balances. The powerful political force behind this drive toward socialist legality finds institutional expression in the Committee on Legal Institutions headed by Peng Zhen—potentially one of the most important committees of the revitalized National People's Congress.

Notwithstanding the arrest of Wei Jingsheng and the unnecessarily severe sentence of fifteen-year imprisonment imposed on him, the case marks a step forward compared to the judicial behavior of the regime even in the period before the Cultural Revolution. The provisions on counterrevolutionary activities remain highly ambiguous and full of loopholes for arbitrary conviction and punishment. But the recognition of the principle that only overt action plus intent constitute a counterrevolutionary crime is a far cry from the indiscriminate earlier use of the label of "counterrevolutionary."

The legal provisions on perjury and false accusation are also intended to prevent the recurrences of both the use of trumped-up charges and the provision of artificially manufactured testimonies either in political movements or in "special case investigations" conducted by the government and the party.

In a very broad sense, democracy can be understood as comprised of institutions established to facilitate inputs and feedback from the society to the government and, more important, to secure the accountability of the government to the society. Whatever its limitations, "socialist democracy" is supposed to provide the same safeguards. The post-Mao trends

70. Ye accused the ultraleftists of suppressing "every social stratum" (Beijing Review, October 5, 1979, p. 18).
71. Ibid., p.19.

stem not only from the tragic experience of most of the current leaders with "feudal fascism" but also from a new appreciation of the positive relationship of a modicum of freedom of person, expression, and association to the major objectives of the regime. Although the slogans "Mr. Democracy" and "Mr. Science" were widely heard during the May Fourth period, in 1979 and 1980 the press publicized the idea that without democracy there cannot be rapid development of science.[72] The relationship between progress in academic research in all fields and political democracy is recognized. Previously, the intellectuals demanded only the drawing of a clear demarcation line between academic study and politics and the grant of freedom of expression on academic questions. In 1979 the view was expressed that, without freedom of speech in the political field as well, there can be no genuine freedom of discussion in science and art. Li Shu, the editor of *Historical Research*, wrote: "To restrict freedom of speech on matters of politics is equivalent to endorsing political autocracy. Once an autocracy is established in political matters, it will definitely not be restricted to politics alone; freedom of speech in the sphere of science and art will also be written off by such an autocracy. This was precisely the case under the cultural autocracy established during the period when Lin Biao and the Gang of Four dominated over the people."[73] To be sure, this is still not the official view, but the fact that it was publicly advocated by an important intellectual is significant.

Although the regime has rejected the slogan of democracy as "the fifth modernization," which was raised by such dissenters as Wei Jingsheng, Ye Jianying in his authoritative speech of September 29, 1979, declared that the reform and improvement of the "socialist political system" and the development of "an advanced socialist democracy and a complete socialist legal system" were "important objectives as well as necessary conditions for the realization of the four modernizations."[74]

The most important reform in the electoral system is the stipulation that the number of candidates nominated through "democratic consultation" should be larger than the number of persons to be elected. An alternative procedure is to have two rounds of voting. The first round is used

72. The term "science" now refers specifically to systematic scientific theory and research, as well as generally to the scientific attitude that was stressed during the May Fourth period as a weapon to attack traditional superstition, attitudes, and values. The term "democracy" can be best understood in the broad sense as a system of freedoms or rights which preceded the establishment in the West of a system of democratic government in the strict sense of the term and made it possible for science to develop even under a monarchical or autocratic government. It refers primarily to "limited government" and only secondarily to "democracy" in the narrower sense.

73. "Academic Freedom and Political Democracy: A Discussion in Academic Research Sponsored by the Beijing Guangming Daily," *Eastern Horizon*, November 1979, p. 6.

74. *Beijing Review*, October 5, 1979, p. 23.

to adopt a list of nominees. In the second round, this list is voted upon. Both represent a partial return to the Yanan practice. The secret ballot has been reinstituted. The election of cadres at the shop level in factories is being tried. Direct election of local representative bodies has been extended from the basic to the county level, and for this purpose sixty-six counties were designated in 1979 as experimental units.[75] Competition for nomination and election is still subject to many political restrictions in practice. But a small formal beginning has been made. In the new election of provincial governors in several provinces, the first secretary of the party committee of the province is no longer always elected as governor. In some cases, he is elected as the chairman of the standing committee of the Provincial People's Congress, the legislature of the province. The party and the government are in the process of reestablishing their separate identities. Experiments with the use of public opinion surveys to determine the support enjoyed by the cadres and to discover the people's reaction to official policies and decisions are being undertaken, in some cases leading to the promotion and demotion of cadres or modification of policies. In the West, democracy is a system in which the state or the party binds itself or precommits itself so that it becomes impossible or difficult to follow certain options otherwise available to it.[76] Socialist democracy in China may in the end incorporate something similar to this feature but in its own way. Ultimately, the significance of these changes in the institutional structure and rules in China under the rubric of socialist democracy depends on the reciprocal effect between them and the developing institutional pluralism inside and outside the party.

Restructuring the Internal Relations of the Party

The fundamental reorientations mentioned above which, taken together, mark a change in the relationship between politics and other spheres of activities are necessarily accompanied by a restructuring of the relations within the party elite and between party and nonparty elites. Although whether it can be maintained for a long period is unclear, collective leadership has replaced the cult of the individual. When Hua Guofeng was concurrently party chairman and premier of the State Council, he was not the most powerful man in China. Within one year of its announcement, his overambitious program of economic development had been replaced by the three-year program of readjustment, restructuring, consolidation,

75. For a concise report on the changes in the system of election and nomination, see *Dagong bao*, February 12, 1980, p. 1.

76. For the notion of "binding oneself" and "precommitment" in a theory of rational choice, see Jon Elster, *Ulysses and the Sirens* (Cambridge: Cambridge University Press, 1979).

and improvement of the economy under the aegis of Vice-Premier Chen Yun, with the strong support of the recently rehabilitated economists and the economic, financial, commercial, and trade bureaucracies. Vice-Premier Deng Xiaoping may be the most powerful man, but even he does not dominate all policy decisions. He has found it necessary to change the timetable in the implementation of his policies and to water down some of their content, as in the case of the trial of the Gang of Four, the convocation of the Sixth Plenum and the Twelfth Party Congress, and the reorganization of the State Council and the Party Center.

Neither Ye Jianying, the most senior military leader, Deng Xiaoping, the nominal chief of staff until early 1980, Wei Guoqing, the head of the Political Department, nor Geng Biao, the secretary general of the Military Committee of the CCP can command and control the PLA as formerly Mao or even Lin Biao did. Hu Yaobang, the general secretary of the Secretariat reestablished in February 1980, does not exercise the same control over the party apparatus that Deng Xiaoping did. His promotion to party chairmanship in June 1982 enhances his authority and power but he cannot dominate the party as Mao did. The post of chairmanship was abolished altogether in September 1982. The State Council under Zhao Ziyang is today a more collegiate body than under Zhou Enlai, although the system of decision by the premier provided by the draft constitution published in April 1982 will undoubtedly strengthen the institutional authority of the premier. Premier Zhao's relationship with Hu is no longer that between a chief lieutenant and a supreme leader. The revitalized and increasingly influential Standing Committee of the NPC represents a new institutional force, the symbol of socialist legality and socialist democracy. The plenary session of the Central Committee now takes place regularly, as it did from 1949 to 1959. The tendency to decentralize power and functions to the provincial-level units to deal with variations in local situations to speed up the four modernizations is likely to loosen up the elite structure still further.

The process of de-deification of Mao has gone so far that it is difficult, if not impossible, for another cult of personality to develop. In the important document adopted at the Fifth Plenum in February 1980, "Guiding Principles for Inner-Party Political Life," Article 2 is concerned with the problem of "firmly upholding collective leadership and opposing arbitrary decision by one individual."[77] A significant editorial in the *Renmin ribao* noted that although the top leader in a unit bears the principal responsibility for any departure from "collective leadership," the blame must be shared by those who always agree with the top leaders on questions of

77. *Hongqi*, 1980, no. 6, pp. 3–4.

principle. The latter are encouraged to think independently and to uphold principles firmly.[78] The promotion of Hu Yaobang and Zhao Ziyang to the Standing Committee of the Politburo, the reestablishment of the Secretariat with eleven new members under General Secretary Hu, and the removal of four of the seven top leaders who had risen to prominent positions during the Cultural Revolution were important steps to prepare for the establishment of a new collective leadership and a repudiation of Mao's practice of cultivating or designating a single successor by the supreme leader.[79] No less important is Article 37 of the new constitution of the CCP to the effect that "Party cadres at all levels, whether elected through democratic procedure or appointed by a leading body, are not entitled to lifelong tenure."[80] This provision, together with the policy of promoting young and middle-aged cadres with specialized skills to responsible positions and the growing practice of more frequent transfers of cadres from one post to another, will help solve the problem of the increased rigidity of the party and government bureaucracies at all levels.[81]

Equally important, the party and the government, which during the Cultural Revolution were fused to a very large extent particularly on the provincial level and below, are now being separated from each other. In many units, the party leader no longer serves as the head of the administration. More specifically, many articles criticize the past tendency for the party committee, particularly the party secretary, to substitute itself or himself for the administrative leadership not only in the government, economic, educational, and other units but also in collective units down to the level of the brigade.[82] A certain degree of institutional pluralism with checks and balances has been restored.

Bureaucratism and the patriarchal style of administration, which had been deeply rooted in the traditional Chinese sociopolitical system and reemerged in the Communist Chinese political system and command economy, will prove to be the most intractable problem. These two evils are considered by the current leaders as a legacy of "feudalism." As a lead article in *Hongqi* put it, the bureaucrats in economic management do not

78. *Renmin ribao*, March 23, 1980, p. 1.

79. Tito may have provided a precedent or example for this new step.

80. "Constitution of the Communist Party of China," *Beijing Review*, September 20, 1982, p. 19. This practice of "being a lifelong cadre" corresponds to the practice of giving an "iron rice bowl" to the workers. In some factories the son or daughter can take over his or her parent's job, if the latter retires.

81. For an early diagnosis of this problem, see the insightful article by Mike Oksenberg, "The Exit Pattern from Chinese Politics and Its Implications," *China Quarterly*, no. 67, September 1976, pp. 501–18.

82. Li Honglin, "What Kind of Leadership by the Party We Uphold," *Xinhua yuebao (Wenzhai ban)*, 1979, no. 11, p. 3. For a report on separating the party committee from the administrative leadership at Nankai University, see *Renmin ribao*, March 29, 1980, p. 3.

follow economic laws "in making decisions" but act "according to the will of their senior officials."[83] The gradual abolition of the practice of being a lifelong cadre will be helpful in combating this tendency. The special privileges of the high officials are a frequent target of attack both inside and outside China. Serious as this problem is, it is merely a reflection of the more fundamental problem of the arbitrary power held by the bureaucrats at all levels, which is used to control the life of the individuals. All these problems are recognized by the Chinese leaders. But whether they can be resolved or mitigated by the new reforms discussed herein remains to be seen.

The redefinition of the class situation in China, the recognition of the positive, manifest functions of the various social groups, and the reestablishment of professional and academic associations inevitably imply a restructuring of the relationship between the party and nonparty elites. The party's united front policy has been refurbished. The machinery of China's People's Political Consultative Conference at the national and provincial levels has been revitalized. The eight democratic parties have been revived. All these institutions serve as channels for the nonparty elites to influence party and government policies and decisions. It is likely that the eight democratic parties and groups will soon die out as their aged leaders pass from the scene, unless the regime adopts new policies to give them a permanent position in the political system and to attract younger persons. But as the economy grows in complexity, science and technology become increasingly sophisticated, and the links with the world market multiply, the professional, academic, and economic associations will gain strength and reinforce the structural foundation of social pluralism in China.

The Limits to Changes

It is important to remember that the repudiation of the features associated with revolutionary-"feudal" totalitarianism has occurred under the

83. Lin Zili, *Hongqi*, December 1979, p. 3. In its March 29, 1980, issue, *Ming bao* carried what purports to be excerpts from a speech made by Vice Chairman Chen Yun at a meeting of the Politburo in July 1979. Chen remarked that the constant guide used by the cadres is not "Marxism-Leninism," but the "will of their senior officials" and the "hints given with the eyes of the upper-level officials." After the Beijing regime publicized a directive to reaffirm the necessity of keeping party and government secrets and noted that much important information about China came back to China from outside, *Ming bao* carried an editorial saying that this speech was given to it by travelers from China and that it could not verify its authenticity. Several days later, the New China News Agency challenged the authenticity of several documents published by *Ming bao*. But the thrust of the remarks cited here is consistent with all the published articles and official statements, although the existence of many expressions and phrases not generally used in China suggests that the document as a whole is not authentic.

sponsorship and indeed the direction of rehabilitated leaders who spent their entire lives revolutionizing Chinese society. Their leadership accounts for the relative success of the reversal thus far undertaken but also sets a limit to how far the reversal will go. In their view, the sociopolitical system built by them during the revolutionary wars and after the capture of power had functioned effectively for long periods of time and had achieved great successes in various fields of endeavors until it was deranged and the fundamental principles underlying it were perverted. The program of rebuilding the institutions, shifting the focus of work, reinterpreting Mao Zedong Thought, and adopting new ideological, political, and organizational lines is considered partly an endeavor to meet new conditions brought about by the achievements as well as the errors of the past.

Thus the process of reversal and the new trend toward institutional and social pluralism have definite limits. This is the meaning of the reaffirmation in March 1979, of the four fundamental principles which are to guide Chinese political and social life. These four principles are: upholding socialism, the dictatorship of the proletariat, the leadership of the party and Marxism-Leninism, and Mao Zedong Thought. Deng Xiaoping, the single most important leader responsible for most of the fundamental changes before that time, played a prominent role, at least in public, in setting these limits at a time when the new changes threatened to get out of hand. Such limits were perhaps thought to be necessary to preserve the unity of the party elite and the stability of the sociopolitical system.[84] It is clear that even the Cultural Revolution did not shake the faith of the veteran leaders in the most basic ideological principles, and they cannot envisage an alternative system that will better perform the tasks of modernizing China. They have too much at stake. For many years to come, the question will be whether a political system set within these limits can perform effectively the function of promoting controlled social change fast enough to satisfy the demands and pressures originating inside China while enabling the state to cope successfully with a threatening international environment.

But for the moment let us observe that the consequences of this reaffirmation of the four principles bear only very superficial resemblance to those that followed Mao's retroactive statement in June 1957 on the six criteria for distinguishing "fragrant flowers" from "poisonous weeds." The present trend toward liberalization in such spheres as the economy, education, science and technology, and relationship with nonparty elites not

---

84. We do not yet have sufficient evidence to show whether Deng set these limits because he was under pressure from the standpatters and his position was momentarily weakened. My guess is that he did so out of conviction.

only continued but further developed in spite of the arrest, trial, and imprisonment of Wei Jingsheng. A careful reading of Ye Jianying's September 29, 1979, speech shows that the four principles are discussed in the context of stressing the role of the people. Ye concludes, "Thus, the source of strength of the four fundamental principles is the people and to give them full scope it is necessary to rely on the people."[85] This familiar and seemingly meaningless rhetoric takes on new significance within the changing framework of current ideological discourse and the shift in the relationship between politics and society noted above. Moreover, the Chinese notion of socialism is vague and broad. To some Chinese leaders, it had only two concrete meanings: first, ownership of the means of production by the state or by collective units; and second, the principle of distribution according to work. Later, a third element, a planned economy was added. The experiment of granting autonomy to the enterprises and the expansion of the use of the market mechanism as a supplement to planning point to the loosening of the system of planned economy. The principle of the dictatorship of the proletariat is a necessary reaffirmation of the CCP's link to Marxism-Leninism. Its main function is to legitimize the leadership of the party, defined as the vanguard of the proletariat. In the draft state constitution, the phrase "the people's democratic dictatorship" replaces the words "dictatorship of the proletariat" in crucial provisions although in one sentence in the Preamble the latter is used as an appositive of the former. The principle of upholding Marxism-Leninism and Mao Zedong Thought also, however, may pave the way to a return to dogmatism and fundamentalism in the future. Alternatively, these principles can all be reinterpreted under the formula of integrating "the universal principles of Marxism-Leninism-Mao Zedong Thought with the concrete practice of socialist modernization and develop it under the new historical conditions."[86]

Undoubtedly, the leadership of the party is the "most basic of the four fundamental principles," as Deng Xiaoping emphasized on January 1, 1980.[87] The theme of the Fifth Plenum held in February 1980 was "to strengthen and to improve the leadership of the party." To strengthen the leadership of the party may mean the strengthening of a "monistic center of power"[88] in the society. But this tendency must also be seen in the context of the granting of a greater degree of autonomy to the various social

85. *Beijing Review*, October 5, 1979, p. 16.
86. See "Communiqué of the Third Plenary Session of the Eleventh Central Committee of the Communist Party of China" (adopted on December 22, 1978), *Peking Review*, December 29, 1978, p. 15. See also Tsou, "Mao Tse-tung Thought," p. 524 [reproduced here as chapter 4 in this volume] for a forecast of this formulation.
87. *Renmin ribao*, January 2, 1980, p. 1.
88. This phrase is borrowed from Linz, "Totalitarianism and Authoritarianism," p. 191.

groups in the society, the elevation of the status of the scientists and specialists, and the growing complexity of the economy, which necessarily strengthens the indispensability and thus the influence of the professional and occupational groups. In other words, the "monistic center of power" will probably be increasingly restrained, influenced, and, indeed, penetrated by the social forces. The recent recruitment of scientists and technicians into the party is an indication of this possibility. In turn, it may be hoped that this possibility may lead to an increase in intraparty pluralism under collective leadership with renewed and widespread popular support.[89]

Yet the strengthening of the leadership of the party still raises the question whether there will be or can be any independent check on the party's power. This question has been underscored by the decision made by the Fifth Plenum to recommend the elimination of the provision in the 1978 State Constitution guaranteeing "big contending, big blooming, big debate and big-character posters"—the so-called "four big freedoms."[90] Later a constitutional amendment was adopted to implement this recommendation. This decision has been criticized even by many sympathetic observers outside China as a sign of a reversal of the trend toward liberalization and as a step to curb popular criticism in order to protect the interests of the party cadres.[91] To be sure, the use of big-character posters and popular protests, particularly in the Tiananmen incident of April 1976, did help the moderate, veteran party leaders first to oust the ultra-leftists and later to curb the influence of the standpatters. But it is a practice incompatible with the emergent pattern of politics in which the party has reasserted its primacy and the state is becoming a more and more im-

89. The future thus contains a wider range of possibilities for good or evil than we can envisage at this time. Yu Guangyuan, a leading theoretician, a vice-president of the Academy of the Social Sciences at that time, and the head of Institute of Marxism-Leninism and Mao Zedong Thought, makes a distinction between realization of the dictatorship of the proletariat *"through the party"* and its realization *"through an organization embodying the entire proletariat."* He attributes to Lenin the ideas that the Communists must create the conditions so that the dictatorship of the proletariat through its vanguard could be advanced to the dictatorship of the proletariat through an organization embodying the entire proletariat. The implication of Yu's idea is that the leadership of the party may one day be downgraded. The downgrading of the principle of party leadership coupled with the emphasis on "an organization embodying the entire proletariat" may in the future provide the ideological foundation of a greater degree of political and economic pluralism (*Xinhua yuebao* [*Wenzhai ban*], 1979, no. 6, pp. 22–31; italics added). One must also point out, however, that this article was published at the high point of the trend toward liberalization. Since 1981, this trend has been checked and even reversed in some specific areas in various degrees.

90. The real issue is the use of "big-character" posters; the other three phrases are mainly rhetorical flourishes.

91. Qi Xin, "Let's Look at How the Chinese Communist Party Strengthens Its Organization," *Qishi niandai* (The Seventies), 1980, no. 4, p. 58.

portant mechanism of regularized control through its new legal codes and revitalized institutions.

In early 1981, in another reversal of the trend toward liberalization, the party suppressed the publication of periodicals and journals by unauthorized groups and organizations. "Bourgeois liberalization" itself has been subject to increasingly harsh attack. It is important to watch whether the party will continue to allow or expand the areas of permissible criticism through the regularized channels such as letters to the editor of the numerous newspapers, the journals published by various associations, the meetings of the masses at basic-level units, the "legislative" organs at all levels, and finally the discussion within the party and government bodies. It is impossible to foresee how far the retreat of politics and the reversal of the trend toward totalitarianism will go. We do not know when the limits imposed by the four fundamental principles will be reached. Nor can we tell whether they will be reinterpreted in such a way that the areas of permissible changes will be enlarged or shrunk. But short of a sharp deterioration in China's international environment, it is possible to suggest that the current formula and the pattern of emergent institutions and policies will permit China to go a long way in the direction of growth and modernization before these limits are reached or before an impasse, and perhaps another upheaval to break it, will occur. The more immediate question, one impossible to answer, is what will happen with the passing of the remaining leaders of the Long March generation and their replacement by the generation of the anti-Japanese war.[92] Can the new generation of leaders, particularly those who had their roots in modern large cities and others who hailed from the rural areas and small county seats, maintain enough unity and cooperation to carry on the work and avoid an irreconcilable split such as overcame the Long March generation and lay at the root of the Cultural Revolution?

In sum, the CCP has been trying to incorporate a carefully limited degree of democracy within the restrictive framework of the four principles that form the foundation of a Leninist party-state. Apparently, it hopes that this limited change will provide a measure of mediation between the party-state and the various social groups, thus strengthening that linkage and enhancing the legitimacy of the regime. Allowing the civil society greater autonomy yet retaining the state's absolute control and leadership over it is one of the most difficult feats of statesmanship.[93] Equally difficult

92. Aside from the problem of political succession, the problem of a generation gap has been raised and discussed in China. For example, see *Zhongguo qingnian* (Chinese Youth), 1980, no. 1, pp. 14–18.

93. See Guillermo O'Donnell, "Tension in the Bureaucratic-Authoritarian State," in David Collier, ed., *The New Authoritarianism in Latin America* (Princeton: Princeton University Press), 1979, pp. 314–318.

is the task of maintaining the delicate balance between two current requirements: first, strengthening all the political institutions to enhance the capability of the state, and second, establishing a system of checks and balances and decentralizing political authority to provide for a higher degree of institutional pluralism and to make government organs more responsive to the multifarious social interests. Most of the political reforms in modern China up to 1977 aimed at satisfying the first requirement. Now the second desideratum must also be on the agenda. These two interrelated feats of statesmanship can meet with success only if necessary structural conditions obtained inside China and the international environment are favorable. Conditions inside China seem at the moment not to be adverse to their success, but a sharp setback in Sino-American relations may have totally unpredictable consequences.

Total Crisis and the Advance and Retreat of the Totalitarian Tendency in Twentieth-Century China

My purpose in this analysis of the post-Mao years is not to answer the questions raised in the last two paragraphs. Instead, I perform this task to seek a new perspective, to look back on political development in twentieth-century China in its entirety, to raise some fundamental questions of interpretation, and to sketch some tentative answers to guide our thinking and research.[94] These questions may be stated as follows: What was the origin of the totalistic response on the part of many intellectuals and political actors to the human conditions in China in the twentieth century which, after a long period of fluctuation, finally culminated in the revolutionary-"feudal" totalitarianism of the ultraleftists? What were the differences between the totalistic response of the Chinese Communists and that of other Chinese intellectuals which led the former but not the latter to develop a totalitarian program? It is obvious that certain elements of the Soviet version of Marxism or Marxism-Leninism-Stalinism provided the seed for a full-fledged totalitarianism in China. But why did this seed fail to grow into a mature plant during the era of revolutionary and foreign wars? Instead, it was precisely during the Yanan period when the CCP succeeded in establishing relatively secure base areas and rapidly expanded its power and influence that the party made important concessions to the social forces, perfected the united front policy, and developed a moderate pattern of inner party struggle.[95] Why did totalitarian tendencies manifest themselves with accelerated speed after 1949, particularly

94. As R. M. MacIver once paraphrased Aristotle, "We can learn the nature of anything only when it has reached—and passed—its maturation. Events and process, theories and actions, appear in a new perspective" (Foreword to Karl Polanyi, *The Great Transformation* [Boston: Beacon Press, 1957], p. ix).

95. The concept of totalitarianism as formulated by most Western social scientists from Friedrich to Linz applies to the regime, not to a revolutionary movement. An implicit as-

after 1957? Why did the resistance by various groups and strata prove to be so weak and so easily crushed? Why did the culmination of these tendencies take the form of the revolutionary-"feudal" totalitarianism of the ultraleftists? And yet why did even this species of totalitarianism never find complete fulfillment? Why was it discredited without too much difficulty? Why has the reversal after 1978 of the trend toward full-fledged totalitarianism been achieved with relative ease?

The answers to these questions take only very tentative and schematic form and are based on a series of simple propositions. In my opinion, the totalistic response developed by many of the foremost intellectuals and political actors in twentieth-century China was not primarily the product of the "persistent Chinese cultural predisposition toward a monistic and intellectualistic mode of thinking" or "intellectualistic, holistic, mode of thinking."[96] Although this cultural predisposition facilitated the emergence of the totalistic response, the decisive condition was the total crisis that confronted Chinese society in both domestic and international affairs.

For our purpose, the point to be emphasized is the obvious fact that a totalistic response does not necessarily give rise to the totalitarian tendencies which are a major feature of twentieth-century China. Hu Shi's totalistic iconoclasm and the idea of total Westernization briefly accepted by him could not have resulted in a totalitarian movement even if they had become the ideology of a party or regime. For the totalistic change he sought was supposed to come about through the development of a pragmatic-scientific attitude and habit of thought leading to a change in research, discussion, debate, methods of conflict resolution, behavior, and institutions. For him, politics did not figure prominently as a means; it was a product rather than a determinant of social and cultural change. Roughly speaking, the same was true of those programs that sought the salvation of the nation through the development of science, or industry, or education, or rural reconstruction advocated by various individuals and groups.

In contrast, the CCP's totalistic response contained two elements that turned it into a potentially totalitarian movement and regime. These two elements are the decisive and central role given to political power and the use of violence as a component of political power by a tightly organized elite that regards itself as the vanguard of a particular class. The CCP

sumption underlying my reformulation of this concept is that it can be extended to discuss the tendency inherent in some revolutionary movements. This extension of the applicability of the concept is also made necessary by the fact that the CCP established its own army, government, and base areas during the revolutionary period and was in fact a state within a state.

96. These phrases are borrowed from Yü-sheng Lin, who uses them to develop a different theme in his outstanding book, *The Crisis of Chinese Consciousness* (Madison: University of Wisconsin Press, 1979), pp. 29, 41.

tried to overcome the total crisis by capturing total power and to re-establish effective political authority in order to bring about a fundamental transformation of the social structure, to establish a new economic system and a new society, and to inculcate new values and attitudes espoused by new men. This approach appealed to many Chinese because it made sense to them. For events in twentieth-century China proved to their satisfaction that education, science, industry, and a new culture could not be developed fast enough to preserve China as a national entity and that they could not be developed without first establishing an effective government. At the same time, an effective system of political authority could not be established without at the same time solving some of the most pressing social and economic problems. Because the approach seemed sensible, its inherent and submerged totalitarian tendency, as well as its many potentially devastating consequences, was overlooked or minimized and rationalized if they were recognized.

The size and fragmentation of China that had made warlordism possible also facilitated the establishment of base areas by the CCP. The Sino-Japanese War of 1937–1945 saw the establishment and expansion of new base areas. In these base areas established before and after 1937, the totalitarian tendency began to raise its head. In various places and units, the ideological remolding campaign of 1942–1944 took a radical turn and threatened to get out of hand in its later phase. Mao's "Talks on Literature and the Arts at the Yenan Forum" was the first systematic statement legitimizing the control of political power over a sphere of professional activity.[97] It was not an accident that what happened in literature and the arts became the harbinger of things to come for other professions and occupations from 1949 to 1976. For literature and the arts bore a direct relationship to ideology, and they were the most effective instrumentality to influence the thinking and attitudes of the reading public and through them the masses. Moreover, during the Sino-Japanese War, writers and artists constituted the largest and most powerful profession in the base areas, which had almost no regular institutions of high learning or modern industry and commercial enterprises.[98]

97. Among other things, Mao asserted that "literature and art are subordinate to politics" (*Selected Readings from the Works of Mao Tse-tung*, p. 221). In the version of Vice-Premier Deng's speech on January 16, 1980, as published in *Ming bao*, Deng declared that "we . . . would no longer raise the slogan that 'literature and art are subordinate to politics' because this slogan can easily become the actual justification for arbitrary interference with literature and art" (*Ming bao*, March 3, 1980, p. 2). For a comment on how Mao's ideas were being pushed step by step to the extreme, see Luo Xun, "Literature and Arts, Life, and Politics." *Wenxue pinglun* (Literary Criticism), 1980, no. 1, p. 2. See also note 40, above.

98. In 1944 there were in the border area of Shaanxi-Gansu-Ningxia, only sixty publicly owned enterprises employing four thousand workers and staff members (*Jingji guanli* [Economic Management], October 1979, p. 46).

But the totalitarian tendency was confined to a small sphere. It was submerged and balanced by other, more powerful currents. Under the policy of the united front, accommodation with various social classes and groups both inside and outside of the base areas reached its highest point since the destruction of the alliance with the Guomindang in 1927. The material interests and felt needs of the people and groups were seriously taken into account in policy decisions and political actions. Persuasion rather than coercive methods were generally used to push reforms in an incremental rather than revolutionary manner. A moderate pattern of inner party struggle emerged, and a set of norms governing it was formalized and practiced under the joint auspices of Mao and Liu Shaoqi. Surrounded by powerful enemies, this was the only feasible way of resolving difference within the party. Otherwise defection to the other side was an alternative readily available to dissenters and opportunists, and a decline in the morale of its members would doom the party to failure. This moderate pattern of inner party struggle was made possible by the establishment of the recognized leadership of Mao.[99] But it is important to remember that the CCP was a minority party leading a minority movement which had to maintain the solidarity of its own rank and to gain the support of various social classes and groups in order to survive and to gain power. This distribution of power within China and the checks and balances among the various political and social forces account for the moderation of the CCP and for the lack of rapid development of the totalitarian tendency inherent in the ideology, the objective to transform the whole society, and the revolutionary use of political power and violence in the CCP's totalistic response to total crisis.

The nationwide victory of the People's Liberation Army brought about a fundamental change in the configuration of political forces. After 1949, the CCP had the monopoly of power. There were no longer any effective external checks and balances. Thus the totalitarian tendency gradually and over a period of years asserted itself and finally culminated in the revolutionary-"feudal" totalitarianism of the ultraleftists, which aimed at the removal of any internal party opposition and at another revolutionary transformation of the society. The Chinese now frequently used the term "feudal fascism" to characterize their program. A Chinese writer went a step farther and charged that they exercised "supra-feudal, supra-fascist 'all-round dictatorship'" over numerous cadres and masses.[100]

99. Frederick C. Teiwes, *Politics and Purges in China*, 1950–1965 (White Plains, N.Y.: M. E. Sharp, 1979). See also Tang Tsou, "Revolution, Reintegration, and Crisis in Communist China: A Framework for Analysis," in *China in Crisis*, ed. Ho Ping-ti and Tang Tsou, vol. 1 , Book 1 (Chicago: University of Chicago Press, 1968), p. 318. [Reproduced as chapter 1 in this volume.]

100. Xu Bing, "On Human Rights and Rights of Citizens," *Xinhua yuebao (Wenzhai ban)*, 1979, no. 7, p. 4.

Moreover, the nationwide victory was achieved by a strategy of surrounding the city from the countryside in a protracted struggle lasting twenty-two years. This struggle relied on the revolutionary momentum of the peasantry, a peasant-based army, and a party and government administration in base areas staffed by a large number of middle and lower-level cadres of rural origin with very little knowledge of urban life and still less of the world outside of China. Many top leaders, particularly Mao, took the peasantry, particularly what has come to be known as the poor and lower-middle peasants, as their responsibility reference groups. At different times, this rural orientation exerted its influence in different ways on the policies and programs adopted by these leaders toward various groups in the urban sectors.

Chinese peasants are very practical persons. But their attitudes and habits have been influenced by the long Chinese traditions rooted in the patriarchal Chinese family structure, such as the custom of sharing though not equality among family members and relatives, arbitrary decisions made by the patriarch, and respect for the aged. Although they welcome the practical benefits of modernization and mechanization, they have no conception of the requirements and consequences of rapid change. They desire their children to move upward in the social ladder, but they have little knowledge of modern culture, science, and technology. Many middle and low-level cadres who dominate the party and government at lower levels and even some top-level leaders have little or no scientific and technological knowledge and little education. A rapid program of modernization oriented toward the urban sector would inevitably undermine their position and render them useless. Yet any policies or measures that jeopardize their vested interests can be opposed or resisted as attacking the interests of the poor and lower-middle peasants and as forgetting their revolutionary contribution.

But there is another paradox. The CCP is a peasant-based party but not a peasant party. It is supposed to be the vanguard of a small, weak, disorganized, and uninformed proletariat—a class that can provide neither strong leadership nor the proper orientation for the entire society. The vanguard is to decide what is good for the nation without any immediate and direct political restraints from the various social forces. Thus the party can take steps that run counter to the immediate perceived interests and the desires of the peasantry, as it did in the acceleration of the program of cooperativization and communization and the abolition or restriction of private plots and rural markets in two different periods and in various localities. The party, or its radical leaders, is perhaps justified in thinking that the transformation of the peasants as a class of small producers is a necessary step in the transition to socialism or modernization. Even so, a proper sense of limits imposed by objective conditions can be, and was, overwhelmed by a desire for haste, by a sense of the omnipotence of political power it monopolizes, by the effectiveness of the organization it built, and by the popular support it once enjoyed.

Viewed from this perspective, political development since 1949 can be understood as a conflict between the inherent totalitarian tendency cum rural orientation and the need to recognize the indispensable roles played by various functional groups in the urban sector in achieving economic growth and modernizing the society and the state. The traditions established in the Yanan period would incline the party to respect a measure of autonomy and preserve the influence and limited authority of these functional groups, but the monopoly of power and the ardent desire to effect a total transformation of the society favored the totalitarian tendency. In the years before 1957, all party leaders, including Mao on one side and Zhou Enlai on the other, were ambivalent about the role of these functional groups, particularly the intellectuals. The party achieved a historic, unprecedented success in handling "national-capitalists." It destroyed them as a class but retained them in their managerial and technical positions and allowed them to perform their necessary functions in the economy. This innovative and ingenious solution now informs its handling of all functional groups in the society.

But in dealing with the intellectuals, who constitute one of the most important functional groups in any modern society, the party instituted a series of policies which finally led to disastrous results in the Cultural Revolution. The party reorganized the system of higher education after the Soviet model, amalgamating some of the universities and dismantling others, destroying their individuality and setting up a highly centralized and uniform system. The principle of party leadership overwhelmed and discredited the principle, advocated by some intellectuals, that professors should run the university. The dissatisfaction of the intellectuals, educators, and scientists which surfaced during the Hundred Flowers period soon brought about the antirightist movement. A similar process of tightening political and ideological control followed by resistance and protests and then by drastic repression of dissent occurred also in literature and the arts.

The rapid collapse of the resistance of these groups and the easy victory of the party were the almost inevitable result of the party's monopoly of power, the weakness of the intellectuals and the professional groups in the underdeveloped economy, and the imponderable might of the peasants and workers who formed the social basis of the party. But in retrospect, one important dimension in this development seems clear. It was that the party leaders did not have sufficient appreciation of the indispensability of the functions performed by the intellectuals and the various professional groups as political and social critics and as constructive forces in economic development. Thus 1957 marked a turning point in the relationship between the state and society. From that time to 1966, no social groups outside the party would offer any active resistance to the party. The penetration of politics into other spheres of society broke through all nonparty barriers. Only internal party restraints existed.

By breaking most of the internal party restraints and suppressing with some success whatever institutional and political pluralism existed within the party, the Cultural Revolution of 1966–1976 marked the culmination of the totalitarian tendency that found expression in the program and actions of the ultraleftists. Political actions undertaken by the Red Guards or mobs mobilized or encouraged by a group of leaders or simply permitted and protected by them broke through almost all restraints, legal, political, civic, social, and traditional, in utter disregard of common decency in an attempt to change man and society. "Politics takes command" degenerated into "politics may assault or overwhelm everything."[101]

The ultraleftists' understanding of the role of political power reflected a nonsensical reductionism that can be reconstructed as follows. From the not totally incorrect proposition that there is a political aspect to every event and to every relationship in society, the absurd conclusion was drawn that politics is everything and power constitutes the only relationship that counts. Thus the ultraleftists urged the workers "not to produce for the wrong [ideological and political] line," "not to produce for the faction of those taking the capitalist road." "We would rather have socialist low ratio of growth than capitalist high rate of growth." "We would rather stop production for two years than stop class struggle for one moment." Zhang Chunqiao was charged with having declared that "I would rather have a laborer without culture than to have an exploiter with culture" and that "it is useless to study."[102]

The general theory of class developed by the ultraleftists was based on a superficial and fundamentally incorrect interpretation of Marx's ideas. Yet many of its political slogans bore a close resemblance to traditional Chinese ideas and practices. It could not have been otherwise. For in attempting to destroy or weaken the party organization and government bureaucracy controlled by their opponents, the ultraleftists had to act in a fashion contrary to the modern organizational norms, rules, and ideas embodied in these establishments. The cult of personality derived strong implicit support from the cult of the emperor although the new cult was attached to a charismatic, revolutionary leader and used to effect revolu-

101. These slogans may or may not have been used by Lin Biao and the ultraleftists. They do accurately describe their mentality.

102. For the documentation of these charges, see Tsou, "Mao Tse-tung Thought." [Reproduced here as chapter 4 in this volume.] There is no way to confirm their accuracy. But they are consistent with the published writings of Zhang and Yao and the articles in *Xuexi yu pipan* (Study and Criticism), a journal under the exclusive control of the ultraleftists.

tionary changes, whereas the traditional cult was an institutionalized practice to preserve the political system. Loyalty to the leader and absolute obedience to him found expression in such ludicrous practices as "asking for instructions in the morning and making a report in the evening," and "loyalty dances." More significant and sinister were such statements as "Every sentence said or written [by Mao] is the truth," "One sentence [by Mao] is equal to ten thousand sentences by us,"[103] "One must obey Chairman Mao's instruction whether one understands it or not." Taken together, such utterances paralleled the leadership principle practiced by Nazi Germany.[104] Chinese Legalism, which had formed the basis of many autocratic and tyrannical practices in the traditional states, was revived by the ultraleftists as the justification for their political program and as an ideological weapon to attack the moderate veteran leaders.

Moreover, one can perhaps justify the proposition that it was precisely the Chinese political tradition which facilitated the development of the tendency for politics to penetrate into all spheres of social life. It can also be said that in the traditional society of China, "politics take command." The system of examination was a more important constituent of the system of social stratification in China than any single political institution was in other societies. It was perhaps as important an element as the ownership of land in the formation of the landlord class. The political bureaucracy had always dominated the merchant and other classes and groups; its belief system achieved ideological hegemony. When the total crisis in the twentieth century demanded total solutions, when a revolutionary party monopolizing power was determined to transform the whole society, and when modern means of communications and control and modern organizational forms and techniques were available, the tradition of politics in command easily and imperceptibly slid into the trend toward totalitarian control.

Thus after a protracted revolution of half of a century to eliminate "feudal" ideas and practices, the CCP found that these very ideas again erupted at the very top of its political system and threatened to overwhelm everything it had fought for. No wonder "feudalism" is now considered by many to be the main source of errors committed in the past and the main obstacle to modernization at the present time.

Nevertheless, the revolutionary-"feudal" totalitarianism of the ultra-

---

103. This statement by Lin Biao was contained in his speech of May 18, 1966 (*Zhonggong wenhua da geming zhongyao wenjian huibian* [Collection of Important Documents of the CCP Great Cultural Revolution] [Taibei: Zhonggong yanjiu zazhi she, 1973], p. 341).

104. In a political system such as that in China, the politics and behavior pattern at the top are immediately copied by those at the lower level and infect the entire system. "A person sent from Chairman Mao's headquarters" was supposed to be obeyed and followed closely. For a vivid account, see Liu Binyan, "Between a Human Being and a Monster," *Renmin wenxue* (People's Literature), 1979, no. 9, p. 85.

leftists did not achieve dominance in the Chinese political system. It had the strong but not complete support of Mao. More important, it was subtly opposed by most veteran leaders, whose outlook, style of work, and institutional commitments were formed during the periods of revolutionary and foreign wars in which ultraradicalism and totalitarian attempts to suppress violently various social classes and groups led to defeat while moderation and accommodation with these groups in a program of incremental and induced change through persuasion produced success. This common experience in the period when the inherent totalitarian tendency in the Chinese Communist movement was held in check by the internal distribution of power in China was strengthened by the urban origin or orientation of some of the leaders, inclining them to appreciate the complexity of the economy, the need for specialization, the imperatives of scientific and technological development, and the importance of the international environment.

This common experience and outlook form the foundation of their alternative program, which they carried out after Mao left the scene. Above all, their personal suffering and difficulties as well as the deepening crisis of authority in the last years of the Cultural Revolution made them fully realize the dire consequences of certain, but not all, ideological and institutional principles endorsed and practiced by them at one time or another when these principles were carried out to their logical conclusion, or in their view, were perverted by the leftward thrust. The result was a rapid, decisive reversal of the trend toward totalitarianism. China now may be approaching the post-totalitarian stage of her political development without having gone through a period of full-fledged totalitarianism. She has come back from the brink of revolutionary-"feudal" totalitarianism.

6

The Responsibility System in Agriculture

In the post-Mao years, particularly since the Third Plenum held in December 1978, China has undertaken a series of reforms in virtually all spheres of political, economic, social, and cultural life. Of all reforms, the most profound and rapid have been those in the policies, institutions, and practices in the countryside. In no other sphere has political control by the upper levels been relaxed to a greater extent; nowhere have relative autonomy and freedom in managing economic affairs on the part of the lowest-level units, the households, and the individual producers been restored more quickly; and nowhere have the market mechanism and individual incentives been given a more important place within the overall framework of national planning. In no other period since 1955, including the three years of agricultural crisis, has the Party Center as a matter of long-term policy accorded households and individual farmers a greater role.

Moreover, these changes have reflected more directly and visibly the wishes of the individuals concerned than in most other fields of social life. They have been the products of a complex process, combining the flow of influence from the bottom to the top and from the top to the bottom. This process has included the official acceptance and then encouragement of many practices adopted by the peasants themselves but previously concealed from officials at the higher levels. It has involved much spontaneous experimentation by peasants and low-level cadres in various localities. It has not been dominated by a single official or a few officials at the highest level of the Party. Indeed, it began as an opposition to the Maoist movement to learn from Dazhai and to build Dazhai-type counties by a combination of forces: peasants in many localities; local officials at various levels up to and including provincial first secretaries (notably those at Anhui and Sichuan); economists, intellectuals, economic plan-

[The paper from which this chapter was extracted was first published in *Modern China*, vol. 8, no. 1, January 1982. The permission by *Modern China* and Sage Publications to reprint part of the article is gratefully acknowledged. The format for documentation and romanization has not been changed. That paper was based partly on Tsou's visit to China from June to September 1980. The willingness of his coauthors, Marc Blecher and Miteh Meisner, to allow him to publish part of the original article in this volume is appreciated.] Tang Tsou wishes to acknowledge the support of the National Endowment for the Humanities for the research project "Political Leadership and Social Change in China at the Local Level From 1850 to the Present."

ners, and officials engaged in agricultural work as well as top party leaders such as Deng Xiaoping and Chen Yun. Despite their shared opposition to the Maoist model, as might be expected, the reformers were not of one mind. Some wanted to push change as far and as rapidly as possible. Others were more concerned with preserving some basic features of the collective system. Many ideas and proposals were advanced and debated. Ultimately, those ideas and proposals which were believed to have produced concrete results in increasing production and improving the peasants' livelihood were adopted. The discovery of new problems which have emerged in the aftermath of the changes has led to the search for new solutions and thus to another round of discussions and debate.

In institutional terms, the central feature of these changes is the evolution of the system of responsibility for agricultural production. This evolution represents not only a change in the method of labor management but also an adjustment in relations of production while maintaining the system of collective ownership of land and other major means of farm production. It involves the most significant change in the direction of developments in the countryside since the beginning of collectivism in 1953, the rapid drive toward cooperativization in 1955, the communization movement in 1958, the launching of the movement of learning from Dazhai in 1964, and the official proclamation in 1975 of the movement to build "Dazhai-type counties." It may lead to a change in the system of the commune, at least to the extent of making it purely a unit of collective economy, while reestablishing a parallel unit for governmental administration at similar levels.[1] From a larger historical perspective, it can even be said that the regime has gone as far as it can in readopting some of the traditional forms of farm practices and relations of production * short of dismantling the system of collective economy established since 1953.

The adoption and evolution of the system of responsibility for agricultural production represents the very antithesis of the movement to learn from Dazhai and to build Dazhai-type counties. The latter movement was in essence an attempt to revitalize the commune system and to encourage a trend toward increasing the size and functions of collective units and minimizing the role of the individual outside the strictly defined

1. There have been proposals for dismantling the commune system. For example, an article in *Jingji guanli* (1981, no. 1: 10–13) suggests that the present system of "three-level ownership with the team as the basic unit or account" be abandoned and that the production teams be changed into independent agricultural producers' cooperatives—a system used in the period between 1953 and 1956.

* Subsequent events show that the regime has gone much further. See chapter 7. The process of reestablishing the township as an administrative political unit and transforming the commune into a purely economic unit was completed by 1985.

collective framework. This was a political movement in which political power and mass mobilization were used to bring about economic development and equality. In contrast, the responsibility system seeks to appeal to the economic self-interests of the individual peasants. Dazhai was held up as a single model for emulation throughout the nation; now the development of a multitude of institutional forms and practices which fit the variations in the Chinese countryside is encouraged. In short, Dazhai as a model was proclaimed to be applicable everywhere and its "success" was trumpeted loudly. Now the tumult to "learn from Dazhai" and to "build Dazhai-type counties" has ended and the Party Center has sanctioned something very different. This article seeks to give an account of the evolution of rural policies since 1977 and a description of the responsibility system. . . .

Adoption of Four Basic Documents Concerning Agricultural Development

In 1977, when outwardly the Dazhai movement reached its zenith, an undercurrent of opposition was already rapidly developing. In two meetings in November and December 1977, opponents stressed the importance of respecting the autonomy of the team; reorganizing the system of management of the communes, brigades, and teams; correcting "equal divisionism" in the distribution of rewards; reviving the system of awarding work points according to fixed quotas of work; protecting private plots; and promoting household sideline occupations. But these proposals were easily suppressed by the highest authorities in charge of agriculture, presumably Ji Dengkui and Chen Yonggui with the support of Hua Guofeng.[2] The turning point was marked by the Third Plenum after a shift in the balance of political forces had been registered in the victory of the reformers in the debate over the epistemological postulate that "practice is the sole criterion for testing truth." That postulate played a prominent part in undermining the Maoist orthodoxy as it had developed during the Cultural Revolution, in destroying the "two whateverism," and in paving the way to a reevaluation of the role of Mao in governing China after 1949.

The Third Plenum agreed to distribute to the lower-level units for discussion and trial use two decisions: "Decisions on Some Questions Concerning the Acceleration of Agricultural Development (Draft)" and "Regulations on the Work in Rural People's Communes (Draft for Trial Use)." The first document of 25 articles still reaffirmed the mass movement to learn from Dazhai and to build Dazhai-type counties. It told the cadres

2. Article by An Gang et al. in *Renmin ribao*, July 9, 1981, page 2. An Gang is a deputy editor of the newspaper.

and peasants to continue to uphold the "basic experience" of Dazhai, but this was now defined merely as the "revolutionary experience of self-reliance and hard struggle." At the same time, it strongly urged them to implement firmly the Party's agricultural and rural economic policies and to learn from useful experiences at home and abroad. It foresaw the emergence of many new models. Dazhai and all the other advanced units of the nation were told to recognize their own shortcomings as well as achievements and to score new successes and create new experiences.

Although the movement to learn from Dazhai was reaffirmed, many of the Party's concrete policies on agriculture and the rural economy as mentioned in the 25 points ran counter to the specific features of the Dazhai-Xiyang model. Point 3 urged collective units at all levels to implement the principle of distributing rewards in proportion to work done and to correct firmly the mistake of "equal divisionism." It stipulated that "giving work points according to fixed work quotas is *permitted* and giving work points according to time spent plus appraisal of work done *is permitted*." Significantly, it added that "under the prerequisite of unified accounting and unified distribution by the production team, [the method of] assigning responsibility for work to work groups, calculating rewards for work by linking them to yield [obtained by the work group], and giving bonuses for surpassing output-quotas *[baogong dao zuoye zu, lianxi chanliang ji-suan laodong baochou, shixing chaochan jiangli] is also permitted*." (*Zhonggong yanjiu*, May 15, 1979: 154; italics added).[3] Implicitly, it discouraged the use of the Dazhai method of "self-assessment and public discussion" and the method of "giving fixed workpoints inflexibly" to the peasants for putting in a day of work. At the other extreme, it specifically prohibited assigning responsibility for production to the household *[bao-chan daohu]*, but this was to gain approval as one of the major forms of the responsibility system within two years. It also proscribed the division of land among households for individual farming *[fentian dangan]*. This latter proscription remains in force with very minor exceptions—for example, in isolated areas in Tibet.

The general and broad provisions in the draft document of 25 articles were not specific enough to guide the development of new institutions and practices. Almost immediately, they were given different interpretations by cadres and peasants in different localities. A debate raged over what was "also permitted" under the phrase, *baogong daozu*. The narrow interpretation supported by the editor of *Renmin ribao* (March 15, 1979 : 1)

---

3. This draft has not been published in China in the newspapers or journals surveyed by us.

In his excellent and immensely detailed study, Frederick Crook (1971: 202) translates the term *baogong* and baochan respectively as "labor contract" and "production contract."

in a comment [on] a letter to the editor printed on the front page on March 15, 1979 was that baogong daozu should be construed as the assignment of responsibility for day-to-day field management to the work groups but not as identical with *baochan daozu* (assignment of responsibility for production to the work groups), accompanied by the allocation of a specific portion of land, farming implements, and draft animals to the latter for their use. Baochan daozu should not be permitted. For under the system of baochan daozu, many work groups had become in effect "small teams" which took on the character of accounting units, and the team had degenerated into an empty shell.

The broader interpretation was adopted in Anhui. Under this interpretation, baochan daozu was considered not essentially different from baogong daozu. Under the system used in Anhui, each work group had the authority to use a fixed amount of land and a fixed number of draft animals and farm implements, but it did not own them. The teams still made a unified plan for cultivation and practiced unified distribution of the produce and cash at the end of the harvest. . . .

This interpretation was advanced by an official of the Agricultural Commission of the Anhui provincial government in a letter to *Renmin ribao*. Apparently the situation was in flux. At the end of the month, the editor of *Renmin ribao* recognized baochan daozu as one form of the system of linking rewards to yield and expressed the view that it should be permitted to continue until the final outcome could be determined. But he still opposed giving the work groups all, as distinguished from a specified percentage, of their above target yield as bonuses (*Renmin ribao*, March 30, 1979: 1). Even so, the first comment of only a few lines by the editor aroused widespread fear and uncertainty among local cadres and peasants that the Party Center was once again changing its policies and reversing the trend toward liberalization and relaxation of political control (*Renmin ribao*, July 2, 1981: 4; Interview in Chengdu, August 1980)—a fear and uncertainty which haunted Chinese in all walks of life.

Anhui scored at least a partial victory over the editor of *Renmin ribao*, whose comment presumably reflected the view of Wang Renzhong, who had replaced Ji Dengkui as the official in charge of agriculture and who was to be replaced in that position by Wan Li, the first secretary of Anhui, a year later. Anhui rested its case on the argument that the peasants in various localities in the provinces were experimenting with diverse forms of the system of responsibility and that whether these forms could promote production could be determined through "practice," thus appealing to the epistemological postulate as their ultimate justification. Moreover, that abstract postulate and the whole atmosphere of relaxation of centralized, upper-level political control legitimized the frequently concealed practices of the peasants which contravened the official policies on work management. It also encouraged a measure of spontaneity in the search for forms of organization and management most suitable to local conditions. In many cases, these forms were first developed by peasants and lowest-level cadres behind the backs of higher-level officials and only later gained the approval of cadres at the county and provincial levels. Finally, they were sanctioned by the Party Center.

Thus, development of the system of responsibility was partly the outcome of an unorganized movement from the bottom to the top. In five districts[4] south of the Yellow River and astride the Huai River in the provinces of Anhui, Henan, and Shandong, the greater part of the teams adopted the system of baochan daozu in 1979, while a very small part of the teams spontaneously developed the system of baochan daohu (assignment of responsibility for production to the household) (*Renmin ribao,* January 23, 1981: 2). As early as 1978, ten teams in one county adopted the system of *da baogan daozu* (*Renmin ribao,* January 28, 1981: 1); in Fengyang county in Anhui, 83% of the teams adopted this system in 1979, which we shall discuss later.

When the Fourth Plenum adopted the final version of the document of 25 articles in September 1979, it deleted the flat prohibition of baochan daohu. In its stead, it declared that "except for certain sideline occupations with special needs and isolated, single households living in remote hilly areas without easy means of transportation, the system of baochan daohu should . . . not be used" (*Renmin ribao,* October 6, 1979: 1). It retained the same language when referring to the assignment of responsibility for work to work groups. It deleted the statement in the draft document that "[the party committees at all levels] must continue to grasp well the mass movement to learn from Dazhai and to popularize Dazhai-type counties." It merely urged them to continue to guide the vast number of cadres and peasants in learning from the "basic experience" of Dazhai, which was now defined in the words of Zhou Enlai rather than the modified formulation widely used during the Cultural Revolution. This change represented the formal termination of the movement to build Dazhai-type counties, after that movement had, for all practical purposes, ceased some months earlier. All this suggests that the impulse for the development of new forms of the responsibility system and their progressive spread came from the bottom and percolated to the top with the indispensable support and championship of Party leaders at the national and provincial levels. As two correspondents of *Renmin ribao* (July 2, 1981: 5) put it, the special feature of this development was that "the bottom level pushes the upper level and the masses push the cadres."

4. In this article the term "district" rather than "prefecture" is used to translate the Chinese term *diqu.*

But one should also not overlook the fact that it was the top leaders who set the tone for reform and created the atmosphere[5] which emboldened the peasants to revive—at first stealthily and later openly—the practices engaged in by some of them in the three years of agricultural crisis, developed first in the early days of the cooperativization drive in 1953 and rooted in the rural tradition. In this atmosphere of reform and relaxation of control, the peasants and lower-level cadres revived many old practices and developed new ones in concrete detail, which were then officially sanctioned by the Party Center in general terms after a period of debate and experimentation.

The permission given by the Party Center in the finalized document to baochan daohu as an exception gave a measure of legitimacy to this form of responsibility system. Its effect was to encourage the peasants to extend the use of this system in localities where economic conditions were very poor, where the collective system was not functioning well, and where the cadres gave themselves excessive work points without effectively discharging their duties to the collective and without doing a fair amount of farm work. As early as 1978, a commune in Yijun county of Jiangxi adopted the system of baochan daohu for the day-to-day management of a newly developed wheat field of 4000 *mu* (*Renmin ribao*, April 7, 1981: 2). In many counties—for example, one each in Anhui, Hunan, and Shandong and three counties in Guizhou—baochan daohu was widely used (*Renmin ribao*, November 5, 1980: 2). In 1979 and 1980, more than 70% of the teams in Funan county of Anhui also adopted it. Many of the teams in these counties are located not in hilly areas but in the plains.

Moreover, a system of devolving responsibility to individual farm workers developed spontaneously, although the teams under unified management still perform collectively many indispensable functions for the individual farm workers. The first and most popularized case was the Mengjiaping team in Shaanxi province. Allegedly created in the spring of 1979 by low-level cadres, this system was known as "division of work according to specialization and assignment of production responsibility to an individual farm worker." In 1979 and 1980, this system, with some variations, was used in a number of teams in widely scattered parts of China. We found reports of its existence in Shaanxi, Liaoning, and northern Jiangsu (*Renmin ribao*, November 5, 1980: 2, December 13, 1980: 1, December 24, 1980: 2). This system was gradually perfected and widely pop-

5. Before and after the two conferences on agriculture in November and December 1977, Deng Xiaoping twice suggested the revival of the various rural policies proven effective in the past, and pointed out that the Dazhai method or awarding work points could *not be popularized* and applied everywhere. The election of Chen Yun as a vice-chairman of the Party at the Third Plenum made him the most powerful leader in managing China's economic affairs.

ularized in Henan in 1979 and 1980 under the simplified name of *lianchan daolao* (linking production quotas to an individual farm worker). By 1981, it was used in 55% of the teams there (*Renmin ribao*, February 24, 1981: 2). Finally, a new form combining elements of the previous methods developed. This form is known as *zhuanye chengbao, lianchan jichou* (contract work for specialized tasks, calculating reward by linking it to yield). In sum, it is obvious that peasants and low-level cadres have taken advantage of the changes in Party Center policies to develop and extend new forms of the responsibility system which yield greater autonomy and promote local self-interest.

Meanwhile, the Fifth Plenum in February 1980 witnessed not only an important shift in top personnel but also the most significant restructuring of organization of the Party Center since 1976. The Secretariat, which had disintegrated during the Cultural Revolution, was reestablished with Hu Yaobang as General Secretary; he was to replace Hua Guofeng as Chairman of the Party 14 months later. Wan Li, the first secretary of Anhui province, was appointed one of the 11 members of the Secretariat. He was put in charge of agriculture. In discussing its reestablishment, Ye Jianying described the Secretariat as an organization which "stood in the first line [of work] with the Politbureau and its standing committee in the second line" (*Liaowang*, April 20, 1981: 9). There is no doubt that the Secretariat soon became the most active (usually it meets twice a week) and effective of all organs in promoting reforms in every sphere. After the reorganization, the Party Center, with the Secretariat as its prime mover, took a series of bold steps. These included a proposal to tackle the economic and political problems of Tibet, a recommendation to reconstruct Beijing, and exposure of the case of the sinking of an offshore oil drilling rig.

Insofar as rural policy is concerned, the Center took two big steps. The first was to launch open criticism of Xiyang county and its responsible person, Chen Yonggui, which led to his resignation as Vice-Premier in September. The other was to send top Party leaders to investigate conditions in the rural areas of several provinces and to commission more than 100 officials engaged in rural work, economists, and theoreticians to study typical localities in ten provincial-level units. These investigations culminated in a symposium held in mid-September in Beijing and attended by the first secretaries of all the provinces, cities, and autonomous regions. The conclusions of this symposium were summarized in a document known as "Certain Problems Concerning Further Strengthening and Improvement of the Responsibility System for Agricultural Production."[6] On September 27, this summary was sent down by the Party Center as document

6. *Banyue tan*, no. 8 (April 25, 1981: 4–10). See also *Zhonggong yanjiu* (March 15, 1981: 110–118). The adoption of this document was immediately followed by the appearance of an

number 75 to the Party committees and groups of leading Party members at the next highest level. This document's adoption was considered by the *Beijing Review* the sixth of ten major events in China in 1980.

Document No. 75 approved baochan daohu (including baogan daohu) as a "necessary measure" in developing production and maintaining links with the masses, not only in remote hilly areas but also in poor and backward regions. But teams in ordinary areas where the collective economy was relatively stable, production was developing, and the masses were satisfied with the responsibility system currently in use were still told not to use baochan daohu. Teams which had already adopted baochan daohu were allowed to continue it so long as the masses did not demand a change. As for those communes, brigades, and teams where economic conditions and management were in the "middle range," they were directed to use a variety of measures to solve their problems rather than confine themselves to baochan daohu alone. The document stressed the merits of zhuanye chengbao, lianchan jichou, as well as the system of lianchan daolao in day-to-day field management. Essentially, the Party Center gave its stamp of approval to the various forms of responsibility system developed spontaneously in different localities, although it had its preferences among them. The fundamental spirit underlying the document was to permit the coexistence of a variety of forms of responsibility system within one area, one commune, or even one team and to allow the team the autonomy to choose among them according to objective conditions and its capacity for managing collective farm work. Implicitly, it also allowed a team to use one form of the responsibility system to govern the relationship between it and its work groups and another form to govern the relationship between the work group and the individual peasants. The dispatch of this document downward had the effect of stabilizing the peasants' and low-level cadres' expectations, but it has not prevented them from further trying various methods to improve their own livelihood.

On March 30, 1981, the Party Center and the State Council jointly issued a circular to transmit a document drafted by the State Agricultural Commission entitled "a Report Concerning Vigorous Development of a Diversified Economy in the Rural Areas" (*Banyue tan*, April 25, 1981: 13–14). Both the circular and the document insisted there should be no relaxation of efforts to increase grain production. But their emphasis was clearly on the importance of developing a diversified rural economy by expanding animal husbandry, fishery, forestry, fruit trees, and many sideline occupations. For this purpose, it authorized the expansion of private plots (including plots to produce feed and fodder for animals) up to a maxi-

---

editorial in *Nongcun gongzuo tongxun* 1980, no. 10, and many articles in that journal and two other journals specializing in agriculture—*Nongye jingji wenti* and *Nongye zhishi*.

mum of 15% of the total cultivated area of a team.[7] Even more surprising to outside observers, it gave approval to what the masses called *ziliu ren*—that is, persons who do not participate in collective farm work and do not draw grain rations from the team but who work only on their private plots and sideline occupations (*Banyue tan*, April 25, 1981: 14, 20).[8] The explicit permission given to individuals to be ziliu ren, or self-employed persons, goes one step further in granting greater freedom to peasants in managing their own economic affairs than the practice, proscribed under the Dazhai model but adopted nonetheless by many teams, under which peasants engaged in transport, handicraft, and similar work in nearby towns and cities receive their grain ration from the team and in turn pay the team a fee out of the cash earned. The report and the circular also sought to promote the development of a diversified rural economy by adopting new proposals of agronomists and economists. These documents at once reflect the state of scientific knowledge in China and urge its use in promoting agricultural development.*

A Scheme for Classifying Various Forms of the Responsibility System

All four documents mentioned so far use terms which are not fully defined and which in practice refer to quite different types of arrangements. Reports and articles in newspapers and periodicals are of some help in describing and classifying the variety of forms included under the rubric of "responsibility system," but unfortunately, not even these sources contain

7. In the summer of 1980, many teams in Sichuan had already allocated more than 10% of their cultivated land for private plots (Interview in August 1980).

8. The circular allows persons with half-labor power or supplementary labor power to be ziliu ren except during busy agricultural seasons, whereas the report did not mention these restrictions.

* Another two important documents were issued in the next three years. (1) "Dangqian nongchun zhengche de rogan wenti" (On Certain Problems of the Current Policy toward the Rural Area). This Central Committee document no. 1 of 1983 sought to stabilize and perfect the system of responsibility for production in the rural area, particularly the contract system linking production and reward with the peasant households and small work groups as the contracting units. It officially encouraged the development of households specialized in a particular line of agricultural or nonagricultural work. It gave permission to households and small groups to hire a small number of short-term workers and workers with specialized skill. It allowed peasants to shift from cultivating the land to engaging in a sideline occupation so long as they did not leave the rural area. See *Renmin ribao*, April 10, 1983, pp. 1–2. (2) "Zhonggong zhongyang guanyu yijiu basi nian nongchun gongzhuo de tongzhi" (The circular of the CCP Central Committee on Rural Works in 1984) (issued on January 1, 1984). This document extended to "more than 15 years" the time limit under which the peasant households could cultivate a specific piece of land in their contract with their teams or brigades. It permitted a peasant to transfer his right under contract to cultivate a particular piece of land to another peasant. It encouraged the gradual concentration of cultivated land in the hands of those peasants who were capable cultivators, *Renmin ribao*, June 12, 1984, pp. 1–2.

all the information necessary, nor do they use the terms consistently. Thus, in piecing together the information from these sources, we sometimes had to fall back on our interpretation of the terms used and our judgment of what the authors meant. A short visit to the villages provides more detailed and concrete information, but a single visitor on a hectic trip is likely to miss important bits of information. Fully realizing all these shortcomings, we have attempted to do our best.

The term "responsibility system" *(zeren zhi)* encompasses a wide variety of forms.[9] What it definitely excludes, at the one extreme, is the "self-assessment and public discussion" method of awarding work points. It is also distinguishable from the system of "fixed [or basic] work points given inflexibly" to the peasants for putting in a day of work *(sifen siji* or *difen siji)*, as well as the system of basic work points plus flexible appraisal *(difen huoping)*. These three systems of distributing rewards are believed ineffective in establishing a direct and visible link between work and compensation, thus creating a drag on the productivity of the individual peasant and making management of collective farming a matter of constantly issuing commands and close supervision. At the other extreme, division of land for individual farming is not considered a form of the responsibility system. These two extremes mark its boundaries.

The various forms of the responsibility system differ according to the degree to which they directly and effectively link the individual peasant's reward and self-interest with his or her work, though obviously the question of effectiveness must be somewhat conjectural and subject to further examination. Some of these forms were developed as far back as the beginning of the cooperativization movement in 1953. Others were adopted in some localities at one time or another since the establishment of the advanced agricultural producers' cooperatives in 1956–1957. Still others are new. Some emerged or reemerged spontaneously at the grass-roots level since 1977 and were later approved by the authorities at the county, provincial, and national levels.

The forms of the responsibility system can be classified in a number of ways, but basically they involve two logical components.[10] One of these

---

9. According to one account, there are more than ten forms of the "responsibility system" *(Renmin ribao,* editorial, November 1, 1980: 1).

10. Chinese economists and reporters generally classify the responsibility system by using the presence or absence of linkage between reward and yield as the primary criterion. They divide it first into two major categories: One does not link responsibility to yield *(bu lianxi chanliang de shengchan zeren zhi)* and the other does *(lianxi chanliang de shengchan zeren zhi).* See the excellent article by Wang Guichen and Wei Daonan in *Jingji Yanjiu,* 1981, no. 1, pages 64–67, and the important article by Wu Xiang in *Renmin ribao,* November 5, 1980, page 2. Instead, we use the level of devolution of responsibility as the primary criterion and the absence or presence of reward-yield linkage as the secondary criterion. Our classification facilitates description of the evolution of the responsibility system and

pertains to the way individuals are remunerated for their labor within any relevant group that shares the responsibility of an assigned task or tasks and where the responsibility is not further devolved to the household or individual. The second involves the level of assignment of responsibilities for production and the methods for regulating the assignment and concomitant economic exchanges between the assigning body (usually the production team and, in a small number of cases, the brigade) and the relevant responsible group or party (that is, a single household or an individual).

In reference to the methods of individual remuneration for labor, the first form to be practiced on a large scale and officially promoted after Mao's death was the awarding or scoring of work points according to fixed work quotas *(ding e jigong)*. For example, a peasant who transplants rice seedlings in one *mu* of land earns a specific number of work points. In many places there are roughly 300 different quotas for agricultural production activities.[11] Thus, the "basic work point" is eliminated, and "task-rate" is in effect substituted for time worked.[12] This system (also known as *ding e jichou* and *ding e baogong)* was first officially authorized and sanctioned in Anhui in November 1977, although it had been used earlier in various parts of China without much publicity. In a refinement of this system, fixed work quotas can also be assigned to a series of tasks related to each other at one time or in a series of steps. This is known as *xiaoduan baogong, ding e jichou*. A system of management using one or both of the methods described above is called management by fixed quotas *(ding e guanli)*.[13] At the end of 1980, this system was used in 50% of the teams in China for day-to-day field management *(Renmin ribao,* December 2, 1980: 3).

The responsibility system implies that production responsibilities can be assigned by a larger collective unit to a smaller subgroup or party.

highlights the *political* problem of the relationship between state and household or individual, while the classificatory scheme used in China calls attention to the *economic* significance of the change, particularly the role of material incentive.

11. Prior to adoption of the system of self-assessment and public discussion *(zibao gongyi)* from 1961 to 1963, there had been 130 to 140 work quotas in Dazhai.

12. Although "piecework" is the common term applied to the fixed work quota system, in some cases the system might better be called "task rate" since the sizes of individual jobs and time required are relatively great. Compare this to the familiar factory or home-industry piecework in which a worker turns out hundreds of small items in a day, usually the same thing (especially in piece-goods work in the garment industry). Moving cartloads of manure may more appropriately be called piecework.

13. Although the Chinese writers subsumed this form of labor management under the category of responsibility system without reward-output linkage, the use of the work point system in itself establishes a remote linkage between performance and reward because the value of the work point is decided only at the end of the year after the harvest, and it fluctuates with the harvest.

There are three possible levels of devolution of responsibilities for production tasks depending on the size of the subgroup. The first level involves the division of a production team into work groups. This division makes the collective unit of responsibility smaller and is an important first step in relating work performance and rewards more directly (in addition to reforms in individual labor remuneration procedures), in making supervision more intimate and easier, and in ameliorating the problem of the "free ride."

At this level, there are three subtypes. The first operates in the following manner. The production team can define for a work group its task (output quota), the standard of quality of its produce, and the time limit in which the task is to be completed. In return, the team gives a specific number of work points to a work group for the completion of this task according to the specifications. The work group will distribute the total work points received to its individual members either by an appraisal of their work performance or according to the fixed work quota which they have fulfilled. This subtype is called "one work group with four specifications" (yizu siding).[14] Under this system, the peasants' reward is linked with output, although still quite indirectly.[15]

In the second subtype, the relationship between the production team and its work groups undergoes an important change, incorporating an element essentially the same as that used in the system of sanbao yijiang adopted in some of the cooperatives in the period between 1953 and 1956 and later during the last two years of agricultural crisis, 1960 and 1961. This element is the provision of a bonus or a penalty for the overfulfillment or nonfulfillment of the obligations specified in an agreement or contract between the team and the work groups. The number and content of these obligations vary from place to place. A common form is siding yijiang (four specifications and one bonus).

Under this system, the work group guarantees the fulfillment of a fixed quota or value of agricultural output at a fixed cost, while the team assigns a fixed number of workers to the group and promises to give the group a fixed number of work points. If the group obtains a higher yield than its output target (presumably staying within the limit of cost), it will have a bonus; but if it fails to reach the target, it will have to pay a penalty. The bonus or penalty is calculated in terms of the percentage of above-target yield or shortfall, but the percentage given to the work group as a bonus is

14. The four specifications usually include task, quality standard, time limit, and the work points to be received in exchange. See article by Wang Gengjin and He Jianzhang, *Jingji yanjiu*, 1978, no. 8, page 18. The provincial authorities in Anhui were among the first to approve this system.

15. This form is classified in China under the category of responsibility system without reward-output linkage.

usually higher than the percentage of shortfalls paid by the work group as a penalty. Bonuses can be as high as 80% or 70%; the penalty can be as low as 20% to 30%. In case of drought or flood, the penalty is usually waived or reduced, depending on the seriousness of the natural disaster.

In spite of the division of the team into work groups, the team remains the basic accounting unit. It adopts a unified production plan for the whole team. It allocates labor power among the work groups. It fixes the workday value or the work point value for the whole team on the basis of the value of agricultural output (which is handed over by the work groups) after deducting taxes, expenses, accumulation funds, welfare funds, and other levies. It gives the bonuses or penalties to each work group by increasing or decreasing the workday value of the members of that particular work group. Thus the system of unified distribution of rewards by the team is preserved. The relationship between the work group and the individual peasants is governed by one or the other method of ding e guanli mentioned above, or both in various combined forms. In some localities, this second subtype is called assignment of output quotas to each work group (baochan daozu).[16]

In the third subtype, all above-target yields belong to the work group, while all shortfalls must be made good by the group from its grain reserve and that of its members. It was the use of this subtype which was disapproved by the editors of *Renmin ribao* as late as March 30, 1979.

The fourth subtype, to which the term baochan daozu is also applied, is more accurately called in some localities "contract work in a big way" or "assumption of total responsibility" (da baogan) by the work group. The most publicized case of a county using this form is Fengyang, Anhui, which has long been known for its poverty. In this specific case, a contract is concluded between a team and each of its work groups. A work group guarantees to fulfill the production plan, fulfill the quotas of farm and sideline products to be sold to the state, and turn over certain amounts of accumulated funds and other levies to the team. After having discharged these obligations, the work group retains all other produce for distribution among its members. But it must also make good all shortfalls. Although the team provides guidelines for the distribution of rewards by the work groups among the members, unified distribution which obtains in the second and third subtypes is not practiced.

Fengyang began to use this system in 1978, without the official sanction of the Party Center but with the support of the Party secretary of the county. In 1979, 83% of the teams in that county adopted this system; in 1980, 93% did so (*Renmin ribao*, January 12, 1981: 4, January 28, 1981: 1).

16. This subtype and all other types of labor management discussed hereafter are classified by Chinese writers as forms of responsibility system with reward-output linkage.

The distribution of rewards by a work group to its members is still handled either under the system of appraisal of work done or under the system of rewarding work points according to fixed work quotas.

Devolving production responsibility to the level of the work groups below the production team has generally gone by the designation of baogong daozu or baochan daozu (fixing work or production responsibility for each work group). It should be recalled that both the draft document on the acceleration of agricultural development adopted by the Third Plenum in December 1978 and the definitive document adopted by the Fourth Plenum in September 1979 permitted almost as an aside the adoption of the first two subtypes [17] but were silent on the third and the fourth. But toward the end of 1980, all four subtypes were promoted by the authorities and widely used in various parts of the country.

Baochan daozu represents another step toward a more direct and effective linkage between an individual peasant's reward and self-interest and his or her work. But in various localities, this linkage is still considered insufficiently direct. Moreover, if team management is not strong enough, the work groups become in effect basic accounting units, while the production team loses its essential functions to the groups.

Hence in some places, the number of teams using the system of baochan daozu decreases as time goes by, and responsibility is devolved to still lower levels: the household and individual (*Renmin ribao*, March 7, 1981: 2). In Fengyang, Anhui, for example, since 1981 responsibility is being further devolved from the work groups to the households.

In this scheme, production tasks are assigned to the household; production and payment arrangements are made with it. This is the second level of the devolution of responsibility. It is known as the assignment of production responsibility to the household or the household responsibility system, *baochan daohu*. [18] There are three subtypes at this level. Under the first, output quotas for only specific kinds of produce are assigned to

17. In granting this permission, the documents used the term *ye keyi* after it gave clear permission *(keyi)* to the system of awarding work points according to work quotas and the system of time work plus appraisal or work done. Thereafter a debate arose at the local level in some areas. One side argued that the best formula was *keyi, keyi, geng keyi* (is permitted, is permitted, and is all the more permitted). The other side, consisting of the opponents to change, argued that the policy should be *keyi, keyi, bu keyi* (is permitted, is permitted, and is not permitted) (*Renmin ribao*, December 24, 1980: 2). Obviously, the proponents of change had won. Moreover, the system or responsibility had by that time extended to the level of a single household and an individual, as we shall see.

18. An article in *Hongqi* expresses reservations about this system. The author fears that it may destroy the system or unified accounting and unified distribution of rewards. He asserts that it should not be classified, without careful examination of its various forms and effects, as one type of "responsibility system." Article by Yu Gudyao, *Hongqi*, 1980, no. 20, pages 12–15, 35.

the household. Under the second, all the land belonging to a team and the output quotas for all farm produce are assigned to households. In both of these subtypes, the team still retains its function of unified accounting and distribution. A system of bonuses and penalties is used. Under the third, the household retains all its produce after paying taxes and selling its grain to the state under the system of unified purchase and after handing over to the team its share of collective accumulation and welfare funds, as well as other levies. This is known as assumption of total responsibility by the household, or household total responsibility system, *baogan daohu,* which is also called *da baogan* but must not be confused with *da baogan* by the work group. Da baogan by either the work group or the household is based on the same principle of incentive (similar to that contained in the agricultural tax system that freezes obligations at fixed amounts of produce calculated in terms of the low yields of the early 1950s): the fixed floor of obligation is an incentive to produce as much as possible above that amount. The government recognizes that this subtype seems to be a step backward from the system used in the advanced agricultural producers' cooperatives. But it stresses that this can bring into play the activism of the peasants and encourage them to cultivate their land meticulously and obtain greater yields (*Renmin ribao,* November 1, 1980: 1). Twenty percent of the teams throughout China use one of these three subtypes of fixing output quotas for each household (*Renmin ribao,* November 5, 1980: 2), a practice which was used in some localities in China during the three years of agricultural crisis but which was banned and condemned from 1964 to late 1977 or early 1978.

Baochan daohu was at first used where the peasant households belonging to a team are widely scattered in relatively poor hilly regions.[19] But there has been a tendency for this form to spread to areas where teams are badly managed or led, peasants are very poor, and agricultural production stagnant. This tendency has been not only permitted but even encouraged by the government in some provinces. As noted earlier, in Funan county in Anhui province, more than 70% of the teams have adopted this system. A two-part dispatch in *Renmin ribao* (January 22, 1981: 2, January 23, 1981: 2) gave strong endorsement to the widespread use of this system in five districts in Anhui, Henan, and Shandong. Through the mouths of the local authorities or in their own words, three correspondents of the Xinhua news agency asserted that of all forms of the responsibility system, baochan daohu establishes the most direct link with the peasants' interests, makes their responsibility most concrete, and is the

---

19. The decision on accelerating agricultural development adopted in September 1979 gave permission to employ this system only among single households living in remote hilly areas and where the special needs of certain kinds of sideline production made it desirable.

easiest method to use. For these reasons, it was said to be very appealing to peasants living under straitened circumstances. It sprang up spontaneously in 1979 in five districts. In 1980, it spread rapidly and has become a major form of the responsibility system there.[20] Baochan daohu, including da baogan, is now regarded not as a mere expedient to overcome poverty but as a "positive measure" to promote production (*Renmin ribao*, August 4, 1981: 2).

In a commune in Jiashan county in this region, some single households, some groups of three or four households, and some work groups have used their own savings to purchase walking tractors (*Renmin ribao*, December 20, 1980: 1). Thus, this important and very expensive farm implement used at the lowest level can now be privately owned. In Guizhou, in 1980 a production team adopted the system of baochan daozu but supplemented it with an allocation of some of its land to the households for production of their grain rations (*Renmin ribao*, December 21, 1980: 3). This is termed *kouliang tian*.

The third level of assignment that has appeared in recent experiments with the responsibility system is the fixing of output quotas for an individual farm worker, *baochan daolao*. An example of this form was given in *Renmin ribao* and has been mentioned in passing above. The Mengjiaping team in Shaanxi had only 16 households, and a population of 64, including 12 male and 8 female farm workers. Its 310 mu of cultivated land were divided in 1979 into eight parts. Eight experienced male farm workers were selected and each was assigned to cultivate one of the eight parts of land under a contract. Each of the eight farm workers was obligated to produce 6,500 *jin* of grain for the collective (that is, 168 jin per mu). Everything produced above this quota belonged to him, but he also had to make up for all shortfalls from his private reserve (*Renmin ribao*, September 28, 1980, October 13, 1980: 1).[21] The remaining farm workers were assigned other kinds of specific jobs such as raising goats and basic farmland construction.

The system of baochan daolao has been further refined, specified, and developed into *lianchan daolao*. A description of this system was given in *Renmin ribao*. Of the 370,000 teams in Henan, about 60% have adopted

---

20. The Xinhua correspondents also contrasted the rapid adoption of this system to the difficulties encountered by the authorities in introducing the Dazhai system of distributing rewards.

21. The ratio between labor and land in this team is low in comparison with many parts of China. Note that a yield per worker of 6,500 jin per year is equivalent to 542 jin per month. If the worker is able to double the rather low output of 168 jin per mu that the quota calls for, the resultant surplus retained is equivalent to a substantial monthly grain ration (*kouliang*). If the worker could attain yields surpassing 500 jin per mu, he or she would receive a high monthly grain ration *plus* around ¥60 in cash (figuring 542 additional jin per month at about ¥0.11 per jin). But these yields may not be possible.

this system (*Renmin ribao*, February 24, 1981: 2, March 7, 1981: 2; article by commentator, March 2, 1981: 1). According to these reports, this system has a dual advantage. On the one hand, it preserves the integrity of the team as the basic accounting unit, without any division into work groups. On the other hand, it links the individual peasant's reward most directly and effectively to his or her work. The team undertakes unified planning, unified tilling of the land, unified investment, and unified allocation and employment of labor, draft animals, and farm machinery and tools of large and medium sizes. All farm tasks that are not easy for the individual peasant to do are done by the team, which organizes persons with specialized skills or small groups to undertake these tasks, which include ploughing, harrowing, raking the soil, building ridges for vegetable gardens, sowing, irrigating the fields, insect control, nursing seedlings, and basic farmland construction. The daily management of the fields throughout the year is assigned to individual farm workers. Each is held responsible for managing a specific sector of the land for one to three years. The worker is obligated to fulfill a production quota, which is generally fixed on the basis of the output of the last year prior to the implementation of this system. The peasant is provided with a fixed amount of chemical fertilizer, insecticides, seeds, and other material inputs and is given a fixed number of work points for the accomplishment of the assigned tasks. But there is also a provision for bonuses for overfulfillment of the production quota and penalties for nonfulfillment. The system under which the farm worker receives a bonus equal to all the above-quota yield and pays the full penalty for the shortfall has gradually replaced the system under which he or she receives a bonus equal to a proportion of the above-quota yield and pays a penalty equivalent to only a proportion of the shortfall. In case of natural disaster, bonuses and penalties are calculated in terms of production quotas readjusted according to the seriousness of the loss. This system has been clarified and stablized after the Party Center's directive on the responsibility system in rural areas was sent down in September 1980. An important article by the commentator of *Renmin ribao* suggests that this system is most suitable for those communes and teams which are neither very poor nor very rich (*Renmin ribao*, March 2, 1981: 1).[22]

In Tibet alone peasants in isolated areas who are confronted with great difficulties are officially permitted to "go it alone" (*dan gan*). Under this subtype, an individual household has no obligation toward the collective unit. It owns its means of production and bears the responsibility for its own profits and losses (*Renmin ribao*, November 15, 1980: 1).

22. In Jiangxi, this system is called the "assignment of responsibility for field management to a farm worker and linkage of rewards and bonuses to yields" (*Renmin ribao*, March 13, 1981: 2).

As we move down the levels of the responsibility system, beginning with those teams which still manage production and pay workers according to the task rate or "ding e" system, to the various subtypes of work group responsibility, then to the level of the household, and finally to the level of the individual worker, the linkage between individual effort and reward would appear to be progressively more direct and visible. (This point is somewhat obscured at the household level, since household management of internal work and pay relations becomes a more private matter; the link between individuals within the household and household management of the responsibility system needs further examination.) In addition, the subject of responsibility moves from the team to the individual at the lowest level, and the peasant's planning initiative and individual incentives are more heavily relied upon. But there is the risk of weakening the collective unit and neglecting collective undertakings, including water conservancy and public welfare. In extreme cases, there is the danger of simply dividing the land and collectively owned machinery and tools among the households. These problems are noted in the press. Measures have been undertaken to solve them, as in the case of the system used in Henan.

There remains one version of the responsibility system which cuts across the logical scheme described above, since it involves specialized work that is available for assignment to any of the three levels mentioned above, utilizing a contract system involving rewards and penalties. This system is known as *zhuanye chengbao, lianchan jichou* (contract work for specialized tasks, calculating reward by linking it to yield). Under this system, special tasks in farming, forestry, animal tending and husbandry, fishery sideline production, and industry and commerce that require specialized skills are assigned to a special work group, a household, or an individual. Thus, work groups, households, and individual farm workers specializing in one task frequently coexist within a team. A contract is concluded between them and the team with provisions for bonuses for exceeding the contractual obligations and penalties for failure to meet them. A simple example of this system is the assignment of milk production by several cows to a household. In more economically developed areas, there is a tendency for teams to make the transition from using the system of contract work for a small number of related tasks to the system of zhuanye chengbao, lianchan jichou (*Renmin ribao*, March 2, 1981: 1).[23] A specialized task is assigned or a contract is awarded to a group, household, or an individual by two different methods. One is self-nomination and public discussion, the other competitive bidding. Recently, the merits of the second method have been stressed in the press.

23. The work groups, households, and individual farm workers who undertake specialized tasks are known respectively as *zhuanye zu, zhuanye hu, and zhuanye ren.*

The document on the responsibility system issued in September 1980 gave zhuanye chengbao, lianchan jichou high praise and compared it favorably with other forms of production contract system on the following grounds: It satisfies the commune member's demand for linking reward to yield; it stabilizes the primary economic position of the team; it integrates in concrete terms the promotion of the individual commune member's activism in production with the development of the superior characteristics of unified management, division of labor, and cooperation; it facilitates the development of a diversified economy, the extension of scientific farming, and the promotion of commodity production; and it eases the task of the members in taking care of sideline occupations (*Banyue tan*, April 25, 1981: 7). This form may be used in economically distressed areas and then developed into a more socialized division of labor among specialized tasks as the forces of production grow and the number of products increases (*Banyue tan*, April 25, 1981: 7; article by Zhan Wu and Wang Guichen, *Jingji yanjiu*, 1981, no. 4, pp. 55–59, 73).

In such work as basic farmland construction and water conservancy projects, a system of individual remuneration sometimes considered marginal to the responsibility system is still frequently used. This is the system of *pinggong jifen*. Sometimes, even *difen huoping* is used. There are attempts to use the ding e system in this kind of work. But the systems of *difen siji* and "self-assessment and public discussion" (*zibao gongyi*) are vigorously attacked as contributing to low labor productivity and difficulties in labor management.

The logical scheme we use also reveals roughly the progression of the responsibility system as it gained the approval of the Party Center and was promoted in the countryside. This trend was described by the officials of the Agricultural Commission of Henan province in terms of "eight breakthroughs" or, to be more precise, eight transformations: (1) from the absence of linkage between reward and yield to the establishment of this linkage; (2) from linkage between reward and yield for work groups to linkage for individual farm workers or households; (3) from linkage between reward and yield in the production of industrial crops to grain production; (4) from linkage between reward and yield in growing autumn grain crops to growing summer grain crops; (5) from linkage between reward and yield in agriculture to linkage in forestry, animal husbandry, sideline occupations, fishery, and so on; (6) from proportionate bonuses and penalties to full bonuses and full penalties; (7) from the adoption of the system by ordinary communes, brigades, and teams to adoption by those with a higher level of production; and, finally, (8) from fixing the production targets for one year to several years without change (*Renmin ribao*, July 2, 1981: 5). But despite this general trend, the main point emphasized is still that a team should adopt a form most suitable to its economic conditions and capability for management.

From our point of view, the seventh "breakthrough" is of utmost significance. It reveals to us how complete is the reversal of the Maoist agricultural policies adopted during the Cultural Revolution. It reflects the reformers' view that the responsibility system can achieve better results even in localities where the implementation of Maoist policies had increased production and improved the peasants' livelihood. This seventh "breakthrough" is forcefully illustrated by a brigade in Sichuan, well known for the strength of its collective economy. Until the end of 1980, all farming activities as well as industrial and sideline production had been under the direct, unified management of the brigade. For farming, the brigade had not been divided into teams or work groups, and no strict system of responsibility had been used. Still the per capita income distributed by the brigade to its members had reached ¥318 in 1980, as compared with the national average of ¥85.9. Seventy percent of its total income came from the profits of industrial and sideline enterprises, which had been highly developed. But according to reports, the high profits covered up the inefficiency in the use of labor not only in farming activities but also in industrial and sideline production. After the autumn harvest, the brigade adopted the system of zhuanye chengbao, lianchan jichou. It assigned two-thirds of its members to fixed, specific posts in its 14 industrial and sideline enterprises. It gave each of its enterprises, their small groups or their individual workers a planned target of output value. The work points earned by each worker were decided on the basis of output value and the cost of the product with bonuses for surpassing the target and penalties for failing to meet it. For field management of farm work, it divided the remaining one-third of its members into seven fixed work groups. As a result, the harvesting of wheat and other produce in spring was allegedly accomplished in half a month without the customary help of 80 to 90 persons hired from other places. In the first four months, the net income of the industrial and sideline enterprises increased more than 56% (*Renmin ribao*, July 3, 1981: 2).

Several other new developments deserve to be mentioned briefly. In some places where baochan daohu was practiced, three to more than ten households voluntarily joined together to purchase farm machinery, to undertake irrigation projects, or to set up small work shops to process farm products. In a small number of cases, several households joined a brigade or team to form an economic enterprise, to which each individual would contribute an equal amount of money as his or her share and the brigade or team would put up the collectively owned land. These enterprises amass their own capital, produce and sell their own products, bear the responsibility for their own profits and losses, select their own personnel, and adopt their own management systems (*Renmin ribao*, July 17, 1981: 4, April 28, 1981: 1, March 21, 1981: 2, March 18, 1981: 1).

The system of responsibility has been extended to the cadres as an experiment. In one county in Ningxia, the Party committee signed contracts with cadres in the communes, brigades, and teams to specify their personal responsibilities with provisions for bonuses and penalties. For example, a contract concluded between the county and a commune used as the base line the averages of total grain production, total amount of grain sold to the state, and income from industrial and sideline production in the past three years. If the commune increased total grain production and grain sold by 10,000 catties or its income from industrial and sideline production by ¥10,000, the county would give the cadres of the commune a bonus of a specified amount. If there was a decrease by 10,000 catties or ¥10,000, the county would deduct from the salaries of the commune cadres a specified amount as penalties. This system was used in 1980 in all 71 brigades and their 564 teams in that county. In settling the account for that year, the cadres in 30 teams received penalties, while those in all other teams were given bonuses of varying amounts (*Renmin ribao*, February 17, 1981).[24] In Guangdong, an association of scientific workers and its local affiliates signed contracts with three backward teams to popularize an improved method of farming. Under the contract, 5% of the increase would belong to the team. Everything above 5% would be divided equally between the two contract parties. Ten percent of the receipts of the association and its local affiliates would be used as bonuses for agricultural technicians who were stationed in these teams. If there was a decrease in production not due to natural disaster, the association would compensate the teams for their losses (*Renmin ribao*, April 12, 1981: 2). In the suburban area of Beijing, 240 contracts between scientific units on the one hand and commune or peasant households on the other were signed in the first seven months of 1981 (*Dagong bao*, August 4, 1981: 1).

The numerous forms of the responsibility system must have been bewildering even to the cadres and the peasants of China, not to say outside observers. In January 1981, Chinese leaders began to sum up, simplify, and systematize their views on the responsibility system. In this summation, two trends in the development of the responsibility system are discernible, aside from those mentioned above. The most important is that increasing stress has been placed on three principal forms of the system of responsibility system with reward-yield linkage: (1) baochan daohu (household responsibility system) and da baogan (household total responsibility

---

24. For use of this system in other localities, see *Renmin ribao*, April 19, 1981; page 1; May 8, 1981, page 2. Leshan, Sichuan also uses this system. In one case, two cadres of the county were assigned to a team. They were promised a bonus if the production of this team increased (Interview in Leshan, Sichuan, 1980). Some localities in Henan adopted a system under which the subsidies given to cadres will be increased 1% if the net income of the brigades and teams increases 1%; they will be decreased 1% if the net income decreases by 1% (*Renmin ribao*, August 11, 1981: 2).

system), (2) *tongyi jingying, lianchan daolao* (unified management [combined with] linkage of the individual worker's reward to yield),* and (3) *zhuanye chengbao, lianxi chanliang jichou* (contract work for specialized tasks [combined with] calculation of rewards by linking them to yields). These three forms are said to fit respectively three different types of localities: (1) economically backward and hard-pressed areas, (2) areas at the middle range of economic conditions, and (3) areas where economic conditions are good and the collective economy is relatively strong. The second trend is that increasing efforts are being made to preserve the collective economy when the first and second forms are used. Even under the household total responsibility system, the production team must—it was stressed in one case—undertake unified planning for cultivation, unified plowing and sowing, and unified irrigating. When the system of linking the individual worker's reward to yield is used, it is specified that the systems of collective ownership, of unified distribution, and of using the team or brigade as the basic accounting unit should not be changed, and that planning for cultivation, plowing, use and control of water, and the care and use of draft animals and agricultural machinery and implements of large and medium sizes should be undertaken under the unified auspice of the team or brigade.[25]

Our classificatory scheme, the cases used as illustrations and our discussion of the trends and processes are all based on official reports which undoubtedly try to justify the responsibility system in terms of the demands, interests, and practices of the masses. At this moment we are not in a position to determine how correctly and accurately these reports reflect the real situation. But given our knowledge of the traditional practices of the peasants and the measures adopted during the three years of agricultural crisis, these reports cannot be totally misleading and deceptive. At the very least, they represent the views of the reformers and the policies of those in charge of agriculture. A few years hence, we shall be in a better position to judge the credibility of these reports, the validity of these views, and the success or failure of these policies. . . .

Continuity and Change: Centralized Political Control, Egalitarianism, and Bureaucracy

Our survey suggests that the evolution of the responsibility system is the product of the endeavor of the Party authorities at all levels to adjust the system of collective economy as it has developed since 1956 to the imme-

---

* This form is no longer important and has been replaced by the other two forms.

25. For Premier Zhao Ziyang's view, see article in *Liaowang*, 1981, no. 2, pages 2–5. For the latest reports, see articles in *Renmin ribao* August 22, 1981, page 2 and September 1, 1981, page 2, and articles in *Nongye jingji wenti*, 1981, no. 6, pages 9–13, 13–17.

diate interests and spontaneous demands of the peasants. In so doing, they have revived and expanded some of the practices adopted during the three years of agricultural crisis and during the initial phase of the cooperativization movement in 1953–1955. They have also developed some new forms, such as lianchan daolao zeren zhi (also known as *tongyi jingying, lianchan daolao*) and zhuanye chengbao, lianchan jichou. This readjustment can be viewed from two different perspectives. In one respect, it represents an endeavor to solve the "free ride" problem and the crisis of motivation which had developed in the system of collective economy and was aggravated by the movement to learn from Dazhai. The value and limits of these institutional changes as measures to spur agricultural growth we shall leave to the future.

These recent reforms, together with the development of rural institutions and practices since 1953, can also be examined as a problem of continuity and change. We wish to suggest the following approach to this problem of historical interpretation. From this point of view, rural society in imperial China can be viewed as having been organized by two institutional arrangements: first, a top-to-bottom control by a centralized bureaucracy down to the level of the county; and second, a system of precapitalist "free enterprise" at the local level. As Philip Kuhn notes (1981: 1–17), the "gentry society" of the late imperial period lacked the support of effective concepts of immanence and representation. It "could generate little more than a pallid parochialism" in view of the immense power of the state and the weakness of a traditional local community autonomy in the sense of local areas generating a truly powerful stratum of indigenous leadership.

Under the post-1949 Chinese state, centralized political control not only penetrated downward to the grass roots but also extended horizontally to the economy and other aspects of social life. The total crisis which engulfed Chinese society and its relations with foreign powers in the first half of the twentieth century rendered the rebuilding of a strong, centralized state and bureaucratic system necessary, or at least made it seem acceptable to many Chinese. It predisposed some Chinese intellectuals to accept Marxism, which is a theory of total crisis. It legitimized the endeavor to make a social revolution which would destroy the traditional class structure; bring about a redistribution of income; reshape social institutions; industrialize the country and modernize its culture and change people's ideas, attitudes, and habits. A strongly centralized Party-state with a planned economy commanding and centrally directing numerous collective economic units emerged. In the rural areas, the communes staffed by officials appointed from above and receiving salary from the state became both political and production units. The brigades and teams below them were penetrated by Party branches, Party small groups, or

Party activists. The central places at the lowest level in the natural system increasingly assumed the character of administrative and political units performing tasks assigned from above. Bureaucratic control overwhelmed spontaneous economic activities.

During the Cultural Revolution, the fractionalization of the Leninist Party at the national summit, the initial destruction of the system of Party committees and governmental units below the Central Committee, and the decreased capability of the rebuilt Party and governmental organs did not weaken the centralizing impulse. Indeed, the impulse found even fuller expression in the leftist revolutionary ideological and political line initiated by Mao and carried to the extreme by the "Gang of Four" with the support of mobilized and aroused masses—at least for a time. The idea of the primacy of politics and the practice of organizational control and mass mobilization were pushed as far as humanly possible. The limited sphere of precapitalist free enterprise in both rural and urban areas which had survived up to this time shrank still further. It was attacked as a "spontaneous tendency toward capitalism" rather than regarded as a survival of precapitalist free enterprise which had developed over centuries. It was not considered a necessary supplement to the farming activities of the peasants in eking out a living under a collective economy in the countryside or to the socialist economy in the cities.

In the countryside, the movement to learn from Dazhai and to build Dazhai-type counties marked the culmination of this trend. The use of a single national model for developing agriculture and organizing rural life was a concrete expression of the centralizing impulse which had been inherent in the political organization of the Chinese Empire but was checked by the economic structure of precapitalist free enterprise at the local level, the technological backwardness of transportation and communications, and the size and diversity of China. Thus, the trend toward centralization, uniformity, and standardization in the performance of all functions and in a program to reshape socioeconomic institutions was pushed forward by a mass political movement led by an apotheosized supreme leader. At the national level, it encountered nothing more than ingenious attempts to prevent it from going to the extreme, endeavors to evade its full impact in the process of implementation, concealed opposition, and hidden dissent. At the local level, however, it met extensive evasion and passive resistance.

But the program to eliminate the remnants of precapitalist free enterprise through a mass political movement in a short time was bound to fail, and the endeavor to use one model ran directly counter to the wide variation in geographical conditions throughout the vast expanse of China, in the traditional pattern of village life, and in the capability of the political organization and leadership in numerous local units of production and governance. Hence, the movement to learn from Dazhai did not bring about the desired result in vast areas of China where conditions were very different from those in Dazhai. It stifled individual initiative. It did not enable the local units to cope with problems specific to them or with newly emergent problems in time. It hindered the effort to improve agricultural productivity and to raise the peasants' living standards.

In the national context of rejecting Mao's ideological and political line of the Cultural Revolution period, the repudiation of both the movement to learn from Dazhai and the post-1966 developments in Dazhai itself marked a reversal of the strong and accelerating trend toward centralization in twentieth-century China, a reversal of the tendency for politics in the form of mass political movements and bureaucratic control to penetrate to the lowest level of society for the purpose of restricting or eliminating what had remained of precapitalist free enterprise in the countryside. The reversal of this tendency and the rehabilitation of some types of precapitalist free enterprise are nowhere more obvious than in the encouragement of household sideline occupations, the protection and enlargement of private plots, and the revival of the rural markets. But the changes go much farther and deeper. The most fundamental change can be found in the promotion and perfection of the system of responsibility in agricultural production, which we have described in this article. The regime has now gone as far as it can in readopting some of the traditional forms of relations of production and farming practices short of a reversion of land and collectively owned means of production to private ownership. It attempts to effect a synthesis of the new institutions and practices adopted since the nationwide movement to organize cooperatives in 1955–1956 with some of the traditional institutions and practices of individual farming. To enable the production team to make these institutional changes in light of its specific circumstances, the idea of autonomy of the team has been underscored and propagated. The reversal of the trend toward increasing centralized political control also finds expression in the provinces, municipalities, and counties and the policy of devolving many more functions to them.

A similar approach can be applied to understand the drive toward egalitarianism in the countryside. It is common knowledge that in the revolutionary process the peasants constituted the major force. Egalitarianism in economic matters was a central feature in traditional peasant rebellions which have been considered by the Chinese Communists as the antecedents of their revolution in a different stage of historical development. To be sure, Mao and other Chinese Communist leaders drew a sharp distinction between "agrarian socialism" and "scientific socialism" or between "populism" and Marxism (for example see Gong Yuzhi, 1981a, 1981b). They rejected "absolute egalitarianism" or "extreme egalitarianism" which characterized the economic program of traditional peasant rebellions. But as the early pronouncements on the communization program, many developments in the Cultural Revolution culminating in the call for the restriction of "bourgeois right," and the movement to learn from Dazhai show, the search for a greater degree of economic equality was a major impetus to continued radical transformation in the countryside as well as its justification.

In their attempt to find the social basis for the Cultural Revolution and the leftist errors in policies since 1957, several Chinese intellectuals trace radical egalitarianism to China's "small producers," particularly the peasants. They call for a new effort to eliminate "peasant ideology" (Wang Xiaoqiang, 1980; Luo Hanxian, 1980). That this line of analysis may have serious and harmful political and social consequences has been noted elsewhere (Tsou, Blecher, and Meisner, 1981). Here we suggest that it is also incorrect—or at least incomplete—in its understanding of the peasants and China's rural society. It also does not help us to understand current developments. If it is true that the rural economy of traditional China can be characterized as a system of precapitalist free-enterprise, the kind of sharing which occurred within the family, the kinship group, the clan, or, to some extent, the village community was very different from the extreme form of egalitarianism which flared up during the peasant rebellions. This radical egalitarianism was nothing less than reaction against the economic inequality produced in the countryside by precapitalist free enterprise. In normal times, the traditional peasants as "small producers" were skillful entrepreneurs rather than extreme egalitarians. The "man from Dazhai," Chen Yonggui himself, was directly quoted to have said: "Only when the peasants are pushed or dragged will they take the socialist road. If left alone, where will they go? Once you relax a little, they will slip toward capitalism" (*Renmin ribao*, July 9, 1981: 2). Chen's analysis is not too far from the truth.

Hence, the extreme egalitarianism which is now condemned by some intellectuals as a natural trait of the peasants was actually a product of the Chinese revolution, which combined elements from the traditional peasant rebellions and modern socialism. The recent revival of many traditional practices in the countryside and adoption of the responsibility system in an attempt to meet the felt needs and spontaneous demands of the peasants are themselves recognition that the peasantry as a whole does not form the social basis of extreme egalitarianism. They also mark the end of the Chinese revolution in the countryside and its replacement by a program of economic development through the use of some of the practices of the system of precapitalist free enterprise. But this revival is taking place within the context of a new ideology, political order, and economic system. If the regime's rural policy succeeds, the relations of production will not revert to the traditional system of individual farming, nor will they develop into commercialized agriculture in a capitalist form. It will be a curious mixture of a modern collective economy and some of the surviving features of precapitalist free enterprise in the countryside. This may represent the Chinese path to modernization in agriculture in the near future. Although "agrarian socialism" is now under strong attack as incompatible with "scientific socialism," it is possible that in the long run a synthesis of these two strands of thought will emerge and represent a creative response to the challenge of modernizing agriculture in China. For egalitarianism was not only rooted in some strands of the Chinese tradition (this point is made in Wang Xiaoqiang, 1980). It is also a modern ideal. The combination of growth with equality is a particularly urgent and inescapable task in a very poor country with a high population-land ratio.

Following a similar line of thinking, we can briefly look at the problem of bureaucratic control in the countryside. During the period of civil and foreign wars, the Party developed not only a mass movement but also a huge bureaucracy. After the victory and through the movements of land reform, cooperativization, and communization, the fighters, activists, and cadres of peasant origin or from small towns and cities in the rural areas staffed the bureaucracy at the levels of the county, commune, and brigade. Indeed, these former peasant rebels and cadres with rural roots led successive mass movements in transforming the countryside in the direction of a greater degree of economic egalitarianism. These mass movements and the elevation of the collective economy to a progressively higher level gave these cadres increasingly great power of control. Their power interests as local leaders and bureaucrats who ran the collective economy must be added to their role as loyal revolutionary Party members as an explanation of the extraordinary pace of the cooperatization movement after 1955 and the excesses in the communization movement. On various occasions Mao undoubtedly wanted to put the responsibility for excesses on the local cadres; there may have been an element of justice in this.

The Cultural Revolution was an attack on the bureaucracy. But the Cultural Revolution itself brought into existence a factional bureaucracy which paralyzed but did not totally destroy the preexisting bureaucratic system. The Dazhai movement increased the control of the leaders at the county, commune, and brigade levels over the production teams and individual peasants. It is probably significant and revealing that the first published self-criticism made by Xiyang county occurred after the Party Center sent down a document on the "experience in Xiangxiang county" in Hunan which denounced the practice of upper-level units in using the labor power, funds, and material resources of the production teams without compensation as well as the enormous increase in nonproductive personnel, work, and expenditure (*Renmin ribao*, July 5, 1981: 7; Xiyang's self-criticism was published on July 21). Shortly thereafter, the Party published another document which condemned the practices of cadres of Xunyi county in maltreating the peasants. Such treatment was frequently the result of cadres trying to prevent the peasants from engaging in selling household sideline products in the rural markets or in other private activities for personal gain (Tsou, Blecher, and Meisner, 1981: 276). Chen Yonggui's leadership style and cadre policy after his seizure of power in Xiyang in 1967 show that even poor and formerly oppressed peasants at the bottom of China's bureaucratic society could consciously or unconsciously take over the political style of the traditional ruling class and succumb to some of the traditional abuses of power after they have risen to positions of authority in a revolution, even if they are simultaneously pushing forward revolutionary, egalitarian, and leftist socioeconomic programs which benefit poor peasants.

Recent changes in the institutions, policies, and practices in the countryside entail a reduction of bureaucratic control and a diminution of local cadres' power. In the context of the acquisition by the peasants, work groups, and production teams of a greater degree of autonomy in managing their own economic affairs, the new system of election with secret ballots and more candidates than positions to be filled may contribute to the development and strengthening of a sense of representation, a new stratum of indigenous leaders, and a tradition of local autonomy. Whether or not this will be the case, there is no doubt that these changes and the current emphasis on the need to adjust institutions, policies, and practices to variations in local conditions will make China's economy, society, and politics much more complex than at any time in its long history. China's fate will hinge on the success or failure of the endeavor to combine this complex system with the goals of political unity and stability and socioeconomic justice in a period of unprecedented change.

References

An Gang et al. (1981) "Zhonghua nongye zhenxing youwang" (There is hope for the vigorous development of Chinese agriculture). Renmin ribao (July 9): 2.

Banyue tan. Beijing.

Crook, Frederick (1971) An Analysis of Work Payment Systems Used in Chinese Mainland Agriculture, 1956 to 1970. Ph.D. dissertation, Tufts University.

Dagong bao. U.S. edition.

Foreign Broadcast Information Service: PRC. FBIS

Gong Yuzhi (1981a) "Pipan nongye shehuizhuyi sixiang de zhongyao wenxian" (An important historical document criticizing the ideas of agrarian socialism). Renmin ribao (March 24): 5.

────── (1981b) "Yizong gengzheng" (A correction). Renmin ribao (April 10): 5.

Jingi guanli. Beijing.

Kuhn, P. A. (1981) "Late Ch'ing views on the polity," pp. 1–18 in Tang Tsou (ed.) Selected Papers from the Center for Far Eastern Studies, No. 4. Chicago: Univ. of Chicago Press.

Liao-wang.

Luo Hanxian (1980) "Lun nongmin shehui zhuyi" (On peasant socialism). Nongye jingji lunchong 1, 1 (November): 58–64.

Nongcun gongzuo tongxun. Beijing.

Nongye jingji wenti. Beijing.

Nongye zhishi. Beijing.

Renmin ribao. Beijing.

Tian Beizhi (1981) "Yige zhiming renwu de luoxuan" (The electoral defeat of a well-known person). Liao-wang 1 (April 20): 20–21.

Tsou, Tang, Marc Blecher, and Mitch Meisner (1981) "Policy change at the national summit and institutional transformation at the local level: the case of Dazhai and Xiyang in the post Mao era." Selected Papers from the Center for Far Eastern Studies 4. Chicago: Univ. of Chicago.

Wang Guichen and Wei Daonan (1981) "Lun baochan daohu" (On the household responsibility system). Jingji yanjiu 1 (January): 64–67.

Wang Xiaoqiang (1980) "Nongye shehui zhuyi pipan" (A critique of agrarian socialism). Xinhua yuebao (wenzhai ban) no. 5: 7–13.

Wu Xiang (1980) "Yangguandao yu dumuqiao" (Open road and single-log bridge). Renmin ribao (November 5): 2.

Yu Guoyao (1980) "Zenyang kan baochandaohu" (How we view the household responsibility system). Hongqi 20: 12–15, 35.

Zhan Wu and Wang Guichen (1981) "Lun zhuanye chengbao lianchan jichou zerenzhi" (On the responsibility system of contract work for specialized tasks, calculating reward by linking it to yield). Jingji yanjiu 4.

Zhang Jinxing and Jin Jiasheng (1981) "Dazhai xin dangzhibu de dansheng" (The birth of a new Party branch in Dazhai). Liao-wang 1 (April 20): 21–22.

Zhonggong yanjiu. Taibei.

7 Political Change and Reform: The Middle Course

Change and Limits to Change in the New Historic Era

A new historic era in China began in December 1978.[1] The signpost of this new era is the Third Plenum of the Eleventh Central Committee, marking not only a decisive break with those ideological and political lines of Mao which culminated in the Cultural Revolution, but also signaling the end of nearly three-quarters of a century of revolutionary ferment and upheavals. The Third Plenum declared that "the large-scale turbulent class struggles of a mass character have in the main come to an end." It issued a call for the shift of the emphasis of the Party's work to "socialist modernization." It urged the Party "to integrate the universal principles of Marxism-Leninism-Mao Zedong Thought with the concrete practice of socialist modernization and develop it under new historical conditions."

Even more significantly historically, this termination of the revolutionary period has been accompanied by a retreat of political power (i.e., the Party-state) from its increasingly deeper penetration into civil society and the economy, thus reversing the fundamental trend of political development since the May Fourth period of 1915–21. Political power is no longer used to effect another transformation in the society's class structure. Class conflict has ceased to be considered "the principal contradiction." A new conception of the existing class structure has emerged, one in which most former landlords and capitalists are considered having been reformed into ordinary members of society and intellectuals are considered a part of "the working class" engaged in mental labor as distinguished from manual labor. Mao's dictum[2] that in certain conditions, relations of production,

1. This paper [first presented at a Conference held in November 1981] was revised in the academic year of 1982–83. During that period, my research was generously supported by the Luce Foundation. I want to express my personal thanks to Ms. Martha Wallace and Mr. Robert Armstrong for their encouragement. In revising the article, I was benefitted by the suggestions of Professors Ira Katznelson, Lowell Dittmer, and Mark Selden. I was grateful to the remarks made by Professors A. Doak Barnett, Robert Scalapino, and Michel Oksenberg. The limitation of space prevented the writer from updating the paper with a detailed examination of events after November 1981. [This paper is reprinted here by the permission of Westview Press, from *China: The 80s Era*, Norton Ginsburg and Bernard Lalor, eds. Copyright © 1984 by Westview Press, Boulder, Colorado.]

2. For a discussion of this idea of Mao's, see Tang Tsou, "Mao Tse-tung Thought, the Last Struggle for Succession, and the Post-Mao Era," *China Quarterly*, September 1977, pp. 498–527 [reprinted in this volume as chap. 4].

theory and the superstructure rather than productive forces, practice, and economic base can and do play the principal and decisive role in social change has been questioned and is no longer invoked. The epistemological postulate that "practice is the sole criterion for testing truth" and the revived slogan "seek truth from facts" have facilitated input and feedback from society to the Party and the state. The sociological postulate—that every sphere of social life and its activities has its special characteristics *(tedian)* and is governed by special laws—is accompanied by the injunction that political leadership can and should create the general conditions favorable to the operation of these laws and even use these laws to promote development, but it cannot violate these laws without suffering serious consequences.

The importance of the perceived needs and material interests of the various groups and individuals in society is also given renewed recognition. The overcentralized, overextended, and stringent system of economic planning, which has proved unworkable in "practice," is being re-examined, partially relaxed, and reduced in scope. The operation of the market is accepted as a supplement to a planned economy, wherein prices, credits, and other mechanisms of the market are selectively used as instruments to spur economic growth. Contract relations have superseded authority relations as the principal method of managing the rural economy at the grassroots level. All of these changes have marked out an irreducible, though still small and vulnerable, element of autonomy in various spheres of social and individual life. In short, civil society is being revived and the relationship between political power and society has changed.[3]

This changing relationship between political power and society has gone hand in hand with endeavors to reform the political system and pro-

3. For a fuller discussion, see Tang Tsou, "Back from the Brink of Revolutionary-'Feudal' Totalitarianism," in *State and Society in Contemporary China*, ed. Victor Nee and David Mozingo (Ithaca, N.Y.: Cornell University Press, 1983) pp. 53–88 [reprinted in this volume as chap. 5].

For a preliminary discussion of my use of the term "totalitarianism," see my paper presented at the Luce Seminar, University of Chicago in May 1980. For the initial formulation of a conceptual scheme for the interpretation of twentieth-century Chinese politics see my unpublished paper, "Political Totalism, Stateness, and Hegemony: A Proposed Theoretical Framework for the Study of the Transformation of a Centralized Bureaucratic Empire into a Communist Regime in China," presented at a seminar at the Northern Illinois University on October 27, 1982. Aside from dealing with other conceptual problems, this paper explains why the term "political power" is frequently used in place of the term "state" in my discussion of the "state-society" relationship.

The literature on totalitarianism and on the relationship between the state and society is too voluminous to be cited in a footnote.

cesses. These endeavors not only stem from the specifically political lessons learned by the Chinese from the Cultural Revolution, but also are tied to the changing relationship between the state and society as well as the changed nature of society itself, which is the product of the forced drive toward economic development partly through the use of political means and mass mobilization. These reforms have stepped up the process of institutionalization, while nationwide mass movements have been abandoned as the favored method of policy implementation.[4] Collective leadership, in contrast to the cult of personality, facilitates input and feedback from society to the uppermost level of politics. So are the attempts to draw a sharper line of demarcation between the functions of the Party and the state, the strengthening of the legislative branch of the government at all levels, and the adoption of an electoral system in which there are more candidates than positions to be filled and a system of a two-step election, used to elect the new Central Committee at the recent Twelfth Party Congress.[5] The streamlining of the government and bureaucratic structure is intended to facilitate decision-making and implementation so that, among other things, the political system can respond more efficiently and adequately to popular demands for action. The plan to abolish life-long tenure for political leaders and subordinate officials alike is linked inseparably with the policy of promoting middle-age and young cadres who have higher levels of culture, knowledge, and technical skills than the old cadres. Both programs reflect the needs of the new and increasingly complex society with a full-fledged, though still backward and inefficient, industrial system. The rapid development of education and science has been made a focal point of the strategy in economic development alongside with agriculture, energy, and transport. All this is well known; but it is important to see these political reforms and policy changes in the context of the changing relationship between the state and society.

As this author noted in a paper written in early 1980, there is a limit to all these changes.[6] Although the trend toward the increasingly deep penetration of political power into society has been reversed, China is only beginning its transition to a posttotalitarian society. This process of transition may well be halted or even reversed. In any case, political power

4. For a discussion of political institutionalization and social mobilization, together with their impact on political stability and order, see Samuel Huntington, *Political Order and Social Change* (New Haven: Yale University Press, 1968).

5. *The Twelfth National Congress of the Communist Party of China: Documents* (in Chinese) (Beijing: Renmin chuban she, 1982) pp. 154–155.

6. Tang Tsou, cf. my aforementioned article, "Back from the Brink of Revolutionary-'Feudal' Totalitarianism: A Preliminary Reflection." [A revised version is printed in this volume as chap. 5.]

continues to dominate society and is the ultimate, unchallengeable arbiter of China's fate. The Party may and does exercise self-restraint as the slogan "For the Party to uphold its leadership, it must improve its leadership" indicates. But even if there is self-limitation of the power of the Party, there are still no organized forces or effective institutions to check and balance its power from outside. Similarly the political reforms and new departures in economic policies still take place within the general political and institutional framework established in 1949.[7]

What this paper is intended to clarify is both the depth and the limits of this change.[8] First, it argues that the change in the relationship between political power and society is uneven in different social sectors. The changes in the relationship between political power and the economy have occurred faster and have gone further than those in the relationship between political power and civil society. Within the economy, changes in the agricultural and rural sector have gone far ahead of other sectors and have followed a steady course. In civil society, the sphere of literature and art has encountered more difficulties than most other professions. Here the relationship has undergone a series of fluctuations. Hence the rural society and the field of literature and art will be singled out for discussion to highlight the problem of changing state-society relations.

Second, in changing the state-society relationship and in reforming the political system and processes, the political leadership has opted for a middle course. This middle course is marked out, on the one hand, by the ideological and political line adopted at the Third Plenum and, on the other, by the affirmation of the "four fundamental principles" (upholding socialism, the dictatorship of the proletariat, the leadership of the Party, and Marxism-Leninism and Mao Zedong Thought) made by Deng Xiaoping in March 1979. This choice of the middle course is most clearly reflected in the abandonment of the notion of "the struggle *between two lines*" and its substitution by the concept of "the struggle *on two fronts*" against both "leftist ideas" and the tendency toward "bourgeois liberalization."

Third, most of the recent political reforms represent efforts at institutionalization and at achieving a modicum of checks and balances within a Leninist Party-state. The more radical ideas of reform have been abandoned either because of political opposition or because of their inappropriateness at this time, but the views of the standpatters have also been

---

7. This author has offered one of the many possible explanations for the simultaneous occurence of rapid and profound changes with the persistence of the overall political and institutional framework in his paper, "Back from the Brink of 'Feudal' Totalitarianism."

8. This paper can be properly viewed as a sequel to the earlier one mentioned in footnote 3.

pushed aside. The aim is to make steady progress only as fast as circumstances permit.

The Party and Literature: The Guardians of Political Society and the Sensitive Souls of Civil Society

The change and limits to change in the relationship between political power and civil society in China can be most vividly seen in the oscillation in official policies and attitudes toward literature and writers, which have become more restrictive than those toward most other professions and professional groups. The reasons are not far to seek. Writers form a sub-group of humanistic intellectuals, as distinguished from the technical intelligentsia.[9] In China, many intellectuals have become leaders in the Party, the government, and the army. Others serve as Party ideologues in all fields, including that of literature. Political leaders have the responsibility of adopting and implementing an ideological and political line. They must perform the function of resolving or mediating the conflicts among all political forces and social groups, of which the writers constitute only one among many. Party ideologues must uphold what they believe to be the ideological framework supporting the regime and society. In a Leninist Party-state, the Party leaders are the guardians of political society.

In contrast, those humanistic intellectuals who are writers not totally coopted by the establishment frequently though not always are the sensitive souls and passionate spokesmen of civil society. They are likely to view society not from the viewpoint of power holders but as ordinary members at the periphery of the power structure or even outside it. Traditionally, Chinese writers have had a deep sense of social responsibility. They are apt to be social critics. Being persons with vivid imaginations, many of them entertain bold visions and lofty ideals which may or may not converge with those of the political leaders or which cannot be realized at this moment but may inspire dissatisfaction with and encourage dissent from the existing socio-political arrangements. Their writings usually have ideological and political implications, direct or indirect. Writers are a self-selected group of intellectuals who value self-expression more than collective actions. In comparison with social scientists or other members of technical intelligentsia, they are less restrained by commonly accepted paradigms, standards, and a course of training. Good writers reach a wider audience and convey a message more effectively than members of the technical intelligentsia, Party ideologues, and Party propagandists. They may produce great literary works which are marks of the level of

9. For this distinction, see Alvin W. Gouldner, *The Future of Intellectuals and the Rise of the New Class* (New York: Oxford University Press, 1979); but the writer has made some modification in the use of these terms.

civilization reached by a nation and become the indestructible treasure of mankind. The mavericks among them are potentially winged steeds.

In the post-Mao era, Chinese leaders wish civil society to rest and rejuvenate itself, while they also aim to develop civilization in China to a high level. Yet, nothing can be done unless political unity and stability can be maintained and the people are willing to work hard and to endure hardship at the present time. In the leaders' opinion, these two conditions can be fulfilled only if the people have faith in the future and confidence in the regime. Hence, the adjustment of the relationship between the Party and the writers is a particularly difficult task. In the post-Cultural Revolution period, this task is further complicated by the ongoing and uncertain search for a viable policy to achieve both goals and by the division of opinion within both the Party and the Army and between them. In China, the role of the Army in the field of literature is a formidable one because it has a huge literary establishment and is engaged in many literary enterprises to an extent unparalleled elsewhere.

Oscillation between the Relaxation and the Tightening of Political Control
Our story unfolds with the Third Plenum which adopted a policy of relaxing political control. It was immediately followed by a proliferation of posters on the well-known "Democracy Wall," the appearance of many privately-published and unauthorized journals or mimeographed sheets, and demonstrations by small groups of people at the most conspicuous places in Beijing and other large cities—all of which were channels for expressing demands for radical changes, voicing long supressed grievances, or asking redress for wrongs inflicted by the regime.

Soon the first swing back toward tightening political control occurred. Although at this time this oscillation affected literature only marginally, if at all, it set the parameters for ideological and political liberalization which have had fundamental significance for China's development in all fields, including literature. On March 30, 1979, at a conference to discuss theoretical, abstract problems sponsored by the Propaganda Department of the Central Committee, Deng Xiaoping himself called for the firm upholding of the "four fundamental principles."

This first swing was followed by two apparently contradictory series of events. One series was: (1) the immediate removal of the "Democracy Wall" from the main thoroughfare in Beijing to an out-of-the-way park; (2) the arrest and trial of Wei Jingsheng and a number of editors of, and contributors to, self-published journals; (3) the adoption by the Fifth Plenum in February 1980 of a proposal to eliminate the constitutional article which provided for the right to engage in "big contending, big blooming, big debate," and to put up "big character posters"; and (4) the final revision of the constitution accordingly at the Third Session of the Fifth [National] People's Congress held in September 1980.

Concurrently ran a second series: (1) the beginning of some basic political reforms; (2) the inauguration of the new economic program of "readjustment, structural reform, consolidation, and improvement"; (3) the continued relaxation of political control over many aspects of society and the economy; and (4) the accelerated liberalization and popularization of the Party-state.

In this historical and political context, in October-November 1979, the Congress of Writers and Artists met for the first time in nineteen years. This Fourth Congress was briefly mentioned in an earlier paper by the author, [reprinted as chapter 5 in this volume] and is now most ably discussed by Professor Leo Ou-Fan Lee in [the volume in which this essay was first published]. Suffice it to mention here that Zhou Yang, the most important Party ideologue in charge of literature from 1949 to 1966 and a victim of the sweeping purge during the Cultural Revolution, apologized publicly to those writers who had been attacked, purged, or oppressed by him. This personal gesture was actually the symbol of the Party's apology to writers for its erroneous policies pursued before and during the Cultural Revolution. The Congress was apparently meant to be a meeting for reconciliation, the rebirth of literature, and the search for new direction. An outpouring of creative writings and a proliferation of journals followed. A period of about 22 months around the Fourth Congress marked the height of liberalization in that field.

Yet another swing toward the reimposition of tighter political control occurred in the early months of 1981, after a period of uncertainty in Chinese politics during the autumn and winter of 1980–81.[10] Many of the political and economic changes pushed by the reformers directly affected the vested interests of the veteran leaders, bureaucrats, and cadres at all levels, particularly those who had risen to higher positions during the Cultural Revolution. The strongest source of opposition seems to have been the Army. During the Cultural Revolution, the position of the Army had been greatly strengthened. Army officers and cadres had assumed increased authority and had been given many more privileges than before. As the principal creator of the Red Army, the primary exponent of its political-military doctrine, and the chief strategist leading it to total victory in the civil war, Mao had always enjoyed higher prestige in the Army than any other political leader. In the protracted revolutionary warfare, Army recruits consisted almost entirely of peasants, and its officers devel-

10. In order to conform with the desire to produce as short an article as possible, most references to the impact of international factors on internal development are omitted.

oped a rural orientation. Both groups had little knowledge about the urban sector and even less about the outside world. The system of responsibility for agricultural production, particularly the total responsibility of the household for farming, directly affected the livelihood of the families of soldiers, officers, and martyrs—families which remained in the countryside and were short of labor power. Meanwhile, the economic program of the reformers and the huge budget deficit in 1980 led to a decrease in the funds allocated to the military.

The opposition of the Army was precipitated by two events. First, the work of drafting a document subsequently known as "The Resolution on Certain Questions in the History of Our Party since the Founding of the People's Republic of China" began in March 1980 under the direct leadership of the standing committee of the Politbureau and the Secretariat. The reformers hoped that this document would settle the major ideological issues once and for all, particularly the problem of Mao's mistakes in his last years, and that it would be formally adopted at the Sixth Plenum planned for January or February of 1981 to be followed immediately by the Twelfth Party Congress. Second, the reformers maneuvered for the removal of Hua Guofeng as the Chairman of the Chinese Communist Party. This was an act inconceivable three years earlier, given the general image of the chairmanship since its inception and given its great authority when it had been occupied by Mao. In addition, Hua had more supporters in the Army than in many other political and social groups. Again, this momentous change was also to be formally accomplished at the Sixth Plenum.

As a preparatory step, a Politbureau meeting was held in mid-November 1980 and lasted several days. At this meeting, Hua's mistakes were examined and subjected to criticism. The Politbureau accepted Hua's resignation from the chairmanship of both the Party and its military commission. Pending formal rectification by the Sixth Plenum, Hu Yaobang and Deng Xiaoping respectively were to take over Hua's duties in handling the work of the Party and the Army, but Hua's resignation under pressure and the drafting of the resolution on Party history raised more controversy and debate than expected. Presumably, most of the reformers' proposals met with reservations, objections, criticism, and direct challenge. The reimposition of tighter control over literature must be understood in this larger political context. As literary works immediately arouse deep emotions and controversy without producing any tangible, material benefits, it is for many people an expendable enterprise and, therefore, it is an easy target for the conservatives in the Army to attack.

The process of tightening control went through two stages. Events in the first stage revealed the differences between the policies advocated by the military as expressed in *Liberation Army Daily (Jiefangjun bao)* and the attitudes of writers, the literary establishment, and some Party leaders as reflected in *The Journal on Literature and Art (Wenyi bao)*. In the second stage, a compromise was reached leaning toward the views of the military. This compromise was sponsored by Deng and the newly elected Chairman of the Chinese Communist Party, Hu Yaobang. It raised the question whether the ideological, political line and the whole package of political and economic programs and policies adopted since the Third Plenum had been or would be reversed. Indeed, it posed the fundamental problem whether or not the political system and process in post-1978 China had remained as they had been under Mao in the period from 1957 to 1976. These questions are so important for understanding recent developments in Chinese politics and for speculation about China's future that we must briefly describe this oscillation, despite our limited knowledge about recent events.

The first stage of this oscillation began with the issuance in early 1981 of documents no. 7 and no. 9 of the Party Center.[11]

According to a report from Hong Kong, document no. 7 imposed fairly strict limitations on creative writing and enjoined writers not to engage in producing "literature on the wounds," which used the anti-Rightist campaign, the Great Leap Forward, and the Cultural Revolution as its subject matter. Document no. 9 reportedly conveyed the decision of the Party Center not to permit "illegal journals" (i.e., self-published journals) and "illegal organizations" (i.e., organizations not specifically recognized by and registered with the regime, including organizations which published unauthorized journals) to achieve legal status. The document also forbade those connected with these "illegal publications" and "illegal organizations" from establishing liaisons with each other and from combining small organizations to form larger ones. In the next few months, there were reports of the arrests of a number of dissenters, including Wang Xizhe, one of the three authors of a famous big character poster during the Cultural Revolution, who had been released in December 1978.

Whatever its specific content, document no. 7 soon found concrete expression in an article published on April 18, under the byline of "a specifically invited commentator of *Liberation Army Daily*," entitled "The Violation of the Four Fundamental Principles Should Not Be Allowed: A Critique of the Film Script 'Unrequited Love.'"* The article was politically significant in that it in effect advocated a reversal of the policy and

---

11. At the time of writing this article in November 1981, I was not able to find the full texts of these two documents which can likely be found somewhere outside China. Document no. 7 was probably sent down around the time of the spring festival in 1981.

* For recently available information on the roles of the Army and Deng in initiating the criticism of Bai Hua's movie script, see Tang Tsou, "The Historic Change in Direction and Continuity with the Past," *China Quarterly*, June 1984, pp. 320–47.

practice of relaxing political control over literature which had been followed up to that time. It condemned "Unrequited Love" as not only "violating the four fundamental principles" but also "going so far as to negate in effect patriotism."[12] Significantly, this film script was published in one of the most innovative literary journals, *Shiyue (October)* in September 1979,[13] during the period of relaxation and in spite of the affirmation in March 1979 of the four fundamental principles. By 1981, it had been made into a movie which was shown to selected audiences but was not yet released to the general public.

What particularly angered the special commentator and the critics was a question posed by the script and its answer: "You love this country of ours. . . . But does this country love you?"[14] The implicit, but forcefully and dramatically expressed, answer in the negative was given by the death of the central figure from hunger, physical exhaustion, and exposure, when he thought he was still being pursued by security forces and radicals just after the downfall of the "Gang of Four." Several newspapers and journals immediately reprinted the article attacking the script.[15] Meanwhile, other writers were criticized or attacked in the press. It was reported in Hong Kong that the authorities of the military region in which the author of the script, Bai Hua, held an official position had asked for his dismissal from the Army and the Party.

This first attack by *Liberation Army Daily* ran into strong passive resistance from a large number of writers and editors of newspapers and journals. Even *People's Daily* did not reprint the article published in *Liberation Army Daily*. This precedent was used by other newspapers and journals to justify their refusal to do so. Moreover, one of Bai Hua's poems was given a prize in late May. *The Journal on Literature and Art*, the official mouthpiece of writers and artists, in an issue published on May 22, carried a short but significant article on "The Criticism of 'Unrequited Love' and Its Response." According to this report, ten of the twelve articles and letters submitted to the journal expressed disagreement with the method used by the special commentator of the Army's newspaper in criticizing "Unrequited Love." They argued that the method used was not sufficiently prudent and produced just the opposite social effect.[16]

According to a report from Hong Kong, Hu Yaobang made the following points at a symposium: The author of "Unrequited Love" had written many good pieces although "Unrequited Love" by itself was "not good"

12. *Liberation Army Daily* is not circulated abroad. But the article was reprinted in *Beijing ribao*, April 20, 1981, p. 2, two days after its publication in *Liberation Army Daily*.
13. *Shiyue*, 1979, no. 3, pp. 140–171, 248.
14. Ibid., p. 167.
15. *Wenyi bao*, 1980, no. 10, p. 29.
16. Ibid.

and "had harmful effects." In general, "bad things" should be criticized, but it was even better to win over the author and persuade him to make a self-criticism. Counter-criticism, or replies to criticism, should be allowed. Articles criticizing a literary work should be published under the byline of individuals rather than Party organizations or editorial boards. A distinction should be made between criticizing a literary work and criticizing its author; these two separate things should not be mixed together. In criticizing a literary work full and good reasons must be given. It was not necessary for all newspapers and journals to publish a particular piece of literary criticism. Some might republish it and others might not. Coercion should not be used to force the latter to publish it. Finally, he asked that the discussion on "Unrequited Love" be calmed down. For some problems, one should not be too hasty in seeking solutions but should put them aside for a while.[17]

These informal remarks by Hu seemed to most outside observers in Hong Kong to have put an end to the case of "Unrequited Love." Yet, events took an unexpected turn toward the reimposition of stricter political control shortly after the Sixth Plenum was held in June 1981. On July 17, Deng Xiaoping, in a talk to leading members of the propaganda organization under the Chinese Communist Party's central committee, said that greater attention should be given to the "lax and weak" leadership of the Party in the sphere of ideological and literary work.[18] He noted,

> Nowadays, erroneous tendencies cannot be criticized; once they are, this is called 'using a big stick.' It is not easy today to make criticisms and self-criticisms, especially self-criticisms.

He pointed out that the essence of the four fundamental principles is the leadership of the Party and that the essence of "bourgeois liberalization" is opposition to Party leadership. In guiding ideological work, criticism and self-criticism should be made of bourgeois liberalization tendencies, as well as "Left" tendencies. In dealing with present problems, the old road should not be taken again; no campaigns should be launched; no concerted attacks from all sides should be undertaken; and the degree of criticism should be appropriate. Yet, he concluded that criticisms and self-criticisms had to be made. In an obvious allusion to Bai Hua, he said that writers, artists, and theorists who were Party members must obey Party discipline; if Party members did not do so, how could the Party lead the masses?

17. *Zhengming*, 1981, no. 8, p. 16.
18. *Renmin ribao*, August 13, 1981, p. 1. The translation used here generally follows the report in *Beijing Review*, September 7, 1981, pp. 13–14. This report did not mention the upholding of the four fundamental principles which was stressed in Deng's talk and mentioned in Hu's subsequent speech.

In late August, the Propaganda Department of the Central Committee called a national meeting attended by more than 300 persons. The topic of the meeting was the strengthening of the Party's leadership in ideological work and the changing of the lax and weak methods used. The specific subject of discussion was Deng's talk. Closely following Deng's talk, Hu Yaobang made it clear that the emphasis should now be shifted to the criticism and self-criticism of erroneous tendencies. He specifically condemned "Unrequited Love" as being harmful to the people and socialism and noted that it was not an isolated problem but on the contrary represented a wrong tendency. He also observed that in making correct criticisms and self-criticisms, one must above all firmly uphold the four fundamental principles which had been recently reiterated by the Sixth Plenum and which constitute the common foundation of unity and consensus of the whole Party, the whole army, and all nationalities in the country. To the writers, journalists, theorists, and editors, he said that the Party Central Committee was now putting forward its earnest hopes and concrete demands for strengthening the Party's leadership in these spheres of work.

For each point emphasizing the tightening of political control, however, we can also find another point limiting the extent of the reimposition of control and the political implications of criticism and self-criticism. Hu made it clear that the purpose of discussing the problem of lax and weak leadership was not to attribute responsibility but to analyze the cause so as to find the correct way to solve it, that "Comrade Bai Hua" had written some good pieces, and that the Party Central Committee was maintaining without any change its policies toward the intellectuals, ideological work, and literature and art.

A few days later, it was reported that a meeting of more than fifty leading cadres, writers, artists, and critics living in Beijing had been held some time before. All those who spoke expressed support for the talks of Deng and Hu. Some made concrete analyses and solemn criticism of "Unrequited Love." The episode involving "Unrequited Love" brought out two distinct attitudes on the part of those officials in charge of literary work who had been persecuted by the ultra-leftists during the Cultural Revolution. One attitude was symbolized by Zhou Yang, who had apologized in November 1979 for his oppression of writers prior to his own downfall, who had became an advocate of the relaxation of control, and who did not follow *Liberation Army Daily*'s lead in criticizing "Unrequited Love." At this meeting, he owned up to "our responsibility" in not conducting "timely and accurate criticism" of that film script. Prior to this meeting, *People's Daily* in an article published on August 18 under the byline of its commentator admitted its mistake of having been weak and lax in literary criticisms.[19] The other attitude was represented by Liu Baiyu, the head of

19. *Renmin ribao*, August 18, 1981, p. 1.

230

the Cultural Department in the General Political Department of the People's Liberation Army, who reportedly was the mastermind behind the article criticizing "Unrequited Love." His basic position was now vindicated, but his methods were not. At the meeting, he said that in literary criticism attention should be paid first to making a clear distinction between the enemy and ourselves, between right and wrong; that one should uphold principles firmly and at the same time be particular about methods; and that if the methods were not good, beneficial results also could not be attained.[20]

After several weeks of delays, *The Journal on Literature and Art* finally published an article criticizing "Unrequited Love" under the byline of two specific individuals rather than under the byline of the journal or its commentator; but this article pointed out that as a national periodical on literary and artistic criticism, the *Journal* had not seized upon this typical case to publish a timely critique and that this failure fell short of the expectation of its readers and could be considered a lesson to be learned. This self-criticism on the part of the Journal was coupled with an admission that it was altogether necessary for *Liberation Army Daily* to take the lead in publishing a criticism of "Unrequited Love."[21]

Finally in November 1981, Bai Hua published a self-criticism. On December 30, Hu Yaobang formally announced that the Bai Hua case had been "successfully concluded." This episode has been fully discussed by Professor Leo Ou-fan Lee in his analysis from the viewpoint of a specialist on literature. Nothing more needs to be added here.

Déjà Vu or an Uncertain Search for a New Form?
With the publication of the article in *The Journal on Literature and Art* and the self-criticism of Bai Hua, the case of "Unrequited Love" came to a close. It marked the end of the beginning of a new cycle of political control. During this period of time, several prominent writers and artists who advocated the relaxation of control over literature and art were also criticized in the press. At the universities and schools, ideological and political work was being pushed. Several relatively pro-Beijing journals in Hong Kong which advocated democracy and attacked the tightening of political control were reportedly classified as "reactionary." Contacts between foreigners and Chinese citizens in China became increasingly difficult. The Foreign Ministry warned foreign journalists not to transgress the proper boundary of journalistic activities. Undoubtedly, the Chinese authorities were particularly intent upon preventing contacts between dissenters and foreigners.

20. Ibid., September 10, 1981, p. 2.
21. The article was reprinted in *Renmin ribao*, October 7, 1981, p. 5. The authors were the deputy editors of the *Journal*, Tang Yin and Tang Dacheng, who had been advocates of liberalization.

The development of the case of "Unrequited Love" after Deng's talk on July 17 and Hu's speech in late August led many observers outside China, including those hitherto sympathetic to Deng's reforms as well as the long-time critics of the Communist regime, to conclude that the new leadership in China had relapsed into old habits and had adopted the familiar pattern of political and ideological control. Explicitly and implicitly, they suggested that the case of "Unrequited Love" was a harbinger of things to come and that the oppression of writers and suppression of creative writing would be intensified and expanded in scope. They concluded that a political movement to suppress deviant and non-conformist ideological views was already in progress in spite of the new leadership's explicit repudiation of the use of political movements to bring about desired changes. Since they had always considered a change in policy toward literature and art the forerunner of a disruptive political upheaval, they were troubled by forebodings for the prospects of political and economic reforms in China.

These analyses called forth a little noticed rebuttal in a short comment in *People's Daily* entitled "The Old Almanac No Longer Works." The author ridiculed the views that the regime had tightened its control over literature, that it had changed its policy toward the intellectuals, and that a cold winter would soon set in. He suggested that China had turned over a new page in history and that the old pattern would not repeat itself.[22] This rebuttal certainly went too far in its denial that control over literature had been tightened. It was indeed true at that time that the Deng-Hu leadership regarded ideological work to curb the tendencies toward "bourgeois liberalization" and to promote a higher degree of ideological uniformity as one of the two most important tasks confronting the regime on a par with economic work. It was obvious that once again, first the Army and then the two topmost leaders themselves, inaugurated the criticism of a piece of writing and called for the correction of wrong ideological tendencies found in literature.

A careful examination of the reports on the remarks by Deng and Hu, as well as a careful reading of the Chinese press, suggests, however, that Deng and Hu have embarked on a search for a new form of ideological control and for new methods to achieve an ideological consensus on the basis of an improvement of the style of Party leadership, a political and economic program attuned to the immediate interests of the people, and a reinterpretation of Marxism-Leninism-Mao Zedong Thought. There is a large element of uncertainty in this search. The top leaders realize that they must break decisively with the past as it was symbolized by the Cultural Revolution; but they know only the general direction in which they

22. Ibid., September 16, 1981, p. 8.

want to proceed. They constantly note the difficulties confronting them: (1) an economy in disarray and a totally unrealistic program of rapid economic growth, both of which they inherited in 1979; (2) a disrupted system of education; (3) a huge gap in the pool of scientists, engineers, managers, and technical personnel of all kinds; (4) an inadequately trained labor force; (5) a decline in the Party's prestige; and (6) a scarcely concealed crisis in Sino-American relations—in short "a heap of problems," to use their own metaphor. They cannot but be aware of the possibility, as many outside observers are, that if their program of reforms does not produce visible results in the next few years, their leadership will be challenged by both the conservative orthodox Maoists and the radical dissenters. They reportedly say that the successful implementation of their program depends on political unity and stability. Translated into our terms, political unity and stability can be maintained only if the top leadership can retain the loyalty of the major political forces in China and maintain a proper balance among the conflicting interests, demands, and views. In particular, the leaders must be able to control the Army by building up the authority of a group of successors to Deng, the only reformer who can now play this role. The new reforms amd new methods of ideological work which are adopted will depend largely on the balance of the politcal forces of the moment. If the reformers succeed, if their authority is strengthened, and if their confidence grows, it is possible that more moderate forms and methods will be adopted, a new period of relaxation will ensue, and the four fundamental principles will be interpreted more liberally. It is equally obvious, however, that the opposite may occur. In other words, the forecasts made by many outside observers may turn out to be correct if the political balance in China continues to shift against the political forces represented by Deng and Hu and if there should be a rupture or even a sharp deterioration in Sino-American relations.

For the moment, let us see whether the new emphasis on ideological work is essentially the same as that in the periods of the anti-Rightist campaign and the Cultural Revolution. Undoubtedly, the aims of ideological work remains unchanged: (1) the strengthening of the leadership of the Party and the preservation of "ideological hegemony"; (2) the promotion of ideological uniformity; (3) the control of tendencies toward "bourgeois liberalization"; and (4) the suppression of dissent which could eventually lead to a change in the nature of the regime. In this sense, developments throughout 1981 up to the moment of writing can be seen as an endeavor on the part of Chinese leaders to define the limits of liberalization in a Leninist Party-state, but it is also true that the forms, methods, and content of ideological work have undergone important changes which have been unduly neglected by outside observers.

A perusal of some major documents and reports reveals the differences between the rhetoric and the methods used in the present and in the past. To be sure, official pronouncements have once again repeated Mao's view that literature and art cannot be separated from politics. Yet, Mao's dictum that literature and art are subordinate to politics was criticized by Hu Qiaomu, then a member of the Secretariat and now a member of the Politbureau in charge of ideological matters, as being unclear and ambiguous and for its adverse influence on the development of literature and art since 1949.[23] The Party Center also decided not to use the slogan that literature and art must serve politics, a slogan which had been derived from Mao's dictum of the subordination of literature and art to politics and had been used since the 1940s. In its place, the Party proposed the slogan that "literature and art should serve the people and socialism." In explaining this change, Wang Ruoshui, the deputy editor of *People's Daily*, asserted that the meaning of the new slogan is much broader than the old. For the people have a wide variety of spiritual needs—education, appreciation of beauty, recreation, and rest. During the Cultural Revolution, moreover, political power was out of the people's control and brought about a catastrophe. When political power is alienated from the people, what would, Wang asked, be the effect of the old slogan? The slogans that literature and art are subordinate to politics and should serve politics could be and were indeed interpreted as subordination and service to the political line or even a specific policy adopted at the moment. They made it impossible for the people to use literature and art to criticize the mistakes of the Party and the leaders.[24] Together with the repudiation of crucial parts of Mao's view on literature, this change in slogan and the explanations offered for the change mark a great step forward for the writers.

The methods used in criticism have also undergone important transformations. Unlike denunciations in the past, current discussions generally adhere to the common sense principle that the condemnation of a particular piece of work by an author does not preclude praise of his other works and by itself does not involve a condemnation of the man himself. It is often reiterated that literary criticism should not take the form of a political movement. According to current rhetoric, counter-criticisms or replies to criticism are also permitted. Although neither the author nor any other writers had published a reply to the criticism of the film script "Unrequited Love" since the conference on ideological work in late August 1981, the strong political attack launched from the left on another movie, "The Romance at Tianyun Mountain," was countered by a defense and a relatively balanced assessment.[25]

23. Article by Hu Qiaomu, in *Hongqi*, 1981, no. 23, pp. 19–20.

24. This article presents the excerpts with some revisions and additions of a speech delivered in August 1980. It was published on April 28, 1982, in the *Renmin ribao*, p. 5.

25. *Wenyi bao*, 1982, no. 4, pp. 76–80; no. 6, pp. 55–60.

Although "Unrequited Love" was criticized by all as a seriously flawed work in its ideological content, the severity of criticism and the ideological criteria used differed from article to article. The criticism by the deputy editors of *The Journal on Literature and Art* did not follow the lead of the "specially invited commentator of the *Liberation Army Daily*" in condemning the script as "*violating* the fundamental principles" and "*vilifying the leadership* of the Party and the state authority of the people's democratic dictatorship," "negating patriotism in effect," and "pointing its spearhead against the *Party*." Instead, they merely charged that it was a glaring example of the ideological tendency of *deviating* from the Party's leadership and the path of socialism, that it *could not be said* to have given expression to patriotism, and that it totally negated the *leader* of the Party (i.e., Mao). The article in *Liberation Army Daily* criticized the theme of the dignity and the worth of man found in "Unrequited Love," while reaffirming "revolutionary humanism." The article in *The Journal on Literature and Art* was silent on the subject. In a third article by Chen Bo, the director of the Bureau of Cinema under the Ministry of Culture, the statements made in the script on human nature and the dignity of man were characterized as incompatible with socialism and realism.[26] In none of the articles consulted thus far was the film script labeled "anti-Party" and "anti-Socialist."

In the criticisms, Bai Hua was called a comrade. Chen Dengke, a famous author living in Anhui, was criticized by name by the Party committee of Anhui, but his work was still published in October in Guangzhou's *Yangcheng wanbao*.[27] More significantly, most famous authors, as distinguished from those Party officials controlling literary work, either remained silent on the case of "Unrequited Love" or merely made some general remarks condemning "bourgeois liberalization" or upholding the four fundamental principles without specifically mentioning the film script itself. In early August, when renewed criticisms of "Unrequited Love" were again in the making, Ba Jin, China's foremost living veteran writer and the acting chairman of the Association of Chinese Writers, wrote a piece praising the editors of *Shiyue* and the periodical itself, which had published the film script and many other innovative literary works. He explicitly expressed his disagreement with the view that "criticism by officials is a form of taking care of the author"—a formula which had been increasingly used once again as one of the justifications for criticizing "harmful" literary works.[28] When Ba Jin was asked about his role in criticizing in 1957 a group of writers as "anti-Party," he said that he would

26. *Hongqi*, 1981, no. 19, p. 31.
27. *Ming bao*, October 13, 1981, p. 3.
28. *Dagong bao*, August 10, 1981, p. 4.

never again play the part of a procurator.[29] Under his leadership, the presidium of the Association of Chinese Writers decided to restore the membership of Hu Feng, a famous writer and literary critic who had been severely criticized by Mao himself in 1955. This decision was most likely meant to be a symbolic move to express the wishes of Chinese writers for the continuation of the trend toward relaxation and to serve as a mild protest against the tightening of political control. Interestingly enough, this decision was made known to the Chinese people on October 14 in *People's Daily* on the same page as a report on a symposium attended by the heads of the departments for culture in the entire Army. Although the participants in the symposium did not fail to note the importance of using correct methods in the conduct of criticism and self-criticism, it is clear that the emphasis fell on opposition to "bourgeois liberalization," the necessity of criticizing the tendency of deviating from the Party spirit and violating the four fundamental principles, and the need to study anew Mao's "Talks at the Yanan Forum on Literature and Art."[30] The difference in the orientations of the Army and the writers can be discerned without too much difficulty.

Nevertheless, the power of the conservatives in the Army is not invincible, particularly when they reach beyond the more controversial field of literature and art. On August 28, 1982, *Liberation Army Daily* printed an article by Zhao Yiya, a long-time propagandist in the Army, entitled "Communist Ideology is the Core of Socialist Spiritual Civilization," which was reprinted on the same day in Liberation Daily (Shanghai).[31] One month later, the editorial department of the *Liberation Army Daily* issued a lengthy self-criticism for printing Zhao's article. According to the editorial department, the focal point of "Comrade Zhao's" article was the denial of the significance of "culture (including education and science)" for constructing socialist spiritual civilization. It neglected the important role played by intellectuals in this task. It ran counter to the Party's policy of building up a force of cadres who are revolutionary in spirit, young in age, and with a high level of knowledge and technical skills. Even more significant, the editorial department declared: "We oppose the abuse of the class viewpoint and class analysis and oppose the characterization of every item of culture, knowledge, and social behavior as having class character."[32] It charged Zhao with having committed the error of propagating "a certain kind of leftist viewpoint" under the pretext of opposing bourgeois liberalization, and it concluded its criticism of Zhao by invoking Hu Yaobang's remark at the Twelfth Party Congress that the Party had to con-

29. *Huaqiao ribao*, September 29, 1981, p. 1.
30. *Renmin ribao*, October 14, 1981, p. 4.
31. *Jiefang ribao*, August 28, 1982, pp. 1 and 2.
32. The article is reprinted in *Dagong bao*, October 17, 1982, p. 5.

tinue to oppose both leftist and rightist tendencies. Around the time of the publication of [the criticism of] Zhao's article, Yu Qiuli, the veteran leader who had played a crucial role in building the Daqing oil field, replaced Wei Guoqing as the Director of the General Political Department of the People's Liberation Army. What is sauce for the goose of writers on the right is sauce for the gander of conservatives in the Army on the left. Education and science obviously occupy a more secure position in civil society than literature and art.

In sum, a survey of the Bai Hua affair and a careful examination of the official pronouncements show that much has changed in the relationship between political power and writers within the unchanging framework of a Leninist Party-state, symbolized by the slogan of upholding the four basic principles. The Party, in effect, apologized for its erroneous policies in the past. It has criticized and abandoned some of the dicta, concepts, and methods of analysis made in or derived from Mao's "Talks at the Yanan Forum." It has begun a process of developing new doctrines and slogans, and resurrected the policy of letting "a hundred flowers bloom and a hundred schools of thought contend" on the basis of the reemphasized epistemological axiom and the newly formulated sociological postulate. It has abolished most of the "prohibited areas" in substantive subjects of writing and literary methods. It has changed its methods of criticism and self criticism in dealing with the writers of those literary works which transgress the boundary of the permissible, has adopted a policy of high rewards and light punishment, and has played a mediating role in the conflict between the writers and the conservatives in the army. Even when the Party finds it necessary to lean toward the conservatives on a specific compromise decision, it still tries to leave a way out for the individual writers under attack and simultaneously allows writers as a group to argue for a more liberalized policy and to take certain symbolic actions to reaffirm their limited sphere of autonomy. Although the Party advocates that literature should depict the bright side of society and its future, it does not arbitrarily prohibit all the writings which expose the dark side, provided that they admit the possibility of correcting those defects under the socialist system.

The writers' attitude and posture toward the Party have also changed. They no longer follow its baton in all literary matters; they have been experimenting with new literary techniques. They have expressed their opinions on literary doctrines, some of which do not conform to Party orthodoxy. They do not automatically chorus the Party's criticism of an individual writer. They no longer feel almost as a conditioned reflex that the Party is right and they are wrong. Formerly, there was little opposition to the tightening of political control. Now whether and to what extent flowers will bloom or wilt depends on the political balance between the reformist writers and the conservatives, with the Party (itself divided) playing a mediating role.

Amidst all these changes, there is one constant. The framework of the Leninist Party-state will not be changed. The supremacy of the Party is not supposed to be questioned. Once announced, the Party's decision must not be publicly challenged. The slogan of "Let a hundred flowers bloom and let a hundred schools contend" is specifically said not to be the only principle or policy dealing with literature and art. Other principles must be taken into account. Some of them have higher status. With still others, there must be a trade-off. There is no question that there has been a tightening of political control, of which the Bai Hua case was the outcome and the symbol. Since 1980, the more politically restrictive atmosphere has affected the writers' creativity and has become a psychological burden for the more innovative authors, as Liu Binyan observed in February 1982.[33] Liu's public remark itself suggests that writers are still fighting for more freedom of expression and publication. The current balance of political forces and the overall political framework impose serious obstacles, but the long-term trend of social development may help them attain their goal.

The Party and the Rural Economy: The Steady Course in the Evolution of the Responsibility System in Agricultural Production

In the old pattern of Chinese politics, a swing to the left or right on one policy was accompanied by a similar swing in most others; and a swing in the ideological sphere was frequently the harbinger of things to come, as in the case of the anti-Rightist campaign which was followed by the Great Leap and as in the case of the attack on the writers in 1964, the Socialist Education Movement, and the criticism of the historical play "The Dismissal of Hai Rui" which were followed by the Cultural Revolution. To those who cannot break the habit of analyzing post-Mao politics by using mechanically their framework for understanding Chinese politics from 1949 to 1976, Chinese political and economic events in the past several years present a paradox. While there has been oscillation in the policy toward literature since 1979, the regime has maintained a steady course in another sphere, perhaps more important to the future of China in the long run than literature and art, that of rural policy.

In this sphere, the policy of relaxing political and administrative control has continued up to the time of writing, in spite of the controversies and doubts generated by it and some indication of opposition from various quarters, particularly the Army. In no other sphere has political control by the upper levels been relaxed to a greater extent; nowhere have rela-

33. *Wenyi bao*, 1982, no. 4, p. 6.

tive autonomy and freedom in managing economic affairs on the part of the lowest-level units, households, and individual producers been restored more quickly; nowhere have market mechanisms and individual incentives been given a more important place within the overall framework of national planning. Moreover, these changes have reflected more directly and visibly the wishes of the individuals concerned than in most other sectors of society. They have been the products of a complex process, combining the flow of influence from the bottom to the top and from the top to the bottom. The process has included official acceptance and encouragement of many practices adopted by the peasants themselves but previously concealed from officials at the higher levels. It has involved much spontaneous experimentation by peasants and low-level cadres in different localities. It has not been dominated by a single official or a few officials at the highest level of the Party. It has been pushed forward by a combination of forces: peasants in many localities; local officials at various levels up to and including provincial secretaries (notably those in Anhui and Sichuan); economists, intellectuals, economic planners, and officials engaged in agricultural work; and top Party officials (such as Deng and Chen Yun).

In the light of their own general orientation in economic affairs, in response to unauthorized developments and spontaneous actions at the lower levels, and on the basis of their assessment of the situation at the grassroots, the top leaders at Party Center secured the adoption of four documents between December 1978 and March 1981 which have reversed the direction of rural policies since the acceleration of the cooperativization movement in 1955–56. Each of these documents went beyond the preceding one in granting a greater degree of flexibility and autonomy to the lowest level units, households, and individuals in managing their own work, as well as in providing them with greater material incentives. Step by step, these documents have led to the firm establishment of what is known as the "system of responsibility for agricultural production."

Since the evolution of the system up to October 1981 has been described in full detail in an article entitled "The Responsibility System in Agriculture" of which the author is a co-author,[34] there is no need to reproduce the discussion here. Only the following points need to be made. First, the steady development has continued at an accelerated pace. In December 1981, it was reported that more than 90 percent of the 5,870,000 production teams had adopted one or the other form of the responsibility system.[35] By April 1982, around 50 percent of all the teams had adopted

34. *Modern China*, January 1982, pp. 41–103. [Reprinted in part as chapter 6 in this volume.]
35. *Wenzhe bao*, December 15, 1981, p. 1.

either the household responsibility system *(baochan daohu)* or the household total responsibility system *(baogan daohu).*[36] By August, this figure became 74 percent.[37] The distribution of this 74 percent of the teams was uneven. In Liuan prefecture in western Anhui, 98 percent of its 56,300 teams adopted the household total responsibility system, and another 1.76 percent adopted the household responsibility system.[38] In Guizhou province, 96.7 percent of the teams had adopted the household responsibility system by early 1982.[39] In Mao's home province of Hunan, around 90 percent of the teams adopted one of the two systems of household responsibility, while in Yueyang prefecture (Hunan), 99.3 percent of the teams adopted the household total responsibility system.[40] A recent article revealed the phenomenally rapid increase in the use of the household total responsibility system *(baogan daohu).* In January 1980, only 0.02 percent of the basic accounting units adopted this system. By October 1981, this figure had become 38 percent, and by late 1982, it had risen to around 70 percent. This system has now become the principal form of the responsibility system in agriculture which links reward to actual yield.[41]

Second, the political-administrative and economic functions of the communes are being separated. The political-administrative functions will be performed by a system of reconstituted township governments. As a collective economic organization, the commune will have exclusively economic functions. In a pilot project in Sichuan, the brigade was abolished, and a village head and a clerk were given all its former administrative responsibilities, while agricultural production in the village will be coordinated by "production officers" sent by the economic organs of the township government.

Finally, from the economic point of view the responsibility system aims at linking reward to work performed. From the point of view of state-society relationship, its significance lies in the devolution of economic functions from the larger units of brigade and teams to work groups, households, and individuals. Under the household responsibility system and the household total responsibility system, the household again becomes the basic unit of production in the countryside. Involved in this change is the replacement of authority relations by contract relations as the principal means of regulating the state-society relationship at the

36. *Liaowang,* 1982, no. 4, p. 8. The term *baogan daohu* can also be rendered into "household comprehensive responsibility system." Under this system, work points are no longer used.

37. *Renmin ribao,* August 22, 1982, p. 1.

38. Ibid., September 16, 1982, p. 4.

39. Ibid., June 5, 1982.

40. Ibid., September 30, 1982, p. 1.

41. Article by Xiang Jiyuan, *Jingji yanjiu,* 1982, no. 12, p. 11.

grass-roots level.[42] Under the household total responsibility system, the household has regained virtually all its former autonomy, and the linkage between reward and work performed is closer than any other forms of the system of responsibility, with the possible exception of the form under which a household engaged in sideline production is given a small field to grow its grain ration.

Institutionalization of the Sociopolitical Structure

The Chinese in the twentieth century have suffered repeated frustrations and disappointments in their search for a stable and viable set of institutions to govern the state-society relationship and in their endeavor to find a smoothly functioning and durable government structure and process. Their experiment with democracy coincided with the rise of warlordism. Under the Guomindang the establishment of Party tutelage for constitutional democratic government produced a one-man dictatorship controlling and manipulating various Party factions. The dictatorship of the proletariat culminated in the personality cult and the arbitrary rule of the supreme leader. The Chinese have never succeeded in finding a set of arrangements in which the formal institutions are firmly established and in which informal relationships are supplements to the formal institutions, enabling the latter to function effectively and efficiently instead of overwhelming them and turning them into empty symbols. The process of institutionalization has constantly been interrupted either by internal or external crisis or by the program to bring about fundamental changes, both of which demanded mobilization of one kind or another. Military mobilization under Chiang Kai-shek to fight the civil war [militated against] the institutionalization of a civilian government. Under the Communist regime, mass mobilization constantly interrupted the process of institutionalization and routinization prior to 1966. During the Cultural Revolution, it destroyed most of the institutions which had become quite firmly established. Now the process of institutionalization has begun anew within the broad framework established since 1949. What sort of institutions will the Chinese leaders want to set up? What has been the outcome up to this point?

Proposals for Changing the Relationships of the Party with the Government, Social Institutions, and Social Groups

Many of these proposals limit the sphere of operations of the Party but not its overall authority. They are made in the spirit of Deng's call for upholding firmly the leadership of the Party by improving it and its style of work. In essence, their general effect is to give a greater degree of operational au-

42. The writer is in the process of writing a paper on this subject.

thority to the government, social institutions, and mass organizations so that the Party can focus its attention on comprehensive and long-term programs and ultimately ideological and political control. In a speech made on August 18, 1980 and approved by the Politbureau on August 31,[43] Deng expressed the view that the over-concentration of power and failure to develop a set of institutions had been the source of China's numerous difficulties and mistakes in the past. He proposed to separate the personnel of the government from the officials of the Party by restricting the practice of a single person holding responsible jobs in both the government and the Party which had led to "the replacement of the government by the Party." It is well known that Hua Guofeng resigned in 1980 from his premiership while Deng and five other leaders resigned from their positions as vice-premiers. Throughout 1980, many first secretaries of the Party or their equivalents at various levels relinquished their concurrently-held positions as chief executive officers; but some served instead as the leading members of the legislative branch. Deng suggested that, henceforth, the State Council and local governments on all levels should discuss, make decisions on, and send out documents pertaining to all work under the jurisdiction of the government, and the Party Center and Party committees on all levels should no longer issue directives and make decisions on these matters.

Deng proposed to change, step-by-step and after having made the necessary preparations, the system of giving responsibility to the factory director or company manager under the leadership of the Party committee of his unit. Instead, responsibility would be given to the factory director or company manager under the leadership and supervision of the factory's management committee, the board of trustees of a company, or the joint committee of joint economic units.

He also suggested that considerations should be given to step-by-step and well-prepared reforms of the present system of giving responsibility to the president of a university, the president of an academy, and the director of a research institute under the leadership of the Party committee. This system has actually concentrated all power in the hands of the Party committee. It is to be recalled that during the brief period of blooming and contending in the first half of 1957, several leading professors and intellectuals proposed that the professors be given greater authority to run the universities. These proposals were rejected, and the outspoken advocates were labeled rightists in the anti-Rightist campaign. But reforming the leadership structure and institutional arrangement of the universities and research organizations was never too far from the minds of the profes-

43. This speech has not been published in China. It can be found in *Zhonggong yanjiu*, July 15, 1981, pp. 106–139.

sionals and intellectuals. Deng seemed to be responding to their wishes, although he did not point to any specific alternatives. In the subsequent reorganization of the Academia Sinica (the Chinese Academy of Sciences) under a new charter, the authority of the scientists was greatly increased. In the powerful presidium of the *xuebu weiyuanhui*, scientists were assigned to two-thirds of the seats, and the other third was to be filled through joint consultation between the Party organizations in the Academy and the related ministries and departments under the State Council. In a final report before stepping down from the presidency of the Academy, Fang Yi declared that the presidency of the Academy should be filled by a scientist. Now for the first time, the president of the Chinese Academy of Sciences is a scientist, elected to a two-year term and eligible for a second term. Whether this reform is the harbinger of things to come in educational and other scientific institutions remains to be seen.

In dealing with various social groups, Deng has always been specially interested in the workers. He urged the extension and perfection of the system of the congress of employees and workers or the assembly of the employees' and workers' representatives in all enterprises and business units. He proposed to give them authority to discuss and make decisions on important problems in their own units as well as to suggest to upper-level units the dismissal of leading executive officials who are derelict in their duties. He even ventured the idea that the congress and the assembly could gradually be given the right to elect a limited number of leading personnel.

Changing the Structure of Party Leadership, the Institutions of Government, and the Cadre System: Proposals and Outcomes

Traditionally, the Chinese held as an ideal the belief that the officials at the top must serve as an example for the people. Recently, the Chinese Communists have constantly stressed that for reforms to take place in the nation, reforms must first be implemented within the Party, particularly at the top level of the Party. Their dilemma is that, as the Party itself admits, many abuses such as the cult of personality, patriarchal rule, the destruction of the system of "democratic centralism," the system of special privilege, and "bureaucratism" were first developed and became most serious within the Party and at its top level. Hence reform of the Party's "leadership institution" and style of work is the first order of business. But this reform together with reform of government institutions has encountered resistance.

Deng's ideas of reforming the Party's "leadership institution" and style of work are most clearly stated in his speech of August 18, 1981. Besides restating the now familiar themes of replacing the cult of personality with collective leadership, restricting the number of concurrent positions held by leaders, and reviving "democratic centralism" to take the place of rule by the first secretary or "number one person," Deng made a remarkable proposal: In addition to the existing Central Discipline Inspection Commission, a new Central Advisory Commission should be established. These two commissions should, like the Central Committee, be elected by the National Party Congress. Each should have clearly-defined tasks and jurisdiction.

In a lengthy report made on October 25, Liao Gailong, a member of the Policy Research Office of the Party Center, a professor in the Institute of Marxism-Leninism-Mao Zedong Thought, and a leading reformer, interpreted and explained Deng's proposal in terms of the familiar Western notion of the separation of powers and checks and balances among the three organs.[44] Liao suggested that the Advisory Commission should be called the Central Control Committee and that its tasks should be to supervise the Central Committee, to examine its work, to make suggestions, and to speed up its implementation of Party policies. Moreover, Liao proposed that the Politbureau be abolished and its function of making policies be performed by a standing committee of the Central Committee, while the Secretariat (*shuji chu*) handles day-to-day work. To put the Central Control Committee on a par with the Central Committee, he recommended that it should also have a standing committee and a Secretariat (*mishu chu*). The position of the Central Discipline Inspection Commission should be elevated. Each of these three organs should be made responsible to the National Party Congress. Disagreements among them should be resolved by a joint meeting. If the joint meeting fails to produce an agreement, the matter will be referred to the Party Congress.

As for Party leadership at all levels, Deng made no specific proposal except to suggest the revival of "democratic centralism," but he did make an important departure in ideological orientation from the past. He endorsed the recent criticism of the slogan of "strengthening the monistic leadership of the Party" (*yiyuan hua lingdao*). He said that throughout the nation, it led to the improper and indiscriminate concentration of all power in the Party committee, and to the concentration of the power of the committee in the hands of a few secretaries, particularly the first secretary. "Thus, the monistic leadership of the Party frequently becomes leadership by a single individual." To institute or revive the system of collective leadership, Deng asked that all important decisions be put to a vote rather than be made by the first secretary alone.

Deng mentioned the possibility of setting up an advisory body at the highest level of government but made no other proposal. Liao, however,

44. Section four of this speech is reproduced in *Qishi niandai*, 1981, no. 3, pp. 38–48. The full text is reproduced in *Zhonggong yanjiu*, September 15, 1981, pp. 108–177.

made sweeping proposals to strengthen the legislative branch of the government. He suggested that the unicameral system of the present be changed into a bicameral one. Under this scheme, the National People's Congress would be divided into two chambers. The "Territorial Chamber" will have only 300 persons to represent the various localities in China. The "Social Chamber" with 700 persons will represent the various professions, occupations, and social strata. These two chambers will jointly exercise legislative power. Thus, Liao accepted the Western idea of functional representation, which was once very popular among liberals and progressives after the First World War. Once again, Liao evoked the idea of checks and balances. Not only will the two chambers supervise the work of the State Council, but they will also check and balance each other. Both will have standing organs of some seventy and eighty persons, and the ministers of the State Council cannot serve in them. Committees on specific policy problems should be set up, with specialists in various fields serving as advisors or forming brain trusts.

How the members of the Party's representative organs and the legislative branch of the government at all levels are elected is a basic problem of the institutionalization and popularization of the political system. It is common knowledge that the secret ballot has been reinstituted and that elections with more candidates than positions to be filled have been tried out. What has been generally overlooked is Deng Yingchao's (Mrs. Zhou Enlai) account of the procedure of nominating candidates followed in the election of the Seventh Central Committee in April 1945.[45] The publication of this account at that time may have reflected the view of the reformers. According to Deng Yingchao, the candidates were not nominated by the upper level of the Party leadership. Their names were first suggested by the delegations representing the Party organizations in various localities. The Presidium of the Party Congress compiled a complete list, but did not determine beforehand the number of central committee members and alternates. Instead, two rounds of elections were conducted. In the preliminary round, all those who received a majority of votes in the Party Congress were declared candidates for election to the Central Committee. Candidates who won in the second round were declared elected, and those who lost became candidates for alternate membership to be added to the candidates on this latter list. Still another round of elections was held. Those who received half of the vote were declared alternate members.

In 1981, a modified version of this procedure was adopted in one district in Shanghai, which was divided into two election districts. In one election district, two persons were to be elected to the People's Congress

45. Article by Deng Yingchao, *Hongqi*, 1981, no. 3, pp. 43–49.

of that district. In the first round of the nomination process, various units in this election district selected 100-odd candidates. In the second round, a preliminary election was held which produced 17 candidates. In the third round, three candidates were officially nominated through a process of "examination and comparison." The three candidates canvassed the voters and expressed their political views. Then the final election took place. As mentioned before, a system of two-step elections was used to elect a new Central Committee at the Twelfth Party Congress.

The abolition of life-time tenure and perfection of a system of retirement for the cadres are the best known ideas and the prerequisite for any reform of the cadre system. Of ultimate importance is the policy that "under the premise of upholding the four fundamental principles," youthful cadres with knowledge and specialized skills should be promoted to responsible positions. Many years before, Deng had attacked the policy adopted by the "Gang of Four" of rapidly promoting inexperienced officials, young rebels, and youthful students to high positions. Now he reversed his position and called for the rapid promotion of new leaders without regard to the past practice of climbing the bureaucratic ladder step-by-step. More than any other reforms, these proposals encountered the most obvious and widespread resistance and opposition.

After these proposals had been made, a new Party Constitution was adopted by the Party Congress in September 1982, and a new state constitution was enacted three months later. Since the Party is above the State, the Party Constitution defines the basic power structure in China, whereas the state constitution fills in the details. We shall briefly mention two major features of the Party Constitution before we proceed to the Constitution of the State. First, in accordance with the widespread demand to eliminate the danger of reviving the cult of personality and to establish collective leadership, the post of the chairman of the Party was abolished. The chairmanship of the Party, established for the first time by the Seventh Plenum of the Sixth Central Committee which met for eleven months from May 1944 to April 1945,[46] was always associated with the cult of Mao. Now the Party is headed by a general secretary, who "is responsible for convening the meeting of the Political Bureau and its standing committee and presides over the work of the Secretariat," Hu Yaobang has retained this position. Second, in accordance with Deng's suggestions, the Party Constitution provides for a Central Advisory Commission to be elected by the Party Congress. Members are to consist of those who have been Party members for over 40 years, have made relatively great contributions to the Party, are relatively experienced as leaders, and have relatively high prestige within the Party. The commission is to serve as the

46. Ibid., 1981, no. 12, p. 32.

assistant and staff of the Central Committee. Quite unexpectedly, however, Deng at its first meeting expressed his view that it was to be abolished in ten to fifteen years.[47] The Central Commission for Disciplinary Inspection is to be elected by the Party Congress, but it is also to work under the leadership of the Central Committee. Thus, there is little doubt that the Central Committee remains the primary organization. The standing committee of the Political Bureau is undoubtedly the most powerful single organ in the Party. According to the Party Constitution, the general secretary, the chairman of the Central Advisory Commission, and the chairman of the Military Commission of the Central Committee must be members of the standing committee of the Political Bureau. It is expected that the first secretary of the Central Commission for Discipline Inspection will be a member of the standing committee. Liao's idea of instituting some sort of checks and balances among the three committees was not adopted. Contrary to widely held expectation, the Party constitution puts no limit on the tenure of Party leaders.

In the Constitution of the People's Republic of China adopted in December 1982, the chairmanship of the state[48] is re-instituted, but its power is sharply reduced. Liao's proposal of a bicameral system was discarded. The National People's Congress remains the sole legislative body, and its authority, particularly of its standing committee, is strengthened. An innovation is the establishment of a Central Military Commission to command the armed forces. The significance of this new institution, however, is diminished by the continued existence of the Party's Military Commission provided for in the Party Constitution. The position of premier of the State Council is enhanced by the stipulation that the premier has overall responsibility for the State Council. Hence, the troika in the government structure consists of the Premier, the chairman of the Central Military Commission, and the chairman of the standing committee of the National People's Congress, with the president of the People's Republic of China serving as the formal head of state without real power. The tenure of the president, vice-president, premier, vice-premier, state Councillors, and the chairman and vice-chairman of the standing committee of the National People's Congress is limited to two consecutive terms of five years each, but a similar provision on the limit of the tenure of the chairman of the Central Military Commission, contained in the draft constitution, was omitted in the constitution finally enacted.

In the months preceding and following the publication of the Party con-

47. Deng's speech before the first plenary session of the Central Advisory Commission, September 13, 1982, *The Twelfth National Congress of the Communist Party of China: Documents* (in Chinese), pp. 170–171.

48. The English version of the Constitution uses the title of "The President of the People's Republic of China."

stitution and the state constitution, a program of streamlining the Party and government bureaucracies has been pushed as far as political circumstances permit. The Party is to consolidate its ranks. Party members who are incompetent will be asked to withdraw from the Party. Some will be purged. This task is to be completed in 1986. A systematic program of retraining cadres in the central Party and government organization is being instituted. It consists of three components: (1) six-months of full-time educational training every three years, (2) part-time study, and (3) self-study or enrollment in night classes. Its aim is to raise after five years all cadres in the central institutions to a cultural and professional level equivalent to secondary school graduates. Special attention is to be given to management and expertise and special knowledge in their own fields of work.

In sum, the Chinese have once again embarked on the course of institutionalization and have abandoned mass mobilization and political movement as methods of governance and change. The passage of history has made the present endeavor different from past attempts in two fundamental ways. First, the present endeavor has followed tragic experiences with the three major political forms in the modern world: democracy, authoritarianism, and the Communist regime. Second, it has been undertaken after the Chinese under the Chinese Communist Party and Mao pushed their revolutionary program almost to its logical extreme. They have belatedly discovered the immovable limits set by the realities in China, even if along the way to the extreme their attempts did produce [some] positive results. This realization is now reflected in a frequently used statement: When truth is pushed even one small step further, it becomes falsehood. We must take account of these two differences when we try to speculate about the probable success or failure of the current effort.

The major premise, as well as the most important goal, of this process of institutionalization is the substitution of collective leadership for one-man rule. Quite possibly, three-quarters of a century after the formal end of imperial absolutism, the Chinese have finally rejected once and for all the legitimacy of arbitrary rule by one man, no matter how it is rationalized or justified. It is frequently said that the cult of personality can no longer replace collective leadership because no future leader can achieve the stature, prestige, and power of Mao. Unwittingly, Mao played a positive role in the final rejection of arbitrary rule by one man. The Chinese must have realized that if a leader as brilliant, politically astute, respectful of reality, and discriminating in the use of power as Mao was in his early years could and did become an arbitrary, dictatorial leader, then the cult of personality and the tendency toward one-man rule must be curbed in its inception and that arbitrary rule by any one man will sooner or later bring about a catastrophe. Many of the institutional changes are based on this premise.

There are other problems for which the Chinese have not reached definitive solutions. Basically, the socio-political structure built by the Chinese Communists from 1949 to 1976 can be conceived as a series of concentric circles. Political power stood at the center of the economy and civil society. The center of political power was located in the Party. The focus of the Party was the Central Committee, the Political Bureau and its standing committee, and the chairman. Mao's arbitrary rule during the Cultural Revolution can be understood as the logical outcome of this concentric-circles system. Now, this concentric-circles system still exists, but with some important modifications. The chairmanship of the Party has been abolished, and the notion of "monistic leadership" *(yiyuan hua ling-duo)* is being challenged. Arbitrary decision-making by the first secretary at any level of the Party is condemned. The idea of maintaining a modicum of checks and balances within a single organ or among institutions has been partially accepted. The evolving relationship and tension between the system of concentric circles and the very different idea of checks and balances as an institutional principle deserves our constant attention.

The currently accepted notion that the Party should be separated from the government, with the Party exercising ideological, moral, intellectual, and cultural leadership while the government enjoys autonomy in matters under its jurisdiction must be constantly adjusted to the framework of the Leninist Party-state. How will the Chinese handle this adjustment?

Finally, there are indications that the Chinese are trying to combine at different levels of their non-Party institutions the principle of collective leadership in policy-making with the principle of one-man management in governmental, industrial, and commercial organs. Article 86 of the Constitution of the State provides that "the Premier has overall responsibility for the State Council" and that "the ministers have overall responsibility for the respective ministries or commissions under their charge." But the "Organic Law of the State Council" clearly stipulates that all important questions must be discussed and decided by the executive meetings or plenary meetings of the State Council. In his speech of August 1980 and elsewhere, Deng seems to have proposed the combination of the two principles for industrial, academic, and some other organizations, as noted above. How this combination will work in practice remains to be seen. All these are unresolved problems in China's search for appropriate institutional forms.

Limits to Reforms

The proposals for reform and the new ideological formulas mentioned throughout this paper reflect the impulses toward a certain degree of liberalization and popularization of the Chinese regime. The term "liberalization" is used here not in the technical sense of "moving toward greater public contestation" which, as used by Robert A. Dahl, rests on a different set of theoretical assumptions and refers to some very specific features of government. It merely means that the regime has become less monolithic and monistic than before, if one may be allowed to abuse the English usage of these two terms which do not admit of degrees. It refers to the following political developments: The immediate interests and spontaneous demands of individuals and groups in society percolate upwards more freely than before. Individuals, mass organizations, professional associations, and small parties and groups are given a larger area of autonomy to manage their own affairs. Their voices are being heard and taken into account more frequently so that their loyalty to the regime can be revived and retained and their exit from the system in the form of passive resistance or inert unconcern about the fate of the nation can be prevented.[49] In the process of policy formation, proposals come from more diverse sources and lower levels of the political system than before. Decisions are made more often through compromise and the aggregation of divergent and sometimes conflicting views. Informal groups, opinion groups, and political tendencies both outside and inside the Party have become more numerous and discernable, as the proliferation of journals, newspapers, published books, and internal publications indicate. Only in this sense has Chinese politics become more pluralistic. The term popularization is used in the sense of the provision of greater participation by individuals and groups in the political process along regularized and controlled channels—a greater degree of participation than in the period from 1957 to 1966 and along more regularized and controlled channels than during the Cultural Revolution.

The limits to reform and, therefore, to the process of liberalization and popularization, are set by the four fundamental principles. The implication of the four principles can be summarized in one simple phrase, the preservation and strengthening of the Leninist Party-state. Reforms in the direction of liberalization and popularization are permitted only within this restrictive framework. Clearly, no individual or group is allowed to challenge the leadership of the Party. No opposition to the Party is allowed to exist. The small parties and groups are permitted to propose but the power to dispose remains with the Party. They are given specific

49. For the ideas of "exit" and "voice," see Albert Hirschman, *Exit, Voice, and Loyalty* (Cambridge, Mass.: Harvard University Press, 1970).

responsibilities in various fields of activities within the overall political, economic, and social programs of the Party-state. Within the Party, the Leninist prohibition against organized factions inside the Party continues to be the norm, in spite of the proliferation of informal groups, opinion groups, and political tendencies.

Given the stringent, well-known rules of the game, the further liberalization and popularization of the Party-state depend on the resolution of the following issue: whether the Party will allow disagreement with and dissent from the Party line and policies to be *publicly* expressed once the Party has made decisions on these matters. Allowing the public expression of disagreement with the Party's line and policies not only would be the next decisive step toward liberalization and popularization, but it would also help the Party-state to subject its line and policies to necessary public criticism and examination, to correct errors more readily, and to have other alternatives to adopt when its line and policies fail to produce the desired results. But at this crucial point the process of liberalization and popularization has stopped. As recently as November 2, 1981, the Party through the authoritative voice of Deng Xiaoping has reiterated the following principle:

> After the Party Center or a Party organization has made a decision and before the Party has changed this decision, Party members and Party organizations at all levels must obey [it]. The opinion which they express must be in accord with the Party's decision. They are not allowed to disseminate at will opinions which express distrust of, dissatisfaction with, or opposition to the Party Center's line, guiding principles, and policies.[50]

It is not clear whether this prohibition applies to the expression of opinions inside the Party as well as outside the Party. In either case, this rule stands as the most important limit to liberalization and popularization at this moment.

After the "Great Transformation," the Middle Course

The middle course adopted by the moderate reformers represents the general direction of policies in all spheres rather than in any specific area, such as literature or rural institutions. It has not been a straight line, but one of twists and turns. It will continue to oscillate. To say that we are seeking to ascertain the parameters of this middle course is to misuse technical vocabulary in a highly impressionistic art dealing with a poorly understood subject. All we can do is to employ metaphors which will perhaps reflect without too much distortion the imprecision of Chinese official discourse and the leadership's groping for ways to achieve its goals.

50. *Renmin ribao*, November 2, 1981, p. 3.

The Two "Zones of Demarcation" Enclosing the Middle Course

The term "zone of demarcation" suggests that there are no precise, well-defined boundary lines marking out the middle course. Instead, the zone itself is a broad, ambiguous, and imprecise area subject to change as the political tide ebbs and flows.

The zone of demarcation on the right side of this middle course is the general orientation adopted by the Third Plenum of December 1978, as well as the developments in that direction afterwards. The specific goals of this orientation as defined by the Sixth Plenum of June 1981 are the four modernizations and the development of a "high level of democracy and civilization," but more important, the fundamental spirit is "to emancipate the mind, to put the brain to work, and to seek truth from facts." This general orientation represents the consensus among top leaders and reformers within the Party that there should be no Cultural Revolution in the future and that there should be a decisive break with the theory and practice which made possible the Cultural Revolution. In this zone are found the impulses toward change and reform. It marks off the middle course from the "two-whatsoeverism" sponsored by Hua, as well as the theory and practice of Chinese Communist policies in the distant past which are believed to have contributed to the "leftist" errors since 1957.

The zone of demarcation on the left side is symbolized by the four fundamental principles. In this zone are found the impulses to preserve continuity with the past and to confine changes and reforms within the framework of a Leninist Party-state. Without this zone, the impulses generated by the Third Plenum may burst asunder all bounds and challenge the existing political system itself. This zone marks off the middle course from "the tendency toward bourgeois liberalization" and "bourgeois democracy." But if it is pushed too far as it was from 1957 to 1976,[51] this orientation can lead to the stifling of necessary reforms and even to the reversal of the process of change. Hence, it is in turn balanced by the orientation established by the Third Plenum. Thus, the two orientations check and balance each other and both form an integral part of the middle course. The translation of the complex relationship between these two orientations into a general program or a specific policy depends on the changing balance of political and social forces over time in general and in that particular policy area.

Reform as "Revolution"

Just as Mao's actions after the anti-Rightist campaign of 1957 rested upon and were justfied by the theory of continuation of class struggle in a so-

---

51. Mao's six criteria of separating fragrant flowers from poisonous weeds can be considered an even more restrictive statement of the four fundamental principles.

cialist society as its principal contradiction, the middle course is based upon the formula that large-scale, tempestuous class struggle is over, but that class struggle still exists within certain limits. The words "within certain limits" are stressed to change the old idea that class struggle "exists everywhere and at all times,"[52] an idea which led to the over-extension of class struggle. The theory of "continuing the revolution under the dictatorship of the proletariat," which was developed with the consent of Mao, has been repudiated because the term "revolution" in this particular slogan meant in effect the overthrow of one "class" by another, whether the target of struggle was defined as the "persons in authority taking the capitalist road" or the "bourgeois headquarters" within the Party (to use Mao's phrases) or as "the bourgeoisie within the Party" (to use the phrase employed by the ultra-leftists). Instead of the struggle between the bourgeois class and the proletariat, the principal contradiction in China after the basic completion of socialist transformation in 1956 is once again defined as the contradiction between the constantly increasing material and cultural needs of the people and backward social production. Avowedly, the revolution is not over, but the term "revolution" is used in the broad sense of "transformation, the substitution of new things for the old such as in the technological revolution."[53] In other words, "revolution" is reform. In many articles on Chinese history, reformism is no longer completely repudiated as counterrevolutionary; on the contrary, its positive role in certain moments of history is now recognized. In the period when Mao's ideas turned progressively to the left, the term "dictatorship of the proletariat" gradually and in the end completely replaced his 1949 formula of "the people's democratic dictatorship" as the label for the form of the Chinese state. Now the latter term, the symbol of a period before the drastic tightening of political and ideological control, has been revived. It contains the word "democratic" to qualify the term "dictatorship," and "people" refers to a broader social base than "proletariat." The satisfaction of the "people's needs" is considered a noble mission of socialist reconstruction.

The Change in the Guiding Principle of Conflict Resolution in Party Ideology and Politics
Shortly after the adoption of the "Resolution on Certain Problems on the History of the Party since the Establishment of the People's Republic of China," a significant article carried by Hongqi noted that the resolution did not call the errors committed by the Party since 1949 "errors in *line*"

---

52. Article by Jie Wen, *Hongqi*, 1981, no. 20, p. 31.
53. Article by Shao Huaze, *Hongqi*, 1981, no. 17, p. 45. Mao himself once used the term revolution in this sense.

and that it did not discuss "the so-called struggle *between two lines*—the correct line and the incorrect line."[54] It pointed out that for more than twenty years, the concepts of "error in line" and "struggle *between lines*" had been universally abused and over-extended, so that a line was either the "revolutionary line of the proletariat" or the "reactionary line of the bourgeoisie," either the "Marxist line" or the "counterrevolutionary, revisionist line," there being no possibility of reconciliation and no possibility of neutrality. This abuse led to extremely bad consequences. Pushing this analysis a step further, another article observed that the method of class analysis should definitely not be simplified into an exclusive search for the class origins of problems arising from erroneous thinking. It is a "metaphysical viewpoint" to try to trace the cause of every error to non-proletarian classes and not to seek it in the Party or in a Marxist leader.[55]

In his report to the Twelfth Party Congress on September 1, 1982, Hu Yaobang declared that ever since the Third Plenum the Party in dealing with all important questions of principles, had conducted timely and correctly an "ideological struggle *on both fronts* in opposition to the leftist and rightist tendencies."[56] Interpreting Hu's remark, Wu Xiang, a writer who had played an important role in explaining and defending the household responsibility system in the mass media, observed that prior to the Third Plenum many people had knowledge only about the "struggle *between two lines*" and no knowledge about the "struggle *on two fronts*."[57] He wrote:

> Our guiding principle ought to be: Taking as our point of departure the realities in different periods, the situations in different localities, and the nature of various problems, oppose the "left" if the "left" occurs, and oppose the right if the right occurs. Our present condition is that although it is easy for the right to appear when we oppose the "left," it is also easy for "leftist" things to raise their heads once again and the force of habit of the "left" cannot be underestimated. Therefore, in opposing the "left" while guarding against the right and opposing the right while guarding against the "left" is an art of struggle which we must learn well at the present time.

The pattern of political conflict which the guiding principle of "struggle on two fronts" seeks to transform and to prevent from resurging is the direct confrontation between the "left" and the "right" with each justifying this confrontation and its own position on the existence of the other and seeking a complete victory over the other. As Worker's Daily *(Gongren ribao)* noted:

54. Article by Jin Chungming, *Hongqi*, 1981, no. 18, pp. 39–41; italics added.
55. Article by Yang Fengchun, ibid., pp. 41–43. Also see articles in ibid., 1981, no. 19, pp. 26–28, 38–40.
56. *Hongqi*, 1982, no. 18, p. 8.
57. *Renmin ribao*, September 28, 1982, p. 5; italics added.

We can frequently see that some who embrace "leftist" ideas and will not give them up seize constantly upon certain mistaken opinions with tendencies toward liberalization as their justification for holding on to their "leftist" mistakes. Similarly, those promoting liberalization constantly seize upon certain "leftist" opinions and the actions of those holding on to the erroneous "leftist" viewpoint and say that liberalization should not be opposed. Thus, we can see that "leftist" mistakes and liberalization appear to be opposed to each other, but in fact "leftist" errors give liberalization a pretext to develop while liberalization in turn furnishes the justification for "leftist" viewpoints to exist. We can say that in a sense, these two tendencies help each other. . . .

Therefore, we must oppose both tendencies. To correct "leftist" errors earnestly can help us in more effectively opposing liberalization; to oppose liberalization forcefully can help us in continuing our opposition to the "left." These two tasks are in fact inseparable. If we deal with the one and neglect the other, we cannot accomplish either of the two tasks very well.[58]

Thus all the above pronouncements suggest that the moderate reformers in the Party have been trying to occupy the middle position in the triangular relationship, playing the two ends against each other in order to effectively pursue the middle course. The political events accompanying the revival of this traditional concept also indicate that they have been endeavoring to rally the middle-of-the-road forces to oppose both the "left" and the "right" and to work out a sensible compromise package of programs and policies which incorporate selected and modified views and demands from both the "left" and the "right" in their ideological and political lines, programmatic principles, and policies on the basis of their judgement of what is the correct and prudent path to follow. They appeal to the general Chinese desire for peace and stability after three-quarters of a century of constant civil wars and life and death political conflicts, to the universal hope for a rising standard of living, and to the widespread wish for uninterrupted progress in Chinese society and civilization. In contrast to the polarization of political forces which was the usual pattern in twentieth-century China and in contrast to the past situation in which a weak third force in politics sought to survive, to maintain its position, and to develop its influence by manipulating the conflicts between the two extremes, the middle-of-the-road forces in both the Party leadership and society now constitute the strongest political force in China. Their programs are hard to oppose and their political tactics are difficult to out-manoeuver.

Viewed in this light, the oscillation between liberalization and repression is neither an accidental occurrence nor a passing phenomenon, nor purely a matter of political tactics. It is a necessary feature of the process

58. Reprinted in *Renmin ribao*, August 22, 1981, p. 4.

of political and economic reforms in the Leninist Party-state in the post-Mao era. To borrow an idea from Robert Dahl but to apply it to a different political situation, we may discern the possibility, though not the certainty, that by suitable dosage of each and by the use of appropriate methods, a skilled leadership may succeed in maintaining a middle course, preserving political unity and stability while pushing forward necessary reforms.[59] If so, one should expect frequent oscillations, advances to be followed by backlashes and repression of the left to be followed by repression of the right, and one should not be surprised by the uneven development of liberalization and popularization and by the differential reimposition of control and repression in different areas of social, political, and economic life. The price of change will always be high and the psychological, political, and human burden of the reformer heavy.

The "Reborn Revolutionaries" and Their Struggle to Redeem an Honorable Place in History

The middle course in changing state-society relations and in improving the political structure is, in substance, a program of reform from above undertaken by a group of veteran political leaders, who, to be sure, have responded to social demands and needs but who have also made authoritative decisions autonomously on the basis of the lessons learned from their past experiences, their new perception of the situation, their preferences, and their world views. The limitation of space does not allow us to discuss the social foundations of this middle course and the inputs from various groups in society, but it is imperative to attempt to discern the inner feelings of those leaders who are pushing forward these changes. All the official pronouncements, the eulogies delivered on the occasion of memorial services for their comrades who passed away or were rehabilitated years after their tragic death, the recently published memoirs, and the short reminiscences honoring friends martyred either at the hands of the enemy or the Party itself suggest that the current leaders have been engaged, both before and after their restoration to power, in an agonizing and searching self-examination. The fundamental question in this reflection must be why a movement for class and human liberalization developed into one of the most oppressive systems in Chinese history or what the Chinese Communists themselves call "feudal fascism." This process of self-examination has been undertaken by those who in their youthful and idealistic days joined the revolution to fight against political oppression, who in their middle age became themselves oppressors, inquisitors,

59. Robert Dahl, "Governments and Political Oppositions," in *Political Science Handbook* volume 3, ed. Fred Greenstein and Nelson Polsby (Reading, Mass.: Addison-Wesley, 1975), p. 129.

and denunciators in order to achieve a revolutionary transformation of society, who in old or late middle age were themselves oppressed, condemned, and denounced by others in the name of still another revolution,
and who in the remaining years of their lives have regained power and
authority. They have indeed been reeducated by the Cultural Revolution
but not in the way intended by its originator. They had viewed the political system created by themselves both from the top and from the bottom,
both from inside and from outside, both as its beneficiaries and its victims. They must have been seriously concerned with their own place in
history. It is this personal experience of the "second liberation" and this
concern of the "reborn revolutionaries" which gives extraordinary poignancy to their self-examination and soul-searching.

One side of their minds and hearts probably shares the view and senti-
ment expressed in the following statements in Robert M. MacIver's foreword to *The Great Transformation* by Karl Polanyi:

> . . .We can learn the nature of anything only when it has reached—and
> passed—its maturation. Events and processes, theories and actions, ap-
> pear in a new perspective. . . .
>
> We see how with a new liberation went a new servitude. . . .
>
> . . .We stand at a new vantage point, looking down, after the earth-
> quake, on the ruined temples of our cherished gods. We see the weakness
> of the exposed foundations—perhaps we can learn how, and where, to re-
> build the institutional fabric so that it may better withstand the shocks of
> change.[60]

The "reborn revolutionaries" who entertain such views and sentiments
are also those who spent their whole life in the arena of power. That the
reform program has been sponsored and directed by them accounts for its
depth and relative success to date; but their minds and hearts have another side, which sets a limit to how far this reform will go. In their views,
the socio-political system which they built up during the revolutionary
and anti-Japanese wars and after the capture of power had functioned
effectively for a long period of time and had achieved great success until it
was deranged and some of its underlying principles were perverted. The
program of rebuilding institutions, shifting the focus of work, reinterpreting Mao Zedong Thought, adopting new ideological, political, and organizational lines is considered partly an effort to restore the true tradition of
the Party and partly an endeavor to meet new conditions which the
achievements as well as the errors of the past have brought about. Thus,
the new trend toward institutional and social pluralism has definite limits.

60. Robert M. MacIver, foreword in Karl Polanyi, *The Great Transformation: The Political and Economic Origins of Our Time* (Boston: Beacon Press, 1944), pp. ix, x, xi.

For many years to come, the questions will be: Can a political system set within these limits perform effectively the function of promoting controlled social change fast enough to satisfy the demands and pressures originating inside China and to allow her to cope successfully with adverse developments in her foreign relations? Will the moderate reformers be able to bring about relatively rapid economic growth, to institute a truly meaningful "socialist democracy" and "socialist legality," and to develop China's civilization to a high level? Will they continue to push forward the process of the liberalization and popularization of their regime so that a new type of polity and society will emerge which will synthesize the best in the long tradition of China, in their own revolutionary experience, and in the institutions and civilization of the modern, democratic West? If they succeed in making a good beginning in this formidable task and in laying a solid foundation for its ultimate fulfillment—in spite of the increasingly unfavorable ratio between population and land as well as the uncertainties in Sino-American relations—they will have found a measure of justification for the tremendous sacrifices incurred by the Chinese people and the blood, sweat, and tears shed during the long years of revolution and reconstruction. They will have been worthy of their martyred comrades. They will have found an ultimate vindication of their long careers. They will have given new meaning to their own lives. They will have redeemed themselves and earned an honorable place in history.

8

Reflections on the Formation and Foundations of the Communist Party-State in China

The Perception of Crisis and the Persistent Problems in State Rebuilding in Twentieth-Century China

After outlining their proposals for institutional reforms in a memorial to the throne submitted on May 2, 1895, and expressing regret that these had not been adopted at an earlier time, Kang Youwei and his copetitioners among the provincial graduates assembled in Beijing for the metropolitan examinations voiced their sense of national crisis in the following words:

> If [institutional reforms] are undertaken now, they can still repair and limit the damage. But if we vacillate, hesitate, drift along day after day, adhere complacently to the old ways, and thus lose the opportunity [for taking corrective actions], then the barbarian nations surrounding us will be watching for their chance. Not a single moment should be lost. If there is a delay of a whole month or of a whole year, some incident will inevitably occur. If later regrets bring about a desire to alter course, the general situation will have deteriorated and cannot be put back in order. Even a sage will not be able to deal effectively with the aftermath.[1]

The crisis perceived by Kang was triggered by China's defeat in the Sino-Japanese war of 1894–95 which was in turn the latest manifestation of the changes in the international power structure and China's place in it. In addition to the sense of crisis stemming from the latest defeat in foreign wars, two other elements in the international environment would, over time, exert a perceptible effect on China, intensifying the sense of crisis, until (at the earliest) the founding of the People's Republic in 1949. These were the influence of Western ideologies and examples ("models," in the terminology of the modern social sciences) and the impact of the capitalist world economy. Though attenuated, this sense of crisis has per-

This essay was originally written for presentation at the Conference on the Foundations and Limits of State Power in China held in May 1983 at the Rockefeller Study and Conference Center in Bellagio, Italy, under the sponsorship of the European Science Foundation. I am grateful to the European Science Foundation, and to the organizer of the conference, Professor Stuart Schram, for permission to publish this expanded version of my paper.

1. Kang Youwei et al., "Gongche shangshu," in Zhan Bozhan and Zheng Tianting, eds., *Zhongguo tongshi chankao ziliao, jindai bufen*, rev. ed., (Beijing: Zhonghua shuju, 1980) 2: 51.

sisted. Even in the four or five years after 1978, some of the most powerful leaders in China still occasionally invoked the possibility of "the extinction of the Party and the state" *(wangdang wangguo)* in their efforts to gain acceptance for their programs of sweeping, fundamental reforms.[2]

In their endeavors to diagnose the causes of China's weakness and in their search for ways to overcome the crisis and to enhance the power and wealth of the nation, Chinese intellectuals and political leaders have, since the turn of the century, come to realize the imperative of developing and mobilizing the energy, capacities, and creativity of individuals and social groups. Benjamin Schwartz concludes his study of Yan Fu by observing that for Yan Fu, "the critical difference [between the West and China] is not a question of matter but a question of energy. The West has exalted human energy in all its manifestations—intellectual, moral, and physical. It has identified spirit not with passivity and withdrawal but with energy and assertion. The West has discovered the unlimited nature of human capacities and has fearlessly proceeded to actualize human potentialities undreamt-of in traditional Chinese culture."[3] During the May Fourth period, awareness of this contrast and the need to liberate individuals and social groups from the visible and invisible restrictions imposed by Chinese tradition in the political, social, and ideological spheres reached its highest point in twentieth-century China. Ever since, the development and mobilization of the energy, capabilities, and creativity of "the people" has remained one of the two most important problems which China has to confront in rebuilding its state and society. The problem has still by no means been solved, as is suggested by the current efforts to provide greater incentives and more autonomy to individuals and social groups so as to spur their "activism" and initiative. These efforts include encouraging a "system of responsibility" *(zeren zhi)* and effecting "structural reforms" *(tizhi gaige)* in the economic as well as other spheres of activity.

Although it has not been fully realized, this requisite of a vigorous political community may, and in fact did, come into conflict with another requisite. This is the rebuilding of a strongly centralized political power that could reunite China and preserve political stability, while increasing its ability to penetrate and control society and the economy. As a matter of fact, this second prerequisite has always been given top priority, and particularly so after the May Fourth movement, while the first has been regarded as a means to achieve the top-priority goal. The reason is not far to

2. For example, *Hongqi*, 1982, no. 6: 3.
3. Benjamin Schwartz, *In Search of Wealth and Power: Yen Fu and the West* (Cambridge: Harvard University Press, 1964), 238.

seek. The primacy of the state (or a high degree of "stateness" in J. P. Nettl's term) and the existence of a centralized system of imperial and bureaucratic authority in traditional China served to sharpen the perception of the crisis of political disintegration during the period of warlordism and the corresponding desire to rebuild a strong state with centralized political power.[4]

Marxism-Leninism and a Leninist Party as a Solution

Internally, this crisis found expression in the collapse of the examination system and of the absolute monarchy and in an abortive experiment with a democratic form of government, followed by the rise of warlordism. During the May Fourth period, it manifested itself in an uncompromising attack on Confucianism and traditional moral precepts and social institutions, while intensifying the search for a solution in foreign ideologies and models. As Clifford Geertz observes on the basis of his study of Indonesian and other cultures,

> It is, in fact, precisely at this point at which a political system begins to free itself from the immediate governance of received tradition, from the direct and detailed guidance of religious or philosophical canons on the one hand and from the unreflective precepts of conventional moralism on the other, that formal ideologies tend first to emerge and take hold. . . . It is when neither a society's most general cultural orientation nor its most down-to-earth, "pragmatic" ones suffice any longer to provide an adequate image of political process that ideologies begin to become crucial as sources of socio-political meanings and attitudes. . . . Whatever else ideologies may be . . .they are, most distinctively, maps of problematic social reality and matrices for the creation of collective conscience.[5]

With a few changes in wording, Geertz's generalization applies perfectly to China in the early twentieth century and particularly during the May Fourth period. In a slightly different way it even helps us to understand the debates since 1978 over the interpretation of Mao Zedong Thought and the search for "socialism with Chinese characteristics."

Extrapolating from Geertz's observation and judging from Chinese political development, one can further suggest that far from serving as an ex post facto rationalization and justification of institutions and policies, ide-

---

4. For the use of the concepts of disintegration and reintegration to analyze Chinese political development in twentieth century China see chap. 1 of this volume. For the value and limitation of these concepts see Introduction to this volume.

5. Clifford Geertz, "Ideology as a Cultural Symbol," in Geertz, *The Interpretation of Cultures* (New York: Basic Books, 1973), 219–20. For a discussion of the salient role played by ideology in contemporary China and the use of Geertz's idea see chap. 1.

ology can play an important role "in creating a new history" and in "collaborating" in the formation of a new system of political authority.[6] One of the ideologies borrowed from outside, and finally triumphant in China, was Marxism-Leninism. In Russia, Marxism as an ideology had already played a unique role "in forging the Bolshevik Party, in endowing it with a dense cohesion, in shaping the Party's tactics and strategy, and in giving it a sense of mission in the making of history."[7] Thus, Marxism and Leninism came to China accompanied by an organizational model. Both were accepted by some Chinese intellectuals who had only a very superficial understanding of the ideology and of the implications of an organized mass party based on Leninist principles.

The reasons why many radical Chinese intellectuals accepted Marxism-Leninism as a solution to China's problems have frequently been discussed. One can also speculate on the question of why Marxism-Leninism met the intellectual and practical demands of the times. Let me repeat some of these interpretations, with additional conjectures of my own, both to prepare the ground for my arguments presented later in this chapter and to guide my own further research. Marxism-Leninism appealed to Chinese intellectuals because, as Schwartz aptly notes, it offered them "the possibility of judging and criticizing the capitalist West from a Western point of view."[8] Marxism is also a theory of total crisis. It envisions a total transformation of the society in the near future. It thus resonated with the Chinese sense or perception of total crisis, and the as yet vague and unstructured demands for total transformation and the desire for immediate political action among radical Chinese intellectuals.[9]

The underlying theory of power in Leninism met the needs of the Chinese radicals in their endeavor to effect a total transformation. As Philip

6. Cf. Norberto Bobbio, "Gramsci and the Conception of Civil Society," in Chantal Mouffe, ed., *Gramsci and Marxist Theory* (London: Routledge and Paul, 1979), 36.

7. Alvin W. Gouldner, *The Two Marxisms* (New York: Oxford University Press, 1980), 4.

8. Benjamin Schwartz, *Chinese Communism and the Rise of Mao* (Cambridge: Harvard University Press, 1952), 15. Chen Gongbo's M.A. thesis at Columbia University (written in 1924, discovered and published in 1966) lends support to Schwartz's conclusion. Chen was one of the thirteen participants of the First Congress of the CCP, held in July 1921, as well as one of the first leaders to become disaffected and leave the Party. Ch'en Kung-po, *The Chinese Communist Movement in China*, ed. C. Martin Wilbur (New York: Octagon Book, 1966). Hereafter cited as Ch'en, *Communist Movement*.

9. Zhang Guotao recalls a conversation with Chen Duxiu on the reasons for organizing a Chinese Communist party. He reports that "we felt that the revolutionary movement led by Sun Yat-sen and his Three Principles of the People were not comprehensive enough, that anarchism was too idealistic and lacked means of practical implementation, and that the parliamentary system advocated by other Socialist schools could not be instituted in China in the foreseeable future." Whether or not Zhang's recollection is accurate, his account can be taken as his analysis of China's needs. Chang Kuo-t'ao, *The Rise of the Chinese Communist Party, 1921–1927* (Lawrence: University Press of Kansas, 1971), 100.

Selznick observes, "Leninist political doctrine rests upon a broad interpretation of the nature of power. In particular, Bolshevik theory and practice recognized that power is *social*, generated in the course of all types of action (not simply the narrowly 'political') and latent in all institutions. This insight stems in part from basic Marxist theory and in part from the overall aim of Bolshevism—a total transformation of society that will invest every institution with political meaning. Leninism views politics as omnipresent."[10] Intellectually, the architectonic and all-embracing structure of Marxism-Leninism was congenial to one unbroken strand of traditional Chinese thought which Lin Yü-sheng characterizes, with some exaggeration, though not without a kernel of truth, as "the powerful and persistent Chinese cultural disposition toward a monistic and intellectualistic mode of thinking," or "a traditionally derived, intellectualistic-holistic mode of thinking"[11] in twentieth-century China. In addition, it supplied radical Chinese intellectuals with a more systematic epistemology and logic (in the form of Marxist dialectics) than traditional thought,[12] as well as a modern economic theory. Its political and messianic messages echoed the tradition of Chinese intellectuals which urged a scholar-official to take all under heaven as his own responsibility *(yi tianxia wei jiren)*.

But the acceptance of a foreign ideology as a "symbolic template," or blueprint, for revolutionary action created its own problems, and ideological orthodoxy and a mechanical application of ideological doctrines to an entirely different society and culture contributed to the disastrous defeats suffered by the Chinese Communist party (CCP) in 1927. These problems were magnified by an organizational model which made the indigenous party a branch of the Comintern and subject to its discipline. To turn defeat into final victory, the foreign ideology had to be adjusted to Chinese realities and traditions in a process known as the sinification of Marxism.[13]

The Leninist party structure came to China in the wake of the conver-

10. Philip Selznick, *The Organization Weapon* (Glencoe, Ill.: Free Press, 1960), 5–6.

11. Lin Yü-sheng, *The Crisis of Chinese Consciousness* (Madison: University of Wisconsin Press, 1979), 41, 156.

Cf. Hao Chang, *Liang Ch'i-ch'ao and Intellectual Transition in China* (Cambridge: Harvard University Press, 1971), 112–14. Hereafter cited as Chang, *Liang*).

12. Ai Siqi's *Dazhong zhexue* was a widely read book among university students in the 1930s. See the publisher's note in Ai Siqi, *Dazhong zhexue* (Philosophy for the masses) (Beijing: Sanlian shudian, 1980).

13. Stuart Schram first made known to Western scholars the notion of "Sinification of Marxism." Benjamin Schwartz in his *Chinese Communism and the Rise of Mao* gave a good description of this process as it developed during the few years following 1927. Mao's reformulation of historical materialism in his statement "in certain conditions, such aspects as the relations of production, *theory*, and the *superstructure* in turn manifest themselves in the *principal and decisive* role" can be considered one of the two basic elements in Mao's sinified Marxism (emphasis added). For a discussion of Mao's reformulation, see chap. 4 of this vol-

sion of some radical intellectuals to Marxism-Leninism. It is not difficult to see why the Leninist party became the single most important collective actor in rebuilding the state and effecting fundamental social change. When the state was undergoing rapid disintegration and when the traditional ruling class of "scholars-officials-landlords"[14] had lost its macropolitical, institutional support with the disappearance of the examination system and the absolute monarchy, the process of rebuilding the state and the political commmunity had to begin in civil society. But the low level of industrialization precluded development of either a powerful bourgeoisie or a strong proletariat. The peasants could not act politically on the national level without leadership from the outside. Elites rather than classes were destined to play the pivotal roles, quite aside from the question of whether even a strong class can become "a class for itself" and act politically without leadership by an elite.

In contrast to the past, the elites were no longer concentrated in the "scholar-official-landlord" class; they ceased to form a recognizable and socially sanctioned hierarchy which defined their authority, prestige, and functions. The bureaucracy was disorganized and disoriented. Bureaucrats' jobs were not secure and there was no definite line of career advancement. Those at the top became free-floating politicians, the agents of warlords and other powerful leaders. Those at the middle and lower levels, having lost their sense of purpose and responsibility, tried merely to cope with the exigencies of making a living. The military emerged for a time as the most powerful group, not only within the governmental structure but also in the society. They lacked the vision, however—though not the ambition—necessary to rebuild the state. Fighting or maneuvering incessantly among themselves, they were unable to build a centralized political organization with a mass base with which to expand their political influence. They failed also to establish organic linkages with civil society except through personal ties to individuals in the upper strata.

---

ume. For Chen Boda's role in the campaign for the "Sinification of Marxism," see Raymond F. Wylie, *The Emergence of Maoism* (Stanford, Calif.: Stanford University Press, 1980).

14. In place of the commonly used term "gentry," I propose, with a great deal of hesitation, to use the hybrid term the "scholar-official-landlord" class. This term will be questioned by Marxists and modern social scientists alike because it does not designate exclusively an economic class or a political class, nor does its rest exclusively on wealth, power, or status. But it does reflect with some degree of accuracy the nature of the ruling class in China, which was based economically on land ownership, socially on a specific skill and on prestige, and politically on selection by the examination system and organization in the bureaucracy. Its strength and persistence in history derived precisely from the direct linkage it established between the state, civil society, and the economy. It was built on the converging interests of the most powerful groups in these three spheres of society. It controlled the state, achieved ideological and political hegemony in the civil society, and dominated the economy.

During the 1910s and 1920s, the intellectuals thus became the most important agents of change. But now the intellectuals were sharply divided among themselves along ideological, intellectual, cultural, social, and political lines. They no longer came largely from one economic class. Their educational backgrounds also varied. Traditional, personal ties could serve as readily available channels of communication among a small group of intellectuals. But these particularistic ties were too restrictive to serve as the framework of a large political organization that could make itself felt in the political arena after the collapse of the older political and institutional structures. Thus, to act politically with any degree of success, they had to find a new basis of solidarity, cohesion, and identification, and a new organizational form—something that could bring a large group of intellectuals to act together in performing their self-imposed tasks of rebuilding the state and transforming the society, and in responding to the demands of the times. This new basis they found in various ideologies imported from foreign nations or formulated under the influence of foreign ideas. And the new organizational form they found in the modern political party.

But why did a Leninist party succeed where liberal parties failed? Conventional wisdom tells us that the hierarchical structure of a Leninist party, its specific criteria of recruitment, and its strict discipline made it an organization capable of taking quick, effective, collective action in a chaotic situation. Lacking these features, the liberal parties were overwhelmed.

This is not the place to repeat all the reasons for the failure of liberal parties to take root in China and for the final triumph of the CCP. Only one point relating to the problem of state rebuilding needs to be made here. Liberal parties of the Western democratic mold presuppose the prior existence of an adequately functioning political system. One of their principal roles is to limit overconcentration of power by means of a system of checks and balances among the three branches of government or between the party in power and the party or parties in opposition. In spite of Michel's iron law of oligarchy, such parties are usually loosely organized and frequently highly factionalized. Given a stable political system, they are often effective in promoting piecemeal, incremental reforms which, over a long period, add up to fundamental changes in the power structure within the society and to alterations in the relationship between the state and the society. But they cannot serve as the main instrument in promoting sociopolitical transformation over the short term. They cannot assuage a sense of urgency rooted in a perception of crisis which demands immediate results.

In China, the Leninist party comprised a strongly centralized system of political authority within a society that lacked any nationwide system of political authority until the Guomindang (itself reorganized on a Leninist model with indifferent success) established its government in Nanjing and brought about the formal, though far from actual, unification of China. In the ensuing civil wars, the Leninist party was able to build a strong state within a state with its own army, government bureaucracy, and territorial base and to compete successfully with the Guomindang for control of China. After 1949, it built a strong state largely in its own image.

The metaphor of hierarchy is frequently used to characterize the Chinese Communist party as a strongly centralized system of political authority, just as the same term is used to describe the traditional bureaucracy. But this metaphor captures only one of its aspects. Another, perhaps more important, aspect can be visualized as a series of concentric circles. Whereas the term "hierarchy" denotes the relationship between different levels of authority, the image of concentric circles suggests the role and the (sometimes explicit) self-perception of the Leninist party in its central relationship to other social groups and organizations, as well as the "horizontal" relationships among various individual leaders and units within the Party structure. During the revolutionary period, the Party was the dynamic center of the civil society, mobilizing and organizing the various social groups around itself to capture power—or so regarded itself. When it built a state within a state, and particularly when it became the party in power, it was the guiding center of the political society and the state, and of the civil society and the economy as well. Following Leninist principles, the Party prohibited the formation of organized factions. Once factional lines were drawn, the struggle tended to become polarized (or was perceived as such) and to result in the victory of one faction and the defeat of the other.[15] Within the Party structure, units at a particular level composed a set of concentric circles, with the Party secretary standing at the center, the Party committee forming the inner circle, and the general membership forming the next one outward. The Party as a whole at that level sought to influence, guide, penetrate, and control the social groups and institutions around them, mobilizing and organizing the social strata, groups, and individuals which had never been actively involved in the political process or had formerly remained passive and inert. Both the hierarchical and the concentric circle models of political power found expression later in the phrase "the monistic leadership of the Party" (*yiyuanhua lingdao*).[16]

15. See chap. 3.

16. The nature of "the monistic leadership of the Party" was most revealingly characterized when Deng Xiaoping criticized this slogan in the context of his advocacy of reforming the leadership institutions of the Party. *Deng Xiaoping wenxuan*, (1975–1982 (Beijing: Renmin chubanshe, 1983), 288–89. Hereafter cited as *Selected Works of Deng*. See also Tang Tsou, "The Historic Change in Direction and Continuity with the Past," *China Quarterly*, June 1984: 340–41.

This hierarchical structure of political power, and particularly its concentric-circle aspect, answered the need and the demand of the Chinese for an effective political authority in a seriously disorganized state and society. It proved to be an efficacious instrument for carrying through a social revolution and reshaping the social system. It facilitated the emergence of charismatic leaders. Its potentiality for fostering an overconcentration and abuse of power was easily overlooked in a society accustomed to absolute imperial power at the macropolitical level and patriarchalism at the microsocial level. This potentiality was to become fully realized only after the Party had captured power.

Social Revolution, Class Struggle, and the Masses in the Process of Rebuilding the State

The total crisis in China brought about not only a national and a political revolution but also a social revolution—a revolution that sought fundamental transformation of the social structure and of man-to-man relations in most spheres of human life. Although the total crisis engendered the revolutionary situation, it was the conscious and purposive activities of individual people that brought about the actual revolution, the outcome of which was always in doubt.[17]

The Chinese social revolution was guided by Marxism-Leninism, understood only vaguely and superficially. It was led by a Leninist party, which developed a specific relationship with the masses during the revolutionary period. A movement that endeavored to effect social, political, and national revolutions simultaneously proved to be better able to survive and prosper in an all-out war with an aggressive modern power—the anti-Japanese war of resistance from 1937 to 1945—than a purely nationalist and political movement. In the sequence of events leading to its final triumph, it effected a fundamental change in the relationship between political power and civil society. It redefined the relationship between that power and all major social groups. It enlarged the scope of political mobilization and participation by establishing an organic link with the peasantry and by seeking cooperative relationships with a wide variety of social groups in a series of concentric circles of alliances. It thus altered the balance of political forces in society and redefined the rules of the political game. It confronted the political coalition of the upper classes in both urban and rural areas with a new and overwhelming coalition of social forces. In the apt metaphor used by Brantly Womack, it turned the political periphery into the political center.[18]

17. Cf. Theda Skocpol, *States and Social Revolutions* (Cambridge: Cambridge University Press, 1979), 16–18.

18. Brantly Womack, *The Foundations of Mao Zedong's Political Thought, 1917–1935* (Honolulu: University Press of Hawaii, 1982), 195.

The state rebuilt on the basis of this transformation could not but have a different foundation from many other states, Marxist or non-Marxist. It has its own special characteristics and its own strengths and vulnerabilities. In this rebuilt political system, the central political problem has arisen from the fact that a Leninist party leading a mass movement has now become the party in power, subject to no external checks by strong sociopolitical forces and lacking unchallengeable, institutionalized limits on its authority and on the power of its leader. Only during the past four or five years has the CCP self-consciously raised the question how it should act and how its authority should be institutionalized, legalized, and routinized after becoming the party in power (zhi zheng dang).

The Marxist concept that led to and legitimized changes between the political power and various social groups (and which after 1957 created new problems for the regime) was that of class struggle. The First Congress of the CCP, which met July 23–31, 1921, declared that "the program [aims] of our Party are as follows: A. With the revolutionary army of the proletariat to overthrow the capitalistic classes, and to reconstruct the nation from the labor class. B. To adopt the dictatorship of the proletariat in order to complete the end of class struggle—abolishing the classes. . . ."[19] The initial attention to the proletariat is vividly portrayed in a recent article that apparently aims at destroying the myth of Mao's infallibility, on the basis of a quoted remark by Zhou Enlai: "On the question of the Chinese revolution taking the path of encircling the cities from the countryside and finally seizing the cities, he [Zhou Enlai] remarked: 'There is a course of development in Mao Zedong's understanding of this question. Once, before the great revolution, Comrade Yun Daiying wrote to Comrade Mao Zedong informing him that Tao Xingzhi and others were working among the peasants. Comrade Mao Zedong replied in his letter: We are now so busy working among the urban workers, how can we have time to work in the countryside? In 1925, when he was at home recuperating from an illness, he made some rural surveys in Hunan. It was only then that he began to pay attention to the peasant problem.'"[20] Zhou's dating of Mao's shift of attention to the peasantry is contradicted by Zhang Guotao's

19. Ch'en, Communist Movement, app. 1, p. 102. The Chinese do not possess a Chinese version of this document. They have a Russian and an English version. They use the Chinese translation of the English version in the quoted passages. This English version is the document printed in Chen's M.A. thesis. See Zhongguo gongchan dang lici daibiao dahui (xin minzhu zhuyi shiqi), compiled by Zhongguo shehui kexue yuan xiandai lishi yanjiu shi (Beijing: Zhonggong zhongyang dangxiao chubanshe, 1982), 15–16, 16 n.1. See also Zhongguo gongchandang dangzhang huibian (Beijing: Renmin chubanshe, 1979), 1, n.1.

20. Shi Zhongquan and Yang Zenghe, "Zhou Enlai on Mao Zedong Thought," Beijing Review, March 1981: 10. Zhou's remark can be found in Zhou's article "Concerning the Study of the Party's Sixth National Congress," written March 3–4, 1944, reproduced in Zhou Enlai xuanji (Beijing: Renmin chubanshe, 1980), 179.

account of the Third Congress, held in June 1923, at which Mao allegedly stressed the importance of the peasant revolution.[21]

But whatever the origin and timing of Mao's advocacy of the centrality of the peasantry and in spite of his unorthodox assessment (in his famous report on Hunan peasants) of the relative contributions made by the peasantry on the one hand and by urban elements and the military on the other, there is no doubt that Mao viewed the rural scene and analyzed the interests of the peasants in terms of the concept of class struggle. In an article entitled "Concerning Rural Investigation," dated September 13, 1941, Mao wrote: "[I] remembered that in 1920, I read for the first time Kautsky's 'Class Struggle,' 'The Communist Manifesto' translated by Chen Wangdao, and 'A History of Socialism' written by an Englishman. Only then did I realize that the history of mankind from the beginning has been a history of class struggle, and that class struggle is the motive force of historical development. I had taken the first step in acquiring a methodology for understanding a problem. Neither Hunan and Hubei of China, however, nor Chiang Kai-shek and Chen Duxiu of China were mentioned in any of these books. From them I took only the four characters 'jieji douzheng' [class struggle] and began conscientiously to study real class struggles."[22] He goes on to mention the progressive understanding of the rural scene he gained in the course of his four months' work with the peasant movement (presumably during the first half of 1925), his Hunan investigation in early 1927, and his land-investigation campaign in 1930.

The idea of the disadvantaged classes overthrowing the privileged classes through interclass struggle naturally entailed the idea of mobilizing the oppressed masses to fight for their own interests against those of the oppressing class. Thus the notion of class struggle led to Mao's stress on the importance of the masses and of mass movements and to what Mao explicitly labeled as the "mass line" in the Yanan period. As Brantly Womack shows, most of the elements of the idea of mass line as a method of leadership and as guide in managing the relationship between the Party and the masses were already present in the theory and practice of Mao in the Jiangxi period. Liao Gailong, one of the leading theorists in China today, maintains that this term cannot be found in any works of Marx, Engels, or Lenin, not to mention Stalin. It also cannot be found in any dictionary of philosophical terms or any textbook published in the Soviet Union. Keeping close contact with the masses is not equivalent to the

21. Chang Kuo-t'ao, *The Rise of the Chinese Communist Party*, 308–9. This account was accepted in the book compiled by the Xiandai lishi yanjiu shi mentioned in footnote 19.

22. Mao Zedong, *Guanyu nongcun diaocha* (September 13, 1941) (Beijing: Renmin chubanshe, 1978), 2. This short pamphlet reproduces the article as printed in *Renmin ribao* on December 13, 1978. It has been reprinted in *Mao Zedong nongcun diaocha wenji* (Collection of Mao Zedong's works on rural investigation) (Beijing: Renmin chubanshe, 1982), 22.

mass line. The mass line is "our Party's basic line in [our] work and [our] understanding [of the objective situation]." The context makes it clear that, in Liao's view, the mass line was Mao's original contribution to Marxism.[23]

Whatever the validity of Liao's claim, I should like to make a few observations here about the three interrelated but analytically distinguishable concepts of *masses, mass movements,* and the *mass line* for the reader's consideration. First, the relationship between the concept of class struggle and the ideas of masses, mass movements, and the mass line is more complex than it is usually understood to be. The mass line is not merely or exclusively a method of implementing class struggle. In actuality, it was an idea which, together with the notion of seeking truth from facts and the impact of the political, economic, and military realities of both the Jiangxi and Yanan periods, led Mao to advocate increasingly moderate policies in many areas. It contributed greatly to the Party's ability to win over ever-larger numbers of the masses and to reduce the size and strength of the opposing forces in Chinese society. In these two respects, it served as a counterbalance to the concept of class struggle, which ordained policies of the most radical stamp.

In the Jiangxi period, Mao adopted a series of policies on land revolution, each more moderate than the last. He abandoned the original policy of nationalizing land and permitted the peasants to rent, buy, and sell redistributed land.[24] He gave up policies which alienated the "middle peasants." He granted to family members of the landlords and later to the former landlords themselves a small share of land. He replaced the policy of giving rich peasants only a small share of poor land with a policy of "taking from those [peasants] who have more land to compensate those who have less" and of "taking away from those who have fertile land to compensate those who have infertile land." This last was at the time justified by Mao as a policy directed against rich peasants and as a measure to achieve equal distribution of land, both as to quantity and as to quality. But he noted later that when this policy was instituted he was castigated by some people for following a "rich-peasant line" *(funong luxian).* He asserted that this policy was the only correct one. As he explained, if the rich peas-

23. Liao Gailong, "Guanyu xuexi 'jueyi' zhong tichu de yixie wenti de jieda." *Yunnan zhehui kexue,* no. 2 (March 1982): 107. A machine copy of this article was given to me by Stuart Schram. The idea of the mass line, if not the exact term, can be traced to the writings of Lenin.

While affirming some of Mao's undeniable contributions, Liao is at the same time one of those high-level officials who played a vital role in demythologizing Mao and pushing sweeping reforms of the party and state structure.

24. In a letter dated February 28, 1931 to the Soviet Government of Jiangxi Province, he directed the provincial government to declare that the redistributed land belonged to those peasants who received them, that others should not violate their right, and that they had the right to rent and to buy and sell the redistributed land.

ants had been given only a small piece of poor land, they would have been "half hungry" and would have been forced to rebel. Poor peasants and hired hands would then have been isolated.[25]

These policy changes in the direction of moderation were accompanied by a gradual development of the elements of the mass line which took into account the immediate interests of the peasants. The changes represented an adjustment of radical policies inspired by the notion of class struggle to the reality of the peasants' perceived interests as detected through the mass line. In other words, it was through the mass line, supplemented later by the policy of the united front, that the CCP succeeded during the revolutionary period in finding and maintaining an adequate balance between the Party's fundamental revolutionary interests, which had to prevail, and such immediate economic interests as were perceived by the peasants and other social groups which should not (or could not) be sacrificed. This state of equilibrium was a prerequisite for the political and military support given by the peasants to the CCP and for the Party's ability to lead the peasants toward its ultimate goals. This complex relationship between the notion of class struggle and the method of mass line is perceived by the current leaders when they find the sources of the Leftist errors in Mao's renewed and intensified emphasis on class struggle on the one hand and the Party's failure to adhere to the mass line on the other.

My second observation points to a problem derived from the concept of masses when it was acted upon in the economically backward area of Jiangxi. When Mao first developed his idea about masses and the oppressed classes, it was linked inseparably with the notion of an overwhelming majority. Professionals and technicians constituted a very small minority in China as a whole and a minuscule group in Jiangxi. Thus, in the formative period, Mao's idea of masses had nothing to do with this minority group, indispensable for the later purposes of modernization. Although Mao underscored the importance of the intellectuals in the Yanan period, his dictum that literature and art are subordinate to politics showed how poorly he understood the role of the professions in modern society.

My third observation on the concepts of the masses, mass movements, and the mass line is, for the purpose of this paper, the most important one. It is common to assert that mass line is a style of leadership, that it is, at its best, a democratic style of leadership, but that it is not equivalent to liberal democracy in the West. For Western liberal democracy consists of an elaborate set of institutions and game rules to implement the principle

25. Mao Zedong, *Guanyu nongcun diaocha*, 3. I am not sure to what extent Mao's idea on the rich-peasant question was fully implemented at that particular time, as Mao was losing influence to the returned-student group.

of "consent of the governed" and to compel rulers to take into account the interests, wants, preferences and aspirations of the citizens more fully than under other forms of government.[26]

Starting from this commonplace, I shall try to make two points.[27] First, an analytic distinction must be drawn between the concept of citizenship on the one hand and the idea of masses and its two derivatives of mass movements and the mass line on the other. These are two different ways of linking the public sector with the private or of linking the state (i.e., political power) with the civil society (i.e., individuals and social groups). The concept of citizenship begins with members of the society viewed as isolated individuals, possessing equally a set of abstract rights, who form themselves into social groups by exercising those rights. These social groups (voluntary associations, corporations, etc.) are the intermediate interests, or *pouvoirs intermediares*, between the state and the individual. The rights of the society's members, rather than their duties, are underscored.[28] In the context of a Western market economy, citizenship provides the political and institutional setting in which the initiative, energy, and capabilities of individuals and social groups are successfully developed and mobilized.

In contrast, the notions of masses, mass movements, and the mass line begin with individuals viewed as members of segments of society possessing not abstract, legal, civic rights but substantive socioeconomic entitlements. The masses, as the overwhelming majority of the society, are members of the lower classes, who are to be mobilized and organized by political activists. It is assumed that their active or latent demands for socioeconomic justice will spur them to political activism, once political leadership is given them. The ideas of masses, mass movements, and the mass line thus underscore active involvement and performance of duties in a political movement. Some intermediate interests are organized by the Party; other intermediate interests are swept away. In all modern societies, both the idea of citizenship and the idea of masses are used to link the state and society, at least on paper. But societies differ in their points of departure and in their emphasis of one or the other form of linkage. The differences produce different patterns of political, social, and economic development—and most specifically, of state building.

26. For a discussion of this aspect of democracy, see Brian M. Barry, *Sociologists, Economists, and Democracy* (London: Collier-Macmillan, 1970), 164, 174.

27. The theoretical foundation of these two points is developed mainly from the following books: Reinhard Bendix, *Nation-Building and Citizenship* (New York: Wiley, 1964), enlarged ed., University of California Press, 1977; T. H. Marshall, *Class, Citizenship, and Social Development* (Chicago: University of Chicago Press, 1977); David Collier, ed., *The New Authoritarianism in Latin America* (Princeton, N.J.: Princeton University Press, 1974).

28. As Bendix writes, "Although citizenship allows for more active participation, there are only a few instances in which it requires positive action. . . . " *Nation Building*, 20.

This last observation brings us to the second point. State building in the modern West, particularly in England, began with the notion of citizenship. There, political, social, and economic development went hand in hand with the extension of citizenship to the lower classes. More important for our purpose is the expansion of the rights of citizenship. As T. H. Marshall notes succinctly, the rights of citizenship can be divided into three categories: civil, political, and social. The formative periods of these three kinds of rights are respectively the eighteenth, the nineteenth, and the twentieth centuries.[29] The notion of citizenship and its expansion have contributed to the ability of liberal democracy in the West to achieve "the compression, at both ends, of the scale of income distribution," "the great expansion of the area of common culture and common experience," and "the enrichment of the universal status of citizenship, combined with the recognition and stabilization of certain status differences chiefly through the linked systems of education and occupation."[30] Economic inequalities and social stratification persist. But as Marshall observes, the expansion of socioeconomic rights has raised even in England the problem of material incentives and of the absence of a sense of obligation "to put one's heart into one's job and work hard."[31]

There is no comparable study of state building and socioeconomic development based on the notion of masses and its derivatives of mass movements and the mass line. This lacuna offers an opportunity to scholars in contemporary Chinese studies—an opportunity that cannot be fully exploited in this short essay. But a few tentative remarks on China's reception of the Western concept of citizenship and its displacement by the ideas of masses, mass movements, and the mass line are not out of place. The question can also be asked whether or not Chinese development under the CCP over the past, present, and future will represent a reversal of the process in the West, in other words, whether it will turn out to be a process that begins with an advance in socioeconomic rights and then shifts to an advance in political and civil rights.

As is well known, the concept of citizenship as consisting primarily of a set of civil rights fell on barren ground in China at the very beginning.

29. Marshall, *Class*, 78–81. By the term "social rights," Marshall refers to "the whole range from the right to a modicum of economic welfare and security to the right to share to the full in the social heritage and to live the life of a civilized being according to the standards prevailing in the society" (p. 78).

Individual nations in the West may have deviated from this general development at specific periods of time. Sidney Verba observed that "the Bismarckian policy for Germany represented an attempt to schedule distribution first and postpone participation." See Leonard Binder et al., *Crisis and Sequence in Political Development* (Princeton, N.J.: Princeton University Press, 1971), 313.

30. Marshall, *Class*, 127.

31. Ibid., 130.

According to Hao Chang, it was Liang Qichao who formulated for "the first time in Chinese history the ideal of citizenship."[32] Contemplating the problem of developing the energy of the Chinese, he came upon "Rousseau's democratic doctrines as the most effective antidote not only to traditional despotism but also to the slavish mentality of the Chinese people."[33] But in the words of Hao Chang, he soon afterwards reached the conclusion that "Rousseau's liberal thought, however splendid otherwise, was not suited to the purpose of China's state-building."[34] In Liang's notion of citizenship, "the public self of the new citizen has almost completely overshadowed his private self."[35]

In his anxiety to create a powerful revolutionary movement and to make China strong, Sun Yat-sen asserted that the Chinese had always enjoyed an excessive degree of individual liberty: the individual, he said, should not have too much liberty, but the nation should possess "complete liberty."[36] Sun's erroneous diagnosis betrays an intellectual confusion, an inability to separate the question of state-society relationship from the problem of political authoritarianism. As a result, within a few pages of a discussion of the "excessive freedom" enjoyed by the Chinese he mentioned the autocratic and unlimited power of the emperor and the severe punishments inflicted on those who endangered the throne. Actually, the "freedom" he referred to was not a matter of civil and political rights but a manifestation of the wide latitude given by the state to social groups and individuals in running their own affairs or of the inability of a traditional state to penetrate deeply into society.

Although Chen Duxiu was far too optimistic about the possibility of establishing political democracy in China, his understanding of the traditional state and society was much more accurate than Sun's. In an article written during his pre-Communist phase, expounding the relevance of Dewey's ideas on democracy to current Chinese problems, he noted that in traditional China an extremely autocratic government at the top coexisted with an extremely large latitude enjoyed by the people at the bottom, who had many kinds of "combinations similar to autonomous associations [in the West]" such as the clan temples, religious associations, philanthropic organizations, local militia, etc. Such combinations (lianhe) could, in his view, serve as the foundation of democratic institutions.[37]

32. Chang, Liang, 214.
33. Ibid., 192.
34. Ibid., 247.
35. Ibid., 218.
36. Sun Zhongshan xuanji, vol. 2 (Beijing: Renmin chubanshe, 1956), 686, 688, 690, or Sun Yat-sen, San Min Chu I, trans. Frank W. Price (Chungking: Ministry of Information, 1943), 205, 210, 213.
37. Chen Duxiu, "Shixin minzhi de jichu" in Duxiu wencun, vol. 1 (Xianggang: Yuandong

Although Chen failed to note the absence of strong theoretical and ideological support for these "parochial institutions,"[38] he seems to have recognized the importance of intermediate groups and structures as a necessary element in the building of a democratic state and society. He also proposed to begin the development of local self-rule at the level of the village and township.

In contrast to Sun, Chen underscored the importance of human rights. In his article "Call to Youth," dated September 15, 1915, he made the theories of the rights of man and of equality the bases of his call on young people to "be independent and not servile." After calling on youths also to cultivate a scientific habit of mind and not to indulge in flights of imagination, he compared science and the theory of human rights *(renquanshuo)* to "the two wheels" of a cart, asserting that in modern Europe science contributes as much as the theory of human rights to the superiority of that society over others. He urged that "if our countrymen desire to leave behind the period of obscurantism, are ashamed of being a people of inferior culture, and wish to rise quickly and catch up [with Europe], then we should put equal weight on science and human rights."[39] This pairing of science with human rights later became the famous slogan "Mr. Democracy and Mr. Science."

But at this time, Chen did not sufficiently realize the intimate relationship between the consolidation of the system of human rights (or, more broadly, of democracy) and party politics in modern liberal, democratic states. He believed that "party politics" would soon be a thing of the past and that moreover it was unsuitable to present-day China. None of the movements sponsored by parties or factions which had developed in China over many years could promote fundamental national progress, in his view. He suggested that these movements should be pushed forward to transform themselves into a "national movement."[40] Within less than five years, Chen became an active organizer of the Chinese Communist

---

tushu gongsi, 1956), 376. This article was discussed in Benjamin Schwartz's "Ch'en Tu-hsiu: Pre-Communist Phase," *Papers on China 1948*, 2: 187–88. See also his article in *Journal of the History of Ideas 2* (1951). See also Thomas Kuo, *Ch'en Tu-hsiu (1879–1942) and the Chinese Communist Movement* (South Orange, N.J.: Seton Hall University Press, 1975), 75.

38. On the lack of ideological support for the autonomy of these parochial institutions, see Philip Kuhn, "Late Ch'ing Views of the Polity" in Tang Tsou, ed., *Select Papers from the Center for Far Eastern Studies*, no. 4 (1979–80): 1–17.

39. Chen, *Duxiu Wencun*, 1:3, 9. This article has been widely read by students of Chinese history in the United States, thanks to its availability in Ssu-yu Teng and John K. Fairbank's *China's Response to the West* (Atheneum, 1954), 240–45. The last two direct quotations used here were omitted from the Teng-Fairbank translation. Chen's term *"zhouju"* is rendered here simply as "cart." It is possible that Chen was also thinking of a river-going side-wheel steamer.

40. Chen, *Duxiu Wencun*, 1:45–47. This article of Chen's was written in January 1916.

party, which dedicated itself to the development of the class struggle and of mass movements.[41]

It was Mao who, in his years of revolutionary warfare and class struggle, developed more fully than any other leaders the ideas of masses, mass movements, and the mass line in his endeavor to mobilize the various social groups, to draw them into the political process as active participants, to take into account their interests in making decisions and to rely on them in the implementation of policies. This group of three interrelated ideas accompanied the more inclusive and more abstract concepts of social revolution and class struggle, and they were used to conceptualize the immediate linkage between political power and civil society. They directed attention to the specific social groups and individuals in particular situations and in the context of particular policies. These groups and their individual members became the points of reference, the subjects and the objects, of policy decisions and implementation. "Mass movement" referred to collective sociopolitical actions in which either a single class or, more likely, several classes and strata participated. The mass line was formulated as a guide for establishing a "correct" relationship between the masses and the leadership. It was believed to be a "Marxist-Leninist theory of knowledge or methodology" in policy making and implementation.[42]

Within the general context of social revolution and class struggle, mass movements were launched to reach specific goals at particular times. Frequently, these specific goals centered in securing the socioeconomic rights of the oppressed masses, as viewed in the light of a particular analy-

41. I have begun to assemble materials for an article or a monograph on the political ideas of Chen Duxiu. I have no answer to the question whether or not Chen at that time realized that a Leninist party and Marxism-Leninism would inevitably impose strict limitations on "human rights" and that as a member of the Party he would have to sacrifice his cherished freedoms. But after his break with the Party and in his last years, he returned to his pre-Communist views on the indispensability of freedom. A convenient compilation of sources is Zhang Yongtong and Liu Chuanxue, eds., *Houqi de Chen Duxiu ji qi wenzhang xuanbian* (Sichuan: Sichuan renmin chubanshe, 1980). Two articles on Chen's later views by Hu Shi and Tao Xisheng can be found in *Chen Duxiu zizhuan*, published in 1969 by Xiandai chuban gongsi in Hong Kong.

42. *Mao Zedong ji* (Tokyo: Hokobo sha, 1971), 9:28. In spite of its practical significance, Mao never attempted a definition of the term "masses" and distinguished it from such categories as "the people" *(renmin)*, *minzhong*, or *renmin dazhong*. ("*Minzhong*" is rendered in Mao's *Selected Works*, vol. 4 as "masses of the people.") The relationship between the concepts of "classes" and "masses" is a particularly difficult one to ascertain. The specific reference of the term "masses" can be determined only when we closely examine the context or when Mao occasionally qualifies the term by an appositive such as "*pin gu nong qunzhong*" (the masses of poor peasants and hired hands). But even a quick rereading of Mao's pre-1949 writing dealing with social policies and governmental organization in the base areas suggests a very important point: i.e., the term "citizen" was very seldom used except in formal, legal and propagandistic documents drafted by him.

sis of class structure. It was believed that these goals could not be attained unless the oppressors were overthrown by violence, the remaining aura of their prestige swept away, and the invincible power of the revolutionary masses vividly demonstrated through collective mass action, sometimes including terror. The CCP's revolutionary experience, ranging from the peasant movement in Hunan in 1926–27, through the land revolution and the land investigation movement, to the land reform movement of 1946–52, clearly show that mass movements were a most effective means of securing socioeconomic rights for the disadvantaged groups. But for our purpose, what needs to be noted is that the process of state rebuilding began with flagrant violation of whatever laws still existed, whatever customary spheres of individual inviolability still obtained in social life, and whatever mutual expectations were still entertained between individuals.[43] Although there was a simultaneous process of enacting new revolutionary laws and establishing a regular pattern of mutual expectations as the revolution moved on, precedents were established that mass movements could legitimately override the law, long-standing traditions, and customary norms. In these circumstances, the establishment of a rule of law and a system of civil rights was not merely a matter of creating something foreign to China's long tradition. It entailed repudiating a strong element of the CCP's revolutionary heritage, as it had grown up during the decades of struggle and warfare. The Cultural Revolution pushed to the extreme Mao's idea of mass movements as an instrument for waging class struggle, flagrantly violated almost all laws and rules, and seriously infringed the civil rights of a large majority of politically powerful or politically relevant individuals, not to say their customary privileges. Understandably, it reawakened their almost forgotten apprehension of the pernicious influence of the long Chinese tradition of authoritarianism and reminded them once more of the painful absence of these rights under the rule of the warlords and of the Guomindang. Paradoxically, it may have given China another chance to begin the quest for a rule of law and a system of civil rights of her own fashioning and in her own way.

In securing socioeconomic rights for the disadvantaged classes, mass movements proved effective in developing the energy and capacities of the masses to pursue military and political goals. In a life-and-death struggle, mass activism and enthusiasm could be sustained by one movement

43. Mao recognized that in 1926 the peasants in Hunan had adopted measures outside the law in attacking the local bullies and bad gentry. But he asserted that these measures were necessary in a revolutionary struggle. "At this time, either the east wind prevails over the west wind or the west wind prevails over the east wind. How can we not but be a little bit stern?" *Mao Zedong ji*, 1:205. See also Mao's "Report on an investigation of the peasant movement in Hunan," ibid., 207–49, "Wei hangwu gongzo gei minxi de yi feng xin," ibid., 3:99–105. "Chatian yundong de chubu zongjie," ibid., 3:341–56.

after another. But this revolutionary heritage had unforeseen consequences when, after 1956, the tasks confronting the CCP became the promotion of steady economic growth and smooth political development—tasks requiring stability of expectations, a measure of freedom and autonomy for individuals and groups to develop their creativity, and constant economic incentives to work hard in everyday undertakings. Thus, mass movements inhibited the development of these prerequisites to building a modern industrialized society. This was especially true as mass movements lost their initial spontaneity and came increasingly under the direction of huge bureaucracies under a regime in which the Party monopolized all power.

Throughout the revolutionary period, mass movements were also employed to destroy the political power of the upper classes and the intermediate social institutions they dominated. In the process of destruction, the Party built up new mass organizations and generated new activists. In turn, these organizations became the basis of new local organs of political power, staffed by the new activists. In more than twenty years of revolutionary warfare, a new bureaucracy of cadres, as distinguished from functionaries, was built up, staffed at the lower and middle levels, and in many instances even at the highest level, by persons with rural roots and orientations. These cadres had little education or knowledge except what they gained through practical experience, political training, and ideological indoctrination. Thus, the vast Party and government bureaucracy established by the time of the nationwide victory in 1949 was ideologically and organizationally strong, but its personnel lacked professional skills and modern knowledge. It has only been in the past few years that the CCP has squarely faced this problem left over from its successful revolution.

In the process of making a social revolution, waging class struggles, conducting mass movements, and fighting a civil war under the guidance of Marxism-Leninism, the Western ideals and universal principles which figured so prominently during the May Fourth period were regarded not as ends in themselves but as expedient means of achieving specific, narrow, political goals. No one made this point more forcefully or more clearly than Mao. In a letter written on May 6, 1943, to Peng Dehuai criticizing Peng's "Talk on Democratic Education," Mao pontificated that "[your] talk took as its point of departure definitions of democracy, freedom, equality, fraternity, etc., rather than the political needs of the struggle against Japan. . . . [You] also did not say that freedom of speech and freedom of the press existed for the purpose of mobilizing the anti-Japanese activism of the people and of struggling for and protecting the political and economic rights of the people. Instead [you] took freedom of thought as your point of departure. . . . [You] said that there should definitely be no unequal legal provisions but you made no distinction between revolutionaries and counterrevolutionaries."[44] Mao's statement was a good summary of the intuitive views held by many CCP leaders and cadres concerning Western institutions associated with or rooted in the concept of citizenship—in spite of the existence of many legal and political documents paying lip service to them.

Three Phases of Chinese Marxism, Shifts in the Structure of Power within the Party, and Changes in the Idea of the Relationship between Political Power and Society

The revolutionary heritage, the problems flowing from it, and the solutions now being proposed cannot be understood unless we firmly grasp the three major shifts in Chinese Marxism and the corresponding phases in the development of the CCP and its policies. The period from 1927 to the years between the second half of 1955 and the first few months of 1957 marked the gradual formation of Mao Zedong Thought and the demonstration of its effectiveness. Chinese Marxism, which was given the label of Mao Zedong Thought in 1943, was an uneasy synthesis of two sets of opposing tendencies: the revolutionary impulse and a prudent respect for sociopolitical reality; class struggle and the mass line; elitist leadership and populism; military power and political primacy; domination by the use of coercive power and hegemony (or political, intellectual, cultural, and moral leadership) achieved through persuasion; mass mobilization and organizational control; and finally political penetration into society and respect for the interests of the masses and of social groups as they themselves perceived them. Its effectiveness derived precisely from this uneasy synthesis, justified in theoretical terms by the notion of unity of theory and practice and in political terms by the idea of struggle on two fronts *(liangtiao zhanxian douzheng).*[45]

But in the following period, from 1955–57 to 1976, this synthesis disintegrated. Chinese Marxism was increasingly dominated by the Leftist tendency. This Leftist tendency had its ups and downs, one climax, in terms of political actions, occurring in 1966–68, and another, in terms of theoretical development, in 1975–76. In the period since December 1978, Chinese Marxism has moved toward the Right in search of a middle course.

The Development of Mao's Synthesis: 1927 to 1955–57

During the first period, one of the most original and widely accepted theoretical contributions made by Mao was his reformulation of historical ma-

44. *Mao Zedong ji*, 9:13.

45. For example, Mao used this term in August 1933 in his article "Preliminary conclusion on the land investigation movement," *Mao Zedong ji*, 3:355. I have not searched the documents for the specific purpose of ascertaining the origin of this phrase.

terialism, which is summarized in the following sentences. "In certain conditions, such aspects as the relations of production, *theory,* and the *superstructure* in turn manifest themselves in the *principal and decisive role.*" "When the superstructure (politics, culture, etc.) obstructs the development of the economic base, political and cultural changes become principal and decisive."[46] This formulation parallels what Norberto Bobbio believes to be one of the two inversions made in Gramsci's conceptual system in relation to the Marxist tradition, i.e., "the prevalence of the superstructure over the structure."[47] Whereas Gramsci's inversion of the Marxist formulation paved the way to a strategy of peaceful transition to socialism, Mao's reformulation represented not only a descriptive generalization of the process of ideological, political, social, and economic changes in twentieth century China, but also a programmatic prescription for revolutionary action which was to lead the Party to nationwide victory in a civil war.[48] It resonated with the revolutionary impulse and was usually thrust into prominence by Mao and his followers when they were pushing for rapid change and revolutionary practices. But in this first period, the dictum was balanced by Mao's emphasis on "practice" and his injunction to "seek truth from facts," which frequently served to temper the revolutionary impulse with prudence. This emphasis and this injunction came into play particularly when realistic political and military strategy and tactics, carefully regulated social change, well thought-out reforms and regulated economic growth were the order of the day. These two tendencies—assigning the principal and decisive role to theory and superstructure (in particular, politics) on the one hand and giving the primary place to "practice" and the economic base on the other—form a unity of opposites. In similar fashion, the universal concept of class struggle was also combined with, and balanced by, the idea of the mass line in particular situations so as to arrive at specific policies.

During the Yanan period, the CCP worked out patterns of combining domination with hegemony (or combining the use of coercion with a reliance on persuasion) in two different political arenas; the base areas and the Guomindang-dominated territories, at a time in the life of the nation when the Party's political and military strength was still far inferior to that of the Guomindang. In the base areas, where the CCP established its own government and had its own army, its unquestioned hegemony over civil society was guaranteed by direct domination. With coercive apparatus always at hand to enforce its will, persuasion and leadership could be relied on to achieve the acceptance of its policies, and overt use of coercion

46. Mao Tse-tung, *Selected Works* (Peking: Foreign Languages Press, 1965–77), 1:336. Emphasis added. For a more detailed discussion, see chap. 4.

47. Norberto Bobbio, "Gramsci and the Conception of Civil Society," p. 36.

48. For a more detailed discussion, see chap. 4.

could be limited to a minimum. When these favorable conditions were combined with effective use of the mass line and the policy of the united front, the Party was able to achieve hegemony while enjoying popular support.

In the areas controlled by the Guomindang, the CCP could only rely on persuasion, establishing alliances, cooperating with various social groups and minor parties by proposing or agreeing to programs that promoted their interests, and by exploiting the population's dissatisfaction with the Guomindang's policies. In other words, it was trying to compete with the Guomindang for hegemony over civil society when state power and the means of coercion were in other hands. Its policies toward the other political parties and groups were popularized and legitimized by the notion of the united front. But even here, its limited success and its popularity rested only partly on the intrinsic merits of the CCP's moderate programs. They also stemmed from the fact that it possessed an independent military force and base areas with which it could back up its demands, as well as the common programs and alliances worked out with the minor parties and various social forces. This was the underlying reality of its united front with the latter groups. The united front with the Guomindang was based on an uneasy combination of two opposites—unity with the Guomindang and struggle against it. As Mao wrote, "In the period of the anti Japanese united front, struggle is the means to unity and unity is the aim of struggle. If unity is achieved through struggle, it will live; if unity is sought through yielding, it will perish."[49] The overall tactics were "to develop the progressive forces, win over the middle forces and combat the die-hard forces."[50]

It was also during the Yanan period that the Party condemned the Leftist tendencies of "mechanical and excessive inner-Party struggle" and "unprincipled disputes and struggles within the Party."[51] It specifically opposed holding "struggle meetings."[52] A pattern of moderate and reasonable inner-Party struggle was established and a set of norms was formalized and practiced under the joint auspices of Mao and Liu Shaoqi. When Kang Sheng tried in the last phase of the *zhengfeng* movement to persecute a large number of cadres under the euphemism of a "rescue movement," Mao called a halt to this and prevented its overextension. (As leader of the *zhengfeng* movement Mao must of course be held at least

49. Mao, *Selected Works*, 2:422.
50. Ibid., Mao also used the phrase "to isolate the die-hard forces." Ibid., 426.
51. Liu Shao-chi, *On Inner Party Struggle* (Peking: Foreign Languages Press, 1957), 23–55. For a good, detailed, and slightly different account, see Frederick C. Teiwes, *Politics and Purges in China* (White Plains, N.Y.: M. E. Sharpe, 1979), 3–101.
52. Liu, *Inner Party Struggle*, 19–20. Holding "struggling meetings" was the normal practice in the early years of the Cultural Revolution.

partly responsible for Kang's action, nevertheless.) In retrospect, the most important norm developed during the Yanan period was that top political leaders should not be executed after they lose out in inner-Party struggle. This turned out to be the principle that enabled many Party leaders to survive the Cultural Revolution and to give the Party another chance to demonstrate its ability to govern China.

This moderate pattern of inner-Party struggle was made possible by the establishment of Mao as the recognized leader of the Party. But there was a larger background factor that shaped this development. The CCP was still a minority party leading a minority movement in its struggle for power against the overwhelming military might of the Guomindang. It had to maintain the solidarity and morale of its own ranks: otherwise defection was a readily available alternative. Moreover, the expansion of the Party and the development of popular support in order to survive and to gain power depended on the attraction and image of the Party. It was this distribution of power within China which, in conjunction with the establishment of a recognized leadership, accounted for the moderate pattern of inner-Party struggle.

But the establishment of the recognized leadership of Mao was not an unmixed blessing, because it contained within itself the potential for replacing collective leadership with a concentration of power in the hands of one man and the development of a cult of personality. It thus contained the seed of eventual total destruction of the system of "democratic centralism." It should be recalled that after the Ningdu Conference, held in early August 1932, Mao lost most if not all of his military power to Zhou Enlai, who in May 1933 was officially named general political commissar of the Red Army. In early 1934 Mao lost his post of chairman of the People's Committee to Zhang Wentian (alias Luo Fu) while retaining the now powerless position of chairman of the Central Executive Committee of the Chinese Soviet Republic, an organ of several hundred members. From 1931 to the eve of the Long March, the Party's Central Committee was effectively controlled by the "returned-students group." From September 1931 to January 1935 Qin Bangxian (alias Bo Gu) served in fact as "head of the Party." But the military strategy adopted and the military operations conducted by the Comintern military adviser Li De (a German whose real name was Otto Braun) under the overall direction of the returned-students group met with utter disaster and ended in loss of the base areas in Jiangxi, Fujian, and Hunan. The Long March began in October 1934.

At the Zunyi Conference, held January 15–17, 1935, Mao's criticism of the military strategy adopted in countering the Guomindang's fifth campaign was upheld. Mao was elected a member of the standing committee of the Politburo. The "three-man group," composed of Qin Bangxian, Li De, and Zhou Enlai, was dissolved. Zhu De and Zhou Enlai were given authority over military affairs, with Zhou as the person responsible for final military decisions. In February Qin Bangxian was replaced by Zhang Wentian as the member of the standing committee in general charge of the Party but without any formal title. In March a "three-man military command small group" (sanren junshi zhihui xiaozu) was established, with Mao, Zhou Enlai, and Wang Jiaxiang as its members.[53]

For the next few years a collective leadership existed, with Mao, hardly more than first among equals, facing formidable challenges from Zhang Guotao and later from Wang Ming. Then the post of general secretary was formally abolished in 1938. As Roderick MacFarquhar points out, "there was then no longer any *organizational position* from which it would be possible to dominate [Mao]."[54] With the defeat of Zhang Guotao and Wang Ming in the power struggle, and particularly with the launching of the *zhengfeng* movement, Mao established himself in an unchallengeable position of leadership. Then the concentration of power in Mao's own hands found formal expression in a reorganization of the leadership institutions of the Party. (This has recently been made known and underscored by current Party reformers as an important step in the erosion of "democratic centralism" and as one of the foundation stones of the Cultural Revolution.) In March 1943, about three months before the formal dissolution of the Comintern, the Politburo in Yanan decided that Mao be made its chairman, specified that the Secretariat be the organ to handle day-to-day work in accordance with the guiding principles adopted by the Politburo, selected Mao, Liu Shaoqi, and Ren Bishi as the three members of the Secretariat, and stipulated that Mao in his capacity as chairman of the Secretariat had the authority to make the final decisions on questions discussed there.[55]

Perhaps not by accident, the term "Mao Zedong Thought" made its public appearance for the first time in an article written by Wang Jiaxiang and published on July 8. It was identified as "China's Marxism-Leninism, China's Bolshevism, and China's Communism." It was characterized as

53. This version of events at the Zunyi Conference and shortly afterwards is based on a newly discovered handwritten note by Chen Yun and is considered by the Party an authoritative account. *Liaowang* (Outlook) March 5, 1984, 40–42, *Renmin ribao*, March 5, 1984: 1. This document has since been published in *Renmin ribao*, January 17, 1985, 1–2.

54. Roderick MacFarquhar, *The Origins of the Cultural Revolution* (New York: Columbia University Press, 1974): 140. Emphasis in the original.

55. Liao Gailong, "Lishi di jingyan he women de fazha daolu" (October 25, 1980), reproduced in facsimile in *Zhonggong yanjiu* 15, no. 9 (September 1981): 142. Liao's information is based on *Dangshi yanjiu*, an internal publication not easily accessible to scholars outside China.

"the product of the integration of Marxism-Leninism with the concrete experience of the Chinese revolutionary movement."[56] At the Seventh Plenum of the Sixth Central Committee, which met intermittently in the period from May 1944 to April 1945, Mao was elected chairman of the Central Committee. The Seventh Congress and the First Plenum of the Seventh Central Committee formally ratified these developments. The new Party constitution declared in its section on the general program that the CCP takes Mao Zedong Thought, characterized as "the ideas integrating the theory of Marxism-Leninism with the practice of the Chinese revolution," "as the guiding principle in all its work."[57] Its Article 34 stipulated that the chairman of the Central Committee shall be concurrently chairman of the Central Political Bureau and of the Central Secretariat." The First Plenum of the Seventh Central Committee, convened on June 19, 1945, elected Mao chairman of the Central Committee and consequently, in accordance with the Party constitution, chairman of the Politburo and of the Secretariat.[58] The power of the chairman was not defined.

After the CCP became the party in power in 1949, Mao's tendency to amass power in his own hands continued. In his written criticisms of Liu Shaoqi and Yang Shangkun on May 19, 1953, Mao ordered that "from now on, all documents and telegrams sent out in the name of the Central Committee can be dispatched only after I have gone over them: *otherwise they are invalid.*"[59] He also said that it was "a mistake and a breach of Party discipline" to issue "resolutions adopted at meetings called by the Central Committee . . . without authorization." But throughout this period efforts were made to preserve a semblance of collective leadership. Furthermore, open and excessive promotion of the cult of personality was not part of the Party's tradition and was not supported by Mao himself. This countertendency bore fruit in the Eighth Party Congress, held in

56. See the note by Chen Wenyuan, in *Hongqi*, 1981, no. 8: 49.

57. See *Zhongguo gongchandang dangzhang huibian* (Beijing: Renmin chubanshe, 1979), 46. Hereafter cited as *Dangzhang huibian*. The wordings translated here are the same as an edition of the Party constitution published in 1949 by Xinhua shudian.

This passage is translated in a recent article as follows: "The Communist Party of China takes Mao Zedong Thought—the thought of unity of Marxist-Leninist theory with the practice of the Chinese revolution—as the guiding principle in all its work" ("How to Define Mao Zedong Thought: Changes over Forty Years," *Beijing Review*, March 2, 1981: 12. In an earlier translation, this sentence reads: "The Communist Party of China guides its entire works by the teachings which unite the theories of Marxism-Leninism with the actual practice of the Chinese revolution—the Thought of Mao Tse-tung" ("The Constitution of the Communist Party of China," reproduced as part 2 of Liu Shao-ch'i, *On the Party*, 3d ed. [Peking: Foreign Languages Press, 1951], 143).

58. Zhonggong zhongyang dangxiao dangshi jiaoyanshi ziliao zu (ed.), *Zhongguo gongchandang lici zhongyao huiyi ji*, (Shanghai: Shanghai renmin chubanshe, 1982), 1:246.

59. *Selected Works*, 5:92. Emphasis in the original. Liao Gailong interprets the phrase "without authorization" as without Mao's authorization.

September 1956, and under the influence of Khrushchev's anti-Stalin campaign. The Party constitution, adopted in September 1956, did not mention Mao Zedong Thought—a decision reportedly pushed by Peng Dehuai.[60] Instead, it contained the statement that "the Chinese Communist Party of China takes Marxism-Leninism as its guide to action," while it also declared that "the Party in its activities upholds the principle of integrating the universal truth of Marxism-Leninism with the concrete practice of the Chinese revolutionary struggle."[61] But this verbal omission did not diminish Mao's power over the Party and did nothing to prevent the promotion of "Mao Zedong Thought" by Lin Biao in the early 1960s and the emergence of an extreme form of the cult of Mao during the Cultural Revolution. Another change made by the Eighth Congress, which continues even now to have important consequences in terms of the CCP's leadership institutions and the fortune of its leaders, was the restoration of the post of general secretary, the selection of Deng Xiaoping to fill that post, and the inclusion of Deng in the standing committee of the Politburo as its sixth, and lowest ranking, member.

The Breakdown of Mao's Synthesis: The Thrust toward the Left from 1955–57 to 1976

By the beginning of the second period in 1955, the CCP had been the party in power for six years, and its sway was no longer checked by other countervailing forces or parties. Mao recklessly pushed forward a series of radical policies: acceleration of cooperativization in agriculture in 1955–56, the anti-Rightist movement of 1957, and the General Line, the Great Leap, and the commune system in 1958. The disaster of 1959 to 1961 and the recovery between 1961 and 1965 revealed two remarkable phenomena. In spite of the disaster, there were no rebellions on a nationwide scale. In spite of a lowering of morale among the cadres and the general public, there was no crisis of authority and no crisis of faith. These two facts suggest that the effectiveness of the Party in achieving nationwide victory and in governing the nation for those first few years had established the legitimacy of the Party-state. This legitimacy persisted in spite of the regime's disastrous errors in the period of 1958–60 and contributed to its ability to resolve the crisis. The recovery was the product of a step-

---

60. According to a Red Guard document, Peng Dehuai opposed at the Eighth Party Congress the inclusion in the Party constitution of the statement that "Mao Zedong Thought should be taken as the Party's guiding thought." Ding Wang, ed., *Peng Dehuai wenti zhuanji*, enlarged ed. (Hong Kong: Mingbao yuekan chubanshe, 1979), 382. An article in *Beijing Review* suggests that before the congress met, Mao himself "proposed once again not to use the formulation 'Mao Zedong Thought'." *Beijing Review*, March 2, 1982: 13.

61. *Eighth National Party Congress of the Communist Party of China: Documents* (Peking: Foreign Languages Press, 1981), 143.

by-step reversal of the policies that had proved disastrous. This reversal was carried out under the auspices of top Party leaders, including Mao himself. The accomplishment suggests that Mao Zedong Thought had not disintegrated totally, in spite of the Leftist direction it had taken.

But as soon as the crisis had been contained, Mao's ideas once again moved toward the Left. In August 1962 he declared flamboyantly that "we must wage class struggle for ten thousand years." He inaugurated the Socialist Educational Movement in 1963 and an attack on writers in 1964. And with the circular of May 16, 1966, the Cultural Revolution was formally launched. It was justified later by the "theory of continued revolution under the dictatorship of the proletariat,"[62] formulated by Kang Sheng and others but approved by Mao.

Revolution is, in Marxist terms, class struggle and the overthrow of one class by another. The central theoretical problem that confronted Mao and the Ultraleftists was how to legitimate turbulent class struggle on a large scale, why the revolution should be continued after the dictatorship of the proletariat had been established, and where one could find a bourgeois class after the means of production had become publicly owned since 1956.

The "gang of four" attacked this problem frontally by giving an exegesis of the term "relations of production" and by underscoring the principal and decisive role of the superstructure and theory. Ingeniously, Zhang Chunqiao distinguished three elements in the relations of production: first, ownership of the means of production; second, the form of distribution; and third, relations between men. Then he asserted: "It is perfectly correct for people to attach importance to the decisive role of the system of ownership in the relations of production. But it is incorrect to attach no importance to whether the issue of the system of ownership has been resolved in form or in reality, to the reaction exerted on the system of ownership by the *two other aspects* of the relations of production—the relations between men and the form of distribution—and to the reaction exerted on the economic base by the superstructure; *these two aspects* and the superstructure *may play a decisive role under given conditions.*"[64]

By the "form of distribution" and the "relations between men" in the economic sphere, Zhang and the Ultraleftists referred to the continued

62. See the article commemorating the fiftieth anniversary of the October Revolution, by the joint editorial departments of *Renmin ribao, Hongqi*, and *Jiefangjun bao, Hongqi*, 1967, no. 16: 15–16.

63. The following passages are based upon chapter 4. They represent a more systematic and selective formulation of the views of the "gang of four," many of which were given explicit or implicit support by Mao. Some modifications and clarifications have also been made.

64. Chang Ch'un-ch'iao (Zhang Chunqiao), "On exercising all-round dictatorship over the bourgeoisie," *Peking Review*, April 4, 1975: 7. Emphasis added.

existence of the eight-grade wage system and of "bourgeois right" in China. They developed their theory on the basis of a rather ambiguous "Important Instruction on the Question of Theory" issued by Mao in early 1975. Mao pointed out: "Our country at present practices a commodity system, and the wage system is unequal too, there being the eight-grade wage system, etc. These can only be restricted under the dictatorship of the proletariat. . . . Lenin said, 'small production engenders capitalism and the bourgeoisie continuously, daily, hourly, spontaneously, and on a mass scale.' This also occurs among a *section of the workers and a section of the Party members*. Both within the ranks of the proletariat and among the personnel of state organs there are people who follow the bourgeois style of life."[65]

The Ultraleftists generalized Mao's reference to the eight-grade wage system and the exchange of commodities through the medium of money into "bourgeois rights."[66] Zhang Chunqiao asserted that in China "bourgeois right . . . is still prevalent to a serious extent in the relations between men and holds a dominant position in distribution."[67] Another Ultraleftist wrote: "If bourgeois rights were not restricted, things like 'material incentives,' 'putting profit in command' and 'free trade' would grow, and that would lead to capitalist restoration."[68] Yao Wenyuan drew the expected conclusion that "the existence of bourgeois right provides the vital economic basis for their [new bourgeois elements'] emergence."[69] These "new bourgeois elements" would become "the new bourgeoisie."[70]

The Ultraleftists were not content to rest their case on the system of distribution and the relations between men in the economic sphere alone. They reinforced their argument by emphasizing the distinction between the form and the actuality of the system of ownership mentioned by Zhang. After reiterating Mao's dictum that superstructure may play a decisive role under given conditions, Zhang observed that "the correctness or incorrectness of the ideological and political line, and the control of leadership in the hands of one class or another decide which class owns a factory in reality."[71] Thus, political leadership determines the actual content and constitutes the reality of the system of economic ownership. The sweeping implications of this sentence had been spelled out earlier by

65. Ibid., February 28, 1975. Mao's remarks were made on December 26, 1974. Emphasis added.

66. Ibid., February 14, 1975: 4. Here and there, the singular term "bourgeois right" is also used in English translation.

67. Ibid., April 4, 1975: 3.

68. Ibid., February 21, 1975: 3.

69. Ibid., March 7, 1975: 6.

70. Ibid., 6–8.

71. Ibid., April 4, 1975: 7.

other Ultraleftists. Chi Heng wrote: "If the revisionist line should become predominent in a unit, this unit would change its nature; in which case, the ownership would be socialist in form but capitalist in reality."[72] Apparently using the "Lin Biao anti-Party clique" as a substitute for his real target, Zhou Enlai, Deng Xiaoping, and their followers, Yao Wenyuan wrote: "In the units and departments under their domination and control they turned socialist public ownership into private property of the Lin Biao anti-Party clique." Whereas Chi Heng was referring to factories and enterprises, Yao's terms "units" and "departments" were applicable to the government, the army, and the Party as well.

When in late 1975 Mao sided with the "gang of four" and dealt a nearly fatal blow against Deng for the second time during the Cultural Revolution, he justified his action by stating that "class struggle is the key link and everything else hinges on it,"[73] thus making his own directive on maintaining unity and stability subordinate to the issue of class struggle. He adopted the term "bourgeois right," which had been popularized by the Ultraleftists in their interpretation of his "Important Instruction on the Question of Theory." Most important of all, he now asserted that "it [the bourgeoisie] is right [here] in the Communist party, those in power taking the capitalist road."[74] Subsequently the Ultraleftists raised the problem that "the bourgeoisie 'is right [here] in the Communist party'" without the specifying phrase "those in power taking the capitalist road," and suggested, in effect, that the term "bourgeoisie" referred to class as an entity.[75]

Six weeks before his death, Mao's statement using the phrase "the class of bureaucratic officials" was published with some alteration to intensify its radicalism. The crucial sentence reads: "the class of the bureaucratic officials [on the one hand] and the working class and poor and middle peasants [on the other hand] are two classes in sharp opposition."[76] This statement served the ideological polemics of the Ultraleftists well. Not only were the bureaucratic officials labeled a "class," they were also implicitly equated with "those leading cadres who are taking the capitalist road" and then identified as "bourgeois elements." They were designated unequivocally "the target of the revolution" and "in the end were bound to be overthrown."

Thus, in these years, two radical strains in Mao Zedong Thought came to a head simultaneously. Together, they blocked any rational solution to

72. Ibid., February 14, 1975: 8. The following quotation from Yao can be found in *ibid.*, March 7, 1975: 9.
73. *Hongqi*, 1976, no.1: 6.
74. Ibid., 1976, no. 4: 1, 15.
75. See chap. 4 of this volume.
76. *Hongqi*, 1976, no. 7: 5.

the problem of organizing the economy. The first was his distrust of bureaucracy as such, not merely a realistic assessment of its defects and unintended consequences. He did not fully realize that bureaucracy is an inherently necessary institution in a system of planned economy based on public ownership of the principal, if not all, means of production. The second was his ideological hostility toward "commodity exchange," and the market as a principle of organizing economic life. In his "Important Instructions on the Question of Theory" published in February 1975, he pointed out that even now China "practices . . . exchange by means of money" and "a commodity system" and "that these can only be restricted under the dictatorship of the proletariat." He could not or would not conceive of an economic structure combining "markets" and "hierarchies" in various sectors and in various degree in different economic spheres. He had nothing positive to offer except ideological purity and mass actions guided by personal leadership.

The political consequences of the radicalized Mao Zedong Thought, particularly as it was interpreted by the Gang of Four, were even more devastating and immediately destructive. Since the bourgeoisie had its sources in both the economic base and the superstructure of the socialist society in China and since the bourgeoisie was right in the Party itself, class struggle had to be waged to suppress the new and old bourgeoisie and to prevent a capitalist restoration. The proletariat had to exercise all-round dictatorship over the bourgeoisie. Since the new bourgeois elements existed in the Party (the persons in power taking the capitalist road), the government (a constituent part of the class of bureaucratic officials), the intellectuals and professionals (the intellectual aristocracy and "the stinking no. 9 category"), the workers (those benefited by the eight-grade wage system), and the peasants (who retained private plots and traded in rural fairs), this all-round dictatorship[77] was exercised over major elements in all social strata. This theory of all-round dictatorship gave precise and practical meaning to the theory of continued revolution under the dictatorship of the proletariat. It extended and intensified the applicability to all sectors of society of the ideas of Yao Wenyuan's article "The Working Class Must Take Leadership in Everything."[78] It provided the justification for the penetration of the political power of the faction in control into virtually every aspect of social life. It became the ideological

77. The term "all round dictatorship over the bourgeoisie" had already been used in the 1967 article cited in n. 62. What had changed since then was the new definition of "bourgeois element" and "bourgeoisie."

78. *Hongqi*, 1968, no. 2: 3–7. This issue was published on August 25, 1968. Yao's article justified the dispatch of the worker's propaganda teams to control all universities. It was after the publication of this article that the term "stinking no. 9 category" *(chou laojiu)* became widely used to refer to the intellectuals.

foundation and guiding idea of what may be called a "revolutionary-'feudal' totalitarian" state. The Yanan synthesis of Chinese Marxism completely disintegrated. No wonder Zhang and his followers were later accused of claiming that the "thought of Zhang Chunqiao" represents the fourth milestone in the development of Marxist thought, following Marx and Engels, Lenin and Stalin, and Mao Zedong.

As I mentioned in chapters 5 and 7, the cult of personality and the concentration of power in the hands of Mao reached their highest point in this period, while the capability of the political system as a whole declined and the political forces under Mao's control were less numerous, less powerful, and less effective than before. All except one of the rules and norms governing inner-Party struggle developed in the Yanan period were discarded. The masses were mobilized by Mao and the Leftists to attack the Party committees, the government bureaucracies, the intellectuals, the professional associations, and the regularly established mass organizations with methods and influenced by feelings similar to those described with approval by Mao in his report on the Hunan peasant movement. Even with their diminished capabilities, Mao and the Leftists sought to extend political control to all spheres of society. The mass line as distinguished from mass mobilization and mass movements became an empty slogan. The immediate interests and perceived needs of the various social groups and of the individual were ignored or even ruthlessly overridden by the imperatives of ideological purity and the demands of another revolution. In the first two years of the Cultural Revolution, the Party-state was partially dismantled. It was not fully rebuilt in the remaining years of Mao's life. Superimposed on this badly damaged structure was a supreme leader supported by masses mobilized or ready to be mobilized and backed by military forces. This pattern of the relationship between political power and society, together with the political structure itself, constituted what we call "revolutionary-'feudal' totalitarianism" or what some Chinese writers called "feudal fascism."

These developments with their stunning twists and turns found symbolic expressions in the statements on "Mao Zedong Thought" in the Party constitutions adopted during this period and the two years of transition. The Ninth Party Congress, of April 1969, adopted a Party constitution which formally designated Lin Biao as Mao's "successor" and which included the following two sentences: "The Communist Party takes Marxism-Leninism-Mao Tse-tung Thought as the theoretical basis guiding its thinking. Mao Tse-tung Thought is Marxism-Leninism of the era in which imperialism is heading for total collapse and socialism is advancing to world-wide victory."[79] When the cult of Mao had passed its zenith after

79. *Peking Review,* April 30, 1969: 36

the death of Lin Biao, the Tenth Party Congress, with Zhou Enlai (on the suffrance of Mao) acting as second highest ranking leader, adopted in August 1973 a Party constitution which retained the first statement but deleted the second statement just quoted.[80] At the Eleventh Party Congress, held in August 1977, under the chairmanship of Hua Guofeng, who was in effect designated by Mao as his heir in a short sentence of six characters in a handwritten note, the new Party constitution adopted essentially the same formula with a slight and inconsequential change in wording but added a characterization of Mao "as the greatest Marxist-Leninist of our time"[81] and a paragraph of fulsome praise of Mao's past leadership.

The Revival and Development of "the Scientific Principles of Mao Zedong Thought" and the Thrust toward the Right in Search of a Middle Course: From 1978 to the Present

Following a fluid situation lasting for twenty-seven months after the death of Mao, the third major period in the development of Chinese Marxism began with the Third Plenum of the Eleventh Central Committee, held in December 1978, as its landmark.[82] It is still continuing.

One of the basic characteristics of the period is the reinterpretation and revision of Mao Zedong Thought to bring it closer to reality—a process which Peter Ludz calls the "refunctionalization of ideology."[83] As is to be expected, the Chinese leaders have repudiated, challenged, or questioned all the Leftist tenets that emerged during the Cultural Revolution, particularly the theory of continued revolution under the dictatorship of the proletariat and all propositions that lent it support or were linked to it. From our viewpoint, the basic change in the theoretical realm consists of the elevation to the position of first importance the postulate which is summarized in the Resolution on Party History in the following terms: "Seeking truth from facts. This means proceeding from reality, combining theory with practice, that is, integrating the universal principles of Marxism-Leninism with the concrete practice of the Chinese revolution." It is characterized as the first of the three basic points of "the living soul of Mao Zedong Thought." It is "the stand, viewpoint, and method embodied in its component parts."[84]

80. Ibid., September 7, 1973.
81. Ibid., September 2, 1977.
82. "On Questions of Party History—Resolution on Certain Questions in the History of Our Party since the Founding of the People's Republic of China (Adopted by the Sixth Plenum of the Eleventh Central Committee of the Communist Party of China)," *Beijing Review*, July 6, 1981: 33.
83. Peter Ludz, *The Changing Party Elite in East Germany* (Cambridge: MIT Press, 1972), 32, n. 53. See also Tang Tsou, "The Historic Change in Direction and Continuity with the Past," *China Quarterly*, June 1984: 329–33.
84. See n. 82 above.

This revived epistemological and methodological postulate took, at first, an extreme and, from the viewpoint of the philosophy of science, untenable form: "Practice is the sole criterion for testing truth."[85] It provided the leading Chinese reformers with a timely and powerful justification for their challenge to and reexamination of the validity of all the theories, concepts, programs, and policies advocated or endorsed by Mao in his last years and pushed to the extreme by the Ultraleftists. It undermined Hua Guofeng's position, stated as late as March 1977 in *Hongqi*, that "whatever the decision made by Chairman Mao was, we will resolutely support; whatever Chairman Mao's directive was, we will unswervingly obey."[86] It also served as a point of departure in repudiating the characterization of the ideological and political lines of Lin Biao and the "gang of four" as "Rightist" or "pseudo-Leftist but genuinely Rightist." It thus paved the way to designate them as Leftist or Ultraleftist.[87] This emphasis on the Leftist errors committed since 1957, as distinguished from the Rightist, "feudal" orientations found in the cult of personality and in the use of "power technique" *(quanshu)*, enabled the reformers to advocate and adopt theories, concepts, programs, and policies which had been condemned during the Cultural Revolution as "revisionist" and "Rightist."

By underscoring "facts," "reality," and "practice," the revived epistemological and methodological postulate justifies, as it did in the first period, the Party's attention to, and orientation toward, the needs, interests, demands, life situations, and behavioral patterns of social groups and individuals. It gives greater weight to the perceived interests and demands of the various social groups and individuals as they impinge upon the Party and the state, especially upon the Party's ideas about these interests and demands. Not accidentally, the mass line as distinguished from mass movements and mass mobilization is characterized in the Resolution on Party History as the second of the three basic points of the "living soul of Mao Zedong Thought." Popular support derived from the practicality and

85. Hu Fuming, "Practice is the sole criterion for testing truth," *Guangming ribao*, May 11, 1978. For a discussion of the origin of this article and an analysis of its political implications, see chap. 5. For its impact on rural policies, see Tang Tsou, Marc Blecher, and Mitch Meisner, "Policy Change at the National Summit and Institutional Transformation at the Local Level: The Case of Tachai and Hsiyang in the Post-Mao Era," in *Select Papers from the Center for Far Eastern Studies*, no. 4, 1979–80, ed. Tang Tsou (Chicago: Center for Far Eastern Studies, University of Chicago, 1981). This principle was challenged on the ground that it cannot explain why Communism should be accepted as truth since Communism has not been proved or implemented in practice. Skeptics in China have also expressed the view that Communism as a goal is distant and vague.

86. Hua's position is called the "two-whatever policy" or "two-whatever doctrine" in English translation. Sometimes the term "two-whateverism" is used by various writers.

87. See articles by Jin Wen, Wu Hui, and Zhang Xianyang, Wang Guixiu in *Xinhua yuebao (wenzhai ban)*, 1979, no. 3: 6–14.

success of policies is thus given priority over ideological purity. Even more important, this epistemological postulate forces the political leaders and factions in conflict to justify their programs in its terms.

The obverse side of the reelevation of this postulate to the position of first importance in Chinese Marxism is the questioning, or at least qualification, of Mao's reformulation of historical materialism. Some theoreticians argue that even when superstructure, theory, and relations of production play the main and decisive role, these principal aspects of contradiction cannot exist without the opposite, admittedly secondary, aspects—the economic base, practice, and the forces of production. The principal aspects should receive emphasis, but the secondary aspects should not be neglected. To emphasize only one aspect to the neglect of the other is an expression of "metaphysical" thinking and does not conform to reality. Others argue that it is the forces of production themselves which bring about the conditions in which relations of production, theory, and superstructure can play the principal and decisive role. Still others feel that Engels's later formulations represent the correct Marxist position and Mao's modification is unnecessary and misleading. No official conclusion has been drawn in this theoretical debate. But there is no doubt that Mao's dictum has been downgraded. It is not invoked as a justification for the Party's program, even when the Party admittedly altered the relations of production in order to develop the forces of production, as in the rapid implementation of the system of responsibility for agricultural production discussed below.

Such is not the fate of other tenets of the Ultraleftists which are related directly or indirectly to Mao's dictum. Even before the Third Plenum, Mao's statement that the bourgeoisie "is right in the Party, those in power taking the capitalist road" was flatly rejected as completely ignoring the minimum common sense of Marx.[88] As to the question of "bourgeois right," it was argued that it can only be limited and cannot be eliminated in one morning, and "as to how and to what extent it is to be restricted, this depends on the material and spiritual conditions at the time."[89]

After the Third Plenum declared that turbulent class struggle on a large scale had basically concluded, Deng in the March 1979 meeting on theoretical work went one step further. He asserted that "we oppose the overextension of class struggle. We do not admit that there is a bourgeois class in the Party. We also do not admit that under a socialist system, after the effective elimination of the exploiting class as well as the conditions mak-

88. *Renmin ribao*, March 14, 1977: 1.

89. *Hongqi*, 1977, no. 2: 16. It was also suggested that the German term which had been translated as "bourgeois right" or "bourgeois rights" should have been translated as "bourgeois interests."

ing exploitation possible, a bourgeois class or any other exploiting class can be produced."[90] The concept of "a class of bureaucratic officials" (guanliao zhuyizhe jieji) was specifically repudiated in a lengthy article, without naming Mao.[91] The authors explained that "class differentiation is based on the criterion of relations of production and system of ownership, not on the criterion of political thinking. If political thinking is used as a criterion to differentiate class, extremely great confusion will be created, the essence of classes will be covered up and the demarcation between classes will be blurred. . . . Throughout human history, it is always classes that produce parties rather than parties that produce classes. Always, parties are parts of classes. We cannot reverse this relationship and say that a class becomes a part of a party."[92] This commonplace in Marxism was explicitly directed against the theory of the "gang of four."

Reexamination of the Cultural Revolution went much further than mere repudiation of the specific tenets just mentioned. It also led to the conclusion that there is a limit to the validity of class analysis, which traces every event or every mistake to its class origin. It brought about the realization that class struggle is not a method to solve all problems. A Chinese theorist alerted us to the fact that the Resolution on Party History did not analyze the Cultural Revolution by tracing it to its class origin. According to his interpretation, that document explained it first by Mao's errors of leadership and then by a set of complex social and historical causes. These causes include the Party's lack of clear understanding of many laws governing social development and socialist reconstruction in a socialist society, its tendency to view as class struggle many new problems and new situations that should not be construed as class struggle, its readiness to continue the use of old and frequently practiced methods of class struggle, and finally China's long "feudal" history. It was, he asserted, a "metaphysical" viewpoint not to admit that Marxists can make mistakes and to find the causes of these errors not in themselves but in other classes. Then he drew three broad conclusions: that class analysis should not be simplified to merely finding the class origin of problems, that while some ideological problems are influenced by classes, others have nothing to do with class influence, and that ideological problems should be resolved by correct ideological work, not by the method of class struggle, which merely intensifies the contradiction.[93]

90. Quoted in the article by Jie Wen, Hongqi, 1981, no. 20: 27. The full text of this speech is now published in Selected Works of Deng (see n. 16 above). This quotation can be found on p. 155.

91. Lin Boye and Shen Che, "Ping suowei fandui guanliaozhuyizhe jieji," Hongqi, 1981, no. 5: 12–18.

92. Ibid., 14.

93. Article by Yang Fengchu, Hongqi, 1981, no. 18.: 41–43. See also article by Fang Qiao, ibid., 1981, no. 23: 29–30.

Since scientific laws are for Marxists the highest form of truth, seeking truth from facts so as to understand and solve some new problem has come to mean searching for the scientific laws governing social development. Just as they believe that the nationwide victory in 1949 came from their discovery and effective implementation of the "laws governing the Chinese revolution," they have been engaged in a search for knowledge of the general laws governing socialist reconstruction and of the specific manifestation of these laws under Chinese conditions, i.e., the specific laws governing Chinese socialist reconstruction in different periods of time and in different areas of activities.[94] In the course of this endeavor, they have downgraded Mao's dictum on the principal and decisive role of the relations of production, theory, and the superstructure, which lies at the heart of the laws of the Chinese revolution, as noted above. This theoretical development necessarily entails restating the relationship between politics and other spheres of social life and reexamining the principle that "politics is in command of everything," which was pushed to the extreme by Lin Biao and the Ultraleftists durng the Cultural Revolution.

This restatement and reexamination takes the form of what we can call a "sociological postulate."[95] This sociological postulate can be reconstructed as follows. Every sphere of social life has its special characteristics *(tedian)* and is governed by special laws of an objective nature. Political leadership can and should create general conditions and a framework favorable to the operation of these laws. It can use these laws to promote the desired development. But it cannot violate these laws without suffering serious consequences. This sociological postulate was formulated first and elaborated and applied most thoroughly in the sphere of economics. In a speech made in July 1978 by Hu Qiaomu, then the president of the newly created Chinese Academy of the Social Sciences and now a member of the Politburo, Hu made the following points: Economic laws are like "natural laws," and "natural laws" cannot be dispensed with. They cannot be altered at the will of the society, the government, or the authorities. "Over and above the economic laws in objective existence, politics itself cannot create other laws and impose them on the economy. In fact, insofar as the laws of economic development are concerned, the mission of correct political leadership lies precisely in making the maximum effort to assure that socialist economic work operates within the scope of these objective laws." In a socialist society, political power can bring "enormous damage to economic development, if it is misused."[96]

94. Article by the commentator of *Hongqi*, ibid., 1982, no. 20: 2–6.

95. The following three paragraphs are drawn with some changes from Tsou, "Back from the Brink of Revolutionary-'Feudal' Totalitarianism," chap. 5 of this volume. Some new information is added.

96. Hu Ch'iao-mu (Hu Qiaomu), "Observe Economic Laws, Speed up the Four Modernizations," *Peking Review*, November 10, 1978: 8, 9.

These objective, economic laws are nothing profound. They merely restore a measure of rationality in economic policy which was overridden by the quest for revolutionary and ideological purity during the Cultural Revolution. The imperatives derived from these laws are succinctly summarized in a short statement by Liu Guoguang: the improvement of the material standard of living of the people and the satisfaction of their cultural needs as the aim of production; the adjustment of the relations of production to the forces of production by encouraging collectively owned enterprises and, within certain limits, individually owned enterprises; recognition of the spontaneous functioning of the "law of value" as a necessary and beneficial supplement to the planned economy; and the deliberate use by the state of the "law of value" within certain limits in the production and circulation of commodities under state plans.[97] Another theorist concludes that the theses "politics should be in command" and "politics must be given first place when compared with economics," are inaccurate or not applicable to the current stage of development.[98]

The current leaders in all spheres of social life, particularly those in the areas of science, education, and literature and the arts, have followed Hu Qiaomu's lead in expressing similar views on the special characteristics in these areas and special laws governing them. The most important political implication of this sociological postulate is that there exist certain areas of autonomy in economic and social life into which political power cannot and should not intrude. It opens up the possibility for specialists and professionals in various spheres to show what these special laws are. Its proclamation coincided with the reemergence of the economists, educators, natural scientists, and social scientists from their suppressed status to positions of greater importance in the political system. It thus symbolizes and legitimizes the reversal of the historic trend toward increasing penetration of politics into all spheres of social life which emerged after the May Fourth period and which reached its zenith during the Cultural Revolution. It has also marked a new beginning in the relationship between political power and society.

But this change is uneven in different social sectors. The changes in the relationship between political power and the economy have occurred faster and have gone further than the relationship between political power and civil society. Within the economy, changes in the agricultural-rural sector have gone far ahead of those in other sectors and have followed a steady course. The Party adopted six documents in the period between December 1978 and January 1984 which reversed the direction of rural policies since the acceleration of the cooperativization movement in 1955–

97. *Hongqi*, 1982, no. 20: 26.
98. Article by Shi Youxin, ibid., 1982, no. 21: 8.

56. Each document went beyond the earlier one in granting a greater degree of flexibility and autonomy to units at the lowest level, to households, and to individuals, for managing their own work, as well as in providing them with greater material incentives. Step by step, these documents have led to the firm establishment of what is called "the system of responsibility for agricultural production,"[99] of which the central feature is a direct link between yield and reward. More than 90 percent of the basic accounting units now use one of the several forms of this system.

Of the various forms used in farming, it is the system of total responsibility of the household, or household comprehensive-contract system *(baogan daohu, or simply da baogan)*, which gives the household the greatest degree of autonomy in managing its own affairs and links reward and yield most directly. Under this system, a household retains all its produce after paying agricultural taxes and certain levies to the production team and sells at fixed prices a definite amount of its produce to the state specified in a contract. An article published in December 1982 revealed the phenomenal increase in the use of this system. In January 1980 only 0.02 percent of the basic accounting units had adopted the system. By October 1981 the figure had grown to 38 percent, and by late 1982, it was around 70 percent. *Baogan daohu* has now become the principal form of the responsibility system[100] and the household has again become the basic unit of production in the countryside. Involved in the development of the responsibility system is the replacement of authority relations by contract relations as the chief means of regulating the state-society relationship at the grassroots levels in rural areas. Another significant policy is the encouragement of "specialized households," "specialized teams," and "specialized villages," marked by a higher degree of division of labor and the production of agricultural and other commodities for exchange rather than for direct consumption by the producers. In the last three years, the regime has been extending the system of responsibility to other sectors in the economy. But the outcome of this effort is still uncertain.

In civil society those engaged in producing works of literature and art have encountered more visible difficulties than most other professionals. In contrast to the steadily accelerating development in agriculture, Party policy regarding writers and their work has undergone a series of fluctuations. (The well-known case of Bai Hua resulted from one such swing.) These oscillations in official policy indicate clearly both the tendency toward change and the limits to change. On the one hand, Mao's dictum, announced at the Yanan Forum, that literature and art are subordinate to

99. For an account of the evolution of this system up to October 1981, see Tang Tsou, Marc Blecher, and Mitch Meisner, "The Responsibility System in Agriculture," *Modern China*, January 1982: 41–103. Parts of the article are reproduced in chap. 4 of this volume.

100. Article by Xiang Qiyuan, *Jingji yanjiu*, December 1982: 11.

politics was officially abandoned. The Party also decided not to use the slogan that literature and art must serve politics—a slogan derived from Mao's dictum and used since the 1940s. In its place, the Party has proposed the slogan "Literature and art serve the people and socialism." On the other hand, the Party retains Mao's view that literature and art cannot be separated from politics. The slogan "Let a hundred flowers bloom and let a hundred schools contend" was specifically declared *not* to be the only principle or policy dealing with literature and art. Other principles must be taken into account. There is no doubt that political control had been tightened since the highest point of liberalization in October–November 1979, at the time of the Fourth Congress of Writers and Artists. But still another swing toward liberalization took place in late December 1984 when Hu Qili, representing the Secretariat of the CCP, gave renewed assurances of greater freedom in creative writing to the writers at the Fourth Conference of the Representatives of the Writers' Association.

Since the Chinese Communists believe that ideological uniformity is the basis of political unity and that the ideological line directly influences the political and organizational lines, it was imperative for them to arrive at an authoritative interpretation of Mao Zedong Thought and the role of Mao in the Chinese Communist movement and the regime, particularly during the Cultural Revolution. This endeavor involved many debates and conflicts which are still hidden from us. But after some delay and under the firm control of Deng,[101] it finally culminated in the Resolution on Certain Questions in the History of Our Party since the Founding of the People's Republic of China, adopted on June 27, 1981, by the Sixth Plenum of the Eleventh Central Committee.[102] Not unexpectedly, the Party now forcefully rejected the "erroneous 'Left' theses" advanced by Mao in initiating the Cultural Revolution as "obviously inconsistent with the system of Mao Zedong Thought, which is the integration of the universal principles of Marxism with the concrete practice of the Chinese revolution." But this "theoretical synthesis of China's unique experience in its protracted revolution in accordance with the basic principles of Marxism-Leninism" was made by "Chinese Communists with Comrade Mao Zedong as their chief representative." In other words, it was not made by Mao alone. After listing its six substantive contributions, which have "enriched and developed Marxism-Leninism," the Resolution concluded that "the stand, viewpoint, and method embodied in its component parts . . . boil down to three basic points: to seek truth from facts,

101. For Deng's role, see *Selected Works of Deng*, 255–74. For a discussion, see Tang Tsou, "The Historic Change in Direction and Continuity with the Past," *China Quarterly*, June 1984: 343–45.

102. *Beijing Review*, July 6, 1981: 10–39. Further quotations in this and the next two paragraphs are all from this article.

the mass line, and independence." The resolution declared that "we must continue to uphold Mao Zedong Thought, study it in earnest, and apply its stand, viewpoint, and method in studying the new situation and solving the new problems arising in the course of practice."

For the period between 1949 and 1957, the Party acknowledged its "shortcomings and errors" in being "over-hasty in pressing on with agricultural cooperation and the transformation of private handicraft and commercial establishments," and in its failure "to do a proper job in employing and handling some of the former industrialists and businessmen." For the ten years before the Cultural Revolution, the Party admitted that "the scope of this struggle [against the Rightists after June 1957] was made too broad." But in upholding the anti-Rightist campaign as "entirely correct and necessary" while in effect rehabilitating all except a handful of the well-known "Rightists," the Party has unwittingly revealed the hollowness of its case. Actually its mistake stemmed from a failure to distinguish the "launching of a resolute counterattack" in the realm of public opinion from the practice of putting an obnoxious label on individuals on account of their opinions and inflicting on them administrative and organizational punishments and discrimination (or, to use an American analogy, failure to distinguish open democratic debate from McCarthyism). Such failure unfortunately has long been the practice rather than the exception in Chinese politics. But the Party made a frank though somewhat understated acknowledgment of Mao's error in "initiating" the criticism of Peng Dehuai. It also mentioned Mao's "theoretical and practical mistakes concerning class struggle in a socialist society," "his personal arbitrariness," and the growth of "the personality cult" along with the undermining of "democratic centralism in Party life." But it rightly accepted its collective responsibility for the failure of "the Central Committee of the Party . . . to ratify these mistakes in good time."

As for the Cultural Revolution, Mao's "principal theses" for initiating it "conformed neither to Marxism-Leninism nor to Chinese reality." His "personal leadership" took the place of "the collective leadership of the Central Committee" and the cult of Mao was pushed to the extreme. To him belongs the "chief responsibility for the grave 'Left' error of the 'Cultural Revolution'" which brought "catastrophe to the Party, the state, and the whole people." But Mao's mistakes took shape gradually over a period of time before the Cultural Revolution. The Party acknowledged once again that the Central Committee "should be held partly responsible" for its failure to check this development. Mao imagined that "his theory and practice were Marxist and that they were essential for the consolidation of the dictatorship of the proletariat. . . . Herein lies his tragedy." But Mao also checked and rectified some of the "specific mistakes" made during the Cultural Revolution while he frustrated the Ultraleftists' "ambition to seize supreme leadership." "For these reasons, and particularly for his vital contributions to the cause of the revolution over the years, the Chinese people have always regarded Comrade Mao Zedong as their respected and beloved great leader and teacher." "Comrade Mao Zedong was a great Marxist and a great proletarian revolutionary, strategist, and theorist. . . . His merits are primary and his errors secondary."

This interpretation of Mao Zedong Thought and Mao's role in its formulation constituted the basis of the statements on Mao Zedong Thought in the Party constitution adopted by the Twelfth Congress in September 1982. On the one hand, the Party constitution states that "the Communist Party of China takes Marxism-Leninism and Mao Zedong Thought as its guide to action."[103] It thus gives deserved credit to the historical contributions of Mao Zedong Thought and recognizes its continued validity when properly interpreted, thus maintaining continuity with the past. On the other hand, it declares: "The Chinese Communists, with Comrade Mao Zedong as their chief representative, created Mao Zedong Thought by integrating the universal principles of Marxism-Leninism with the concrete practice of the Chinese Revolution. Mao Zedong Thought is Marxism applied and developed in China; it consists of a body of theoretical principles concerning the revolution and construction in China and a summary of experience therein, both of which have been proved correct by practice; it represents the crystallized, collective wisdom of the Communist Party of China."[104] This statement gives proper credit to Mao as the systematizer and codifier of, as well as the chief contributor to, the theory and practice which led the Party to victory. But it recognizes the contributions of other leaders to various parts of this system. It implicitly repudiates the cult of Mao while explicitly preserving the integrity of Mao Zedong Thought, which has taken deep roots in China, providing a common framework for political analysis and a common language for political discourse. It rejects posthumously Mao's claim, accepted by others in the past, to be the authoritative interpreter of Mao Zedong Thought. It implies that the Party as a whole, or its collective leadership, is the authoritative interpreter. It lends support to the conclusion that Mao in his last years deviated from the true Mao Zedong Thought and that the present leadership has taken steps to revive the real nature of that system of theory and practice by eliminating mistakes and returning to the correct path. Above all, it legitimizes the decision that China is to search for its own road to socialism and modernization.

But ideological debates and political conflicts can never be ended by the adoption of supposedly authoritative documents. Within a year, an-

103. *Beijing Review*, September 20, 1982: 8. This statement is similar but not identical to that in the 1945 Party constitution.
104. Ibid.

other oscillation in the sphere of ideology and literature occurred. It may be recalled that ever since 1978 many Chinese reformers had gone back to the ideas of Marx in their search for answers to questions about the past, present, and future. Many articles had been published on the early manu-scripts of Marx, particularly on Marx's idea of humanism and his notion of alienation. Zhou Yang's long article on Marxism, published on March 16 1983, in commemoration of the one hundredth anniversary of Marx's death, can be taken as a summary of the conclusions reached by a group of reformers within the Party. Zhou pointed out that the early Marx had affirmed humanism. Although Marx rejected Feuerbach's *anthropologis-mus*, he never basically rejected humanism as such. Later, his formula-tion of historical materialism and his theory of surplus value put his ideas on humanism on a more scientific basis and did not constitute any aban-donment of them. Marxism includes humanism. It affirms the value of man. Paralleling Wang Ruoshui's earlier article, Zhou suggested that aliena-tion can exist in socialist society. The outcomes brought about by the stu-pid mistake of failing to understand objective economic laws constitute alienation in the economic realm. The abuse of power given by the people to public servants but used by them to become the people's masters is alienation in the political realm, or the alienation of power. The cult of personality is the most typical case of alienation in the ideological realm.[105]

Suddenly, in conjunction with its campaign of Party rectification and of purging unrepentant Leftists, the Party launched an attack on "spiritual pollution," with "bourgeois liberalization," "bourgeois humanism," "the abstract theory of human nature," and the concept of alienation as its ideological targets. Thus, the Party center intervened once again in an ideological debate among the reformist followers of Deng Xiaoping. But this attack was contained. Its scope was sharply restricted, and its ferocity declined within a few weeks. Even on the difficult abstract questions of ideology, so important to the Chinese, a compromise was reached by January 1984. In a significant article, Hu Qiaomu firmly rejected use of the theory of alienation in analyzing the problems of a socialist society. But he accepted "humanism" as "an ethical principle and a moral norm" while repudiating it as "a world view and a philosophy of history."[106] Pre-sumably, the combining of humanism as an ethical principle with histori-cal materialism as a philosophy of history is the content of "socialist hu-manism," or "Marxist humanism," which is said to have its antecedent in the "revolutionary humanism" developed during the period of the revolu-tionary civil wars. Soon writers seized upon Hu Qiaomu's remarks to

105. Zhou Yang, "An examination of several theoretical problems concerning marxism," *Renmin ribao*, March 16, 1983: 4, 5. Wang Ruoshui's article was published in *Xinwen zhan-xian*, 1980, no. 8: 8–12.
106. *Renmin ribao*, January 27, 1984: 1–5.

stress the importance of "socialist humanism."[107] Thus the earlier period of liberalization and academic debate has left an indelible imprint on the current ideological line.

But amidst these ideological shifts and the changing relationship between political power and society, there is one constant. The framework of the Leninist Party-state is not and will not be altered. The supremacy of the Party is not supposed to be questioned. Once announced, the Party's decision must not be publicly challenged. This constant is the concrete meaning of the slogan of firmly upholding the four basic principles.

Thus the shifts in ideology since the Third Plenum and the reaffirmation of the four fundamental principles form two zones of demarcations, defining the middle course along which the Party seeks to maintain its continuity with the past and at the same time to achieve the "four modernizations," to establish socialist legality, and to bring about "a high level of democracy." This new synthesis of Chinese Marxism is the diametrical opposite of Mao's ideas advanced during the Cultural Revolution and pushed to extreme by the Ultraleftists. But it is also different in many substantive aspects from Mao's synthesis during the first major period, including the Yanan era. Many of his theories and dicta have been abandoned or downgraded. But in one basic aspect and in its fundamental spirit, it adheres to Mao's synthesis. It tries to confront new situations and to solve new problems by a basic epistemological and methodological postulate which looks simple on paper but which raises more questions than it answers when it is applied to complex problems.[108] The question remains whether the current leaders will be as successful in reconstructing and modernizing China as Mao and his colleagues were in making the Chinese revolution.

The Party, the State, and the Citizens: Reforming the Political Institutions and Searching for a "Democracy on a High Level"

The Cultural Revolution left China with a profound authority crisis, which many outside observers describe as combining a crisis of faith in socialism, a crisis of confidence in the future, and a crisis of trust in the Party-state *(sanxin weiji)*. Although the top leaders officially deny the existence of these three crises, they frequently warn Party members that improvement of the Party's working style is a question of life or death, of the continued existence or the extinction of the Party *(shengsi cunwang)*. In response to this crisis there has developed among some of the top Party leaders a powerful impulse to reform the Party, the state system, and the

107. Ibid., April 18, 1984: 3.
108. It is not accidental that the Chinese are extremely interested in Western theories of scientific decision making. See Xia Yulong et al., "Lun juece kexuehua," *Zhongguo shehui kexue*, 1982, no. 3: 3–25.

economy, as well as to redefine the relationship between the Party-state and society. If the reforms and the reformist impulses of the first three decades of the twentieth century can be said to have facilitated rather than forestalled revolution, then the series of Chinese Communist revolutions culminating in the "continued revolution under the dictatorship of the proletariat" has assuredly led to sweeping reforms in all areas of sociopolitical life within the framework of a Party-state. These reforms are precisely the changes that the Cultural Revolution was supposed to prevent and to forestall. They would not have gone so far and been undertaken so soon if the Cultural Revolution had not driven home the devastating consequences of certain ideas of Mao and some features of the Party-state itself when these were pushed to the extreme by Mao and the Ultraleftists. Yet at the same time, the Cultural Revolution left many legacies that make adoption and implementation of the reforms difficult.

These self-imposed changes have stemmed from a learning experience of the Party, particularly of its top leaders. In the realm of political action, learning is frequently based on the experience of defeat and victory, success and failure, in the past. The history of the Chinese Communist movement and regime has highlighted this aspect of the learning process. The Party admits that as its knowledge of the "laws governing the Chinese revolution" and now the "laws governing socialist construction in China" is based on both "positive and negative experiences," just as its reformist programs and policies are. But as we saw in chapter 7, this present learning experience has taken place among the top leaders under very special circumstances. In their youthful and idealistic days, these leaders joined the Party to fight against political and social oppression. In their middle age, they became the oppressors, the persecutors, and the inquisitors. In their old age or late middle age, they were themselves oppressed, condemned, and denounced by others in the name of still another revolution. Now in the remaining years of their lives, they have regained their power and authority. They have viewed the political system they themselves created both from the top and from the bottom, from the inside and from the outside, as its beneficiaries and as its victims. It is this learning experience that has shaped current programs and has provided the impetus behind them. But this learning experience has occurred within a definite historical context: the changes wrought in the economy by both the Party's correct and its incorrect policies, the rise of two new generations to top and middle positions in the Party and society, and a vastly different international environment—an environment characterized by a changed relationship with the two superpowers and by the contrast (since 1959) between China's slow rate of economic growth and the relatively speedy growth in other developing countries.

In this latest period of Chinese Marxism, the process of emergence, adoption, and implementation of the Party's political programs and policies is different from that of the period 1927–57; rather it parallels that of the period 1917–27. That is to say, ideological debates have preceded, or in some instances, immediately accompanied, the adoption and implementation of concrete programs and policies. One common feature, however, has characterized Chinese development throughout the twentieth century. The reforms, as distinguished from the revolution itself, have always been pushed from above. To be sure, the top leaders have responded to social demands and needs, but they have always made authoritative decisions autonomously, on the basis of lessons learned from the past.

In concrete terms, these reforms fall into three categories, which I shall discuss in the following three sections of this essay. They are first, reforming the leadership institutions and the cadre institutions of the Party; second, redefining the relationship between the Party and the state while reforming the state institutions; and third, searching for "socialist democracy" and "socialist legality" while taking the concept of citizenship more seriously than before.

Involved in all these reforms are four underlying processes. The first consists in self-criticism, self-improvement, self-discipline, and self-renewal, by which the Party hopes to avoid abuse of power by its leaders, particularly by a single leader at the highest level; seeks to revitalize its links with the masses; and attempts to replace the old technically incompetent and poorly educated cadres with younger, technically competent, and better-educated functionaries. The second process is self-limitation and precommitment on the part of the CCP in its relationship with the state.[109] The third is the search for a new balance between a strong Party-state and the need to develop the initiative, energy, creativity, and capabilities of the individuals and groups in society.[110] The fourth and fundamental one is the resumption of the process of institutionalization and the abandonment of mass mobilization so as to reestablish a stable political order in a period of rapid social change.[111]

Reforming the Leadership Institutions and Cadre Institutions of the Party

At no time since 1949 have the Party leaders themselves come to realize as fully as now the ease with which political power can be abused by both the top Party leader and the Party itself, at all levels of the political sys-

---

109. See Jon Elster, *Ulysses and the Sirens* (Cambridge: Cambridge University Press, 1970), 36–47, for a discussion of the importance of precommitment and binding oneself. Elster's terms are used here without some of their technical meanings but in reference to the ideas developed in his discussion.

110. See the first section of this chaper.

111. See Samuel Huntington, *Political Order and Social Change* (New Haven, Conn.: Yale University Press, 1968), for a general discussion of this fundamental process.

tem. They have self-consciously and repeatedly raised the question of how a party in power should behave, institutionalize its authority structure and its decision-making processes, and regulate its relationship with the state, society, and the individual citizen. Since they continue to reject both the two-party system and Western-style democracy, their reformist programs pose the following questions: To what extent can they accomplish the task of maintaining the delicate balance between the two requisites for China's political development in the twentieth century—strengthening all political institutions to enhance the capability of the state and developing the energy, capabilities, and creativity of individuals and social groups within a strong state? To what extent can they maintain a Leninist Party-state and at the same time adopt a measure of checks and balances within the political system, as well as a relatively decentralized arrangement of political authority and some degree of "institutional pluralism"? How can such a Party-state prevent or at least minimize the chances of power being abused and make Party and government organs more responsive to the multifarious social interests?

In the area of reform of the Party and state, particularly the reform of leadership institutions, Deng Xiaoping has played a decisive and indispensable role. Here the direction, the pace, and the limits of change have been firmly in his hands. Deng wished to eliminate the faults of the leadership institutions and cadre institutions while strengthening the one-party system. He charted a middle course of action by the simultaneous use of two slogans: (1) In upholding the Four Cardinal Principles, "the crucial thing is to uphold Party leadership" (i.e., other parties and groups serve the socialist cause only under the precondition of recognizing the leadership of the CCP) and (2) "In order to uphold Party leadership, we must strive to improve it."[112] The ills of the Chinese political system were diagnosed by Deng as "bureaucratism," "excessive concentration of power," "the patriarchal system," the "system of life tenure of cadres in leading posts," and "special privileges of all sorts."[113]

Bureaucratism is, Deng recognized, rooted in Chinese tradition. But he stressed three factors that distinguish contemporary bureaucratism from that of the past. One is the Party's long-held view that the socialist system and the system of planned management require that there be at the Party center a high concentration of power over the economy, politics, culture, and society.[114] The second is the absence of any set of strict administrative laws and rules and of any firm system of individual responsibility in leading organs in all fields. The third is the lack of regular, ac-

112. See "The Current Situation and Tasks," *Selected Works of Deng*, 230–32
113. "The Reform of the Leadership Institutions of the Party and the State," ibid., 287.
114. Ibid., 287–88.

cepted ways of dealing with recruitment, reward and punishment, retirement, resignation, and dismissal.

An excessive concentration of power develops, according to Deng's admission, when under the guise of strengthening the monistic leadership of the Party (yiyuanhua lingdao),[115] powers are improperly and heedlessly concentrated in the hands of the several secretaries, particularly the first secretary. As a result of this concentration the first secretary takes command of everything and makes all decisions. "The monistic leadership of the Party thus becomes the leadership of an individual." He found the sources of this phenomenon in China's "feudal despotism," in the tradition of the other Communist parties during the Comintern period, and in the history of the CCP itself.

When Deng criticized the overconcentration of power in Party committees, he was not referring merely to power within the Party. In effect he was referring also to the Party's penetration into and control over all other sociopolitical spheres. He observed that on several occasions in the past the Party had attempted to divide power between the Party center and the local units, but it had never faced the problem of defining the Party's sphere of authority on the one hand and that of "the government, economic organizations, mass organizations, etc.,"[116] on the other. He placed special emphasis on solving the problem of the failure to separate the Party and the government and of the displacement of the government by the Party. He also suggested that, in state enterprises, the system of giving responsibility to the head of a factory or the manager *under the leadership of the Party committee* be gradually replaced by the system of giving responsibility to the factory head and manager *under the leadership of the management committee of a factory or the board of trustees of a company.*[117] He expressed his belief that the excessive concentration of power

115. Ibid., 288–89. The phrase *yiyuanhua lingdao* is generally translated as "unified leadership." This translation does not fully express either the literal meaning or the political implications of the Chinese phrase.

116. Ibid., 289. For the importance of the boundaries between political power and other spheres of social life, see Michael Walzer's *The Spheres of Justice* (New York: Basic Books, 1983).

117. Deng's speech delivered on August 18, 1980, as reproduced in *Zhonggong yanjiu*, July 15, 1981: 135 (emphasis added). The rapidly changing situation in China and the shifts in policies are vividly revealed in the following developments. This suggestion to reduce the authority of the Party committee does not appear in his speech as printed in *Selected Works of Deng*, published in July 1983. But in his report on the work of government delivered on May 15, 1984, Premier Zhao Ziyang declared that the system of giving full responsibility to the head of a factory or the manager of a company should be gradually implemented. Zhao has apparently gone further than Deng's earlier suggestion in giving more power to the head of a factory or manager of a company when he said that the *state* entrusts the factory head or company manager with full authority and responsibility over the direction of production,

in the Party is no longer suitable to the development of the socialist cause because the tasks of socialist reconstruction have become extremely arduous and complex. For this outside observer, Deng's criticism of the principle of monistic leadership of the Party and excessive control by the Party over other sociopolitical spheres points to one of the most significant but little discussed aspects of "the historic change in direction."

Deng's criticism of the "patriarchal style" was directed against any individual's putting himself above the organization, thus using the organization as his instrument, replacing collective leadership with the cult of personality, demanding absolute obedience, making others appendages to himself, and ordering them to perform tasks in contravention of the Party constitution and of state laws. He listed life tenure for leading officials as one of the major faults of the system and said that its elimination was a pressing item of business on the agenda for immediate action.

Finally, he defined "special privileges" broadly, as any political and economic privileges that are not specifically granted by legal or institutional arrangements. He traced again their existence to the lingering influence of "feudalism" and the absence of a tradition of democracy and of legal institutions. He affirmed the principle that "all citizens are equal before the law and all Party members are equal before the Party constitution and Party discipline." [118] He no longer believed, he said, that merely changing the style of work and the thinking of the cadres constitutes an adequate solution. The emphasis should be placed on "effectively reforming and perfecting the institutions of the Party and the state." [119] Thus the need for institutionalization has finally been given top priority after the CCP has been in power for over thirty years and after it has been taught an unforgettable lesson by the Cultural Revolution. The lesson is, in Deng's words, that "although one cannot say that individuals should not bear their share of responsibility [for what has happened and will happen], one must say that the problems in the leadership and organizational systems are persistent, long-term problems of fundamental and overall importance." [120]

The concrete steps proposed by Deng for reforming of the system of Party leadership included reestablishment of the Secretariat and establishment of an advisory commission, to be elected by the Party Congress. Surprisingly, *Selected Works of Deng Xiaoping* contains no specific statement by Deng on the question of abolishing the Party chairmanship, al-

---

management, and administration. See *Renmin ribao*, June 2, 1984: 2, and the short editorial in *Renmin ribao*, June 23, 1984: 1.

118. "The Reform of the Leadership Institutions of the Party and the State," *Selected Works of Deng*, 292.

119. Ibid., 296.

120. Ibid., 293.

though it is generally believed that he advocated or at least strongly supported this decision. He proposed to institutionalize the principle of combining collective leadership with individual responsibility in Party committees at all levels. He suggested the elimination of life tenure for leading officials in the Party. He advocated the establishment of a measure of separation between the Party and the government. With regard to the question of the relationship between the Party and the state, there is in *Selected Works* no statement by Deng which corresponds exactly to a remarkable sentence in the preamble to the Party constitution: "the Party must conduct its activities within the limits permitted by the Constitution and the laws of the state,"[121] the importance of which will be discussed later.

As early as December 1980 Deng endorsed the principle of the "institutionalization of democracy and its codification into laws," as well as the principle of the inseparability of "socialist democracy" and "socialist legality."[122] In recommendations made in August 1980 Deng supported proposals for revising the state constitution to enable the people to enjoy full rights of citizenship and to improve the system of people's congresses at all levels.[123] This general endorsement made possible the adoption of the many detailed provisions in the state constitution on these matters.[124] But Deng was also one of the strongest advocates of the elimination of the so-called "four great freedoms," the removal of "Democracy Wall," and the suppression of "illegal" journals and "illegal" organizations through the use of "socialist laws" and the socialist legal system.[125] For him, socialist democracy is "definitely not a democracy which discards the socialist legal system, the Party's leadership, and discipline and order."[126]

On the basis of these ideas, most of which were made known to the Party in a speech delivered on August 18, 1980, at an enlarged meeting of the Politburo, Liao Gailong, a leader of the liberal wing of the Party and its leading spokesman on reforming the political institutions of the Party-state, endeavored to push political reforms in a liberal direction. In a report made on October 25, he proposed the establishment of a central executive committee, a central control committee, and a central committee

121. *Beijing Review*, September 20, 1982: 10.
122. "Thoroughly Carry Out the Programmatic Principle of Readjustment, Ensure Stability and Unity," *Selected Works of Deng*, 319; *Beijing Review*, September 13, 1982: 27.
123. "The Reform of the Leadership Institutions of the Party and State," *Selected Works of Deng*, 299.
124. Articles 37, 38, 67, 96, 100, 103, 104, 135.
125. "Firmly Uphold the Four Cardinal Principles," *Selected Works of Deng*, 159–62; "The Current Situation and Tasks," ibid., 218.
126. "Thoroughly Carry Out the Programmatic Principle of Readjustment, Ensure Stability and Unity," ibid., 319.

for disciplinary inspection, all of which were to be elected by the Party Congress. They were to have equal status. They were all to be the central committees of the Party. They were to check and balance each other. They were to supervise each other. They were all to be responsible to the Party Congress. Disputes and disagreements among these three committees would be resolved by a joint meeting. If they could not be resolved at the joint meeting, they would be decided by the Party Congress, which, unlike the present system, would be a "standing organization" *(changren zhi)* that could meet at any time.[127]

The radical nature of Liao's proposal stemmed from the fact that he suggested substituting a system of checks and balances at the uppermost level of the Party for the concentric-circle structure of political power, which had been the norm rather than the exception from the very beginning in the history of the CCP. It is therefore not surprising that this proposal was rejected. Instead, the new Party constitution adopted on September 6, 1982, continues to reaffirm the primacy of the Central Committee while defining the Central Advisory Commission as the "political assistant and consultant" of the Central Committee. Although the members of the Central Advisory Commission itself are elected by the Party Congress, the Advisory Commission's election of a chairman, vicechairman, and standing committee from among its own members must be reported to the Central Committee for approval (Article 22). Moreover, Deng suggested that the Central Advisory Commission was a transitional institution and would be abolished in ten to fifteen years.[128]

Thus, in formal terms, the concentric-circle structure at the top remains the Party Congress, the Central Committee, the Politburo, and the standing committee of the latter. According to the Party constitution, the general secretary of the Central Committee, the chairman of the Military Commission, the chairman of the Central Advisory Commission, and the first secretary of the Central Commission for Discipline Inspection must be members of the standing committee of the Politburo.[129] But this new concentric-circle structure is different from that which existed at various periods in the past. It is a concentric-circle structure lacking a one-man center, according to the provisions of the Party constitution. The chairmanship, which was one of the foundations and symbols of the cult of Mao, has been abolished. The formal head of the Party is the general secretary, whose duties are defined as "convening the meetings of the Politburo and

---

127. Liao Gailong, "Lishi de jingyan he women de fazhan daolu," reproduced in *Zhonggong yanjiu*, September 15, 1981: 108–77.

128. *Zhongguo gongchandang di shi-er ci quanguo daibiao dahui wenjian huibian* (Beijing: Renmin chubanshe, 1982), 171. Hereafter cited as *Wenjian huibian*.

129. Articles 21, 22, and 43, *Beijing Review*, September 20, 1982: 15, 20.

its Standing Committee and presiding over the work of the Secretariat." Many commentaries make it clear that the term "convene" (*zhaoji*) does not have the same meaning as the term "preside over" (*zhuchi*) and does not imply the power to decide. In terms of real power, Hu Yaobang, the current general secretary, is not even first among equals in the collective leadership. Instead, Deng, chairman of the Party's Military Commission and concurrently chairman of the Central Advisory Commission, is the most powerful leader in actual practice. But he is not the formal head of the Party and repeatedly expresses his own wish to relinquish his real power in favor of his successors. No cult of personality has developed.

Insofar as day-to-day decision making is concerned, the current practice departs from the concentric-circle structure specified in the Party constitution. A. Doak Barnett reported in a remarkable article based on an interview with Premier Zhao Ziyang that "the standing committee no longer meets as a body and that the full Politburo now meets only irregularly and infrequently," "probably three or four times a year." Barnett concludes that "Mr. Hu [Yaobang]'s secretariat and Mr. Zhao's State Council run the Party and the government on a day-to-day basis, in close consultation with each other and Deng Xiaoping.[130] Thus, the "first line" in policy making has in effect superseded the "second line," and the concentric-circle structure specified in the Party constitution has been replaced by two separate circles. These are linked by the informal participation of Premier Zhao in the meetings of the Secretariat, as well as by the presence of Deng, who has ultimate decision-making authority over the most important questions but does not concern himself with other problems. Thus, the structure of authority at the very top of the Party has been loosening up. Whether this is a temporary arrangement, to last until the old, veteran leaders now holding membership in the standing committee of the Politburo have left the scene or whether it will become a permanent system remains to be seen. It is quite possible that when Deng is gone, the general secretary, in the person of Hu Yaobang or someone else, will become first among equals in a collective leadership.

At some later time or in a period of crisis, a general secretary or the chairman of the Military Commission may rise above the status of first among equals to become the dominant leader of the Party. But it is unlikely that another Mao will ever again emerge. If this is true, then it seems that after a series of revolutions beginning in 1911, China has finally departed from the age-old tradition of rule by one man at the very top of the political system.

The Party leaders now reiterate frequently that in the Party structure at all levels the system of collective leadership must be fully implemented.

130. *New York Times*, August 13, 1984.

Decision must be made by a majority vote in the Party committee and not by the first secretary. If a first secretary departs from the system of collective leadership, all members of the committee and not he alone must bear the responsibility. The reformers also believe that the probability of over-concentration of power in the hands of one man can be further minimized by two institutional arrangements: limiting the number of terms an office-holder may serve and limiting the number of positions a single individual may hold. As it turned out, the Party found it politically inexpedient or impossible at the Twelfth Party Congress to adopt strict provisions limiting the tenure of top Party leaders. And the Party constitution as adopted did not specify any limitation on the number of positions to be held concurrently by one leader. But these two principles are still reaffirmed as guiding ideas for future reforms. The first principle is incorporated in the Party constitution: "Leading Party cadres at all levels, whether elected through democratic procedure or appointed by a leading body are not entitled to lifelong tenure, and they can be transferred from or relieved of their posts."[131]

The tightening of Party discipline and the restoration of the Party tradition regulating inner-Party life constitute a response to a series of problems inherent in a party in power which the Cultural Revolution was designed to resolve but actually aggravated. These defects are loss of the revolutionary ideal; a decline in Party spirit; bureaucratism, particularly the avoidance of responsibility, pursuit of special privileges, selfishness, and a corresponding lack of public spirit; absence of mutual trust between Party members; lack of creativity in policy making and implementation; failure to use criticism and self-criticism in appropriate ways; and the absence of new blood, as seen in the aging of the Party at its upper and middle levels. The establishment in December 1978 of a Central Commission for Disciplinary Inspection (selected by the Central Committee) was the first step in solving these problems. The provision in the 1982 Party constitution for the election of the members of this commission by the Party Congress is designed to elevate its status and authority. The Party constitution imposed stricter demands and discipline on Party members and cadres in the ideological, political, and organizational spheres than any previous party constitution had done. As a supplement to these provisions, it retained the more detailed "Guiding Principles for Inner-Party Political Life," adopted in February 1980.

The Party decided upon a two-pronged program to renew the membership of the Party. First, the Party was to spend three years, beginning in the latter half of 1983, conducting an all-round rectification of one sector after another—in other words, a purge of the Party conducted in a

131. Article 37 of the 1982 Party constitution, *Beijing Review*, September 20, 1982: 19.

planned, regularized manner, using normal organizational channels. This rectification campaign is designed to purge the Party of remaining unrepentant Leftists, some of whom occupy positions of authority at the middle and lower levels. In the course of this campaign, the banner of a thorough repudiation of the Cultural Revolution has been raised.[132] Second, the Party will build a contingent of cadres of individuals who are revolutionary in spirit, young, knowledgeable, and skilled in various specialized fields. To achieve this purpose, a policy of promoting such existing cadres, retraining old cadres, and persuading others to retire has been adopted.

The building of a contingent of such cadres is the core of organizational reform[133] which, together with reform of economic institutions, constitutes the first of the four tasks outlined by Deng. This first task is to be "tightly grasped," for a long period of time, at least until the end of this century. "Organizational reform" is to take place not alone in the Party but also in the government bureaucracy and all other non-Party, nongovernmental organizations. This means, of course, the rationalization of organizational structures and operational procedures. From the long perspective of the history of the Chinese revolutionary movement and regime, it has another significance, even more far-reaching and consequential: it is an effort to develop quickly and on a large scale an orientation toward professional and other specialized forms of knowledge in the predominantly "ideologically and organizationally oriented bureaucracy" that has existed thus far. Whereas the latter has been staffed largely by cadres of rural origin or outlook, encouraging the new orientation will increase the number and enhance the authority of functionaries of urban origin or training, possessing knowledge of the modern world.[134]

Redefining the Relationship between the Party and the State while Reforming the State Institutions

For the sake of simplicity, the relationship between the Party and all other institutions in the society can be characterized as the Party's self-

132. *Renmin ribao*, July 1, 1984: 1.

133. *Wenjian huibian*, 4. "Organizational reform" is not an adequate translation of the Chinese term *jigou gaige*.

134. For a discussion of "organizationally oriented bureacracy" and "professionally oriented bureaucracy" as two ideal types, see Bernard Silberman's unpublished and untitled paper circulated at a seminar at the University of Chicago in winter 1982. For the purpose of analyzing the historical transformation of the Chinese bureaucracy, I modify his first concept by adding the word "ideologically" and suggest that the Chinese are now trying to develop "an ideologically-organizationally and professionally oriented bureaucracy." The present and future development of the Chinese bureaucracy depends on how the tension and complementarity between these two orientations will work themselves out.

limitation of its power over the latter.[135] Insofar as the relationship between the Party and the state is concerned, the fact that the adoption of the Party constitution was followed by the enactment of a state constitution suggests an additional feature—that the Party "binds itself" or "precommits itself" to follow a certain course of action and to refrain from doing other things.[136] The Party constitution adopted in September 1982 declared in its general program that "the Party must conduct its activities within the limits permitted by the constitution and the laws of the state."[137] In his report to the Twelfth Party Congress, Secretary General Hu Yaobang characterized this stipulation as "a most important principle" and then added: "It is impermissible for any Party organization or member from the Central Committee down to the grass roots, to act in contravention of the constitution and laws. The Party is part of the people. It leads them in making the constitution and laws which, once adopted by the supreme organ of state power, must be observed by the whole Party."[138] Then in the preamble to the state constitution enacted the following December it is stated that "the peoples of all nationalities, all state organs, the armed forces, *all political parties* and public organizations and all enterprises and undertakings in the country must take the constitution as the basic norm of conduct, and they have the duty to uphold the dignity of the constitution and insure its implementation."[139] An editorial in the December 5, 1982, issue of *Renmin ribao* on the new state constitution explicitly noted that the term "all" means "there can be no exception whatsoever" and that "our Party is the party in power, and occupies the position of leadership in the political life of the state, but before the constitution and laws, our Party, like all other parties, groups, and organizations, must conduct its activities within the limits permitted by the constitution and the laws."[140] In other words, the Party bound itself first, and then the state constitution was adopted, with a provision that incorporated this precommitment.

A rigorous propaganda campaign was launched to publicize the state constitution, including this stipulation on the relationship between the

135. The term "self-limitation" (or autolimitation, autodetermination, and autoobligation) is borrowed from the theory of sovereignty without its technical legal meaning.

136. The terms "binds oneself" or "precommits oneself" are borrowed from Jon Elster, again without its technical meaning in the theory of rational choice. Elster, *Ulysses and the Sirens*, 35–47.

137. *Beijing Review*, September 20, 1982: 10.

138. Ibid., September 13, 1982: 27.

139. *Beijing Review*, December 27, 1982: 12. Emphasis added.

140. The editorial is reproduced in *Zhonghua renmin gongheguo diwujie remin daibiao dahui diwuci huiyi wenjian* (Beijing: Renmin chubanshe, 1983), 327. Hereafter cited as *Huiyi wenjian*.

Party and the state. This unprecedented stress on the dignity of the constitution and the need to obey the laws of the state followed a period of utter lack of respect for the constitution and state laws, not only in actions of the Party leaders and cadres, but also in their pronouncements and attitudes. This disrespect for the law received powerful (and unprecedented) support from Mao's remark that he was "a monk holding an umbrella," i.e., for him there was no law and no heaven to restrain him.[141] During this propaganda campaign, many articles noted that people frequently asked whether the Party or the law is superior or even whether "the Party Committee of a county (*xian*) or the constitution has higher authority."[142] The writers asserted that these questions had now received a definitive answer, and that mistaken attitudes toward the constitution and the laws of the state must be uprooted.

This self-limitation and precommitment implies that there should be a measure of separation between the Party and the government. This principle has been referred to repeatedly. What it means, however, is simply that Party organizations at all levels should avoid interfering in the day-to-day decisions of governmental units or taking over any of their functions, let alone displacing them completely as they did in many cases during and immediately after the Cultural Revolution. At first, the role of the Party vis-à-vis the state and society was defined in terms of exercising "political and ideological leadership." Later, the term "organizational" was added.[143] Since the term "organizational leadership" usually implies the power over personnel—including appointment, promotion and demotion, removal, transfer, discipline, and dismissal—the "leadership" of the Party over the state remains direct and unequivocal. In addition, the four fundamental principles are reaffirmed in the preamble of the state constitution. As the

141. The (here unspoken) phrase that follows this proverbial expression is "no hair [a homonym for 'law'], no heaven." The monk has no hair (i.e., he obeys no law), and his umbrella shuts out the sight of heaven. This attitude toward law (but not toward heaven) was deeply rooted in one strand of the Chinese political tradition that the emperor had the ultimate authority to make laws and that imperial dictates should be obeyed without question. Du Zhou, a famous official of western Han said: "Whatever the earlier rulers thought was right they wrote down in the books and made into statutes, and whatever the later rulers thought was right they duly classified as ordinances." Quoted in Ping-ti Ho, "Salient Aspects of China's Heritage," in Ho and Tsou, *China in Crisis*, vol. 1, bk. 1, p. 19. This attitude was also widespread among the folk heroes and rebels. It was reinforced by the CCP's revolutionary tradition. All this is recognized by the current leaders. For example, see the editorial in the *Renmin ribao* of December 5, 1982, in *Huiyi wenjian*, 326–27. As for the repudiation of Mao's remark without naming Mao, see ibid., 337. "Scientific laws" of Marxism-Leninism and Mao Zedong Thought have taken the place of heaven.

142. See article by Song Renqiong, *Hongqi*, 1982, no. 24: 11.

143. As finally formalized in the general program of the Party constitution of 1982, the statements reads: "Party leadership consists mainly in political, ideological, and organizational leadership."

Chinese leaders stress, the core of these principles is the leadership of the Party.[144] Thus, the nature of this leadership over the state depends in the last analysis on the Party's self-limitation or self-restraint.

Yet there are still some *symbolic* changes in the state constitution which reflect the desire to achieve a measure of separation between the Party and the state. First, the older provision (in Article 15 of the 1975 constitution and Article 19 of the 1978 constitution), that the chairman of the Central Committee commands the armed forces of the whole nation is omitted. Instead, under the 1982 constitution, a Central Military Commission is to be established by the National People's Congress [NPC] (Article 62) and to direct the armed forces of the country (Article 93). Also eliminated is the provision in Article 17 of the 1975 constitution and Article 23 of the 1978 constitution to the effect that the NPC decides on the choice of the premier of the State Council upon the recommendation *(tiyi)* of the Central Committee of the CCP. Instead, under the new constitution he is to be nominated by the president of the People's Republic (Article 62). As we all know, these are all symbolic changes. In actuality, the Party will continue to control the People's Liberation Army (PLA) and the selection of the top leaders of the state.

To what extent the self-limitation and precommitment of the Party will hold, particularly during a serious internal or external crisis, remains to be seen. But there is no doubt that for all those who suffered from the lawlessness and the utter disregard of simple human decency during the Cultural Revolution, the new state constitution is for them a precious document. Wang Guangmei, the widow of Liu Shaoqi, probably expressed the feeling of a large majority of the people when she said that "this new constitution was paid for by blood."[145]

Let us then turn to the provisions of the constitution for an examination of the current Chinese concept of the state. The Chinese make a distinction between the form of the state *(guoti)* and the form of the government *(zhengti)*, and between the form of the state *(guoti)* and both the state institution *(guojia zhidu)* and the organizational form of political power *(zhengquan zuzhi xingsi)*.[146] For them the form of the state is determined by class relations, i.e., which social class or classes control the state and occupy the dominant position in society. The constitution defines the form of the state in Article 1 as follows: "The People's Republic of China is a socialist state under the people's democratic dictatorship led by the working class and based on the alliance of workers and peasants." The

144. For a discussion of the inclusion of the ideology of a single party in a state constitution in the history of constitution making in twentieth-century China, see my original paper as presented at the Bellagio Conference, May 1983, 60–62.

145. *Minzhu yu fazhi*, 1983, no. 1: 6.

146. Article by Lu Zhichao, *Hongqi*, 1982, no. 21: 14–15.

term "dictatorship of the proletariat" used in the corresponding article in the constitutions of 1975 and 1978 is abandoned, but the wording of the 1954 constitution, "a people's democratic state," is not restored either. What it does is to reinstate Mao's term, as employed in his article "On the People's Democratic Dictatorship," which had been completely displaced by the term "dictatorship of the proletariat" during the Cultural Revolution. But to maintain the Marxist orthodoxy that found expression in the term "dictatorship of the proletariat" as far back as the "Program of the CCP," adopted at the First Congress in 1921, the "people's democratic dictatorship" is said in the preamble to be "in essence the dictatorship of the proletariat." [147] Elsewhere, it is stated that the dictatorship of the proletariat may assume many forms and that the people's democratic dictatorship is one of them.

But the change in Article 1 does have its significance. As is frequently pointed out by Chinese commentators, the reinstated phrase contains the word "democratic," and so underscores the notion of democracy among the people in contrast to dictatorship over enemies. The term "people" has a much broader connotation and many more referents than "proletariat." It includes the peasantry, the intellectuals (who are now classified as part of the working class), and the socialist working people *(laodongzhe)* (i.e., some former national bourgeois and petty bourgeois), and all patriots who support socialism (i.e., some other former national bourgeois and petty bourgeois). Hence, many Chinese writers assert that the scope of democracy in China has been vastly expanded while the scope of dictatorship has contracted. At least, the phrase "people's democratic dictatorship" stands as a symbol for "socialist democracy" and for the aim to establish "democracy on a high level." It legitimizes the new emphasis on the civil rights of the citizens, to be discussed later.

The insertion of the word "intellectuals" in the preamble—that "in building socialism it is imperative to rely on the workers, peasants and *intellectuals*" [148]—was the result of strong advocacy during the nationwide discussion of the draft constitution by the intellectuals with the support of some Party leaders, their intention being to elevate their status and underscore their contributions. The idea that the People's Political Consultation Conference should be specifically made into an organ of the state in a separate article was rejected. But its position in the political system as "a broadly representative organization of the united front" is affirmed in the preamble. [149]

147. *Beijing Review*, December 27, 1982: 11.
148. Ibid. Emphasis added. The draft constitution of April 1982 did not contain this sentence. For the text of the draft constitution see *Renmin ribao*, April 28, 1982: 1, 3, 4.
149. Ibid.

So far as the state structure, or form of government, is concerned, Liao Gailong's proposal of a bicameral legislature[150] was rejected. The provision of the 1954 and 1978 constitutions to the effect that "the National People's Congress is the highest organ of state power" was reenacted without the qualifying phrase in the 1975 constitution, "under the leadership of the Communist party of China." Also omitted is the statement in article 2 of both the 1975 and 1978 constitutions that "the Chinese Communist party is the core of leadership of the whole Chinese people."[151] However, these changes are balanced or even nullified by the reaffirmation of the Party's leadership in the preamble. But in the purely legal and formal sense, it can now be said that the National People's Congress (NPC) has sovereign power. The important point for our purpose is that this provision rejects once again the principle of the separation of powers at the highest level of governmental structure in favor of the supremacy of the legislature. This is driven home by the power of the NPC to elect or to decide on the choice of the highest officials in the other two branches as well as the power to recall or remove these officials. It also has the power to amend the constitution.

Increasing the authority of the Standing Committee of the NPC is an innovation. It is now given legislative power, whereas formerly it only had the power to adopt individual decrees and to revise individual articles in the existing laws.[152] It retains the power to interpret the constitution, given to it for the first time in Article 25 of the 1978 constitution, but it now has the explicit authority to supervise the enforcement of the constitution. It is at this level that a measure of separation of powers is instituted, by the provision in Article 65 that "no one on the Standing Committee of the National People's Congress shall hold any post in any of the administrative, judicial or procuratorial organs of the state."[153]

Whether or not it makes any difference in the actual operation of the state institutions, the introduction of a measure of separation of powers at this level is nevertheless of some significance in formal and legalistic terms if we look back at the tradition of constitution making under the Chinese Communists. As far back as the Central Soviet Republic established in late 1931 in Jiangxi, the Chinese Communists adopted the fusion

150. Liao's article as reproduced in *Zhonggong yanjiu*, vol. 15, no. 9 (September 15, 1981): 164, 165. But some of the other principles and concrete proposals contained in his speech have been incorporated in the Party and state constitutions.

151. *Peking Review*, January 24, 1975: 13, March 17, 1978: 6.

152. Article by Zhang Youyu, *Renmin ribao*, January 14, 1983: 5. Article by Wang Xiangming, ibid., January 20, 1983: 5.

153. Liao Gailong proposed in his speech that ministers should not serve concurrently as members of the Standing Committee. Liao's article as reproduced in *Zhonggong yanjiu*, vol. 15, no. 9 (September 15, 1981): 165.

of legislative and executive powers as a principle in their state institutions. The Draft Outline of the Fundamental Law (Constitution) of the Soviet Republic proposed by the Party center provided explicitly for "a fusion of the legislative organ and executive organ."[154] The Outline Constitution of the Chinese Soviet Republic adopted in November 1931 provided for the election by the National Congress of Workers', Peasants', and Soldiers' Soviet of a Central Executive Committee, under which a People's Committee (renmin weiyuanhui) was organized.[155] The National Congress on November 7, 1931, elected a Central Executive Committee. The Central Executive Committee in turn elected Mao Zedong as its chairman and Xiang Ying and Zhang Guotao as its vice-chairmen.[156] It organized the People's Committee again with Mao as the chairman and Xiang and Zhang as vice-chairmen. The Organic Law of the Central Soviet proclaimed on February 17, 1934, provided for the election by the National Congress of Soviet Representatives of a Central Executive Committee of no more than 585 persons, which in turn was to select the members of a People's Committee and its chairman from its own members.[157] By this time Mao had lost much of his power. He was reelected chairman of the Central Executive Committee but Zhang Wentian was elected chairman of the People's Committee.[158] The center of the concentric-circle structure of government was loosening up. But the principle of the fusion of legislative and executive powers remained. The state constitutions of 1954, 1975, and 1978 did nothing to modify this principle. Now with the introduction of some separation of powers at the level of the Standing Committee of the NPC, the executive branch no longer forms, in constitutional theory, the inner circle of a structure of concentric circles within the legislative branch.

This stipulation concerning the separation of executive and legislative powers holds for the members of the Standing Committee of a local people's congress at and above the county level who are barred from holding any post in the state administrative, judicial, and procuratorial organs (Article 103). As applied to the governmental structure at the local level, it is a new departure not found in the previous constitutions. It was not even found in the draft constitution of April 1982. It stands in contrast to Article 37 of the 1975 constitution which made the local revolutionary committee concurrently the standing organization (changshe jiguan) of

154. Han Yanlong and Chang Zhaoru, eds., Zhongguo xinminzhu zhuyi geming shiqi genjudi fazhi wenxian xuanbian (Beijing: Shehui kexueyuan chubanshe, 1981), 1:3. No date was given for this document. It was probably adopted in October or early November 1931.
155. Ibid., 9.
156. Mao Zedong ji, 3:43–45.
157. Han and Chang, Genjudi fazhi, 2:87–88.
158. Mao Zedong ji, 4:298–99.

the local people's congress and the local people's government—a provision which accentuated the principle of fusion of power at this level of government. But it had a precedent in a law adopted on July 1, 1979, by the NPC.

In formal terms, the NPC is, under the 1982 constitution, "the highest organ of state power" and the State Council is "the executive body of the highest organ of state power; it is the highest organ of state administration." In practice, actual political power is concentrated in the State Council rather than the NPC or its Standing Committee. There is another institution which wields formidable political power and is formally parallel to the State Council, as its chairman is directly elected by the NPC. This is the Central Military Commission. Its formidable power is also derived from the widely reported arrangement under which its membership will be identical with that of the Military Commission of the Party's Central Committee.

Within the NPC itself and as it projects its influence beyond its boundary, the NPC will most probably reflect a concentric-circle structure. Its power and influence will be concentrated in its Standing Committee. The power and influence of the latter will be concentrated in its chairman and vice-chairmen, with the Chairman as the center of these three concentric circles. The same will probably be the case within the State Council and the Central Military Commission. But in formal and legal terms, there exists some ambiguity regarding the position of the premier. In the Chinese versions of both the draft constitution and the constitution as finally enacted, the words regarding the authority of the premier are the same. Both stipulate in article 86 that the State Council *"shixin zongli fuzezhi"* and in article 88 that the Premier directs the works of the State Council. But the interpretation of Article 86 underwent an important change after the adoption of the draft constitution and before the enactment of the new constitution in its final form. Shortly after the draft was adopted, Article 86 was interpreted in the following terms. Zhang Youyu asserted that the State Council is an executive organ and that it need not follow the rule of the minority's yielding to the will of the majority but should implement the system of *zongli fuzezhi*. [159] He explained that collective discussion would certainly take place in the executive and plenary meetings of the State Council but that collective discussion would not stand in contradiction with the authority of the premier to make final decisions (*zongli you zuihou juedingquan*). Hence the official English translation of 86 in the draft constitution reads: "The State Council applies the system of *decision*

---

159. See article by Zhang Youyu, in Zhang Youyu et al., *Xianfa lunwenji* (Beijing: Qunzhong chubanshe, 1982), 2:3. Zhang Youyu is a prestigious jurist in China. For a less explicit statement see the article by Xu Qiongde, *Hongqi*, 1982, no. 11: 24.

by the Premier."[160] In contrast, the official translation of the same words in the constitution as finally enacted reads: "The Premier has overall responsibility for the State Council."[161] The significance of this change in translation can be seen in the Organic Law of the State Council, adopted on December 10 by the NPC to implement the new constitution. This law provides that "important questions involved in the work of the State Council must be discussed and *decided* by either the executive meetings or plenary meetings of the State Council."[162] The same change in the English translation is made with regard to the position of the chairman of the Central Military Commission. The process of interpreting the various wordings of the constitution has already begun. In any case, the governmental structure has, in actuality, a troika structure at the very top, consisting of the chairman of the Standing Committee of the NPC, the premier, and the chairman of the Central Military Commission, with the president of the People's Republic as the formal head of state, who has no real power but could probably play a useful mediating role among the three most powerful government leaders.

The policy of limiting the tenure of the top leaders, which could not be written into the Party constitution, was adopted in the state constitution. The president and vice-president of the Republic, the premier, vice-premiers and state councillors, the president of the Supreme People's Court, and the procurator-general of the Supreme People's Procuratorate may not serve more than two consecutive terms. But a provision in the draft constitution which also applied this limit to the chairman of the Central Military Commission has been omitted in the constitution as finally enacted. It is quite possible that when the draft was adopted in April 1982 its authors still expected the Party to impose a limit on the tenure of the top leaders, including the chairman of the Party's Military Commission. But this expectation was not fulfilled. It is also generally believed that the same person will serve as the chairman of both military commissions.[163] Hence, it was necessary to omit the limit on the tenure of the chairman of the Central Military Commission of the State.

Searching for "Socialist Legality" and "Socialist Democracy" and Taking More Seriously the Concept of Citizenship

Although restructuring the "leadership institutions" of the Party and of the state is of fundamental importance at the present time, China's most

160. *Beijing Review*, May 10, 1982: 41. Emphasis added.
161. *Beijing Review*, December 27, 1982: 23.
162. *Huiyi wenjian*, 272. Emphasis added.
163. For a succinct account of the evolution of the Party's Military Commission and the government's Military Commission, see Zhu Chengjia, ed., *Zhonggong dangshi yanjiu lungwen xuan*, vol. 3 (Hunan: Hunan renmin chupanshe, 1984) 567–87.

significant problem in the long run is the establishment of "socialist legality" and "socialist democracy." The challenge here is to make meaningful the constitutional guarantees of civil and political rights which have always existed on paper. Earlier in this chapter I distinguished between the concept of the masses and the concept of citizenship as different ways of linking the public sector with the private—political power with civil society. I further observed that state building in the modern West was based on the concept of citizenship and cited T. H. Marshall's view that civil rights, political rights and socioeconomic rights[164] were achieved in that order in the course of the eighteenth to the twentieth centuries. I finally raised the question of whether Chinese development under the CCP will prove to be a process that begins with an advance in socioeconomic rights and then shifts to advances in political and civil rights. Let me explain further why I raised this question.

In spite of the problem of unemployment,[165] the advances achieved in socioeconomic rights during the past thirty-three years have been impressive, notwithstanding the serious setback that followed the Great Leap Forward and the economic dislocations caused by the Cultural Revolution. The provisions on socioeconomic rights in Articles 91–94 of the 1954 constitution were not merely empty words. One can even argue that in the cities, the "iron rice bowl," "eating from a common pot," overstaffing, and underutilization of the labor force were in part expressions of the Party's preoccupation with these rights. In the countryside, the land reform of 1946–52 must be considered to have been a great success in promoting the socioeconomic rights of the poor and middle peasants, although it was achieved at the expense of the socioeconomic rights of the landlords and rich peasants and led to a reign of mass terror directed against the latter. Mao's ill-conceived policy in 1955–56 of accelerating the process of cooperativization and his disastrous program of communization were both intended to raise the socioeconomic level of the poor and lower-middle peasants—the most disadvantaged group in the nation—but in the process all the peasants were deprived of many of the socioeconomic rights granted them since the land reform. The fact that both measures proved to be counterproductive does not denigrate Mao's intention. The process of learning through experience finally led in 1978 to the progressive development of the (apparently successful) system of responsibility in agricultural production. In the course of this development many of the socioeconomic rights taken away since 1955–56 have been returned to peasants of all strata.

164. T. H. Marshall's term is "social rights" but he meant economic rights as well.
165. For the number of persons unemployed and the percentage of these people in the total urban labor force, see *Beijing Review*, March 28, 1983: 21.

In contrast, whatever civil and political rights citizens have actually enjoyed in any period has depended totally on the ideological and political line of the Party. During the Cultural Revolution, the constitutional guarantees of political and civil rights were even more ruthlessly and shamelessly violated than before.[166] The question must be raised whether or not the adoption of the new state constitution makes any difference. In terms of the guarantees on paper, the 1982 constitution omits some significant provisions of the earlier constitutions. The statement in Article 87 of the 1954 constitution that "the state guarantees to citizens enjoyment of these freedoms [of speech, press, association, procession, and demonstration] by *providing the necessary material facilities*" is omitted,[167] just as it was in the 1975 and 1978 constitutions. Also omitted in the 1982 document is the freedom to strike, which was guaranteed on paper from 1975 up to that time.[168] The provision in Article 45 of the 1978 constitution guaranteeing the right to "speak out freely, air their views fully, hold great debates and write big-character posters"[169] had already been eliminated by a constitutional amendment adopted by the NPC on September 10, 1980. Naturally, it is not restored in the 1982 constitution.

But the new constitution does contain significant changes which advance civil rights on paper. It restores (with an interesting modification) the provision of the 1954 constitution which in translation reads: "citizens . . . are equal before the law." Whereas the Chinese version of this provision in the 1954 constitution reads "gongmin zai falu *shang* yilu pingdeng," the new provision now reads "gongmin zai falu *mianqian* yilu pingdeng," which is also officially translated as "citizens . . . are equal before the law."[170] The former provision was omitted in both the 1975 and 1978 constitutions because it ran afoul of the Maoist doctrine there that cannot be equality between the proletariat and the exploiting class,[171]

166. For a recount of the pathetic attempt made by Liu Shaoqi to defend himself by invoking the constitution, see the article by Yu Haocheng, Zhang Youyu, et al., *Xianfa lunwenji* 2:276. This episode was first reported in Red Guard publications.

167. Emphasis added. For a weak attempt to defend this omission by noting the roughly tenfold increase in the number of copies of newspapers and periodicals printed, see the article by Wu Jie, ibid. 180. An interesting article by Zhang Zonghou and Sun Xupei indirectly criticizes this omission. Zhang Youyu et al., *Xianfa lunwenji*, (Beijing: Qunzhong chubanshe, 1982) 1:187–89. China does not use the system of censorship (shixian jianchazhi) in ordinary times. But there are other restrictions on the freedom of the press. Ibid., 195–201.

168. The freedom to strike appeared for the first time in Article 28 of the 1975 constitution.

169. This right first appeared in Article 13 of the 1975 constitution.

170. Emphasis added.

171. I have not been able to ascertain the relationship between the rejection of this provision and the attack on Peng Zhen's dictum that "everyone is equal before the truth." According to Yu Haocheng, this constitutional provision, together with many others, was openly criticized as early as the anti-Rightist movement of 1957. Article by Yu Haocheng, in Zhang Youyu et al., *Xianfa lunwenji*, 2:275. See also the article by Wang Liming and Qui Min, ibid., 83–84.

and, more broadly, of the doctrine of the class nature of law.[172] The new Chinese wording is less vulnerable to the charge that it makes no provision for class differences. The defenders of this modified provision explain that while in *legislation* the state may and does treat different classes or categories of people differently, in the *application of law*, particularly in the judicial process, everyone should be treated equally.[173]

For the first time in the history of constitution making in China, the new constitution provides (Article 38): "The personal dignity of the citizens of the People's Republic of China is inviolable. Insults, libels, false charges or frame-ups directed against citizens by any means are prohibited." It strengthens a similar provision in the draft by adding the words "false charges or frame-ups." The protection of the freedom of person is also enhanced by the addition in Article 37 of the sentence that "unlawful deprivation or restriction of citizens' freedom of person by detention or other means is prohibited; and unlawful search of the person of a citizen is prohibited." These new provisions are obviously aimed at preventing any repetition of the widespread abuses that occurred during the Cultural Revolution, and which were rationalized by invoking Mao's report on the investigation of the Hunan peasant movement. The protection of the freedom and privacy of citizens' correspondence is also strengthened.

Provisions concerning the judicial and law-enforcement organs exhibit some progress, as well as one step backward. In connection with our discussion of the political system, the most interesting change is the introduction, in Article 135, of the idea of checks and balances among the people's courts, people's procuratorates, and public-security organs.[174] The independence of the courts in deciding cases is insulated from mass opinion by the deletion of similar but not identical provisions in the 1975 and 1978 constitutions concerning the mobilization of the masses for discussion and criticism in major counterrevolutionary cases. The 1975 provision on the application of "the mass line" in "procuratorial work and in trying cases" is also omitted. For our purposes, the significance of these omissions is that they highlight the difference, and in this case the incompatibility, between the idea of masses and the concept of citizenship.

172. Article by Wu Buyun, *Faxue yanjiu*, 1980, no. 5: 15.

173. Article by Li Buyun in Zhang Youyu et al., *Xianfa lunwenji*, 2:114–23. Although there are several questionable statements in this article, the author's explanation is not greatly different from what C. Herman Pritchett writes regarding the concept of "equal protection of the law" in the United States. Pritchett writes: "The principle of equal protection does not mean that all class legislation or legal discrimination is invalid. . . . But what equal protection does demand is that all persons in the same situation have the same privileges and be subject to the same legal obligations." *The American Constitutional System* (New York: McGraw-Hill, 1971), 111.

174. The system of procuratorates was in effect abolished by the 1975 constitution. According to Article 25, "the functions and powers of procuratorial organs are exercised by the organs of public security at various levels."

Though not written into the constitution, the system of review by Party committees of cases pending before the courts or of decisions of the courts before their official announcement was abolished by the Party center some time during the past three or four years. But it is also clear that the Party organizations in the people's courts must report to, and ask instructions from, the Party committees at the same level. They must follow the Party leadership strictly and win its support. The same rule applies to the procuratorates.[175] Hence, the Party's control is simply not as specific or as direct as before.

A retrogression from the 1954 constitution[176] can be found in Article 133 of the 1982 constitution. This reads: "Local people's procuratorates at the different levels are responsible to *organs of state power* at the corresponding levels which created them and to the people's procuratorates at the higher level."[177] The local organs of state power referred to are the local people's congresses and, at the county level and above, the Standing Committees of local people's congresses.[178] A Chinese author has noted that in practice this dual system of leadership usually means that the local organs of state power play the primary role. Local cadres frequently interfere illegally with the independent exercise of procuratorial power by the local procuratorates. Many of them still substitute their superiors' or their own opinions for law. Particularly in the case of exercising procuratorial power over economic work or transgression of law by cadres, there is no real guarantee of the independence of the local procuratorate.[179] Yet even this author emphasized that the abandonment of the dual system of leadership and the restoration of the system of perpendicular, unitary leadership by the procuratorates at a higher level (both of which he proposed) would not affect the Party's leadership because the Party organizations in the local procuratorate are led by the local Party committees.

This discussion of the system of courts and procuratorates again raises the question whether in practice anything has changed since the Third Plenum. The answer is that the individual citizen now enjoys greater pro-

175. Article by Jin Mosheng on the people's courts and people's procuratorates, Zhang Youyu et al. *Xianfa lunwenji*, 1:266–67.

176. Article 83 of the 1954 constitution reads: "In the exercise of their authority local organs of the people's procuratorate are independent and not subject to interference by *local organs of the state.*" Emphasis added. The underlying idea was that the supremacy of the legislature *does not* apply to the organs of law enforcement.

177. Emphasis added. Here, the underlying idea is that the supremacy of the legislature *does* apply to the organs of law enforcement.

178. Article 104.

179. Article by Jin Mosheng, *Minzhu yu Fazhi*, 1982, no. 6 (June 25, 1982): 3. He was commenting on the identical provision in the draft constitution. Apparently the system of procuratorates at the local level was completely restored only in 1980.

tection than before against the actions of the masses, other private individuals, individual Party cadres, specific Party units, non-Party organizations, and administrative organs that are not authorized by the Party. So far as the Party as a whole is concerned, his civil rights are protected, in the last analysis, only by the self-limitation and the precommitment of the Party. The Party now realizes that after their experience in the Cultural Revolution all Chinese have a new appreciation of the importance of civil rights. It also recognizes that a system of civil rights is an important factor in increasing the "activism" of the Chinese people, that is, in developing their energy, capabilities, and creativity. We cannot ascertain, however, to what extent the Party knows or takes seriously the fact that Chinese citizens are skeptical about the protection provided by the constitution for their rights. Some Chinese writers hope that changes other than the provisions in the new constitution may in the long run help to promote the civil and political rights of the citizens. Two Chinese authors express their belief that the system of responsibility in agriculture and the enhanced autonomy of industrial enterprises provide broader conditions for freedoms of speech and the press than before.[180] The same conclusion probably can be drawn with regard to the effects of the increasing importance of the intellectuals, professionals, specialists, and technicians in a society that aims at rapid economic growth and at achieving a "high level of spiritual civilization."

Political rights have made some advance. The second session of the Fifth NPC on July 1, 1979, provided for the direct election of the people's congresses at the county level by secret ballot. It adopted a rule under which at any level the number of nominees must exceed the number of deputies to be elected to a people's congress. It also allowed the voters or the people's congresses to adopt a list of nominees through a "preliminary election" (yuxuan)." But the deputies to the NPC and the people's congresses at the provincial level are still elected indirectly. There is an interesting feature which institutionalizes the political power of the People's Liberation Army (PLA). The PLA will elect 265 deputies to the NPC.[181] Assuming that the total number of personnel in the PLA is 4,200,000, each deputy would represent roughly 15,849 persons,[182] whereas each non-PLA deputy represents 1,040,000 persons in rural areas and 130,000 persons in cities and towns.

During the years since the Third Plenum, the Chinese have synthe-

180. Article by Zhang Zonghou and Sun Xupei in Zhang Youyu et al., *Xianfu lunwenji*, 1:186.

181. *Huiyi wenjian*, 310.

182. If the term PLA in the constitutional provision includes all persons working in the PLA establishment, this number of 15,849 will be increased. This is a point on which I shall seek more information.

sized the two concepts of "socialist democracy" and "socialist legality" into the formula of the institutionalization of socialist democracy and its codification into law.[183] In his speech at the Twelfth Party Congress, Hu Yaobang declared that "we must closely link the building of socialist democracy with that of the social legal system, so that socialist democracy is institutionalized and codified into laws."[184] In an article anticipating Hu's statement, Wang Jingrong underscored the notion of democracy in the following conclusion: "The socialist legal system takes socialist democracy as its premise. It is the result of the institutionalization, and codification into law, of socialist democracy."[185] In addition, Hu Yaobang declared that "to attain a high level of socialist democracy is therefore one of our fundamental goals and tasks."[186] Whatever "socialist democracy" means in a Leninist Party-state, these and other statements reflect a large step forward. First, democracy is no longer considered an expedient means of achieving narrow and immediate political goals as Mao did in his criticism of Peng Dehuai.[187] Second, it is no longer conceived as merely a "style of work," but as a political principle that should be institutionalized and codified in law. Third, the achievement of "democracy on a high level" is considered to be a fundamental aim and basic task. Fourth, the pronouncements and the accompanying discussions have in effect affirmed the rule of law and repudiated the long tradition of rule by men. Fifth, although the class nature of the whole system of law in a society is forcefully reaffirmed, it is also said that "class nature is an important attribute of law but not its only attribute," that law should not be viewed as "simply a means of class struggle," and that "the class nature and the social nature of law form an organic unity rather than exclude each other."[188] The will of the ruling class of workers in alliance with the peasants must predominate but it should be expressed through the form of law. The incompatibility of mass political movements and the legal system has been recognized.[189] Finally, the Chinese belief that political democracy, economic democracy and social democracy must go forward hand in hand, each helping the other, may prove significant over the long term if serious attempts are made to implement the principle at all levels of society, particularly at the grass roots. But all these verbal changes must be first internalized.

183. See article by Wang Jingrong in *Faxue yanjiu*, 1982, no. 1, pp. 1–5.
184. *Beijing Review*, September 13, 1982: 27.
185. *Faxue yanjiu*, 1982, no. 1: 5.
186. *Beijing Review*, September 13, 1982: 26.
187. See above, end of section 3 of this chapter.
188. Article by Sun Guohua and Zhu Jingwen, *Faxue yanjiu*, 1982, no. 4: 24–27. The last statement is utterly ambiguous and reflects the uncertain and unsatisfactory status of the current debate on this question. But again this uncertainty must be seen from the perspective of the past when the class nature of law was considered its exclusive attribute.
189. Article by Chen Shouyi, Liu Shengping, and Zhao Zhenjiang, *Faxue yanjiu*, 1959, no. 4: 4–5.

The Chinese believe that socialist democracy is "democracy on a high level," that is, superior to bourgeois democracy. If it has taken the West three centuries, however, to move from the establishment of civil rights through the achievement of political rights and to the implementation of socioeconomic rights, how long will it take for the Leninist Party-state in China to achieve "a democracy on a high level" under much less favorable conditions?

Summary and Conclusion: "Scientific Laws," Popular Support, and Legality

The Chinese Party-state is the final product of China's response to the crisis confronting her throughout the twentieth century. This crisis expressed itself most forcefully in the political sphere, but the political crisis was also rooted in both the civil society and the economy, and externally was affected strongly by the international environment—China's changing position in the international power structure, the challenge as well as the "models" provided her by the "advanced" countries, and the impact on her of the capitalist world economy. As conventional wisdom puts it, China has had to confront simultaneously and to solve in decades problems that the West encountered and dealt with seriatim over the centuries: commercial revolution, industrial revolution, the Enlightenment, political revolutions, and the more recent, incremental changes and reforms within the political, social, and economic realms. In China, the crisis was total, and the time allowed for overcoming it was short, limited as it was by the need of the nation to survive in a hostile international environment.

Total crisis and a sense of urgency precluded the possibility of piecemeal, incremental reforms. They ruled out evolutionary approaches which sought to tackle fundamental problems one by one and in isolation—the problems of industrialization, education, cultural "renaissance," and the promotion of science and technology—in the hope that political unity, stability, and progress would then ensue and could be put on a solid foundation. Moreover, it became obvious that none of these problems could be resolved without first building up a strong, centralized state, which would then deal with these fundamental problems in a coordinated fashion. Hence political power had to take command.

In the highly disorganized society of early twentieth-century China, where the traditional order had collapsed and there was no agreement on fundamentals to take its place, political power had to be built on the basis of an explicit ideology and around a new organizational structure. Given China's position in the world, both had to be borrowed in toto or in part from abroad. Marxism-Leninism and the Leninist party structure were adopted by a group of radical, alienated intellectuals. They then sought a total transformation of Chinese society in terms of that ideology. The concept of class struggle fitted the Chinese political and social scene, where conflicts were endemic and deeply rooted in the disorganized structure. It helped the Party to discern and exploit these conflicts in its search for power. It made easier the Party's task of legitimizing its policies, strategies, and tactics. In this it was far more convincing than Chiang Kai-shek's revival of such Confucian concepts as harmony, sincerity, and adherence to traditional moral rules at a time when he was constantly fighting civil wars, playing power politics, and indulging in underhand maneuvers of all sorts.

Class struggle and social revolution involved the use of violent means. Military power in the final analysis decided the fate of all political parties, groups, and individuals. But military power had to be built on a sociopolitical foundation. Thus both class struggle and the quest for military power led the Party to penetrate civil society in order to mobilize and organize the masses. Social revolutions brought about through political-military power and mass movements carry within themselves a totalitarian tendency,[190] a social revolution guided by Marxism-Leninism and led by a Leninist party inevitably so. Through most of the revolutionary period, the inherent totalitarian tendency was checked by the overwhelming military might of the Guomindang. The CCP found that recognition and promotion of the perceived interests of the masses led to success and that moderation in its program was the necessary basis for building a large coalition of social forces. But with the final victory of the civil war in 1949, it became the party in power in a Leninist party-state. There were no countervailing forces outside the Party to check and balance its power. In the program to transform the system of social stratification and to establish socialism, the Party-state penetrated civil society ever more deeply and imposed increasingly tight control over various social groups and individuals while ignoring their interests in the pursuit of its revolutionary program. The Party's rules and the norms governing inner-party political life which had been established in the Yanan period proved inadequate to

---

190. I have followed N. S. Timasheff's use of the term "totalitarianism" to denote the "unlimited extension of state function" and to designate "a trait isolated by means of abstraction and apt to appear in society of various types." N. S. Timasheff, "Totalitarianism, Despotism, and Dictatorship," in Carl J. Friedrich, ed., *Totalitarianism* (Cambridge: Harvard University Press, 1954), 39. For a more extended discussion, see my paper presented at the Luce Seminar at the University of Chicago (May 1980), "Back from the Brink of Revolutionary-'Feudal' Totalitarianism: A Preliminary Observation." A slightly shortened and revised version was published in Victor Nee and David Mozingo, eds., *State and Society in Contemporary China* (Ithaca, N.Y.: Cornell University Press, 1983). It is this version that is republished as chap. 5 in this volume. See also Introduction, *supra*, pp. xxii–xxvi.

prevent the abuse of power which was concentrated in the hands of its top leader. During the Cultural Revolution, the totalitarian tendency reached its highest point and was justified by the theory of continued revolution under the dictatorship of the proletariat and its corollary of all-round dictatorship over the bourgeoisie—"bourgeoisie" being defined ever more broadly to cover, during the last year of Mao's life, elements in all major social classes and strata, including the working class and the peasantry, which enjoyed "bourgeois rights" and thus became "bourgeois elements." As a result, the Cultural Revolution drove home the realization that this centralized system of political power, penetrating the social fabric and controlling more and more strictly the life of the individual, suppressed the energy, initiative, and creativity of all individuals and social groups. And by so doing, the system proved self-defeating by stifling civil society and preventing the continued development of the capability of the state itself.

The extremism of the Cultural Revolution brought about a profound crisis of authority. It also prompted the disgraced and then rehabilitated leaders to reexamine some of the ideological tenets and "guiding ideas" which underlay the social, political and economic programs and which they had once espoused or supported as well as various parts of the Party structure and the political system which they had helped to build.

Just as the Cultural Revolution marked the culmination of that trend toward increasing penetration of society by the political power which had developed after the May Fourth period, the fundamental significance of the Third Plenum of the Eleventh Central Committee was that it signaled the reversal of this trend. This can be seen in the shift of focus from class struggle to socialist modernization, the approval of the debate on the criterion for testing truth, the reinterpretation of Mao Zedong Thought, the initiation of a process of demythologizing Mao and repudiating the cult of personality, the rapid reestablishment of the mass organizations and professional associations with a greater degree of autonomy than before the Cultural Revolution, the change in the direction of policies on agriculture and rural institutions, and the beginning of the process of rethinking the status of the former landlords and rich peasants, as well as that of the intellectuals. All these betokened a retreat of political power from deep penetration of society and a relaxation of political control so that civil society could be revived, and the energy and creativity of social groups and individuals released. Shortly afterward, the four fundamental principles were reaffirmed in order to maintain continuity with the past, to reestablish a strong political authority, and to keep the trend toward liberalization and relaxation from getting out of control.

Thus, the Third Plenum line and the four fundamental principles serve as two zones of demarcation bordering a broad middle course along which political, social, and economic reforms have been pushed forward. The reforms that have finally taken definite form in the Sixth Plenum, the Twelfth Party Congress, and the Fifth Session of the Fifth National People's Congress fall into three categories: first, reforming the leadership institutions and cadre institutions of the Party; second, redefining the relationship between the Party and the state while reforming state institutions; and, finally, searching for "socialist democracy" and "socialist legality" while taking more seriously the concept of citizenship. But all these reforms take place within the framework of a Leninist party-state which is not supposed to be questioned. Institutionalization is the fundamental process underlying all these reforms—a process that works also to strengthen the Leninist party-state.

Political life in China is now governed by a new "paradigm" which is the product of the century-old confrontation between China and the West. In this paradigm, traditional and modern elements, the old and the new, foreign examples and Chinese reality, Western knowledge and Chinese mentality are sometimes merely juxtaposed, sometimes combined in unstable mixtures, and sometimes fully integrated. But the paradigm is mainly modern in its totality, its explicit orientation, its substantive contents, and its posited goals, even though it is traditional in some of its parts, its implicit supports, its structural forms, and its methods.

The principles of legitimation of the Party-state which also serve as the sources of its guiding ideas in regulating its relationship with society and individuals rest on three concepts: "scientific laws," popular support, and legality. For Marxists, "scientific laws" are the highest form of truth. They embody what non-Marxists would call rationality of both ends and means. They deal with both values and facts. Marxist general laws of social development point to an inevitable outcome of human evolution in which the highest values are realized: the vague and undefined utopia of Communism. The manifestations of these general laws under the specific conditions of China become the laws governing the socialist reconstruction in China. They justify the search for a Chinese path to socialism. They legitimize the concepts and forms of the Chinese state and governmental structure. The current emphasis on the existence of "special laws," which arise from the special characteristics in different spheres of socioeconomic life in China, is a most significant departure from the past in post-Mao China,[191] for it furnishes a theoretical basis for the relative autonomy given various social groups and professions.

191. Although Mao recognized a long time ago the existence of "special laws" governing war, he did not extend this notion of "special laws" to other realms of human affairs. Moreover, Mao's military strategies and tactics, as well as his principles of army building, were governed by the primacy of politics. See chap. 5.

From the long perspective of Chinese history, "scientific laws" have replaced the age-old notion of Heaven and the neo-Confucian concept of *li* as the ultimate source of legitimate authority. This statement is a commonplace, but it is beyond my intellectual capacity to discuss. The recent emphasis on "scientific laws" in China does raise a fundamental question regarding the political implications of a Marxist party's claim that it can possess sure knowledge of these laws and use them to guide the political, social, and economic development of a nation. It is generally thought that the belief in these laws is both the basis of the authoritarian or totalitarian tendency of a Marxist party and the impetus constantly pushing this tendency forward.

Chinese development since 1978 suggests that this commonplace needs additional explication. There are three points I should like to make in that connection. The first point is compatible with the commonplace just mentioned, but it should be underscored if we are to understand the development in China. This point is that the more certain the Party or Party leaders are about their knowledge of these laws, and the more specific and operationalized are the laws, the more authoritarian or totalitarian are their implications. The curbing of political power and the relaxation of control since 1978 have stemmed in part from the Chinese repudiation of the "scientific laws" formulated by Mao and the "gang of four," from the renewed search for other laws to replace them, and from the continued reformulation and testing of these laws.

But this uncertainty does not explain everything. Equally if not more important is the content of these laws, particularly the special laws governing the different realms of social life. This is my second point. To be sure, the Chinese have reaffirmed the law leading ultimately to Communism, and have forcefully refuted the view that Communism as a theory about a society in the future has not been tested by practice and that the future of Communism is distant and uncertain. But the relaxation of political control and the grant of a greater degree of autonomy to peasant households, to various enterprises, and to individual Chinese citizens have been justified by the specific economic laws as summarized succinctly by Liu Guoguang. The aim of socialist reconstruction has been defined as developing the forces of production and satisfying the material and spiritual needs of the people. Thus, the content of the "scientific laws" does matter.

My third point concerns the sources of these "scientific laws", namely, who formulates them and whose voice is decisive or at least plays an im-

---

Following Clausewitz, he considered, quite rightly, that "war is an extension of politics," but he pushed this principle much further. It is not incorrect to suggest that for him the "special laws" for war were governed by and subordinated to politics. The current leaders' conception of these special laws and their relation to politics is very different.

portant role in defining them. There is no doubt that the ultimate authority resides in the Party and in the Politburo. But economists such as Xue Muqiao, Sun Yefang, Liu Guoguang, and Xu Dixin, who are supported at the very top by Chen Yun, a Party specialist on economic problems, have played an unprecedented role in the formulation of these laws. Now a group of younger economists are emerging under the leadership of Premier Zhao and Vice-Premier Li Peng. An even stronger case can be made with regard to science and technology. In other areas, the situation is less clear. But there is no doubt that even in the ideologically and politically sensitive field of literature, writers have exerted much greater influence than at any time since the Yanan Forum on Art and Literature. The latest episode in the debate over ideology—the campaign in the autumn of 1983 against "spiritual pollution"—revealed a deep split among reformers on fundamental theoretical questions of Marxism. Hu Qiaomu, taking an orthodox view and actually speaking for the Party center, condemned the application of the theory of alienation to socialist society but accepted a compromise in affirming the validity of "humanism" as an "ethical principle and moral norm" within the framework of historical materialism as "a world view or conception of history." The preceding period of liberalization and debate have not been totally without positive results. Though they were dissatisfied with various parts of Hu Qiaomu's article, the reformers seized upon the compromise to spread humanistic ideas. Meanwhile the writers continued to demand freedom in creative writing. The Party responded in late 1984 by accepting this principle and urged Party leaders at all levels to respect the "scientific laws" governing the development of literature and art. Thus the "science" of Marxism need not always lead to the obliteration of the individual. Indeed, the withdrawal of political power and the relaxation of control in China since 1978 have been effected in the very name of the "scientific laws" of Marxism-Leninism and Mao Zedong Thought.

In the modern world, there is nothing unusual about popular support as a principle of legitimacy for any regime, be it democratic, authoritarian, or totalitarian. What is interesting about the Chinese case is how the CCP succeeded in building up widespread popular support during the period of the civil and foreign wars, lost it during the Cultural Revolution, and then began to regain it after 1978. This process of regaining popular support has been intimately associated with the Party's reaffirmation of the epistemological postulate of seeking truth from facts, proceeding from reality, and combining theory with practice. Elevation of this postulate to a place of first importance has reoriented the Party's attention toward the needs, life situations, and behavior patterns of social groups and individuals. In addition, the epistemological postulate shapes the search for "scientific laws," as the greater attention to perceived interests contributes to the content of some of the laws. This process represents a "refunctionalization of ideology" to link it to the functional requirements of a modernizing society and of economic growth. In turn, the refunctionalized ideology and the "scientific laws" help strengthen popular support in the following way. The imperatives of the scientific laws, as well as the judgments concerning social reality and relationship embodied in them, form the basis of specific public policies. The latter in turn generate support for the Party-state and create a vested interest in their own continuation and expansion, and thus in the stability of the regime.

To regain popular support, the mass line has been underscored while mass political movements and mass mobilization have been abandoned as methods of implementing policies. The referents of the terms "people" and "masses" have been vastly expanded by reclassifying the overwhelming majority of "former landlords" and "former peasants" as ordinary members of their local communities. The intellectuals are defined as a component part of the working class who labor with their minds. The ranks of the enemy shrink. The mass line once again becomes a method of finding and maintaining an adequate balance, or acceptable compromise, between the Party's fundamental political interests, which have to prevail, and the immediate socioeconomic interests perceived by the people, which should not and cannot be sacrificed—just as it was with Mao's synthesis in the period from 1927 to 1955–56.

The emphasis on legality, or the sanctity of law, as a principle of legitimacy and as a guiding idea in regulating sociopolitical behavior is a new departure for the CCP. Although it is based solely on the Party's self-limitation and consequently is less well grounded than the other two principles, the patterns of political authority and process are now institutionalized more firmly and specifically than ever before in a new state constitution and a series of laws and regulations. The will of the state, which is under the leadership of the Party, is supposed to be expressed through laws. The enactment and enforcement of laws has replaced mass movements as a method of defining and implementing policies. In the constitutional system, the notion of citizenship and its corollary concept of civil rights have occupied a more prominent place and have been taken more seriously than before. Political rights have been extended on paper, and they may become more meaningful in reality, although they are still kept within the framework of a Leninist party-state. The ideas of "socialist legality" and "socialist democracy" have been synthesized in the formula of the institutionalization of socialist democracy and its codification in law. "Socialist democracy" is supposed to become a part of the content of laws. Some Chinese reformers are advocating the view that state law is the legal expression of "scientific laws." If this view gains acceptance, law will be given a sanctity which it never had before. For some, the rule of law, which is seen as an expression of the rule of impersonal, unalterable "scientific law," is placed far above the rule by men, which is frequently vitiated by their idiosyncracy, unpredictability, unreliability, and susceptibility to error. For others, it is to replace the latter altogether.

The incipient emphasis on legality means the development of a pattern of regular expectations and predictability in the political life of the nation. The institutionalization and codification in law of the fundamental rules governing the political structure, the state-society relationship, and the position of the citizens in the Chinese state suggests that after a period of thirty-three years, the process of routinization may finally have set in. Even if this is so, it has taken the Chinese revolution a much longer time to reach this stage than most other revolutions, contrary to the expectation and hope of many observers. It may be that the protracted revolutionary civil war built up a powerful momentum and generated a large group of radical revolutionaries, and that this momentum and this group retarded the process of routinization and then reversed it after it had started. It is also important to realize that in recent Chinese history the process of routinization must be characterized not as "routinization of charisma" but as routinization through the repudiation of charisma.

Before "socialist democracy" can be achieved, institutionalization, routinization, and acceptance in principle of the rule of law must first take place. All this is now being attempted. But how long will it take the Chinese to actualize "democracy on a high level" and "spiritual civilization on a high level"? Could it be that Chinese development in the twentieth century and beyond is like the journey of the traveler depicted in the well-known Chinese verse:

> Mountains multiply, streams double back—
> I doubt there's even a road;
> willows cluster darkly, blossoms shine—
> another village ahead![192]

192. Translated by Burton Watson, *The Old Man Who Does As He Pleases: Selections from the Poetry and Prose of Lu Yu* (New York: Columbia University Press, 1973), 3.

The reader may want to recall or look up some significant articles published recently in China in which this verse is used or alluded to in one way or another.

Chronology

1894   *August 1*
              China and Japan declare war on each other. During the
              war, China suffers disastrous military defeats.

1895   *April 17*
              The first Sino-Japanese war ends with the signing of the
              Treaty of Shimonoseki. China recognizes the indepen-
              dence of Korea, cedes Taiwan and Penghu (the Pesca-
              dores) to Japan, promises to pay 200 million taels for
              reparations, and accepts Japan's other demands.
              May 2
              Kang Youwei and copetitioners among his fellow provin-
              cial graduates assembled in Beijing for the metropolitan
              examinations submit a memorial to the throne in which
              they propose immediate institutional reforms.

1905   *September 2 (Lunar calendar, August 4)*
              In response to a memorial submitted by Yuan Shikai,
              an imperial rescript is issued to abolish the examination
              system in 1906.

1911   *October 10*
              The Wuchang uprising against the Manchu dynasty
              starts.

1912   *January 1*
              Sun Yat-sen is inaugurated as the provisional president
              of the Republic of China.
              February 12
              The Manchu dynasty abdicates.
              March 10
              Yuan Shikai is inaugurated as president of the Republic
              of China.

1915   *September 15*
              The first issue of *Qingnian Zazhi* (Youth magazine) ap-
              pears. It is published and edited by Chen Duxiu. (In
              this volume this date is taken as the beginning of the
              May Fourth period.)

1916   *June 6*
              Yuan Shikai dies. The period of warlordism begins.
              September 1
              Qingnian Zazhi is renamed *Xin Qingnian* (New youth).

1919   *May 4*
The May Fourth incident occurs. Students in Beijing
stage a demonstration to demand that the Chinese warlord government refuse to sign the Versailles Treaty and
to punish the three top officials handling foreign affairs.

1921   *July 23–31*
The First National Congress of the CCP meets. (In this
volume 1921 is taken as the end of the May Fourth period.) Twenty years later (1941) July 1, 1921, is designated as the official date of the founding of the Chinese
Communist Party.

1922   *July*
The second National Congress of the CCP declares that
the CCP is a branch of the Comintern.
August 17
The second "Westlake Conference" of the CCP meets.
The Comintern representative Maring invokes the au-
thority of the Comintern to overcome the opposition by
several Chinese leaders to the policy of joining the
Guomindang. The conference decides that a small num-
ber of Chinese Communist leaders should join the
Guomindang in their individual capacity and that the
Party should later persuade all its members to join.

1923   *June 12–20*
The third National Congress of the CCP meets. It declares that Guomindang should be the central force in
the national revolution and should occupy the position
of leadership. It decides that all members of the CCP
should join the Guomindang in their individual
capacity.

1924   *January 20*
The First Congress of the Guomindang meets in
Guangzhou. It makes the official decision to accept Chinese Communists in their individual capacity as members of the Guomindang.

1926   *July 9*
The northern expedition of the Guomindang to unify
China begins.

1927   *March 28*
Mao Zedong's "Report on an investigation of the peas-
ant movement in Hunan" is published.
April 12
Chiang Kai-shek stages a coup in Shanghai to purge the
Guomindang of Chinese Communists.

April 18
Chiang Kai-shek establishes his Nationalist government in Nanjing.
July 15
The Guomindang at Wuhan under Wang Jingwei's leadership purges the Chinese Communists from the Party.
August 7
The August 7 Conference is held under the leadership of Qu Qiubai, who has replaced Chen Duxiu as the actual leader of the CCP three or four weeks earlier. It adopts a policy of armed uprising and land revolution.
September
The Nationalist government at Nanjing is reorganized, and the three major factions of the Guomindang are temporarily reunited.
October 1927 through October 1934
The Jiangxi Period.
October 27
Mao Zedong establishes a base area in Jinggangshan, Jiangxi.

1928   *June 18–July 11*
The Sixth National Congress of the CCP meets in Moscow under the direct guidance of the Comintern.
December
The northern expedition of the Guomindang ends.

1931   *January 7*
The Fourth Plenum of the Sixth Central Committee meets under the guidance of Pavel Mif, the Comintern's representative. The "returned-students group" with Wang Ming as their leader gain dominant influence over the Central Committee of the CCP
November 7–20
The First Congress of All-China Soviets meets in Ruijin, Jiangxi. The "Outline Constitution of the Chinese Soviet Republic" is adopted.

1932   *June 16*
The Guomindang's fourth campaign of encirclement and annihilation begins against the Chinese Communists.
August
The Ningdu Conference is held, and Mao loses most of his authority over military affairs.

1933   *March*
The Guomindang's fourth campaign of encirclement and annihilation ends in failure, as had the first three campaigns.

October 2
The Guomindang's fifth campaign of encirclement and annihilation of the Communists begins.

1934   *October*
The Guomindang's fifth campaign of encirclement and annihilation ends in total victory.
October 16
The Long March begins.

1935   *January 15–17*
The Zunyi Conference accepts Mao's criticism of the military strategy adopted by the Chinese Communists during the Guomindang's fifth campaign of encirclement and annihilation. It also reorganizes the top organs of the Central Committee.
March 11 (ca.)
"A three-man military command small group" consisting of Mao Zedong, Zhou Enlai, and Wang Jiaxiang is established to direct military affairs.
August 1
This is the date given to the declaration drafted in Moscow by the CCP's delegation to the Comintern under the guidance of the Comintern leaders. It is approved personally by Stalin and Dimitrov and issued under the name of the Central Committee of the CCP. The "August First Declaration" calls for the establishment in China of a united front of all political forces to resist Japanese aggression and to oppose Chiang Kai-shek.
October 19
Mao Zedong's forces reach northern Shaanxi and link up with the Communist guerrilla forces there.

1936   *October*
All major Communist forces reach northern Shaanxi. The Long March ends.
October 1936 through 1947
The Yanan Period.

1937   *July 7*
The Sino-Japanese War begins.
September 22–23
The second united front between the Guomindang and the CCP is formally established by parallel statements by the two parties.

1942   *February 1*
The Zhengfeng movement is launched by Mao to oppose subjectivism and sectarianism. It seeks to eliminate the ideological influence of Wang Ming and the

"returned-students group" and to establish ideological
and political unity in the Party.
May 2 and 5
Mao Zedong gives two talks at the Yanan forum on art
and literature. He declares that "literature and art are
subordinate to politics."

1943   *March*
The Politburo decides that Mao Zedong be made chair-
man both of the Politburo and of the Secretariat.
June 10
The Comintern is officially disbanded.

1944   *April 12*
The Zhengfeng movement ends with Mao Zedong's
speech "Our study and the current situation."
May 21, through April 20, 1945
The Seventh Plenum of the Sixth Central Committee
meets intermittently for almost a year. It elects Mao
chairman of the Central Committee. On April 20, 1945,
it adopts the Resolution on Certain Questions in the
History of Our Party.

1945   *April 23–June 11*
The Seventh National Congress of the CCP meets.
June 11
A new Party constitution is adopted at the Seventh National Party Congress. It contains the statement that
"the Communist Party of China guides its entire work
by the teachings which unite the theories of Marxism-
Leninism with the actual practice of the Chinese revolution—the Thought of Mao Zedong." It provides for
the election by the Central Committee of a chairman of
that committee who shall be concurrently chairman of
the Central Politburo and chairman of the Central
Secretariat.
June 19
The First Plenum of the Seventh Central Committee
elects Mao Zedong chairman of the Central Committee. According to the Party constitution adopted eight
days earlier Mao also serves as chairman of the Politburo and of the Central Secretariat.
August 14 (August 15, Far Eastern time)
Japan accepts the American terms of surrender. The
Sino-Japanese War ends.

1946   *June 26*
The Third Revolutionary Civil War begins.

1949   *October 1*
The founding of the People's Republic of China is
proclaimed.

1951	*December 1951 through the summer of 1952* The "Three-Anti" and "Five-Anti" campaigns take place.
1954	*September 20* The first state constitution is adopted.
1955	*July 31* Mao Zedong gives a speech on the question of agricultural cooperation. This is the beginning of the acceleration of cooperativization.
1956	The transformation of capitalist enterprises to joint state-private enterprises is completed. *May 26* Lu Dingyi gives his speech "Let a hundred flowers bloom, a hundred schools contend." *September 15–27* The Eighth National Congress of the CCP adopts a new Party constitution. It refers to Marxism-Leninism as its guide to action. The explicit reference to Mao Zedong Thought is deleted. The post of secretary general is restored, and Deng Xiaoping is named to fill it.
1957	*February 27* Mao Zedong gives his speech "On the correct handling of contradictions among the people." *May 15* Preparations are made for the anti-rightist campaign. *June 8, 1957, through August 1958* The anti-rightist campaign takes place. *June 18* Mao's speech "On the correct handling of contradictions among the people" is published. Six criteria for distinguishing "fragrant flowers" from "poisonous weeds" are added.
1958	*May 5* At the second session of the Eighth Party Congress, Liu Shaoqi makes a speech "The present situation, the Party's general line for Socialist construction and its future tasks." The Great Leap Forward is launched. *August 29* The Central Committee adopts the resolution on the establishment of people's communes in rural areas.
1959	*July 2–August 6* The Lushan Plenum meets. Peng Dehuai criticizes the commune system and the Great Leap Forward. Mao denounces Peng for his criticism. The campaign against the "Rightist tendency" is launched. One month later, Peng is dismissed from his post of defense minister.

1960	*November 3* The Party issues Emergency Directives on Rural Work. This document confirms the policy of modifying the commune system and retreating from the Great Leap.
1962	*September 24–27* The Tenth Plenum of the Eighth Central Committee meets. Mao calls on the Party never to forget class struggle.
1963	*May 1963 through May 1966* The Socialist Education movement takes place.
1966	*May 16* The Party center sends down a circular formally launching the Cultural Revolution. *August 1–12* The Eleventh Plenum of the Eighth Central Committee meets. The decision concerning the Great Proletarian Cultural Revolution is adopted.
1969	*April 1–24* The Ninth National Congress of the CCP meets. The Party constitution declares that "the Communist Party of China takes Marxism-Leninism-Mao Zedong Thought as the theoretical basis guiding its thinking." Lin Biao is designated as Mao's successor.
1971	*September 13* Lin Biao dies.
1973	*April* Deng Xiaoping reappears in a public function and is being groomed by Premier Zhou Enlai as his successor. Zhou is suffering from incurable cancer. *August 24–28* The Tenth National Congress of the CCP is held. Wang Hongwen is named a vice-chairman of the Party, ranking below Zhou Enlai but above the other three vice-chairmen. Jiang Qing, Zhang Chunqiao, and Yao Wenyuan are elected to the Politburo.
1975	*January 5* Deng is appointed a vice-chairman of the Military Commission of the Central Committee and the chief of staff of the People's Liberation Army. *January 8–10* The Second Plenum of the Tenth Central Committee meets. Deng is elected a vice-chairman of the Party. *January 13–17* The second session of the Fourth National Congress is

held. A new state constitution is adopted. Deng is con-
firmed as the ranking vice-premier.
November
The veiled attack on Deng begins.

1976   *January 8*
The Tiananmen Incident takes place in Beijing to honor
Premier Zhou Enlai dies. Hua Guofeng is subsequently
named acting premier and put in charge of Politburo
work by Mao Zedong.
April 5
The Tiananmen Incident takes place in Beijing to honor
the memory of Zhou Enlai, to oppose the "gang of
four," and to support the followers of Zhou, including
Deng Xiaoping.
April 7
The Party center dismisses Deng Xiaoping from all his
posts.
September 9
Mao Zedong dies.
October 7
The "gang of four" is arrested.
October 7
Hua Guofeng becomes chairman of the Party and chair-
man of the Military Commission of the Party.

1977   *July 16–21*
The Third Plenum of the Tenth Central Committee
meets. Deng Xiaoping is restored to all his former
positions.
August 12–18
The Eleventh National Congress of the CCP meets.
August 19
The First Plenum of the Eleventh Central Committee
elects Hua Guofeng chairman of the Central Commit-
tee and Ye Jianying, Deng Xiaoping, Li Xiannian, and
Wang Dongxing, vice-chairmen.

1978   *March 5*
The Fifth National People's Congress adopts a new state
constitution.
May 11
The article "Practice is the Sole Criterion for Testing
Truth" appears in *Guangming ribao*, starting a nation-
wide public discussion of the theory of knowledge.
December 18–22
The Third Plenum of the Eleventh Central Committtee
meets. It endorses the national discussions on the crite-
rion for testing truth. It shifts the emphasis of the
Party's work from class struggle to socialist moderniza-
tion, and elects a Central Commission for Inspecting
Discipline.

1979   *March 30*
Deng Xiaoping calls for the firm upholding of the Four
Fundamental Principles.
June
Premier and Party Chairman Hua Guofeng declares at
the second session of the National People's Congress
that landlords, rich peasants, and capitalists no longer
exist as classes.
September 29
Vice-Chairman Ye Jianying says in a speech that class
struggle must not be magnified or created out of
nothing.
October 30-November 16
The Fourth Congress of Writers and Artists meets. It is
the first meeting of the congress in nineteen years.

1980   *February 23–29*
The Fifth Plenum of the Eleventh Central Committee
meets, and reestablishes the Party's Secretariat. It decides to recommend to the National People's Congress
the elimination of the constitutional article providing
for the right to engage in "big contending, big blooming, big debate" and to put up "big character posters."
August 18
Deng Xiaoping delivers a speech entitled "Reforming
the leadership institutions of the Party and the state."
In it, he states that the overconcentration of power
and the failure to develop a set of institutions were
the source of China's numerous difficulties in the past.
November through January 1981
The "gang of four" is tried and convicted.
November
The Politburo examines Hua Guofeng's mistakes and ac-
cepts his resignation from the chairmanship of both the
Party and the Party's Military Commission. Hu Yaobang
and Deng Xiaoping take over those respective posts.

1981   *April 18–December 30*
A public debate over Bai Hua's *Bitter Love* takes place.
It ends with the publication of Bai Hua's self-criticism
and Hu Yaobang's statement on the conclusion of the
case of Bai Hua.
June 27–29
The Sixth Plenum of the Eleventh Central Committee
meets. Hu Yaobang is elected chairman of the Central
Committee and Deng Xiaoping, chairman of the Mili-
tary Commisssion of the Central Committee. Hua
Guofeng is demoted to be one of the vice-chairmen of
the Central Committee. The Resolution on Certain
Questions in the History of Our Party since the Found-
ing of the People's Republic of China is adopted on
June 27.

1982   *September 1–11*
The Twelfth National Congress of the CCP meets. The
post of party chairman is abolished, and a new Party
constitution is adopted. The Party constitution declares
that "the Party must conduct its activities within the
limits permitted by the constitution and the laws of the
state."
September 12–13
The First Plenum of the Twelfth Central Committee
elects Hu Yaobang general secretary of the Central
Committee. Hua Guofeng loses his position on the Politburo but retains his membership on the Central
Committee.
December 6
A new state constitution is adopted. The chairmanship
of the state is reinstituted, but with its power sharply
reduced. The state constitution declares that "all the
peoples of all nationalities, all state organs, the armed
forces, all political parties and public organizations, and
all enterprises and undertakings must take the constitution as the basic norm of conduct, and they have the
duty to uphold the dignity of the constitution and insure its implementation."

1983   *July 1*
Selected Works of Deng Xiaoping is published.
October 11–12
The Second Plenum of the Twelfth Central Committee
meets. In conjunction with the ongoing Party Rectification campaign, Deng Xiaoping warns the Party against
the danger of "spiritual pollution." In the next few
weeks, this speech is interpreted as a call to eliminate
"spiritual pollution" and to criticize "bourgeois humanism," the concept of alienation, and "the abstract theory of human nature."

1984   *January 27*
Hu Qiaomu's article "On the questions of humanism
and alienation" is published in *Renmin ribao*. The publication of this article signals the approaching end of the
campaign against "spiritual pollution."
July 16
The commentator of Hongqi calls for the "thorough repudiation" of the Cultural Revolution, and this is defined as a precondition for the success in consolidating
the Party.

Index

Index

as criterion, 187; practice as criterion, xxxviii, 153–54, 191, 220, 280, 291–93, 342. *See also* "Two-whatever policy"
Cult of personality, xxxiv, 24–25, 78–79, 82–83, 91, 147, 186–87, 221, 241, 243, 246, 282, 284–85, 290, 292, 299, 301, 307, 329

Dahl, Robert A., 8, 250, 256
Dahrendorf, Ralf, 67
Deng Tuo, 19–20, 23, 32, 44, 56n, 58
Deng Xiaoping, 78, 141–42, 173, 226, 239, 341–44; prior to the Cultural Revolution, 45, 55, 78, 285, 340; at the beginning of the Cultural Revolution, 55, 86; Reform program in 1974–75, 119, 129–32, 341–42; Maoists' attack on Deng in 1975–76, 129–38, 288, 342; emergence as the preeminent leader, 141–42n, 153, 161, 173, 176–77, 222, 224, 226, 239, 243–44, 246, 249, 293, 298, 301, 306–10, 312, 342; on the criterion for testing truth, xxxviii, 153–54, 291–92, 298, 342; on the four fundamental principles, xxxix, xl–xli, 176–80, 222, 224, 229, 233, 250–53, 302, 305, 329–30; and middle course, xxxix–xl, xli, 222, 251–53, 255–56, 279, 302, 305, 329–30; on the defects of the political system, 244, 305–8, 311, 343; and reform of leadership and cadre institutions, 173–75, 243–51, 304–12, 317, 330, 343; and reform of relationship between party, state, and society, 220–21, 241–51, 295–99, 312–20, 330, 343; and freedom of expression and democracy, 176–78, 224, 227, 229–30, 232–33, 250–51, 255–56, 258, 308, 343; and other reforms, 161, 176–77, 199, 222, 224–25, 227, 239, 242–47, 321–27, 333–34; and limits to reform, 161, 176–80, 190, 222, 224–25, 227, 239, 242–47, 250–51, 305; and the reevaluation of Mao, 154, 173, 191, 232, 257, 291, 300, 329; and "Resolution on History" (1982), xxxviii, 142n, 291, 298–300
Deng Yingchao (Mrs. Zhou Enlai), 245
Deng Zihui, 71
Deutsch, Karl W., 3
Dictatorship of the proletariat: xxxix, 8, 14, 127, 130, 142n, 176–77, 241, 253, 268, 286–87, 289, 291, 303, 316; continued revolution under, xxiii, 253, 329; over the bourgeoisie, xxiii, xxxvii, 120, 121n, 123, 129, 136, 147, 183, 289, 329
Ding Ling, 149

Egalitarianism, 132, 214–16
Elite or ruling class: disintegration of, in traditional China, xxiii, xxxiii–xxxv, 8–9, 14, 63, 187, 212, 217, 263–65; in communist China, xxxii, xxxiv, 8–9, 13–14, 25, 28–30, 38–39, 41–42, 63, 67–69, 362; class of bureaucratic officials, xxxvii, 121, 134–38, 288–89, 294; and the masses, 5, 9, 13, 25–30, 41, 67, 69, 74; and political community, 5, 8–9, 25–27, 63; and state rebuilding, xxiii–xxv, xxxiii, 67–69, 260–61, 264–65
Elster, Jon, xxxvin, 172n, 304n
Engels, Friedrich, xxxvi, 83, 112–14, 139, 154, 290, 293

Factional model: formal organization and factions, 97–99; fundamental assumption of Nathan's model, 99; alternative constructs, 105–7; and informal groups, xviii, 97–99; behavior of informal groups in CCP politics, 99–102, 107–11; factions and policy-making, 103–4. *See also* Chinese Communist Party
Factions, xviiin, 39, 90, 92–93, 98n, 118, 129, 140, 266, 281, 289, 293
Fang Yi, 243
Feng Ding, 19, 52
"Feudal fascism," 148, 171, 183, 256, 290
"Feudalism," 147–49, 174, 187
Friedman, Edward, 141

Gang of Four, xviii, xxiii, xxv–xxvi, xxx, 124, 128, 129n, 130, 133, 139–43, 171, 173, 213, 228, 246, 286–89, 292, 294, 331, 342, 343
Gao Gang, 41, 43, 102
Geertz, Clifford, xxi, 7, 261
Geng Biao, 173
Gittings, John, 48
Gouldner, Alvin W., xvin, 223n, 262n
Gramsci, Antonio, xl, 113n, 280
Great Leap Forward, 13, 16, 19, 30–31, 34–35, 43, 50, 55n, 69, 78–81, 94, 227, 238, 321, 340, 341
Guomindang (GMD), xvi, xxxv, 11, 18, 41, 103, 109, 183, 265–66, 277, 280–82, 336, 338

Historical Materialism, xxxvi, xxxvii, xxxviii, 113, 114, 116, 118, 121, 138, 139, 332. *See also* Mao Zedong Thought, modification of historical materialism
Hua Guofeng, xl, 133, 139, 141–42, 163, 172, 191, 196, 226, 242, 252, 290, 292, 342–44
Hu Feng, 236
Hu Fuming, 153
Humanism, 301–2, 332, 344

347

Index

Index

Middle course, xxxiv, xl, xli, 222, 251, 252, 253, 255, 256, 279, 302, 330. *See also* Deng Xiaoping
Moore, Barrington, Jr., xxiii n
Munro, Donald, 51

Nathan, Andrew, xviii, 96–105, 107–10
National People's Congress, 119–20, 170, 172, 225, 244–48, 320, 322, 341, 342, 343; Standing Committee of, 9, 118–19, 173
Nettl, J. P., xxii, 261
Nie Rongzhen, 33
Nie, Yuanzi, 91

Peng Chong, 150
Peng Dehuai, 41, 47–48, 50, 51 n, 78, 80, 102, 124, 278, 285, 299, 326
Peng Zhen, 51 n, 56, 85–86, 93, 97 n, 103, 170
People's Liberation Army (PLA), 47, 61 n, 107, 124, 153, 173, 224–28, 231–33, 236–38, 315, 325, 341; PLA and the Cultural Revolution, 58, 62, 89–90, 107; Mao and the PLA, 16, 18–19, 22–23, 35–36, 41–42, 46–52, 58–59, 61–62, 81, 89–90, 105, 107, 173, 225–26, 282–83; Lin Biao and the PLA, 21–23, 47–50, 89; PLA and the writers, 225–27, 230, 236–37
Pluralism: institutional, xlii, 172, 174, 176, 180, 186, 257, 305; social, 175, 176, 257
Primacy of politics, xxii–xiv, xxxviii, xxxv, 154–55, 186–87, 213, 261, 279, 293, 295–96, 327

Qi Benyu, 50 n, 87 n
Qin Bangxian (alias Bo Gu), 282–83
Qu Qiubai, 337

Rao Shushi, 41, 43, 102
Red Guard, xxxvii, xxviii, 25, 27, 45–46, 57–59, 65, 71, 73, 79–80, 82–85, 87–94, 162, 186
Ren Bishi, 283
Returned-Students Group, xxxvi, 282, 337, 339
Revolution, xx, xxv, xxxv, xxxvii, 6, 14–15, 24, 38–39, 113–14, 124, 140, 145–46, 151, 154, 163, 187, 212, 215, 252–53, 257, 267, 274, 276, 278, 291, 295, 298, 300, 302–3, 327–28, 334

Schram, Stuart, 18 n, 114 n, 263 n, 270 n
Schurmann, Franz, xxix, 30
Schwartz, Benjamin, 34, 260, 262
"Scientific laws" of Marxism and Mao

Zedong Thought: 295–96, 303; as a principle of legitimacy, 327, 330, 334; "Scientific laws" and totalitarian tendency, 331–32; "specific scientific laws" governing specific spheres, xxxii, 154–55, 295–96
Selznick, Philip, 262–63
Shao Zhuanlin, 52, 53
Skocpol, Theda, xxi, xxix
Socialist democracy, xliii, 170–74, 258, 304, 308, 316, 320–21, 326, 330, 333–34
Socialist Education Movement (1963), 70, 77, 81, 121, 286, 341
Socialist humanism, 301, 302, 332
Socialist legality, xliii, 170–73, 258, 302, 304, 308, 320–21, 326, 330, 333–34
Stalin, 24, 27, 32, 45, 83, 106, 155, 269, 290, 338
State Constitutions, 148, 178, 246, 249, 313–15, 320, 322, 325, 340, 342, 344
State Council, 9, 118, 133, 173, 197, 242–45, 247, 249, 310, 314, 319, 320
State rebuilding and reintegration of political community. *See* Chinese Communist Party and Chinese Communist Movement; Citizenship; Class struggle; Crisis; Elite; Ideology; Masses, Mass-line and Mass movement; and State-society relationship
State-society relationship (political power-society relationship): in traditional China, xxxiii, 212–16, 274–75; and state rebuilding, 37, 260–61, 277, 302, 327; Leninist Party and state-society relationship, xxv, 219, 249, 263–67; and social revolution, xxxv, 146, 212, 267, 276, 328; retreat of political power, xxxix, 146–47, 151, 159, 214, 219–22, 329; as reflected in ideological discourse, 151–57, 169–71, 220, 291–96; as reflected in the perception of class structure, 159–64, 219; as reflected in the relative autonomy of social organizations, 161–63, 175, 241–43; as reflected in the restructuring of the economy, xli, 165–69, 177, 222, 331; uneven development in different social spheres, xli–xlii, 222–24, 238–41. *See also* Totalitarianism, xv, xxii, xiv, 37
Sun Yat-sen, 163, 274, 275, 335
Sun Yefang, 44, 332

Theoretically informed and theoretically relevant case study, xvi–xxvi
Third Plenum of the Eleventh Central Committee (December 1978). *See* Chinese Communist Party's meetings

350